No More States?

No More States?

Globalization, National Self-determination, and Terrorism

Edited by
Richard N. Rosecrance
and Arthur A. Stein

ROWMAN & LITTLEFIELD PUBLISHERS, INC.
Lanham • Boulder • New York • Toronto • Plymouth, UK

ROWMAN & LITTLEFIELD PUBLISHERS, INC.

Published in the United States of America
by Rowman & Littlefield Publishers, Inc.
A wholly owned subsidiary of The Rowman & Littlefield Publishing Group, Inc.
4501 Forbes Boulevard, Suite 200, Lanham, Maryland 20706
www.rowmanlittlefield.com

Estover Road
Plymouth PL6 7PL
United Kingdom

British Library Cataloguing in Publication Information Available

Library of Congress Cataloging-in-Publication Data
No more states? : globalization, national self-determination, and terrorism / edited by Richard N. Rosecrance and Arthur A. Stein
   p. cm.
Includes bibliographical references and index.
ISBN-13: 978-0-7425-3943-3 (cloth : alk. paper)
ISBN-10: 0-7425-3943-1 (cloth : alk. paper)
ISBN-13: 978-0-7425-3944-0 (pbk. : alk. paper)
ISBN-10: 0-7425-3944-X (pbk. : alk. paper)
1. Globalization.   2. Self-determination, National.   3. Terrorism.   4. State, The.
5. United States—Foreign relations—2001.   6. World politics—1995–2005.
I. Rosecrance, Richard N.   II. Stein, Arthur A.
JZ1318.N6 2006
320.1—dc22
                    2006014795

Printed in the United States of America

♾ ™ The paper used in this publication meets the minimum requirements of American National Standard for Information Sciences—Permanence of Paper for Printed Library Materials, ANSI/NISO Z39.48-1992.

Contents

Preface and Acknowledgments

The UCLA-Harvard project on the likely creation of new states (under conditions of pervasive economic globalization) began with the support of the Carnegie Corporation of New York in the summer of 2000. It endeavored to offer new theoretical perspectives as well as case investigations of countries which might possibly split apart. After three major conferences and a wide range of discussions, we have reached the tentative conclusion that few new states will be created in the years ahead. Indeed, a reverse political-economic trend may well have set in, with states getting bigger, rather than smaller in size. Consolidation through new international or supranational organizations may become the rule rather than further division into smaller entities. We have to thank numerous colleagues and research organizations for supporting us including the Department of Political Science, UCLA and the Belfer Center for Science and International Affairs at Harvard. Luisita Cordero offered invaluable research assistance as well as contributing a chapter to our labors. Mike Lofchie gave us financial assistance and Department facilities at UCLA. Graham Allison and Joseph Nye lent help with activities at the Kennedy School of Government. Steve Del Rosso and Vartan Gregorian of Carnegie were moving forces in originating the program and they lent important support throughout. We owe them a great debt. We would also like to thank Teri Barnard and Nancy Blumstein who helped to administer the program.

The Editors

I

GENERALIST FORCES

1

Globalization and Its Effects: Introduction and Overview

Richard N. Rosecrance, Etel Solingen,
and Arthur A. Stein

GLOBALIZATION—MORE NEW STATES?

In 1997–98 Thailand, Korea, and Indonesia were attacked by international financial interests convinced that the countries were not running their economies properly. The trio had borrowed heavily in hard currency, and were unable to repay their debts, at least in the short term. Money flowed out of Bangkok, Seoul, and Jakarta; currencies plummeted in value and interest rates went sky-high; unemployment spurted upward. The Indonesian government fell, and the others barely averted collapse. The IMF insisted on draconian measures before providing financial assistance. With much greater reserves, even China and Japan skated near financial peril. The lesson was clear: no country is large enough to withstand huge financial drains imposed by the globalization of the world economy. To paraphrase the English poet, John Donne: No country is an island entire unto itself. Each is part of the main.

Globalization has the effect of incapacitating states as autonomous units. Under its influence, states have come to rely on distant markets for raw materials, production, and finance, and have thereby become dependent on economic forces they do not control. In a globalized world, national governments are not able to insulate their citizens from the effects of world inflation and depression, causing unemployment and low growth.

Reacting to these problems, groups of citizens within particular states may seek full independence from their erstwhile homeland. But they then face opposed incentives. On the one hand, a new state will confront the same pressures as the previous inclusive metropolitan state did. It will probably be weaker, and it will be even more reliant on the international economy. On the other, as long as tariffs are low, even small states can become viable. Even countries with a small national market can still sell overseas. Much depends upon whether they can attract liquid capital or foreign direct investment to increase their production capability to send exports abroad. But no country has enough cash to withstand all assaults, and when periodic crises occur, each is at the mercy of the international market. The dissatisfaction of a province therefore can lead in two directions: toward greater dependence on the metropolitan government and an acceptance of lesser status, or toward independence in hopes that the international economy will treat the fledgling state kindly. There is also another possibility, heavily resorted to in the 19th century—sending one's disgruntled citizens overseas. Migration provides a safety-valve for domestic discontent as the Irish, liberal Germans, and dismayed Italians showed in the 1840s and 1850s. But if the discontented remain at home, globalization magnifies the size of the problem a group confronts in considering a movement toward independence.

From a historical perspective, new movements toward independence are not surprising. Since the days of Joseph Mazzini in the mid-19th century, dissidents have been encouraged to form new states, and many have done so. Nationalism is only two centuries old, dating back to the times of Napoleon and the French Revolution. Scholars disagree about what creates nations, but for our purposes it is the desire for self-rule expressed through popular influence on government that is at the heart of nationalism. In the 19th century it was a largely integrative force, uniting the separate German and Italian provinces. In the 20th century, however, nationalism became a disintegrative force as peoples fought for independence from colonial rule. As a result the number of states in the international system grew rapidly. At the end of the First World War, previously repressed communities split off from the Ottoman and Hapsburg Empires to form new states. After the Second World War, the Dutch, British, French, Belgian, and Portuguese empires collapsed, leaving a host of new nations in their place. The dissolution of the Soviet Union and Yugoslavia in the 1990s similarly added new countries to the international system. There were 50 states in 1900, 75 before World War II, and about 200 today. And today there remains plenty of combustible material that might ignite a demand for additional states; dissatisfaction with economic and political outcomes abounds. Kurds, Kashmiris, Tamils, Basques, and Palestinians are among their number. In addition to political and economic grievances fostered by globalization, there are more than 8,000 different dialects spoken in the world today. If even a tiny additional fraction of these were organized into political units, the total number of nations would multiply.

The surprising conclusion of this book, however, is that few new states will form in the next generation.[1] This is not because demands for national self-determination do not exist. They occur, and they remain powerful. Three factors, however, bar the way. The first is the increasing ability of metropolitan governments, faced with nationalist dissent, to buy off the discontented or to induce them to submit. Globalization may have blunted economic sovereignty, but it has not dulled governmental tools to keep dissidents within the metropolitan fold. Governments have spent more in the wake of globalization, and they are willing to use these funds to keep their country together.[2] In addition, governments are ready to concede high degrees of autonomy to their dissident provinces. They will not agree to independence, but they are much more willing to meet the discontented half-way than governments in the past. In the 19th century, imperialism linked a metropole in Europe with colonies in Africa and Asia. Today, the discontented live in provinces contiguous with the central core of the state. Because of greater propinquity, metropolitan governments can threaten greater punishments as well as offer greater rewards to those who are dissatisfied.

Second, as we have seen, discontented voters have another alternative—a safety valve for the metropole: they can migrate to another country. When there were vacant places to be filled up, new territories and new states could be easily established abroad. Now that the world's surface is already organized, the discontented can still seek residency or citizenship in another—from their point of view—better-governed country. Nineteenth-century emigration from Europe to America, Canada, and Australia was one great example of this phenomenon. It continues today with large-scale emigration from Latin America, Africa, the Middle East, and East Asia to Europe and North America. If this safety-valve performs adequately, there is no need for ethnic dissenters to form new states. They can find a home abroad in already established polities.

Thirdly, international opinion and Great Power support for self-determination and the creation of new states have lessened. As governments have perforce embraced globalization, they have also become leery of dissidents who reject it. Even more significant, dissenters who use the methods of international terrorism to gain attention for their plight have thereby generally discredited themselves. Thus, the international climate of opinion and action has now turned against axiomatic national self-rule for every dissident group. In some cases, the Basque separatists or Scottish nationalists may hope that they can gain admission to the European Union and that they will fare better in the EU than they did as provinces of Spain, France, or Britain. They are, however, likely to be disappointed. Nor will a restive Quebec be able to choose NAFTA and an alliance with the United States as an alternative to provincial autonomy within Canada. To join a new international organization or customs union, dissident nations need the consent of existing members, and they will by no means automatically receive it. The informed approval of the international community is less likely to be given.

Globalization has made all states less strong, but it has made things especially difficult for new states unless low tariffs exist across the board. Factors of production and flows of finance can get into a new state, challenging its industries, but those industries are not always able to sell to the outside world, discharging the obligations thus incurred. The financial crisis of 1997–98 was a case in point. Asian nations had heavily borrowed abroad, but their ability to repay depended upon general acceptance of their exports. When this came into question in 1996–97, debts accumulated and foreigners removed their money. Through contagion effects, one crisis led to another, and Thailand, Indonesia, Malaysia, and Korea were thrown into crisis and most of them had to kneel at the altar of the IMF, accepting devaluation and higher interest rates as a result.

In the result, therefore, globalization has produced differential effects— weakening metropolitan governments but making life even more difficult for fledgling states. Under the circumstances, nationalist movements have generally agreed to remain within the protections of the central regime in their country.

Can new small states emerge? In theory this is possible. But there will be no investment or trade, if wars of national liberation ravage the countryside. To do their job, private traders and investors rely on continued peace and stability. Wars of national liberation, depending as they always have done on external support, therefore, are unlikely to receive it. There is no bipolar division of the world to keep those struggles going. Thus, there may be few new states emerging under such conditions.

Globalization, of course, increases the viability of even small states. In the past, national self-determination was rarely granted unless the emerging state would be deemed economically "viable." But in an open world economy— where all comers can buy and sell freely—states do not have to be large to be viable. Thus candidates for self-determination like Scotland or Quebec would not be prohibited from independence solely on grounds of viability. If admitted to free trade arrangements, they might stand on their own. But the pattern of globalization favors bigger players, with a greater supply of cash. Trade is less free than capital movements whose outflow can penalize a country without deep pockets. In addition, provincial units receiving benefits and subsidies from the center can do better inside than they might as independent units exposed to sudden economic shifts.

WILL GLOBALIZATION WITHER?

This outcome could change if globalization were negated or transformed. A decline in globalization would almost certainly enhance the national power of states, as it did in the 1930s. This in turn could lead to greater oppression of subject minorities, as occurred then. But it would also augment incentives for independence. The globalization of today, then, probably in the net helps repressed minorities within most states, even if it provides few opportunities for them to declare independence. If globalization gave way to new economic nationalism, it would scarcely benefit regional minorities. The result, therefore, is that globalization may be a force for restraint in creating new nation-states. If it were reversed, the pressures for further self-determination would likely increase. Will this happen?

Since 9/11, the international economy and global relationships have been under assault. In its aftermath, policymakers have worried that terrorism might soon be directed at world trade, metropolitan centers, or once again at the capitals of international finance. Weapons of mass destruction—nuclear radiation weapons, or biological agents—might be delivered against major cities. If these weapons were used, parts of cities might be destroyed; seaports could be severely disabled or shut down.[3] Planes might be attacked by shoulder-fired surface-to-air missiles, rendering air travel hazardous. The exchange of goods, persons, and money might be curtailed. The foundations of globalization could then begin to crumble.

In addition—so it is said—Great Power rivalries might themselves write "finis" to the further spread of commerce and investment. As China grows stronger, tension between the United States and China could lead to economic conflict or even military conflict over Taiwan or other issues.[4] Despite high economic interdependence between them in 1913, rising Imperial Germany came into collision with Great Britain. Facing the possibility of a similar clash with China, some Americans believe that the United States should act now to cut China's growth rate, interrupting its global economic ties, and weakening global trade. Greater globalization might not prevent this conflict.[5]

To be sure, terrorism and power rivalries could theoretically disrupt the world economy. These things have happened in past ages—during the vast internal and external struggles of the Thirty Years' War, for example. Nonetheless, they do not presently appear likely to halt the ongoing globalization process.[6] The basic characteristic of globalization has been its flexibility—its power to adjust to checks or barriers and find new ways to continue the exchange of goods, persons, and information. The attacks on New York and Washington in 2001 did not disable their telephonic or financial operations. Back-up systems and new methods of routing calls and finance were created very quickly. Today international shipping remains unimpeded though only a small percent of its containers are inspected. Nations are, however, fashioning new supplier-receiver arrangements which maintain the integrity of the shipment from packing to arrival. (Canada, the Netherlands, Singapore, China, and the United States are negotiating arrangements to achieve this result.) The movement of persons from country to country has been monitored and restricted, but it has not come to a halt. This does not mean that a large-scale terrorist attack could not have devastating consequences.[7]

But would it shut down the entire apparatus of international commerce? At present this seems quite unlikely. Even the use of nuclear weapons would not certainly disable international trade. There are many ports and many cities through which commerce could continue to proceed as the attacked nation—with the assistance of powerful allies—scours the world for the perpetrators.[8] Those harboring the terrorists—whether organized or "failed" states—would not be immune to attack, nuclear or other. And in terms of the long-term Great Power competition, the U.S. rivalry with China is not best advanced by termination of civilian investment or trade.[9] Countervailing economic sanctions would be inimical to both nations.

If globalization does continue and expand—which appears the most likely eventuality—policymakers will have to consider and deal with its pervasive effects. As more countries enter the world economy and communications system, diverse regions are impacted in different ways. Some countries and regions wish to benefit from the new global ties, others to withdraw from or restrict them. Still others may wish to put on tariff or capital controls to limit globalization's effect. The U.S. presidential election campaign in 2004 questioned whether outward foreign direct investment in manufacturing has hurt the home economy. In response, some have advocated penalties for companies which "outsource" manufactured goods. Yet cooler heads have observed that "outsourcing" does not disadvantage the economy as a whole —it helps it, even when particular sectors are adversely affected.[10]

Still, as globalization proceeds, some provinces may be more affected and more dissatisfied than others. Some may be tempted to seek independence to pursue economic and political policies different from those of the metropolitan regime. They may petition the international community for assistance in their quest.

The study which follows is an attempt to chart the likely outcome. Will new states continue to be formed? Or will the international community generally inveigh against independence and particularly against the use of terrorism to achieve self-determination for dissident groups? While the future remains uncertain, we believe few states will be created in the near future.[11] East Timor and, more uncertainly, Palestine may be among the last exceptions to a general rule against further independence of potentially dissident provinces. A summary of our analysis follows.

GLOBALIZATION—THE MOBILITY OF GOODS, CAPITAL, AND INFORMATION

In our definition, globalization is the growing mobility of factors of production—capital, labor, information, and goods—between countries. Since 1945 world trade has been growing more rapidly than world gross domestic product (GDP). Capital movements have also risen rapidly in recent years. Few regions of the world are now immune to inflows or outflows of capital or labor. If the world economy continues to spread, formerly autarchic regions like Outer Mongolia, Xinjiang, land-locked African states, and central Asian countries will eventually be brought into contact with the forces of globalization. Their labor forces and raw materials will then be priced according to international market valuations, and capital and labor will begin to move in and out accordingly. This will affect social patterns in the hitherto untouched states and cause a political reaction. This reaction has already occurred in Latin America and East Asia, leading in most cases to adjustment to the new flows. In some cases, disaffected regions may seek power to ameliorate the effects, as in Chiapas or Aceh. In other cases regions like the Punjab or Catalonia will want more of globalization's effects. The question, however, is whether the metropolitan or the international community will support autonomy or independence for disaffected provinces. As we shall see, independence for such regions is becoming less and less likely.

The trade in goods has spread around the world. Consumers in many developed nations, particularly the United States, have demonstrated a voracious appetite for the products of other nations. This puts income into the hands of exporting nations which now include East Asian countries as well as Europe and Japan. Given their low labor costs, Third World nations have increasingly become manufacturing powerhouses—exporting goods back to developed country markets. As outsourcing continues, even more First World industrial facilities will move to less developed locations. Certain software activities will also shift to the Third World. This process will cause a greater equalization of GDP between North and South. As a result, a growing number of nations will participate in world trade; commerce will increase in size and scope.

In contrast to goods, capital has not spread uniformly around the world. Since World War II, capital transfers have typically occurred between developed countries. Only recently has this transfer been extended to include East Asia, Latin America, and India. Beginning in the 1980s, the failure of capital to spread more widely has caused a greater pressure for migration, but this pressure has been resisted in Europe and Japan and to some extent even in the United States. In theory, the failure of capital to move to Southern countries could be made up in economic terms by the migration of labor from South to North. In theory, factor price equalization then might occur.

In practice, however, migration has not fully compensated for capital's failure to shift locations. Real wages remain low in the Southern Hemisphere and in relative terms perhaps too high in the Northern Hemisphere.[12] If less developed states undertook to do more manufacturing, inequality between countries would be reduced.[13] The outsourcing of services will also help equalize growth rates between industrial and developing countries. Foreign direct investment (FDI) proceeding from North to South would then partly substitute for migration flows from South to North, and Third World manufacturing production based on FDI could serve as the basis for exports to developed economies. Under these conditions, trading nations would become producers of manufactured goods as well as services.

Moving to the next stage of industrial progress, previous low-cost producers like Hong Kong, Korea, Taiwan, and Singapore could then become designers and financiers of products produced in even lower wage locations—like China, India, Mauritius, Indonesia, and Bangladesh.[14] Then, differences between North and South would be further reduced as "virtual states" emerged among developing economies.[15]

Until this happens, inequalities may be one of the causes of tensions between nations. In addition, globalization may favor particular regions within a country, giving rise to internal conflicts. As a result of their participation in global trade, the Punjab and Kerala did particularly well in India while other provinces were relatively disadvantaged. In Spain, Catalonia and the Basques were favored by international economic flows, but Castile was not. In China, Guangdong and Dalian benefited, but Xinjiang did not. Under these circumstances even relatively advanced countries may contain less favored regions which seek to break out of metropolitan control and achieve independence. States with restive populations include: Sri Lanka (Tamils), India (Punjabis, Mizos, Nagas, and Kashmiris), Mexico (Chiapans), and Indonesia (with dissident populations in Aceh, Ambon, and elsewhere).[16] Thus the failure of capital to move to areas of labor abundance, and the simultaneous inability of labor to move to areas of capital abundance, will cause inequalities and perhaps lead to greater subnationalism of the affected regions. In this way capital as a factor in globalization may stimulate tensions.

As domestic security problems are resolved within the Third World, however, capital will generally resume flowing to areas of capital scarcity and labor abundance. If this occurs, globalization of capital will provide an equalizing tendency between if not within nations.[17]

Finally, the spread of information is becoming a worldwide phenomenon, and it is the hardest to stop. Engulfed by information flows from other countries, individuals may become dissatisfied as they compare their present situation with known life-possibilities available elsewhere. A revolution of rising expectations may be stimulated by new information sources on the quality of life in other countries. But a more uniform spread of information does not mean a proportional increase of terrorism or movements seeking national self-determination. If everyone in a social system is affected equally by these global tendencies, ethnic self-determination and terrorism are unlikely to erupt. Also the government takes advantage of the new opportunities in information technology to control dissidents. By and large, ethnic inequalities or regional differences must be present to stimulate the disadvantaged to seek redress. If these emerge, self-determination movements and terrorists can use internet and information networks to further their cause.[18]

CONTROLS ON GLOBALIZATION EFFECTS

This does not mean, however, that globalization in different regions will automatically produce a negative, separatist reaction. Much depends on what national and international authorities (national governments, the IMF, WTO, NATO, ASEAN, and G-8) do to contain the response. Globalization, of course, enlists or at least attracts a large number of cooperators—governments, labor movements, bureaucracies, and business organizations, to say nothing of consumers. The middle classes and local reservoirs of technical expertise benefit from the rising investment and cheap consumer goods that are provided by the global economy. In this way, globalization may help to co-opt potential dissidents. In addition, the disenchanted populations may be spread evenly throughout the country, preventing the buildup of regional centers of opposition. New subnationalism will not then be formed. Governments, moreover, can influence the settlement patterns of their minorities.

In addition, modern governments, particularly those in Europe, seek to assure welfare for groups that might be disadvantaged by the globalization process. Groups in the major cities may benefit from worldwide production, trade, finance, or information. In the hinterlands, where infrastructure is lacking, globalization may bypass local interests, but the national government can compensate the neglected provinces with subsidies or benefits, especially where potential dissidents might be concentrated. Quebec, Scotland, the Punjab, and the Basque regions of Spain and France have not suffered as a result of their regional distinctness or distance from the metropolitan center. They have been generously compensated for losses by the central authorities. Taiwan is now receiving de facto economic benefits—even subsidies—from Beijing which may partly assuage Taipei's failure to achieve international recognition of its separate sovereignty. Taiwanese elections show that sentiment in favor of independence has not declined, though the Democratic People's Party (which favored sovereignty) has been losing ground to the Kuomintang (see Richard Baum in chapter 15).

In some cases, like Chechnya, Kashmir, or Aceh, however, benefits provided by the central government have been insufficient to overcome ideological-religious hostility or the active assistance of hostile foreign elements directing insurgent attacks against the central regime. To cope with continuing strife, national governments have used force to contain dissident provinces, with partial success. In addition, the international community may inveigh against independence for dissident regions. It has been hostile to independence or autonomy for Chechnya and Kashmir at least since the September 11,

2001 attacks on the World Trade Center. In Indonesia, Aceh and Ambon have not enlisted international sympathizers akin to those who supported independence for East Timor. For many outside powers, the prospect of a major state unraveling under the pressure of regional self-determination has stimulated a conservative reaction. Palestine is one of the few emergent nation-states that still garners international support, though that support may be lost because of Hamas's dominance of local politics in the West Bank and Gaza. Hamas has not yet shown any indication to control terrorism directed against Israel.

GLOBALIZATION AND SELF-DETERMINATION— A THEORETICAL MODEL

Many factors condition the acceptance or rejection of continuing metropolitan rule of dissident provinces. There are at least four variables that influence the dependent region: (1) the degree of globalization itself; (2) the acceptance of globalization by metropolitan rulers; (3) the acceptance of globalization by major international actors (who could support or oppose independence for the region); (4) the dependent province's attitude toward globalization. We hypothesize that the most likely case for independence— or an increase in the potency of the self-determination movement (SDM)— would occur when the metropolitan government is isolated in its stance on globalization, being opposed by both foreign actors and the dissident province itself. Independence would also be more likely when preceded by a crisis enveloping the central government (such as economic or financial collapse) (see table 1.1).

On the contrary the metropolitan bond with the dependent region would hypothetically be strengthened when the dissident provinces position on globalization was similar to that of the metropole and of leading international actors (see table 1.2).

In case 1 a dissident modernizing province supported by international actors seeks independence from a retrograde government. The Punjab in the 1980s might have constituted such a case, but since then the Indian government has itself modernized. Kashmir is not such a case, because Kashmiri

Table 1.1. Cases 1 and 2

State of Globalization	Metropolitan Policy	International Policy	Dissident Group
1. High	Against G	For G	FG-dissatisfaction
2. Low/moderate	For G	Against G	AG-dissatisfaction

Table 1.2. Cases 3 and 4

State of Globalization	Metropolitan Policy	International Policy	Dissident Group
3. High	For G	For G	FG-satisfaction
4. Low/moderate	Against G	Against G	AG-satisfaction

dissidents aided by Pakistan are Islamic traditionalists and they have only limited support from the international community. (See Deepak Lal in chapter 9.) In case 2 with globalization low, a modernizing regime seeks to keep a traditional province that is supported by anti-global international actors within its national fold. Chechnya does not constitute such a case because the international community has become pro-globalist. (See Reppert-Shevchenko in chapter 8.) In fact, if there were such cases in the past, there are no obvious examples of them today.

Case 3 in which governments, dissidents, and the outside world are all in favor of globalization is much more typical and is becoming the characteristic outcome, even where there are cultural differences between province and metropole. Scotland and Quebec are examples as we shall see. Case 4 is again an anachronistic outcome, involving low globalization and anti-globalist policies all round. Today, few if any regions of the world are free from the pressures of globalization. It is difficult to think of relevant current examples of case 4. In the past, however, President Sukarno of Indonesia faced a "backlash" coalition of dissidents even when he shared their fundamental antipathy toward globalization.

The appendix lists the twelve other possible outcomes.

THE INDEPENDENT VARIABLES

In seeking independence, dissidents seek to capitalize on a situation in which their metropolitan government is out of harmony with three other elements in the picture: (1) the strength of globalization, (2) the international support for globalization, and (3) their own position on globalization. Chechnya is opposed to modernization, and Moscow is in favor. If major international actors were against it, and if globalization were weakening, these trends would favor self-determination for Chechnya. But, as we know, globalization is not apparently lessening, nor is international support for it declining, so independence becomes even more unlikely (see Reppert-Shevchenko in chapter 8). (Given their support of terrorism, Chechen nationalists have become more isolated still.)[19] Chechen separatist attacks have only solidified international opposition to their designs. The Beslan school massacre in North Ossetia constitutes a leading case in point.

In the past, dissidents in the Punjab sought independence and/or greater autonomy from India. The movement wanted more freedom to participate in the international economy without controls from Delhi. Most international actors favored globalization. But the need for Punjabi autonomy/independence declined when Delhi came to support globalization as well. India succeeded with a policy which combined local repression with greater globalization. In the Basque case the dissidents favored globalization, but Spain and France were also its partisans in political as well as economic terms. Despite their cultural differences with Castile, Basques had few economic grievances, and support for ETA declined. Before Spain's entry into the EU and the Euro-zone, Basques might have argued for independence plus EU membership; now, however, independence without such membership looks quite unattractive. Since Basque separatists want French as well as Spanish territory, they face an uphill fight. In this respect, their position is analogous to the Kurds' failure to achieve an autonomous or independent nation-state of their own comprising territory from Iraq, Iran, and Turkey.

Those likely to remain within the metropolitan bond include Scotland and Quebec because Canada and Great Britain are as globalist as the outside world. Nor would independence necessarily lead (as some dissidents believe) to either an American or a European embrace of the seceded province. The Parti Quebecois has staged a partial comeback though the new Conservative government is unlikely to be any more hospitable to Quebec than the Liberals were. This issue of negotiations, however, remains open. In addition, the French-speaking region has benefited from generous government subsidies from Ottawa. Public opinion surveys indicate that separatist opinion in Quebec was largely strategic in character, seeking greater influence in Canada, whether or not independence was granted.[20]

In the Scottish case, Glasgow has received a considerable devolution of power—a parliament, the Scottish pound, and an independent legal system—and like Scotland, Britain remains in the globalization camp. Britain has also given a disproportionate share of benefits to Scotland. Glasgow may (vainly) hope that it could fare even better if the EU offered it membership, but this prospect is quite unlikely. The EU has too many candidate-members already, and Britain would strongly oppose its admission.[21]

Cyprus has been granted EU membership, but the Turkish part of the country has been left in abeyance, pending agreement with Greek Cypriots who have vetoed an international accord. The Greeks will have to change their stance over time because Turkish Cypriots, with the support of Ankara, have accepted a federal solution. This settlement will pave the way for negotiations leading to Turkish membership in the European Union.[22]

In summary, metropolitan and international forces typically embrace globalization.[23] If the dissident province does not do so, its independence will rarely be supported and may not succeed. If the dissident province favors globalization, its independence is in a degree unnecessary. In this way, the interaction of variables typically favors the retention of the dissident province within the metropolitan frontier.

THE AMOUNT OF GLOBALIZATION

There may be more or less globalization. Some believe that globalization will moderate in the aftermath of the attacks on the World Trade Center of September 11, 2001. That is not our conclusion, however. (See Deepak Lal in chapter 3 and John Mueller in chapter 4.) Despite questions concerning port security, world trade has not lessened. The flow of capital resumed as the world recession diminished. Our study concludes that more countries will now be affected by international financial flows than previously. In the 1960s many Third World nations could stand aside from globalization, but few can do so today, dependent as they have become on selling abroad and receiving capital from the outside world. The greater the globalization, the harder it will be for dissident movements to reverse economic pressures even if they are opposed to them. After the deposition of the Shah in 1979–80, the Iranian mullahs sought to restrain globalist pressures, but they succeeded only partially. Underneath the surface of Iranian religiosity, a pro-globalist citizenry resides.

In more general terms, the amount of globalization which varied significantly in past ages seems to be secularly increasing today. Some areas of Africa, South Asia, and the South Pacific may still be largely unaffected by global trade and capital movements, but most areas of the world are strongly influenced by them.

THE SOCIAL RESPONSE TO GLOBALIZATION

If global factors generally intrude into social affairs, it is necessary to examine society's response to them. To test for the influence of domestic social factors, one can begin with the assumption that the response to globalization will generally depend on the political/economic status or development of the particular society. An urban, politically-participant electorate in Caracas or Mexico City will apparently be far more affected than rural peasants in Nepal or nomadic herdsmen in Outer Mongolia.[24] Non-participation can be either in class or regional terms. If the mobilized part of society is excluded from political participation either vertically (in class terms) or horizontally (in regional terms), it may well react to demand greater autonomy or benefit.

Is there a threshold (in terms of domestic social development) between acceptance and rejection of global influences? At least two different issues are involved in answering this question: what is the nature of the target society; and what is the degree of penetration by global economic forces? As to the first, how much of the society will be able to adjust to incoming capital and technology and gain (not lose) jobs?[25] What proportion will be unemployed? As to the second question, the entry of overseas capital will depend in the long term on the legal safeguards in place in the target society. Do citizens enjoy property rights, and are their rights protected? How stable is the government? Russia failed the stability test in 1998, and many Latin American countries do not accord property rights to their impoverished citizens. Russia also does not fully protect the property rights of its people. (The treatment of the oil company, Yukos, by the Russian regime is a case in point.) Infrastructure and literacy will also be involved. A literate and trained population together with a developed infrastructure of roads, ports, communications, and air routes may also be needed to attract foreign capital. Equally, class and income differences within the society should not be so extreme as to restrict consumption. In more general terms, one might expect that globalization will be accepted by more modernized societies and rejected by more traditional ones. The amount of literacy, infant mortality, and years of schooling would presumably also affect a country's reception of globalization.

Yet a brief comparison of local social characteristics and the indicators of globalization (such as trade/GDP ratios) demonstrates few robust correlations. This suggests that there are few intrinsic barriers to the spread of global influences. (See Cordero-Rosecrance in chapter 2.) Urban population, schooling, life expectancies, and female literacy are associated with globalization effects. But these do not represent strong or necessary relationships in all cases. It appears that some governments favor a movement toward globalization even when their country's social characteristics remain fairly traditional, even backward.[26]

Two such examples are Brazil and Indonesia. These two countries are struggling to meet requirements of the "Washington Consensus"—low inflation, restrained government deficits, and a stable currency—yet they are not fully modern societies. As Etel Solingen demonstrates, countries do not have to be democratic to attract capital.[27] There are some authoritarian societies in which liberalizing coalitions seek foreign investment on the basis of improved contract-law safeguards and greater political stability.[28] General Park Chung Hee foisted globalization on South Korea when there were few local characteristics which favored it. In the Indonesian case, elites have accepted globalization, though the masses have not yet done so. Islamists have vied with Christians in various provinces, but it is unlikely that dissidents will be given independence. This relationship is further explored in chapter 10.

A general conclusion is that the policy of the metropole is the single most important independent variable in charting the acceptance of globalization. A country's participation in the globalization process may be determined more by a willing government than by the social "ripeness" of the population itself.

THE METROPOLITAN RESPONSE TO GLOBALIZATION

The response of the domestic government is critical to the success of both globalization and self-determination for a regional minority. Some domestic governments have been quite effective in channeling or reducing the effect of globalization upon their populations, seeking to prevent new dissident movements from rising. Increased governmental expenditure can mitigate the inequalities foisted upon low income countries by globalization. In previous years, Iraq's Saddam Hussein kept the Kurds in the north and the Shiites in the south in check by preventing foreign (globalist) influences from intruding. His approach was largely a punitive one. The Indonesian response to Aceh under Megawati Sukarno-putri also mixed military repression with blandishments. This will likely continue with General Adhoyono in power. In other cases governments have typically rewarded potential dissidents, hoping to keep them within the fold. Canada, Spain, and England have offered rewards to dissidents in Quebec, the Basque areas, and Scotland. The Russian government combined carrots and sticks to influence Chechnya, but the conflict continues to simmer with terrorist actions in Russian cities and nearby provinces. Aside from Chechnya, Vladimir Putin has used the prospect of benefits as well as political pressures to keep disparate regions in line.[29] In more general terms, when aided by the international community, the metropolitan government has been able to prevent self-determination in a very wide range of cases. King Hussein and King Abdullah in Jordan were able to persuade Islamist elements in the legislature to accept effective central rule from Amman.

INTERNATIONAL RESPONSES TO GLOBALIZATION

The outcomes of national self-determination struggles are also strongly influenced by the amount of international support they receive. If key independence movements are assisted by Great Powers, they will be more successful. Croatia became independent largely because of German and then European support. Slovenia was assisted by the European Union in achieving independence. Macedonia retains its territorial integrity largely because of help from the United States, the United Nations, and the European Union—otherwise its northern region might have become part of Kosovo. America and Russia supported the independence of Israel in 1948 against the wishes of the British government. The United Nations, the Great Powers, and sometimes even the previous colonial power paved the way for national self-determination for new African states from the 1950s to the 1970s. On the other hand, the United States has not encouraged an independent Quebec, and international forces do not support independence for either Scotland or Wales. East Timor, however, moved to independence from Indonesia with the support of Australia and other countries.

DISSIDENT ATTITUDES TOWARD GLOBALIZATION

In some cases dissident attitudes toward globalization can be very important in garnering international support. Slovenia convinced many observers that it was an eligible nation-state because of its already high degree of economic and political advancement. As the rest of Yugoslavia fell into chaos, Slovenia was seen as a new and viable economic entity. The key here appears to be the dissidents' congruence with international pressures as compared with their acceptance by the metropolitan regime. If international powers support globalization and the metropolitan government does not, a globalist group of dissidents may win support. In a traditional society, if international powers stand against globalization and the domestic regime also opposes it, a liberal dissident group may have difficulty winning autonomy. The Punjab faced such problems initially.

THE DEPENDENT VARIABLE—SELF-DETERMINATION OUTCOMES

The reaction against globalization extends along a continuum which ranges from terrorism (the weapon of the weak) at its lower end to devolution, autonomy, independence, and nationalist assertion at its higher end. Each of these objectives reflects a successively higher degree of nationalist ambition and/or response. Nationalist aggressors and seekers of independence are the most demanding responders, and under favorable circumstances can become the most successful modifiers of the status quo. But if full independence and/or nationalist expansion cannot be achieved, dissidents may have to be satisfied with autonomy or a lesser devolution of power. If none of these is within reach, terrorism may be the default response. It can occur at the beginning and/or at the end of a (failed) struggle for independence. It is theoretically possible that a decisive failure of the Parti Quebecois to win independence from Canada could regenerate the FLQ in Canada and Quebec. The Basques and the Kurds have failed to achieve statehood, but they continue with terrorist tactics of ETA and the PKK. If Taiwan were forced to amalgamate with China against its will, it might direct terrorism against Beijing. In chapter 2, our study seeks to chart the domestic political/economic variables which will help decide the reaction to globalization. If the regime in power rejects global influences and a dissident group wishes to participate in a wider international society, tension may increase and generate international support for the group in question. But full autonomy will depend upon the policies, strength, and stability of the metropolitan government as well as the response of the Great Powers and the international community more generally.

Another variable which appears to foster globalization is the participation of a candidate-state in a regional security arrangement (see Etel Solingen in chapter 10). ASEAN has paved the way for globalization and an end to military conflicts in East Asia. No such organization exists in the Middle East, and the region's acceptance of globalization has been spotty at best. In Europe, NATO and EU have paved the way for globalization and peace, but there is yet no similar organization in South Asia. In Etel Solingen's terms, "backlash coalitions" (directed against globalization) are more likely where there is no accepted security cluster to provide for regional acceptance of global influences.

CONCLUSIONS—THE OUTLINE OF THE ARGUMENT

Globalization will continue and deepen. Neither terrorism nor Great Power rivalry is likely to halt its expansion.

There will be continuing movements toward self-determination, but these will generally not achieve independence. NGOs may assist locals to propound their political claims, but terrorism will not be an acceptable means of advancing the cause of independence. In Africa, diamonds, oil, and minerals will draw dissident elements to particular provinces, but countries will fight to prevent their secession. If so, few new states will likely be created. Few additional empires are in the market for collapse.[30] Nationalism of the state regime, however, will be a continuing feature of the international political scene to control potential dissidents.

Thus states, even states with ethnic minorities, will not generally split apart.

There will be no independence for Aceh, Kashmir and Chechnya (see table 1.3).

Palestine may become independent with outside peacekeepers stationed there. But this depends upon a domestic consolidation within the Palestine

Table 1.3.

Negative Sanctions	Positive Sanctions
Aceh	Scotland
Kashmir	Quebec
Chechnya	Basques

Authority to control terrorism, which under Hamas's dominance appears unlikely. In Africa the Southern Sudan may possibly split from the North if an agreement is reached to end the civil war. But few other instances of successful subnationalism are likely to be found in the next few years.

Global terrorism will continue, irrespective of globalization, though globalization will make terrorist success more difficult. Partisans of globalization will increase in number, favoring open trade, open markets, and financial flows. They will not wish to see these transactions disrupted by international terrorism. As a result, an increasing number of state supporters of globalization (including the United States and Europe) will cooperate to reduce the prospects of terrorism. The United States cannot do this alone, for there are no superpowers in the struggle against this international evil. Equally, the fight against terrorism could facilitate stronger Great Power links, including links with the People's Republic of China.

APPENDIX

	State of Globalization	Metropolitan Policy	International Policy	Dissident Group
(5)	High	AG	FG	AG
(6)	Low	FG	AG	FG
(7)	High	FG	FG	AG
(8)	Low	AG	AG	FG
(9)	High	AG	AG	AG
(10)	High	FG	AG	FG
(11)	Low	AG	FG	AG
(12)	High	FG	AG	AG
(13)	Low	FG	FG	AG
(14)	Low	FG	FG	FG
(15)	Low	AG	FG	FG
(16)	High	AG	AG	FG

In most of these intermediate cases (with the exception of 9, 12, 14, and 15) the dissident group is opposed by international policy actors, making its struggle more difficult. In addition, the dissident region agrees with the government on globalization in cases 5, 6, 9, 10, 11, 14. This also reduces its incentive to withdraw. Only in cases 9 and 14 is the dissident province's attitude on globalization supported by both the government and the international community. But this would in turn further mute its support for independence. Liberalizing coalitions in such countries would likely opt to remain inside the metropole.

In case 7 the dissident province is out of harmony with both the government and the international community's attitude on globalization. In case 8 a weaker globalization is resisted by both government and the international community. The dissident province is more modernist, but remains isolated in its struggle. This case could only occur in an area or continent isolated from global trends. Perhaps the case of Ibo Biafra fighting against Nigerian traditionalists in the 1960s would be one past example. Nonetheless, as globalization spreads, and case 7 becomes more characteristic, dissident provinces like Chechnya or Aceh will not garner international support.

NOTES

The authors would like to express thanks to Barbara Rosecrance, Amy Davis Stein, and Luisita Cordero.

1. The long-term future of states in Africa, however, cannot be fully foreseen. Today, with perhaps the exception of the southern Sudan, Kosovo and Montenegro, no new states appear likely to be formed. For an alternative point of view, see Alberto Alesina and Enrico Spolaore, "On the Number and Size of Nations," NBER Working Paper #5050 (March, 1995).

2. See Geoffrey Garrett, "Capital Mobility, Trade, and the Domestic Politics of Economic Policy," in R. Keohane and H. Milner, eds., *Internationalization and Domestic Politics* (Cambridge: Cambridge University Press, 1996), 80–81.

3. See Graham Allison, *Nuclear Terror* (2005).

4. See John Mearsheimer, *The Tragedy of Great Power Politics* (New York: Norton, 2003).

5. But see Richard Cooper in chapter 5.

6. The relative immunity of present-day globalization to break down as a result of terror attacks is testified to by John Mueller, Richard Cooper, and Deepak Lal.

7. As demonstrated by the attacks on Madrid railways in 2003. Studies by former Secretary of Defense William Cohen suggest the continuing possibility of large-scale terrorist attacks.

8. In the sixteenth century Antwerp was sacked and blockaded, but this only stimulated the emergence of Amsterdam as a hub of commerce.

9. See Richard Cooper in chapter 5, and Council on Foreign Relations, "Chinese Military Power" (2003).

10. The Council of Economic Advisors under Gregory Mankiw frequently elaborated this case. See also *Principles of Economics* (Mason, OH: Thomson/South-Western, 2004).

11. See Graham Allison in chapter 6.

12. In contrast, labor mobility made for a greater equalization of real wages between England and the United States during the second half of the 19th century. (See Kevin O'Rourke and Jeffrey Williamson, *Globalization and History* (Cambridge, MA: MIT Press, 1999).

13. This would not necessarily diminish inequality within countries, however.

14. See the reference in footnote 3.

15. Virtual states are countries which shift their production overseas, retaining design and research facilities at home. See Rosecrance, *The Rise of the Virtual State* (New York: Basic Books, 1999).

16. The way to prevent this is to invest more in the disadvantaged province—in terms of both carrots and sticks.

17. See Robert E. B. Lucas, *International Migration and Economic Development: Lessons from Low Income Countries* (Cheltenham, UK: Edward Elgar, 2005).

18. See John Mackinlay, "Globalization and Insurgency," International Institute for Strategic Studies (London, 2002). Governments also use such networks to enhance their control of separatists.

19. But see also the work of Matthew Evangelista, *The Chechen Wars: Will Russia Go the Way of the Soviet Union?* (Washington, DC: Brookings Inst., 2002).

20. See Alan Alexandroff in chapter 13.

21. See Richard Rosecrance and Arthur Stein in chapter 14.

22. These negotiations began in October, 2005.

23. The Middle East and Africa remain exceptions here.

24. In Argentina, however, urban populations are sometimes more opposed to globalization than are the agricultural population (whose fate is tied to farm exports).

25. See Adrian Wood and Kersti Berge, "Exporting Manufactures: Human Resources, Natural Resources, and Trade Policy," *Journal of Development Studies* (October, 1997).

26. There are many anomalies here. General Park Chung Hee forced globalization on South Korea when the society's latent and rural characteristics were not fully supportive of such a change. King Hussein in Jordan and President Yoweri Museveni in Uganda also fostered greater globalization than their populations may have been initially ready for.

27. There is, however, a "democratic efficiency" argument. See UNDP, "Arab Development Report" (2002).

28. See Fareed Zakaria, *From Wealth to Power: The Unusual Origins of America's World Role* (Princeton, NJ: Princeton University Press, 1998).

29. See Daniel Treisman, *After the Deluge: Regional Crises and Political Consolidation in Russia* (Ann Arbor: University of Michigan Press, 1999).

30. Russia, Indonesia, and India might be thought to be continuing candidates for dismemberment, but this outcome seems increasingly unlikely.

2

The "Acceptance" of Globalization

Luisita Cordero and Richard N. Rosecrance

International relations are not simply a state of anarchy. There are profound elements of hierarchy in the international system, and even authority relationships. Some countries obey others or duly constituted international organizations—even if they are not coerced to do so. Globalization contributes to the weakness of states by reducing state-centric controls of the national economy. Countries sway this way and that, according to the vicissitudes of global economic winds. In this way, all states have lost the ability to set interest rates and exchange rates on an independent basis. But the market—even the international market—does not thereby gain authoritative control over their actions. National governments not only retain political authority, they maintain the ability to discipline dissatisfied provinces. They also can cushion the effects of globalization on different regions of the country.

At the same time globalization makes independence for such regions a less attractive option. Alberto Alesina argues that free trade can hold out export possibilities for newly independent states, perhaps stimulating their growth and thereby increasing the incentive for self-determination, augmenting the number of states.[1] But international trade is not completely free. New exporters face barriers in selling in developed-country markets. New countries can easily borrow abroad, but they cannot always sell enough to repay the debts they have incurred. Under these circumstances subject provinces contemplating independence may decide to rely on the domestic market in their own country even if they are not entirely happy with the policies of the home government.

In this particular respect, globalization has reinforced central power and made independence more risky. In addition, the international community, international organizations, and most Great Powers favor the extension of globalization to most areas of the world. A dissident province which rejected globalization (as terrorist provinces or "failed states" do) would not find much support internationally.

How rapidly will globalization be extended? This depends upon the local context in which it occurs. In theory at least, some countries and social contexts may be more prone to globalization than others. Is there a socio-economic threshold differentiating the acceptors from the rejecters of globalization? In this chapter we examine this question.

As a first approximation, we begin by considering the possibility that a country's embrace of globalization depends more on international than domestic factors. Next we look at the influence of internal factors on globalization. Third, we offer data to help us decide among the contending hypotheses, and finally we offer some relevant conclusions. Broadly speaking, we conclude that the size of a country conditions its acceptance of globalization, and that globalization is likely to be more successful where there is higher female educational achievement. Size, however, is not a variable that can be easily manipulated by governments to produce increased globalization. From a policy standpoint, the most important variable is regime preferences, influenced by success of other countries. The emulation of the practices of other countries, therefore, remains a very important factor in the decision to accept globalization.[2]

THE INTERNATIONAL DETERMINANTS OF GLOBALIZATION

In this section we look at hypotheses which suggest inter alia that the country's position in the international hierarchy of power and security might determine its "acceptance" of globalization. But other international influences might also apply. A country's foreign economic policy may depend on patterns of leadership and emulation. How would such factors affect the relationship of trade and GDP—our measure of globalization?

The well-known "hegemonic stability argument" contends that an open trading system needs a hegemon to hold the reins and provide liquidity and markets to countries in trouble. Stephen Krasner found evidence of this phenomenon in the role of Britain in the 19th century and America in the 20th century. More recently, Edward Mansfield has tested the impact of the distribution of power on trade. He concludes that an equal division of power offers few incentives for any state to seek windfall gains by imposing tariffs. As inequality increases, however, powerful nations may raise tariffs. But when extremely high levels of inequality are reached, Mansfield claims that the dominant state may refrain from imposing tariffs despite the potential for sizable economic gains.[3] It may then come to act as the hegemonic leader of the system.

Elaborating further, Joanne Gowa points out that a country may hesitate to trade with a potential adversary if the latter's benefits from trade may be turned into a military advantage. Thus, trade among allies should be greater than that among rivals. Bipolar relationships which cement intra-bloc ties should conduce to greater trade than would occur under strict multipolarity.[4]

Conflict or war will also influence international trade. Political conflicts may spill over to economic relations and impede commercial dealings. Conflict can also dampen trade indirectly by discouraging economic actors from pursuing business opportunities in an environment of higher risk and uncertainty. War can also cause supply shortages, hikes in transport costs, loss of access to markets, and even losses of territory.

James Morrow and his colleagues examined international determinants, but also included regime type in their analysis of bilateral trade. According to their findings, regime type turns out to be very important with trade increasing as countries become more democratic. If country relationships improve—that is, international cooperation rises—this also increases trade, but the occurrence of militarized disputes (not involving war) does not disrupt trade very much. Morrow and his colleagues also disagree with Gowa; they conclude that bipolar alliances do not necessarily enhance trade within the bloc and that there is little difference between the effects of bipolarity and multipolarity on trade outside it.[5]

We concur with the tenor of most of these contributions, and would stress that leadership matters in the choice of globalization. Leadership factors may explain why sudden leaps in trade levels occur in isolated countries even when there is no change in their underlying social and economic conditions. Sometimes decision-makers move to integrate a country into the global market. Note the decisive roles here of Lee Kuan Yew of Singapore, Park Chung Hee of South Korea, and Deng Xaio-ping of China, for example. Such decisions may be prompted also by the influence of liberalizing coalitions, and may also result from international circumstances. There may be an externally induced crisis or a fresh opportunity when a rapidly growing neighbor seeks greater trade. Countries also emulate each other as leaders of one country see another forging ahead economically and seek to adopt the same winning formula.

Emulation is just one possibility accounting for the spread and acceptance of globalization. Beth Simmons hypothesizes that a generalized diffusion of new ideas favoring democracy and open markets in recent decades has facilitated the diffusion of globalization. Countries may adhere to liberal economic policies to obtain external sources of financing. Well-known "structural adjustment" programs have been pressed on recipients by the IMF and the World Bank. Countries have also opened up to attract investment. Network externalities or the positive spillovers from being part of a group whose individual members have adopted similar policies may also foster openness and globalization. In short the acceptance of globalization is determined by emulation, ideas, leadership, and political stability.[6] Despite the hegemonic stability argument, relative power does not appear to determine acceptance of global influences, since both large and small states are prepared to open themselves to trade and capital movements.

INTERNAL DETERMINANTS AND GLOBALIZATION

Another possibility is that domestic factors may position a country to accept or reject globalization. These characteristics fall under three broad headings: a country's geography and physical environment, its socioeconomic conditions, and its political features.

Economic Conditions

The gravity model relates the size of the economy and a society's wealth to the level of trade between trading partners. According to it, larger economies trade less. In contrast, smaller countries—which have to export to live—rely more on foreign trade because their domestic market is too small.[7] Second, wealthier countries have higher levels of trade presumably because they can indulge a greater variety of consumer tastes. Third, the gravity model posits that the closer countries are to one another, the greater the trade, other things being equal. But it is also true that technology and infrastructure can compensate for distance between trading partners. The more developed the infrastructure of a society and the higher its level of technology, the more likely it is to trade regardless of distance from suppliers or markets. In addition, the presence of legal frontiers may reduce trade. In the absence of a customs union, trade is diminished if it has to cross international frontiers.

Social Conditions

Social modernization also plays a role in charting the response to globalization. The degree of social mobilization of a society as measured by mass media, literacy rates, urbanization, and manufacturing will affect the acceptance of globalization. Karl Deutsch and his associates argued that increasing modernization and mobilization moved countries in two different directions. In the early stages of mobilization and industrialization, a country's dependence on external trade and finance increased. When industrialization matured, however, nations, according to Deutsch, became less dependent on trade because they could provide for most of their own needs. Deutsch believed that Britain, Germany, and Japan went through this two-step—rise and decline—process.[8]

Despite Deutsch, there is little indication of such an outcome today. Even the most highly industrialized countries are heavily dependent on international trade and financial flows. Deutsch's outcome also differs from the gravity model's prediction of a linear relationship between wealth and trade.[9] Deutsch concluded that there was a reduction in international trade as a percentage of GDP after World War I, but this result may very well be explained by the distorting effects of war, not by the attainment of full industrialization by the trading parties concerned.

Urbanization and increasing education also have a positive effect on a country's propensity to trade, paralleling that of wealth. More educated populations are more likely to have a broader range of consumer tastes and preferences than less educated ones, contributing to increasing trade. In addition, reducing the gap in educational and economic opportunities between men and women may also broaden the impact of globalization. The expansion of opportunities for women and their entry into the labor force is one vital aspect of social mobilization. This essay goes on to test such social factors and their influence on trade. Proceeding beyond Deutsch's conclusions, recent work suggests a reason for associating urbanization with an increase in trade. Under assumptions of increasing returns, one society may gain a distinct edge over another in terms of labor and manufacturing capacity. This would then lead the second society to send labor to and/or buy goods from the first. Paul Krugman presents a model in which the prospect of increasing returns induces trade even between two countries with identical factor endowments (in contrast to the usual Heckscher-Ohlin theory in which trade emerges from differences in factor abundance). Path dependence then becomes crucial. Krugman posits that an increase in trade may be associated with countries undergoing urbanization where there is a particular concentration of individuals in and around city-centers. Countries may then trade on the basis of urban-rural differences. For countries which restrict immigration, the flow of goods may substitute for labor inflows.[10]

Political Conditions

To turn now to a final set of characteristics that might occasion an acceptance of globalization, we observe that domestic political variables may also influence a country's propensity to trade. First, skewed income distribution may divide a society into competing camps that either favor or resist greater international trade. The amount of trade may relate to socioeconomic divisions. Because owners of abundant factors stand to benefit more from trade according to the Heckscher-Ohlin theory, they would be expected to favor openness, while the owners of scarce factors would be more protectionist. The Heckscher-Ohlin theory assumed full mobility of economic factors internally. On the other hand, the Ricardo-Viner model questions this assumption. If there are differences in the internal mobility of factors, owners of the more mobile factor will expect to gain more from international exchange and in turn would be more likely to favor free trade. Equally, owners of specific factors (which are less mobile) would be more protectionist. As Ronald Rogowski shows, economic theory only indicates what political groups might form, not why and under what conditions one would prevail over another.[11] In addition, domestic political cleavages change gradually, far too slowly to account for the rapid change in the amount of trade countries have experienced, weakening any relationship with globalization.

Regime type may also influence a country's propensity to trade. One might suppose that countries with liberal political institutions might adopt more liberal trading practices. Democratic nations would then engage in trade more than would non-democracies. Democratic governments, however, have not always embraced free trade. Australia, Canada, and the 19th-century United States imposed high tariffs. Oppositely, authoritarian governments have been known to encourage trade and to maintain economic openness, despite their undemocratic character. Depending on the presence of "liberalizing coalitions" in their midst, Etel Solingen shows that even authoritarian states may engage in free-trading relations.[12] Thus, regime type might not predict a country's propensity to trade.

As we have seen in the contemporary American reaction to "outsourcing," even liberal governments may sometimes discourage capital outflows and foreign trade inflows. According to one theory, democratic governments may focus on short-term election cycles more than authoritarian ones do, perhaps favoring higher tariffs. On the other hand, economic closure also imposes costs on particular sectors of the economy, so democratic governments might shrink from it as readily as their authoritarian counterparts. Hence, regime type alone may not determine either the content of trade policy or its long-term trend.

Refining this argument, Garrett and Lange hypothesize that democracies may be more able to alter policies, while authoritarian governments can make more drastic shifts in policy. Where fairness prevails, less costly and less risky policies are apt to be preferred. In contrast, where the views of a particular group are privileged, the less favored can be forced to bear a disproportionate share of the costs. Since fairness is higher in democracies, high-risk policies of economic brinkmanship are more likely to be pursued by more authoritarian governments.[13]

A countervailing argument, however, is that uncertainty favors democracies. Because information flows more freely in democracies, they should experience less of the uncertainty that reduces interstate cooperation (including trade) than corresponding authoritarian states.

EMPIRICAL TESTS

We have now offered various theoretical possibilities which need to be investigated in concrete empirical terms. In this section, we use data from 1995 to 2002 from the World Development Indicators to test the hypotheses discussed above. We employ indicators of governance devised by Kaufmann et al.[14] From various "enterprise, citizen, and expert respondent surveys," they have derived indicators that typify different aspects of governance. In this chapter we use their indicator for political stability; this variable ranges from –2.5 to +2.5 on a scale of governance where higher values mean better governance. We also draw from the Polity IV and the Correlates of War data sets to study the effect of regime type and international conflict on trade. The first specifies a polity score indicating the mix of democratic and autocratic characteristics of a state; it ranges from –10 (full autocracy) to +10 (full democracy) (see Marshall and Jaggers). The second provides data on inter-state conflicts in which hostilities have been marked by the use, rather than the mere threat, of force.

The Baseline Model

Our baseline model (model 1) examines the well-documented influence of country size and wealth on trade. Because trade and wealth are likely to influence each other, we used the log of the average of per capita GDP from 1995 to 1999 to predict the average share of trade in GDP from 2000 to 2002. The log of the average land area from 2000 to 2002 is a measure for country size. Trade should decrease with higher values of area and rise with higher values of per capita GDP.

The coefficient of –.10 for size is statistically significant, but that of wealth is not. A 10 percent increase in land area translates into a 1 percent fall in the share of trade relative to GDP. A 5 percent hypothetical decrease in the size of Ukraine would leave it about the size of France.[15] Such a decrease implies an increase in the share of trade in GDP by .5 percent (or half a percentage point). Suppose Indonesia were to lose Aceh province, which is roughly 3.2 percent of its land area; this implies a .32 percent increase in the proportion of trade to GDP.[16] The dissolution of the former Czechoslovakia hints at the salience of country size to trade. The split represented a loss in area of about 38 and 62 percent respectively to the Czech Republic and Slovakia. Only at such magnitudes would size predict more noticeable changes at 3.8 and 6.2 percent in the level of trade.

Technology and Human Capital

Next we examine in model 2 how communications technology might overcome the impediment of distance by including the logged average cost of a

Table 2.1. Summary Statistics

Variable	Obs	Mean	Std. Dev.	Min	Max
2000–2002 Average Trade as Proportion of GDP (in %)	161	86.51	43.49	20.18	290.71
Log of 2000–2002 Average Trade as Proportion of GDP	161	4.338	0.506	3.005	5.672
1995–1999 Average GDP per Capita (in constant $US)	175	6,028	9,778	102	48,278
Log of 1995–1999 Average GDP per Capita	175	7.535	1.579	4.627	10.785
Land Area (in sq. kms.)	183	709,588	1,916,146	160	16,900,000
Log of Area	183	11.539	2.433	5.075	16.642
1995–1999 Average Cost of 3-Min. Call to the United States (in $US)	136	5.81	4.11	0.80	26.86
Log of 1995–1999 Average Cost of Call to the United States	136	1.566	0.622	−0.223	3.291
1995–1999 Average Female Illiteracy (in %)	132	29.52	26.30	0.20	92.62
Log of 1995–1999 Average Female Illiteracy	132	2.676	1.510	−1.595	4.528
Female Secondary Gross Enrollment Ratio (in %)	171	62.64	36.75	4.01	163.11
Landlocked	182	0.2	0.4	0	1
1996–1998 Political Stability Indicator	162	0.0	0.9	−2.6	1.6
Degree of Democracy in a Polity	157	3.1	6.6	−10	10
Involvement in Militarized Inter-State Dispute Using Force	189	0.4	0.5	0	1

3-minute telephone call to the United States and expect trade to rise as this figure falls. We find that only size remains a significant predictor of trade with a coefficient of −.11, which is almost the same as in the previous model. The effect of the logged cost of a call to the United States, which is correlated with a country's wealth, on trading levels is indistinguishable from zero.

As an alternative to the cost of a call to the United States, we use the logged average number of mobile and fixed phone line subscribers from 1995 to 1999.[17] Not surprisingly a higher number of phone subscribers correlates strongly with higher trade. Its .15 coefficient is significant at the .01 level and implies that a 10 percent increase in phone subscribers increases the share of trade in GDP by 1.5 percent.[18]

Human capital, indexed by level of education, might be expected to be a predictor of trade. It is difficult to verify this however. Many have contended (see Solingen and others) that female literacy and enrollment might be more

Table 2.2. Regression Results

	Model 1	Model 2	Model 3	Model 4
Log of 2000–2002 Average Trade as Proportion of GDP in %				
Log of 1995–1999 Average GDP per Capita	0.03	0.05	−0.02	−0.09**
	0.02	0.04	0.04	0.04
Log of Area	−0.10***	−0.11***	−0.10***	−0.11***
	0.01	0.02	0.02	0.02
Log of 1995–1999 Average Cost of Call to the United States		0.01		
		0.09		
Log of 1995–1999 Average Female Illiteracy			−0.11***	
			0.03	
Female Secondary Gross Enrollment				0.01***
				0.002
Landlocked				−.07
				0.09
1996–1998 Political Stability Indicator				0.09
				0.06
Polity				−0.01**
				0.006
Involvement in Militarized Inter-State Dispute Using Force				−0.13
				0.08
Constant	5.28***	5.25***	5.90***	6.07***
	0.28	0.58	0.44	0.38
Observations	157	121	116	135

sensitive measures, as they would pick up patterns of discrimination or inequity in the labor force that might inhibit globalization. But the independent variables wealth, technology, and human capital are correlated and cannot be represented in the equation at the same time.[19]

If we include only the logged values of area, per capita GDP, and female illiteracy as in model 3, the effects of size and illiteracy are as expected and significant at the .01 level. The coefficient of area is the same as in model 1. Per capita GDP is seen as varying inversely with global trade, but is not statistically significant. If female illiteracy declines by 11 percent, then trade increases by 1 percent. A decline in female illiteracy by one standard deviation from the mean of 30 percent to about 3 percent implies about a 10 percent rise in the share of trade in GDP.[20] A decrease in female illiteracy by one standard deviation to the mean of 30 percent implies a 5 percent increase in the proportion of trade to GDP.[21]

International and Domestic Politics

Lastly we look at the influence of political stability, regime type, and conflict, along with some of the previous domestic variables, in model 4.[22] We expect trade to increase with higher political stability and less international conflict and for regime type to have no discernible effect. Size, per capita GDP, secondary school enrollment ratio for females, and extent of democracy seem to be significant. A 10 percent increase in size decreases trade by 1.1 percent as in the previous models. Contrary to what we expect, wealth is negatively related to trade, but seems to have a weak effect. A 10 percent increase in per capita GDP leads to a less than 1 percent increase in the share of trade to GDP. Democracy too is negatively related to trade, but its impact is negligible.[23] The relation between trade and hostilities among states involving the use of force appears negative, but the effect of such disputes is indistinguishable from zero.[24] Political stability and whether a country is landlocked or not have no apparent effect.

Female secondary enrollment is positively related to trade. Consider Ecuador and Thailand—two countries, one low-trading and another high-trading—which have about the same female secondary enrollment ratio of 55 percent. An increase of 10 percent in female secondary enrollment implies an increase in trade for Ecuador from 63 to 67 percent and for Thailand from 124 to 132 percent—an improvement of 4 and 8 percent respectively.[25]

CONCLUSIONS

In conclusion, our surprising result is that few domestic variables have a sizable and unambiguous correlation with globalization. The only two variables which clearly influence trade as a proportion of GDP are country size and female educational achievement. Other things being equal, we find that the shorter the geographic boundaries, the greater the trade. It appears that the larger the country, the less the trade, but there is contradictory evidence on whether the richer the country, the greater its trade. Degrees of democracy and autocracy are not strongly correlated with indicators of globalization. This suggests that governments have a considerable degree of latitude in opting for or against globalization. Globalization will not necessarily fail in authoritarian polities, nor will it axiomatically succeed in democratic, liberal ones.

This result affects our findings concerning the future likelihood of national self-determination. Globalization can influence many different social, economic, and political systems, and it may be embraced by different political regimes. Regimes which wish to prevent their dissident provinces from becoming independent can become more globalized and thus win international adherents to their cause. As we have seen in chapter 1, cases where both the government and international actors support globalization will win out against a province which stands against it. Provinces which appeal to global forces to gain support may be confronted by a metropolitan regime which also goes global. Under the circumstances, the mere existence of globalization will not be decisive in favor of independence for the dissenting province. As we have seen elsewhere, dissident groups which have to use terrorism to gain recognition for their cause will usually be blocked when they seek international support. This would reinforce the broader conclusion that few new independent states will be created in the years ahead.

A key implication is that one of the reasons for the diminution of national self-determination outcomes has been the ability of the metropolitan regime to adopt a pro-globalization stance and then gain international support to keep a dissident province within the fold. In this case globalization emerges not as an independent, but as a partly dependent variable, supporting our general finding that regimes may have considerable latitude in keeping their dissidents under national control.

NOTES

1. See Alberto Alesina and Enrico Spolaore, *The Size of Nations* (Cambridge, MA: MIT Press, 2003).

2. See Beth Simmons, Geoff Garrett, and Frank Dobbin, "The International Diffusion of Liberalism," ms. 2003.

3. Edward D. Mansfield, *Power, Trade, and War* (Princeton, NJ: Princeton University Press, 1994). This would appear to go against the "optimum tariff" argument and may be questionable. A hegemonic state would reduce optimum tariffs only when other countries had become competitors and were no longer "price takers." See, inter alia, David Lake, *Power, Protection, and Free Trade* (Ithaca, NY: Cornell University Press, 1988).

4. Joanne Gowa, "Bipolarity, Multipolarity, and Free Trade," *American Political Science Review* (December, 1989).

5. James Morrow, Randolph Siverson, and Tressa Trabares, "The Political Determinants of International Trade," *American Political Science Review* (September, 1998).

6. Beth Simmons and Zachary Elkins, "The Globalization of Liberalization: Policy Diffusion in the International Political Economy," *American Political Science Review* (January, 2004).

7. See Alexandra Guisinger, "Patterns of Trade Protection and Liberalization: Is There a Role for Diffusion?" Conference on the International Diffusion of Democracy and Markets, UCLA, March, 2003.

8. See Karl Deutsch and Alexander Eckstein, "National Industrialization and the Declining Share of the International Economic Sector, 1890–1959," *World Politics* (April, 1961).

9. See Edward Leamer, *Sources of International Comparative Advantage: Theory and Evidence* (Cambridge, MA: MIT Press, 1984).

10. See Paul Krugman, *Geography and Trade* (Cambridge, MA: MIT Press, 1992).

11. See Ronald Rogowski, *Commerce and Coalitions* (Princeton, NJ: Princeton University Press, 1989).

12. See Etel Solingen, *Regional Orders at Century's Dawn* (Princeton, NJ: Princeton University Press, 1998).

13. Geoffrey Garrett and Peter Lange, "Internationalization, Institutions, and Political Change," *International Organization* (December, 1995).

14. Daniel Kaufmann, Aart Kraay, and Massimo Mastrucci, *Aggregate Governance Indicators, 1996–2002*, Research Project, World Bank.

15. Ukraine and France are 579,350 and 550,100 square kilometers respectively.

16. The share of trade in GDP averaged about 72.5 percent from 2000 to 2002 in Indonesia. The hypothetical loss of Aceh barely increases trade to almost 73 percent of GDP.

17. Although the cost of a call to the United States better captures "technology," we also used the number of phone subscribers to increase the number of observations.

18. The sign on the coefficient of per capita GDP, however, becomes negative at −.12, albeit significant at the .05 level. Note that per capita GDP and the number of phone subscribers are also highly correlated.

19. A regression that adds the log of female illiteracy to model 2 shows the cost of a call to the United States to be insignificant, as is per capita GDP. When the number of phone subscribers, however, is used in place of the cost of a call to the United States, its coefficient is positive and almost significant at the .10 level, but that of per capita GDP −.12 changes sign and is significant at the .10 level. Whichever technology indicator is used, the coefficients for area and female illiteracy are statistically significant and their values are similar to those for models 2 and 3.

20. That corresponds roughly to a fall in female illiteracy from the level of Equatorial Guinea or the Congo to that of Romania or Croatia.

21. That corresponds to an improvement in female literacy from the level of Zaire to that of Kenya.

22. Instead of a technology indicator, this model uses a dummy variable for landlocked countries to capture the hindrance posed by geography to trade. We do this to minimize problems arising from strong correlations among per capita GDP, female secondary school enrollment, and the number of phone subscribers or the cost of a call to the United States.

23. Recall that the regime-type variable ranges from −10 to 10. A 20-point swing from the most autocratic to the most democratic polity produces only a .2 percent *decline* in the ratio of trade to GDP.

24. To interpret the coefficient, the difference between the absence and the presence of hostilities involving the use of force weakens the ratio of trade to GDP by only −.12 percent.

25. The mean enrollment ratio is about 63 percent and its standard deviation is 37 percent. Consider an improvement in female enrollment by one standard deviation in three countries, whose trade levels are about the same, but whose female secondary enrollment ratios vary. A 37 percent improvement in Kenya's female secondary enrollment ratio from 25 to 62 percent implies an increase in the trade ratio from 60 to 75 percent. The same change in enrollment for Panama with intermediate enrollment at 71 percent improves trade from 59 to 74 percent. Finally, a one-standard-deviation increase in Spain's high enrollment ratio of 119 percent raises the share of trade in GDP from 62 to 77 percent.

3

Will Terrorism Defeat Globalization?

Deepak Lal

Globalization is the process of creating a common economic space. It leads to a growing integration of hitherto relatively closed economies through increasingly free movements of goods, capital, and labor. It is not a new process. It has usually been associated with the creation and maintenance of empires. The latter have been created in part to provide "order" in the larger economic space, by suppressing various threats to the productive and sedentary ways of life of civilizations from various roving bandits, who today are called terrorists. An elaboration of these points will allow us to answer the question posed in the title of this paper.

One of the features of a closed economy is that goods and services do not enter international trade—they are non-traded. Their prices are set by domestic demand and supply. The efficiency gains which accrue from differences in the domestic and international prices of traded goods in an open economy cannot be obtained. These gains can be decomposed into the consumption gain, which allows consumers to obtain their consumption bundles at lower cost, and the production gain, which arises from the specialization in domestic production on the basis of comparative advantage, allowing countries to use the more productive "technology" provided by international trade to raise their output from given resource endowments.

Goods can be non-traded because natural barriers raise transport costs or because tariffs prohibit trade. In the millennial past when costs of communication and transport were very high, only high-valued non-bulky goods entered into long-distance trade. This trade was always threatened by pirates and bandits of every kind. They imposed a further cost in addition to natural barriers to trade. If the costs of piracy were high enough, trade would cease as happened when the Great Powers' attempts to control the bandits failed.

Further, given the costs of doing international business, most traded goods were not locally produced. Domestically produced goods rarely faced foreign competition because they were not traded. The major gain from foreign trade was thus the consumption gain. But the spice trade—which involved transfers between East Europe and the tropics—did lead to production gains because meat from East Europe was stored for later shipment during long northern winters. This demanded new storage technology which was produced locally. Luxuries and the instruments of war were the major items involved in this long-distance trade. But the realization of these gains required a modicum of order enforced by military power.

With the Industrial Revolution, and the creation of a British-led international economic order policed by the Royal Navy, there was an expansion in the goods traded around the world. This period of globalization saw the growing integration of nearly the whole world into an international economy. The predators were kept at bay by the exercise of direct and indirect control over a vast economic space by British naval and military power. Nevertheless, there were still terrorists, mainly fueled by nationalism as well as the romantic revolt against capitalism, who did disturb domestic order in the metropole and its dependencies.[1] This terrorism did not, however, raise the costs sufficiently to undermine the processes of globalization. As long as the imperial peace was maintained, it was at worst a local irritant.

During this 19th century liberal international economic order there were substantial consumption and production gains from the free mobility of goods, capital, and labor. It was only during the first half of the 20th century, with the decline of the British Empire and the ravages of the interwar years, particularly the Great Depression, that domestic economic policy led to growing barriers to foreign trade in many countries, converting many previously traded into non-traded goods. These inward-looking policies had predecessors, most notably China in the Middle Ages and Japan under the Tokugawa Shogunate. Such regimes had completely banned foreign trade as they looked upon the accompanying foreign influences as sources of domestic disorder.

Order is required to maintain three elementary and universal goals that any society must pursue if any social life is to exist. These are, first, to secure life against violence which leads to death or bodily harm; second, that promises once made are kept; third, the stabilization of possessions through rules of property. These are the minimal functions that any state in its domestic domain needs to perform. But, for international trade and commerce, there is also the need to protect the trading networks: to maintain international order. In an anarchical society of equally matched states, there is always the danger that internecine warfare will disrupt these trading channels. Given the high value of the objects traded in the past, taxing long-distance trade has always provided an important source of revenue for states. It has been in their interests to protect these channels.

But, as Jack Hirshleifer pointed out, in economics there is also the "dark side of the force."[2] For one can make a living by either making or taking. Disrupting or stealing a rival's long-distance trade can therefore form part of a country's strategy, of which war is the most extreme alternative. So state-sponsored terrorism, as we now call it, to both directly "take" as well as damage the "making" of a rival's income has also been a constant feature of human history.[3]

If an asymmetric advantage in military technology permits one state in an anarchical society of states to achieve hegemony, the resulting imperial state has usually been best able to provide the order over a larger geographical space, which is a necessary condition for the benign economic processes of "globalization" to operate. For these empires reduce the threats to these processes from roving bandits—either private or state-sponsored. In fact most of the ancient empires arose because of the threat posed by roving bandits to their sedentary ways of life. In long-term historical perspective, terrorists are best looked upon as roving bandits. They have threatened the sedentary civilizations of Eurasia for millennia. This is because these civilizations which arose in the ancient river valleys of the Tigris and Euphrates in Mesopotamia, the Nile in Egypt, the Indus in India, and the Yellow River in China, were sandwiched between two areas of nomadic pastoralism: the steppes to the north, and the Arabian desert to the south. The nomadic pastoralists in these areas had not given up the hunter-gatherer instincts of their forefathers. They periodically mounted raids on the sedentary civilizations and sought to turn their inhabitants into chattel like their cattle.[4] All the sedentary civilizations had a common response to this terrorism. They sought to extend their frontiers to some natural barriers which would keep the barbarians at bay—thus creating their empires—and maintained specialists in warfare to protect them from the periodic barbarian invasions. They created manmade barriers and fortifications to protect their heartlands, of which China's Great Wall is the most notable example. They also invested in the latest military hardware to keep up with the nomadic Joneses.

Quite often the barbarian roving bandits turned themselves into stationary bandits by taking over the sedentary civilizations they had attacked and creating their own empire. The earliest example is the conquest by Sargon of Akkad in Mesopotamia in c 2340 BC, who then created the first Sumerian empire. The one which reverberates to our day is the early Arab empire. These nomads from the southern fringes of antiquity fired by the messianic zeal of their prophet Mohammed, as well as their age-old desire for booty, smashed the world of antiquity. Unlike their nomadic cousins from the north—who were absorbed by the ancient civilizations—they created a civilization of their own. Osama bin Laden's daring raid on the heartland of the current metropole on September 11, 2001 is resonant of these earlier nomadic raiders who created a new empire.

The motives for creating these imperial states, apart from this defensive one, have also included the desire for glory (Alexander the Great, Genghis Khan), booty (the Mesopotamian empires, the early Arab empire, the Iberian empires), and the messianic desire to convert heathens (the early Arab empire, the Iberian empires). But, once established, all these empires have by providing an Imperial Pax reduced if not altogether eliminated roving bandits, thereby facilitating the processes of globalization. Thus, the long period of the Pax Romana allowed commerce to develop under the most favorable conditions. It eliminated the piracy and brigandage which had continued to threaten commerce in the Hellenistic era, and the Mediterranean became the major artery for trade and commerce. Though the Romans did not place a high value on commerce in their cosmological beliefs,[5] nevertheless their Pax, and the associated development of Roman law which spread with the expansion of the empire, created a large economic space with a coherent legal framework for economic activity.

Similarly, the Abbasid Empire of the Arabs linked the world of the Mediterranean and the Indian Ocean, the Mongol empire linked China with the Near East, the various Indian empires created a common economic space in the subcontinent, while the expanding Chinese empire linked the economic spaces of the Yellow River with those of the Yangtze. Finally, after their victory at Waterloo, the British created the first truly global empire, linking the whole world. In all these cases they provided protection against brigands and other predators. Together with the institution of an empire-wide legal system, the British promoted trade and commerce over a wide economic space, leading to those gains from trade and specialization emphasized by Adam Smith and generating what I call Smithian intensive growth.[6] Thus, from the historical record, it would seem that suppressing international piracy and brigandage (terrorism) has been important for globalization to occur throughout the ages. Second, the international order required for globalization has usually been provided or at least assisted by a strong hegemonic power.

Since the Second World War, the United States has forged a degree of stability in world politics which has led to the current period of globalization. This has come about both with the demise of the "evil empire" of the Second World which challenged the global capitalism that is the hallmark of the new international economic order, and with the gradual acceptance by the Third World that its postwar "inward looking" policies were dysfunctional and needed to be reversed. Since the 1980s it too has joined the global bandwagon, with two major exceptions: Africa and much of the Middle East have remained aloof.

In this current period of globalization, with the revolution in communications, there have been further falls in "transport costs." So that hitherto non-traded goods like various back-office services are now being traded. The call centers in India are part of the trend in outsourcing these services. At the same time the growing trade in components has led to the fragmentation of the production of goods: with parts being produced in the lowest-cost "country" and being shipped for assembly for final consumption all around the world. This is leading to a finer and finer global division of labor.

But this global division of labor depends even more than in the past upon an intricate web of global communication networks, which are susceptible to damage by pirates and brigands as of yore. But do these terrorists pose more of a threat than did those when Pax Britannica held sway in the 19th century? One way of answering this is to see what the gains were from suppressing piracy and brigandage (terrorism) in the past, and then to see how current terrorist threats might affect the international order required for globalization to proceed.

We do not have any quantitative estimates of what the gains from the Imperial Pax in suppressing piracy and brigandage (terrorism) were for pre-modern times. But we do have some estimates made by Douglass North of the gains from suppressing piracy once the British navy came to rule the waves in the late 18th and 19th centuries. North estimates that from the mid-17th to the end of the 18th century there was a large increase in the productivity of shipping due to the suppression of piracy. Without any change in technology, freight rates on the Atlantic trade fell by a half, and from 1814 to 1850 before the technological revolution associated with steamships, productivity in shipping increased by 3.5 percent per year. The decline in piracy with the extension of the British international order also reduced insurance costs by about two-thirds between 1635 and 1770.[7] Who are the current international pirates and brigands, and do they have the means to erode the current hegemonic system and thereby the processes of globalization? Four major sources for these undesirables can be distinguished. The most important is provided by militant Islam. Its objectives are messianic and cannot be met with any compromise. If someone wishes to use the sword to establish their divine Kingdom on Earth, those reluctant to convert have only one option—to contain or kill the relevant purveyors of terror.

The second are sundry nationalists who in the name of a separate ethnicity or of religion wish to use terror to gain political ends—normally secession from an existing state and the creation of one of their own. They pose a difficult problem for the current imperial power. For since one of its high priests—Woodrow Wilson—pronounced the end of the Age of Empires and the dawn of that of Nations, its rhetoric has emphasized the principle of self-determination as the highest moral principle.[8] When does a freedom fighter become a brigand and a terrorist? This is a question which the proconsuls of the current hegemonic arrangement have great difficulty in answering. But the damage these terrorists do is more to their own people and those from whom they want to separate. The domestic disorder they breed rarely spills into international disorder which would damage the processes of globalization.

But, as the failing state of Afghanistan shows, they can provide succor and shelter to terrorists of various other hues.

The third are closer to past pirates and brigands. These are the international Mafias linked to trade in illegal substances and humans. They are the result of particular policies adopted by states. The War on Drugs, for example, increases the price of banned substances and heightens the criminal return. Current policies also curtail the 19th century's liberal international economic order's free movement of people through immigration controls. The latter are in turn due to the creation of welfare states in developed countries which, through restrictions, makes citizenship itself an issue of great material and political importance. Changes in these drug and immigration policies would suck the lifeblood out of the brigands who feed on them. They do not however pose a direct threat to globalization. For as they live by trade and commerce—albeit illegal—their interests do not lie in fouling the networks through which they operate.[9] Their threat is indirect. They can, however, promote domestic disorder leading to failed states, and by providing illegal and thereby secret sources of funds for the "nationalist" and "messianic" terrorists, help them in furthering their brigandage. The profits from drug smuggling by the Taliban in Afghanistan helped to support the state as well as to finance terrorism, for example.

Finally, there are the IT terrorists: the computer nerds whose motive is generally one of creating mischief for fun, but also increasingly theft—of money and identities—for personal gain. There is nothing new about theft, except in the mounting costs of the arms race between the law and thieves. IT technology provides a new avenue for cheating, which in turn requires further resources to countervail the thieving. This has further raised the dead-weight costs associated with policing.

So the major threat, if any, to globalization remains that of the messianic terrorists. These at present are mainly Islamists. How serious is the damage they can do? Considering their most spectacular terrorist act to date, the destruction of the World Trade Center, what were the effects on the U.S. and global economy? It is difficult to separate out the effects of the global recession which coincided with the collapse of the Twin Towers in New York. But one crude indicator is that after 9/11 the consensus forecast for U.S. real GDP growth was instantly downgraded by 0.5 percentage points for 2001 and 1.2 percentage points for 2002. The implied projected cumulative loss in national income through the end of 2003 amounted to 5 percentage points of annual GDP, or half a trillion dollars. The total loss for the three years was estimated at $630 billion. But, as Alice Rivlin has pointed out, these estimates certainly overstate the effects, largely because with the puncturing of the dot-com bubble and the sharp decline on Wall Street, New York was already going into a recession. Nevertheless, even if we take the expected loss for U.S. GDP based on the changed forecasts after 9/11 as having been realized, this would still be only about 5 percent of U.S. and a much smaller fraction of world GDP.

The specific damage from 9/11 has been estimated by Peter Navarro of the University of California, Irvine, as between $10 and 13 billion for property damage (the costs of the lost buildings, aircraft, public works and infrastructure, and corporate property like office equipment and software); the economic value of the lost lives in the range of $40 billion; the lost economic output in the immediate aftermath in the range of $47 billion (from lost airline and cargo shipping revenues, lost hotel industry revenues, lost advertising revenues in the first days during commercial-free TV and radio, two-day work stoppage, lost consumer spending and retail sales). This gives a total of $100 billion which is less than 0.8 percent of U.S. GDP. Thus the economic damage from 9/11 to the U.S. and the world economy was fairly small.[10]

Nor did New York's economy—the worst-hit by the immediate aftermath of the collapse of the Twin Towers—suffer a long decline as many had feared. Research by a team at the Russell Sage Foundation found that, comparing New York's performance before and after September 11 with its performance in past recessions, with the performance of the rest of the country before and after September 11, and with the experience of other large cities, it was not knocked off track in any fundamental way by 9/11.[11] Moreover, and most importantly, the communications networks on which globalization depends did not collapse. Trading recommenced very speedily. The damage was to the U.S. psyche.

What of future threats from biological and chemical weapons or a dirty bomb? Of these, for various reasons, the danger of a dirty bomb is the most pertinent. Biological and chemical weapons are not easy for private agents to use. They are more likely to be used by states and state-supported terrorists. But a dirty bomb is relatively easy to produce. It is difficult to estimate the damage, but most likely it would be to the real estate in the large area which was made radioactive. (See Graham Allison in chapter 6.) I guess its effects would be similar to that of a massive earthquake in California. Being localized, its damage would again be more to the psyche than to the world economy.

A worse nightmare for globalization would be if there were a series of explosions in the main shipping ports around the world in containers holding dirty bombs. It is difficult to estimate the damage this would do to shipping and commerce, but some estimate can be made from the costs of the insured losses from other recent disasters. Navarro provides estimates of these insured losses (adjusted for inflation). They are $5 billion for the 1989 Hurricane Hugo, $844 million from the 1992 Los Angeles riots, $16.9 billion from the 1992 Hurricane Andrew, $542 million from the 1993 World Trade Center bombing, $13 billion from the 1994 Northridge, California earthquake, and $127 million from the 1995 Oklahoma City bombing. Again, though tragic, these were not catastrophic losses.

The most serious costs associated with continuing terrorism are the general increase in the uncertainty associated with doing business that it might cause. But equally serious costs arise from preventive measures taken in a society seeking to be risk free from overreacting to the terrorist threat. (See John Mueller in chapter 4.) Besides the direct costs of homeland security there are for instance the costs imposed on travelers in terms of the opportunity costs of the time lost in long security searches at airports. Navarro estimates these costs at between $16 and 32 billion annually. But while all these costs will reduce the gains from the ongoing developments in and spread of communication technology in the globalization process, they are unlikely to hinder the globalization process.

The most serious threat to globalization arises from the Islamist terrorists, not because of the direct physical damage they can cause—as this is likely to be fairly localized—but because of their desire to sap the will of the metropole in maintaining its imperial sway. This could in theory succeed. To prevent this, it is important to realize that, despite protestations to the contrary, America presides over an informal empire. Since it overtook the British Empire in economic and military strength towards the first quarter of the last century, it has been the natural successor to the British in maintaining a global order. It can be argued that many of the bloody events of the last century were due to its failure to take over these responsibilities which Britain was too weak to carry out. Realizing this error, the post–World War II foreign policy elite has surreptitiously built an informal agglomeration of power.[12] But many including President George W. Bush remain frightened of the "E" word. It goes against the American self-image.

It is claimed that the U.S. is a hegemon but not an imperial power. Hegemons seek control over only the foreign policies of their dependencies. Empires seek control over both their domestic and foreign policies.[13] But in the current "war on terror" it is the domestic policies of states—providing money and succor to Wahhabi madrassas which breed terrorists, channeling money through Islamist charities to finance terrorist operations, building nuclear power plants which can be used to produce nuclear weapons as in Iran—that need to be controlled. Instead of the distinction between hegemony and empire, a much more meaningful distinction is between formal and informal empire. Of these an informal empire is always to be preferred as it is less costly in maintaining an imperial order. The British knew this. A predatory choice—despite nationalist historiography denigrating British imperialism for being exploitative—was never the option. Direct imperialism was only reluctantly taken to control what would today be called "failed states." The informal route was always the preferred route. For instance, in areas of indirect British control, the Imperial Pax was maintained through gunboats and Gurkhas.

The same choice faces the U.S. in maintaining its imperial order. But in making it and still retaining domestic political legitimacy, it is essential to be clearheaded in recognizing that the American order involves imperial responsibilities. Perhaps the greatest inadvertent service Osama bin Laden's 9/11 raid has done is to make it easier for the foreign policy establishment to come clean about America's international role and responsibilities. The recent Bush doctrine with its acceptance of preemptive strikes is a departure along these lines, as is the war in Iraq. In maintaining the Pax which is essential for the processes of globalization, the U.S. will have to continue to bear the burden with probably changing "coalitions of the willing." The Wilsonian dream of securing the peace through collective security enforced by the United Nations was always a dream, and the Iraq war should have made this obvious. The UN only wishes to tie Gulliver down with a million strings. Relying on this ineffectual and increasingly redundant institution will only promote international disorder.

It is nonetheless true that maintaining an informal U.S. hegemony is costly in terms of men and materiel. It also requires (as the British discovered and the U.S. is currently learning in Iraq) the equivalent of a colonial service with the requisite political and administrative skills to run an empire. But today, the United States' role is the necessary though perhaps not the sufficient condition for globalization to operate. It is the hope of the messianic terrorists that the American people will not have the necessary will to bear the burden of empire. It is their attempt to sap American will through their acts of terror which constitutes the greatest threat to globalization from terrorism. But an overreaction to the terrorist threat will also indirectly play into their hands. As the British discovered as an imperial power, the American homeland will continue to be subject to terrorism. The IRA has not yet given up its quest for reunion with Ireland, and has in the past bombed Britain to demonstrate this. But the British populace has learned to live with this threat for nearly a century without overreacting by restricting civil liberties—including the freedom to travel without restraint—and without giving in to terrorism. The citizens of the new U.S. informal empire will have to learn to do the same.

NOTES

1. See George Dangerfield, *The Strange Death of Liberal England* (Stanford, CA: Stanford University Press, 1935).

2. Jack Hirshleifer, *The Dark Side of the Force: Economic Foundations of Conflict Theory* (Cambridge: Cambridge University Press, 2001).

3. The Royal Navy which created and maintained the British Empire was itself the result of the state-sponsored pirates who had previously raided the Spanish Main. See A. Herman, *To Rule the Waves* (New York: Harper Collins, 2004).

4. See William H. McNeill, *The Human Condition* (Princeton, NJ: Princeton University Press, 1980).

5. The distinction between the material and cosmological beliefs of a culture is outlined and discussed in D. Lal, *Unintended Consequences* (Cambridge, MA: MIT Press, 1998). The former are concerned with ways of making a living, the latter with, in Plato's words, "how one should live."

6. This implied a rise in per capita income based on the Smithian gains from trade. But it was bounded because the ancient agrarian economies depended upon a fixed factor of production—land. The Industrial Revolution converted these agrarian economies into mineral energy economies which were no longer bounded by land but could use the near unlimited stock of fossil fuels for energy. This unleashed modern economic growth which allows a sustainable and continuous rise in per capita income. These two forms of *intensive* (with rising per capita incomes) are to be distinguished from *extensive* growth (where output grows pari passu with population, leaving per capita income unchanged), which has been ubiquitous through human history. See D. Lal, *Unintended Consequences*.

7. Douglass North, "Sources of Productivity Change in Ocean Shipping, 1600–1850," *Journal of Political Economy*, no. 5 (1968).

8. The fatuity of this principle was noted by Dean Acheson in a speech at Amherst College on Dec. 9, 1964. He said this high-sounding moral principle of self-determination "has a doubtful moral history. He [Woodrow Wilson] used it against our enemies in the First World War to dismember the Austro-Hungarian and Ottoman Empires, with results which hardly inspire enthusiasm today. After the Second World War the doctrine was invoked against our friends in the dissolution of their colonial connections. . . . On the one occasion when the right of self-determination—then called secession—was invoked against our own government by the Confederate States of America, it was rejected with a good deal of bloodshed and moral fervor. Perhaps you will agree it was rightly rejected" (Acheson, "Ethics in International Relations Today," in D. L. Larson, ed., *The Puritan Ethic in U.S. Foreign Policy* [Princeton, NJ: Van Nostrand, 1966], 134–35).

9. The illegal drug trade was estimated to be about $400 billion in 1997, compared with a value of legal world exports of $5 trillion that is about 8 percent of the value of legal world trade. The profits from the trade are enormous. Thus, a kilogram of cocaine base sells for between $650 and $1000 in Bolivia or Peru. It can be processed into cocaine hydrochloride for export for between $900 and $1200, which sells for between $13,000 and $40,000 wholesale in the U.S. before reaching consumers at a retail price of between $17,000 and $172,000. Heroin from Burma begins its progress at $70 per kg to the Burmese producer, to $3000 after processing in Thailand, whence it is exported from Bangkok at $6000–$10.000. It sells wholesale in the U.S. for between $90,000 and $200,000, and at retail for nearly $1 million (A. Krueger and C. Aturupane, "International Trade in 'Bads'," in H. Giersch, ed., *Merits and Limits of Markets* [Berlin: Springer, 1998]). The direct budgetary costs of enforcing the prohibition of drugs in the U.S. have been estimated to be over $20 billion per annum. Yet the war shows no sign of succeeding. There is a strong case for legalization, while Krueger and Aturupane rightly contend that following the theory of trade and welfare, the correct policy is not to prevent production by the most efficient worldwide producer, but only to seek to tax or prohibit domestic consumption.

10. P. Navarro and A. Spencer, "September 11, 2001: Assessing the Costs of Terrorism," *The Milken Institute Review.*

11. See A. Krueger, "New York's Economic Resilience," *New York Times* (September 16, 2004).

12. See Deepak Lal, *In Praise of Empires* (New York: Palgrave, 2004).

13. See M. Doyle, *Empires* (Ithaca, NY: Cornell University Press, 1986).

4

Terrorism, Overreaction, and Globalization

John E. Mueller

The chief danger for globalization from terrorism comes not from the terrorists themselves, but from the reaction—or overreaction—terrorism often inspires in those it threatens or seems to threaten.

This chapter begins by considering terrorism's destructiveness and argues that this has been and could well remain quite limited. It then examines the costs and consequences of the reactions to terrorism by governments and individuals, suggesting that this is often decidedly overwrought and unnecessarily costly. Finally, it proposes some guidelines for developing a sensible policy toward terrorism, stressing efforts to reduce the often costly fears and anxieties it characteristically inspires. The chapter also assesses the impact on globalization of terrorism and overreaction, concluding that, while troublesome in some areas and instances, the effects are unlikely markedly to hamper, much less set back, globalization unless overreaction goes too far.

THE LIMITED DESTRUCTIVENESS OF TERRORISM

"The chances of any of us dying in a terrorist incident are very, very, very small," filmmaker-provocateur Michael Moore happened to remark on *60 Minutes* on February 16, 2003. His interviewer, Bob Simon, promptly admonished, "But no one sees the world like that." Both statements, remarkably, are true—the first only a bit more so than the second.

For all the attention it evokes, terrorism, in reasonable context, actually causes rather little damage and, as Moore suggests, the likelihood that any individual will become a victim in most places is microscopic. Those adept at hyperbole like to proclaim that we live in "the age of terror." However, the

47

number of people worldwide who die as a result of international terrorism is generally only a few hundred a year—tiny compared to the numbers who die in most civil wars or from automobile accidents. In fact, until 2001 far fewer Americans were killed in any grouping of years by all forms of international terrorism than were killed by lightning. And except for 2001, virtually none of these terrorist deaths occurred within the United States itself. Indeed, outside of 2001, fewer people have died in America from international terrorism than have drowned in bathtubs.

Even with the September 11 attacks included in the count, however, the number of Americans killed by international terrorism since the late 1960s (which is when the State Department began its accounting) is about the same as the number killed over the same period by lightning, or by accident-causing deer, or by severe allergic reaction to peanuts.

Some of this is definitional. When terrorism becomes really extensive, we generally no longer call it terrorism, but war or insurgency. But Americans and others in the developed world are mainly concerned about random terror, not sustained warfare. Moreover, even using an expansive definition of terrorism and including domestic terrorism in the mix, it is likely that far fewer people were killed by terrorists in the entire world over the last hundred years than died in any number of unnoticed civil wars during that century.

TERRORISM AND WEAPONS OF MASS DESTRUCTION

Obviously, this could change if international terrorists are able to assemble sufficient weaponry or devise new tactics to kill masses of people, and if they come to do so routinely—and this, of course, is the central concern. The weapons most feared in the hands of terrorists are so-called weapons of mass destruction, a phrase that has been systematically and extensively embellished after the Cold War to embrace chemical and biological weapons as well as nuclear ones. This rhetorical expansion is highly questionable.[1]

Chemical arms do have the potential, under appropriate circumstances, for panicking people; killing masses of them in open areas, however, is beyond their modest capabilities.[2] Although they obviously can be hugely lethal when released in gas chambers, their effectiveness as weapons has been unimpressive, and their inclusion in the weapons-of-mass-destruction category is dubious unless the concept is so diluted that bullets or machetes can also be included.[3]

Biologist Matthew Meselson calculates that it would take a ton of nerve gas or five tons of mustard gas to produce heavy casualties among unprotected people in an open area of one kilometer square. Even for nerve gas this would take the concentrated delivery into a rather small area of about 300 heavy artillery shells or seven 500-pound bombs.[4] And this would usually require a considerable amount of time, allowing many people to evacuate the targeted area.[5] As the Gilmore Commission, a special advisory panel to the President and Congress, puts it, it would take a full ton of Sarin gas released under favorable weather conditions for the effects to become "distinctly greater than that attainable by such traditional terrorist means as conventional explosives."[6]

Properly developed and deployed, biological weapons could indeed, if thus far only in theory, kill hundreds of thousands, perhaps even millions, of people. The discussion remains theoretical because biological weapons have scarcely ever been used. Belligerents have eschewed such weapons with good reason: biological weapons are extremely difficult to deploy and to control. Terrorist groups or rogue states may be able to solve such problems in the future with advances in technology and knowledge, but, notes Russell Seitz, "bio-terrorism is easy on paper, but the learning curve is lethally steep in practice."[7]

For the most destructive results, biological weapons need to be dispersed in very low-altitude aerosol clouds: aerosols do not appreciably settle, and anthrax (which is not easy to spread or catch and is not contagious) would probably have to be sprayed near nose level.[8] Moreover, 90 percent of the microorganisms are likely to die during the process of aerosolization, while their effectiveness could be reduced still further by sunlight, smog, humidity, and temperature changes.[9] Explosive methods of dispersion may destroy the organisms, and, except for anthrax spores, long-term storage of lethal organisms in bombs or warheads is difficult, and, even if refrigerated, most of the organisms have a limited lifetime. Moreover, the use of such weapons can take days or weeks to have full effect, during which time they can be countered with civil defense measures.

The basic knowledge about the destructive potential of chemical and biological weapons goes back decades, even centuries in some respects—the English, for example, made some efforts to spread smallpox among American Indians in the French and Indian War.[10] Not only has the science dealing with these weapons been known with considerable sophistication for more than a century, but that science has become massively more developed over the last hundred years. Moreover, governments (not just small terrorist groups) have spent considerably over decades in an effort to make the weapons more effective. Yet, although there have been great increases in the lethality and effectiveness of conventional and nuclear weapons during that time, the difficulties of controlling and dispersing chemical and biological substances seem to have persisted.[11]

Perhaps dedicated terrorists will, in time, figure it out. However, the experience in the 1990s of the Japanese cult Aum Shinrikyo is unlikely to be encouraging. The group had some 300 scientists in its employ and an estimated budget of $1 billion, and it reportedly tried at least nine times over five years to set off biological weapons by spraying pathogens from trucks and wafting them from rooftops, hoping fancifully to ignite an apocalyptic war. These efforts failed to create a single fatality—in fact, nobody even noticed that the attacks had taken place. The group then abandoned its biological efforts in frustration and instead released Sarin nerve gas into a Japanese subway in 1995, the attack caused thousands of casualties, but only 12 deaths (though a more skillful attack conceivably might have killed more).[12]

In the meantime, the science dealing with detecting and ably responding to such attacks is likely to grow. Although acknowledging that things could change in the future, the Gilmore Commission concluded, "as easy as some argue that it may be for terrorists to culture anthrax spores or brew up a concoction of deadly nerve gas, the effective dissemination or dispersal of these viruses and poisons still presents serious technological hurdles that greatly inhibit their effective use."[13] Interestingly, if chemical and biological attacks are so easy and attractive to terrorists, it is impressive that none have so far been used in Israel. Although there have been plenty of terrorist attacks there, all have used conventional explosives.

Nuclear weapons, most decidedly, can indeed inflict massive destruction, and it is certainly reasonable to point out that an atomic bomb in the hands of a terrorist or rogue state could kill tens of thousands of people. But it is also essential to note that making such a bomb is an extraordinarily difficult task. As the Gilmore Commission stresses, "Building a nuclear device capable of producing mass destruction presents Herculean challenges. . . . A successful program hinges on obtaining enough fissile material; . . . arriving at a weapon design that will bring that mass together in a tiny fraction of a second, before the heat from early fission blows the material apart; and designing a working device small and light enough to be carried by a given delivery vehicle." It emphasizes that these are "the *minimum* requirements. If each one is not met . . . one ends up not with a less powerful weapon, but with a device that cannot produce any significant nuclear yield at all or cannot be delivered."[14]

Warnings about the possibility that small groups, terrorists, and errant states could fabricate nuclear weapons have been repeatedly uttered at least since 1947.[15] It has now been three decades since terrorism specialist Brian Jenkins published his warnings that "the mass production and widespread distribution of increasingly sophisticated and increasingly powerful man-portable weapons will greatly add to the terrorist's arsenal" and that "the world's increasing dependence on nuclear power may provide terrorists with weapons of mass destruction."[16] We continue to wait.

Actually, it is somewhat strange that so much emphasis has been put on the dangers of high tech weapons at all. Some of the anxiety may derive from the post–September 11 anthrax scare even though that terrorist event killed only a few people. The bombings of September 11 by contrast were remarkably low tech, and could have happened long ago: both skyscrapers and airplanes have been around for a century now.

EMBRACING THE WORST CASE

Two careful reports from the late 1990s—one from the Gilmore Commission, the other from the General Accounting Office—stress the great difficulties a terrorist group would have in acquiring and developing devices with the capacity to cause mass casualties, and they pointedly warn against the worst-case scenarios "that have dominated domestic preparedness planning."[17] The 9/11 attackers did not use weapons more sophisticated than box cutters, and the subsequent anthrax terrorism killed only a very few people. Nonetheless, those events have caused people to neglect more sensible warnings.

Thus, recent books by Graham Allison and Joshua Goldstein issue dire warnings about nuclear terrorism. Of particular concern in this are Russia's supposedly missing suitcase bombs even though a careful assessment by the Center for Nonproliferation Studies has concluded that it is unlikely that any of these devices have indeed been lost and that, regardless, their effectiveness would be very low or even non-existent because they require continual maintenance.[18] And in 2004 testimony, CIA adviser and arms inspector Charles Duelfer stressed that "nuclear weapons development requires thousands of knowledgeable scientists as well as a large physical plant."[19] It is also worth noting that, although nuclear weapons have been around now for well over half a century, no state has ever given another state—even a close ally—much less a terrorist group, a nuclear weapon that the recipient could use independently. There is always the danger the weapon would be used in a manner the donor would not approve—or even, potentially, on the donor itself. Allison thinks a dedicated terrorist group could get around these problems in time and eventually produce or procure a "crude" bomb itself, but it would be one that, by Allison's admission, would be "large, cumbersome, unsafe, unreliable, unpredictable, and inefficient."[20]

Goldstein is alarmed because he considers nuclear terrorism to be "not impossible," and Allison more boldly declares his "own considered judgment" that, unless his policy recommendations (which include a dramatic push toward war with North Korea) are carried out, "a nuclear terrorist attack on America in the decade ahead is more likely than not."[21] Allison's declaration is far more likely to be remembered if it proves true than if, more probably, it goes the way of C. P. Snow's once-heralded broadside published in 1961:

> We are faced with an either-or, and we haven't much time. The *either* is acceptance of a restriction of nuclear armaments. . . . The *or* is not a risk but a certainty. It is this. There is no agreement on tests. The nuclear arms race between

the United States and the U.S.S.R. not only continues but accelerates. Other countries join in. Within, at the most, six years, China and several other states have a stock of nuclear bombs. Within, at the most, ten years, some of those bombs are going off. I am saying this as responsibly as I can. *That* is the certainty.[22]

George Will, working from the musings of Gregg Easterbrook, has come up with "Easterbrook's Doomsaying Law": "Predict catastrophe no later than 10 years hence but no sooner than five years away—soon enough to terrify, but far enough off that people will forget if you are wrong."[23] Allison and Snow seem to have got the point.

AL-QAEDA'S CAPACITIES

In 1996 Osama bin Laden issued a religiously oriented proclamation which is usually taken to be a personal declaration of war on America—though actually the document seems to restrict bin Laden's wrath to the Americans stationed in Saudi Arabia and is entitled "Declaration of War against the American Occupying the Land of the Two Holy Places." Writing in *The Skeptical Inquirer* a year after 9/11, astronomers Clark Chapman and Alan Harris quite reasonably expressed incredulity that anyone would take seriously a declaration of war promulgated by a single individual. Under the emotional impetus of the 9/11 attacks, a considerable portion of the readership even of that magazine apparently did so.[24]

Fears of and anxieties about the twenty-foot-tall terrorist seem reminiscent of those inspired by images of the twenty-foot-tall Communist in the 1950s. By contrast, Gilles Kepel's extensive assessment of the radical Islamic movement finds this reaction to be singularly unjustified. Although a fringe element, radical Islamists did expand their influence in Iran, Sudan, and Afghanistan in the 1980s and early 1990s, and they fought viciously to do so in Algeria. But the pattern since has been mostly one of retreat or utter collapse in all those places (in Iran, they have in effect been overwhelmingly voted out of office twice). Moreover, their acts of spectacular terrorist violence, he concludes, far from spurring "the masses into a general upheaval" as they hoped, have proved "to be a death trap for Islamists as a whole, precluding any capacity to hold and mobilize the range of constituencies they need to seize political power." In this view, "the attack on the United States was a desperate symbol of the isolation, fragmentation and decline of the Islamist movement, not a sign of its strength and irrepressible might."[25] After more than three years of intense hunting, the FBI noted in a secret report that it had been unable to identify a single true al-Qaeda sleeper cell anywhere in the country.[26] B. R. Myers's image of Osama bin Laden "sharing a tent with a mountain goat and a well-thumbed Koran" may be a bit too glib, but it does vividly bring the menace, such as it is, back down to earth.[27]

SEPTEMBER 11: HARBINGER OR ABERRATION?

It should also be kept in mind that 9/11 was an extreme event: until then no more than a few hundred people had ever been killed in a single terrorist attack. The economic destruction on September 11 was also unprecedented, of course.

In 2004 Charles Krauthammer characterized the post-9/11 period as "three years in which, contrary to every expectation and prediction, the second shoe never dropped," and Allison noted that "in the weeks and months following 9/11, the American national security community focused on what was called the question of the 'second shoe.' No one believed that the attacks on the World Trade Center and the Pentagon were an isolated occurrence."[28] Perhaps such popular, if knee-jerk, expectations, predictions, and beliefs will continue to be confounded: extreme events often remain exactly that—aberrations, rather than harbingers.

Thus, a bomb planted in a piece of checked luggage was responsible for the explosion that caused a Pan Am jet to crash into Lockerbie, Scotland in 1988. Since that time, hundreds of billions of pieces of luggage have been transported on American carriers and none has exploded to down an aircraft. This doesn't mean that one should cease worrying about luggage on airlines, but it does suggest that extreme events do not necessarily assure repetition—any more than Timothy McVeigh's Oklahoma City bombing of 1995 has prompted emulators. Some sort of terrorist inoculated Tylenol capsules with cyanide in 1982, killing seven people; however, this frightening and much publicized event (which generated 125,000 stories in the print media alone and cost the manufacturer more than $1 billion) failed to inspire much in the way of imitation.[29] After its alarming release of poison gas in the Tokyo subway in 1995, Aum Shinrikyo seems to have since abandoned the terrorism business, and its example has not been followed. Moreover, although there have been many terrorist incidents in the world since 2001, all (thus far, at least) have relied on conventional methods.[30]

This should not be taken to suggest, of course, that all extreme events prove to be the last in their line or that nothing bad ever happens. At the time, World War I, called the Great War for decades, was the worst war of its type. Yet an even more destructive one followed. Moreover, while Aum Shinrikyo and Colonel Qaddafi may be under control, al-Qaeda and like-minded terrorist groups are unlikely to die out any time soon. Like the Communists during the Cold War, they appear to be in it for the long haul: September 11, after all, marked their second attempt to destroy the World Trade Center. In addition, the suicidal nature of many attacks, while not new, can be very unsettling because deterring by threatening punishment to the would-be perpetrator becomes impossible. And, of course, terrorism itself will never go away: it has always existed and always will.

A central issue, however, is whether such spectacularly destructive terrorist acts will become commonplace and will escalate in their destructiveness. The American Communist Party comprised a dedicated band of conspirators in league with foreign enemies who were devoted to using subversion and violence to topple democracy and capitalism, and, if successful, they would presumably have established a murderous tyranny. The intent was there, but not, as it turned out, the capacity. In the present instance, one should not, as Seitz suggests, "equate the modern ubiquity of high technology with terrorists becoming omniscient or infallible." Although there is no reason to think al-Qaeda will never strike again, the record suggests that it will find it difficult to match or top what it accomplished on 9/11 and that terrorism's destructiveness, despite the creative visions of worst-case scenarists, may well fail to escalate dramatically. As Seitz continues, "9/11 could join the Trojan Horse and Pearl Harbor among stratagems so uniquely surprising that their very success precludes their repetition," and "al-Qaeda's best shot may have been exactly that."[31] Moreover, the extreme destruction of September 11 has raised the bar, possibly reducing the impact of less damaging attacks.

OVERREACTING TO TERRORISM

The costs of terrorism very often arise mostly from the fear and consequent reaction (or overreaction) it characteristically inspires. That is, they commonly come much more from hasty, ill-considered, and overwrought responses to it than from anything the terrorists have done.

For example, when two American embassies in Africa were bombed in 1998, killing over 200 people (including a few Americans), Bill Clinton retaliated by bombing a suspect pharmaceutical factory in Sudan, the loss of which may have led to the deaths of thousands of Sudanese over time. Also bombed were some of Osama bin Laden's terrorist training camps in Afghanistan, which caused the Afghan government, the Taliban, to renege on pledges to extradite the troublesome bin Laden to Saudi Arabia, made him into an international celebrity, turned his al-Qaeda organization into a magnet for funds and recruits, and converted the Taliban from reluctant hosts to allies and partners.[32]

REACTING TO SEPTEMBER 11: THE COSTS

The costs of reaction outstripped those inflicted by the terrorists even in the case of the 9/11 attacks, which were by far the most destructive in history. The direct economic costs of 9/11 amounted to tens of billions of dollars, but the economic costs in the United States of the much enhanced security runs several times that. The yearly budget for the Office of Homeland Security, for example, is approaching $50 billion while state and local governments spend additional billions,[33] and the United States now spends $4 billion a year on airline passenger screenings alone.[34] The costs to the tourism and airline industry have also been great: indeed, three years after September 2001, domestic airline flights in the United States were still 7 percent below their pre-9/11 levels,[35] and one estimate suggests that the economy lost 1.6 million jobs in 2001 alone, mostly in the tourism industry.[36] Moreover, safety measures carry additional consequences: economist Roger Congleton calculates that requiring people to spend an additional half-hour in airports costs the economy $15 billion per year. For comparison, total airline profits in the 1990s never exceeded $5.5 billion per year.[37] The reaction to the anthrax attacks will cost the United States Post Office alone some $5 billion dollars— that is, one billion for every fatality inflicted by the terrorist.[38]

The reaction to 9/11 has even claimed more—far more—human lives than were lost in the terrorist attacks. Out of fear, many people canceled airline trips and consequently traveled more by automobile than by airline after the event, and one study has concluded that over 1,000 people died in automobile accidents in 2001 alone between September 11 and December 31 because of this.[39] If a small percentage of the 120,000-plus road deaths subsequent to 2001 occurred to people who were driving because they feared to fly, the number of Americans who have perished in overreaction to 9/11 in road accidents alone could well surpass the number killed by terrorists on that terrible day. Moreover, the reaction to 9/11 included two wars—one in Afghanistan, the other in Iraq—neither of which would have been politically possible without 9/11. The number of Americans—civilian and military— who have died thus far in those enterprises probably comes close to the number killed on September 11th. Moreover, the best estimates are that the war in Iraq resulted in the deaths of 100,000 Iraqis during its first eighteen months alone.[40] This could represent more fatalities than were inflicted by all terrorism, domestic and international, over the last century.

In addition, the enormous sums of money being spent to deal with this threat have in part been diverted from other, possibly more worthy, endeavors. In the words of risk analyst David Banks, "If terrorists force us to redirect resources away from sensible programs and future growth, in order to pursue unachievable but politically popular levels of domestic security, then they have won an important victory that mortgages our future."[41]

THE TERRORISM INDUSTRY

Thus far at least, terrorism is a rather rare and, in appropriate context, not a very destructive phenomenon as argued above. Nonetheless, the most common reaction to terrorism is the stoking of fear and the encouragement of overreaction by members of what might be called the "terrorism industry," an entity that includes not only various risk entrepreneurs and bureaucrats, but also most of the media and nearly all politicians. Thus, a problem with getting coherent thinking on the issue is that reporters, bureaucrats, politicians, and terrorism experts mostly find extreme and alarmist possibilities much more appealing than discussions of broader context and statistical reality.

There is no reason to suspect that George W. Bush's concern about terrorism is anything but genuine. However, his approval rating did receive the greatest boost for any president in history in September 2001, and it would be politically unnatural for him not to notice. His chief political adviser, Karl Rove, in fact was already declaring in 2003 that the "war" against terrorism would be central to Bush's reelection campaign the next year.[42] It was, and it worked. The Democrats, scurrying to keep up, have stumbled over each other with plans to expend even more of the federal budget on the terrorist threat, such as it is, than President Bush.

Meanwhile, Bush's hastily assembled and massively funded Office of Homeland Security seeks to stoke fear by officially intoning on the first page of its defining manifesto that "Today's terrorists can strike at any place, at any time, and with virtually any weapon."[43] This warning is true in some sense, of course, but it is also fatuous and misleading. As Benjamin Friedman notes, "Telling Kansan truck drivers to prepare for nuclear terrorism is like telling bullfighters to watch out for lightning. It should not be their primary concern. For questionable gains in preparedness, we spread paranoia." Such warnings, continues Friedman, also facilitate the bureaucratically and politically appealing notion that "if the threat is everywhere, you must spend everywhere," and they help develop and perpetrate "a myth of the all-knowing, all-seeing terrorists." Threat exaggeration is additionally encouraged, even impelled, because politicians and terrorism bureaucrats also have, as Jeffrey Rosen points out, an "incentive to pass along vague and unconfirmed threats of future violence, in order to protect themselves from criticism" in the event of another attack.[44]

Since 9/11 the American public has been treated to endless media yammering about terrorism. Politicians and bureaucrats may feel that, given the public concern on the issue, they will lose support if they appear insensitive to the dangers of terrorism. The media claim that they present fair and balanced coverage of important public issues. As has often been noted, however, the media appear to have a congenital incapacity for dealing with issues of risk and comparative probabilities—except, of course, in the sports and financial sections. If a baseball player hits three home runs in a single game, press reports will include not only notice of that achievement, but also information about the rarity of the event as well as statistics about the hitter's batting and slugging averages and about how many home runs he normally hits.

I may have missed it, but I have never heard anyone in the media stress that in every year except 2001 only a few hundred people in the entire world have died as a result of international terrorism.

Even in their amazingly rare efforts to try to put terrorism in context—something that would seem to be absolutely central to any sensible discussion of terrorism and terrorism policy—the process never goes very far. For example, in 2001 the *Washington Post* published an article by a University of Wisconsin economist which attempted quantitatively to point out how much safer it was to travel by air than by automobile even under the heightened atmosphere of concern inspired by the September attacks. He reports that the article generated a couple of media inquiries, but nothing more. Gregg Easterbrook's cover story in the October 7, 2002 *New Republic* forcefully argued that biological and especially chemical weapons are hardly capable of creating "mass destruction," a perspective relevant not only to concerns about terrorism, but also to the drive for war against Iraq that was going on at the time. The *New York Times* asked him to fashion the article into an op-ed piece, but that was the only interest the article generated in the media.

Moreover, the response to 9/11 has created a vast and often well-funded coterie of risk entrepreneurs. Its members would be out of business if terrorism were to be back-burnered, and accordingly they have every competitive incentive (and they are nothing if not competitive) to conclude it to be their civic duty to keep the pot boiling. "Dependent on the public for status and recognition," notes Rosen, terrorism experts have an "incentive to exaggerate risks and pander to public fears."[45]

It is tricky to try to refute doomsayers in part because there is more reputational danger in underplaying risks than in exaggerating them. People routinely ridicule futurist H. G. Wells's prediction that the conflict beginning in 1914 would be "the war that will end war," but not his equally confident declaration at the end of the Second World War that "the end of everything we call life is close at hand."[46] Disproved doomsayers can always claim that caution induced by their warnings prevented the predicted calamity from occurring. (Call it the Y2K effect.) Disproved Pollyannas have no such convenient refuge.[47]

Not only are failed predictors of doomsday rarely held to account, they have proved remarkably agile at creative nuance and extrapolation after failure. Thus, in 2004, the terrorism industry repeatedly insisted that some Big Terrorist Event was likely in connection with a) the Athens Olympics, b) the Democratic Party convention in Boston, c) the Republican convention in New York, d) the election campaign, and/or e) the presidential vote in November. For example, the widely published pundit Michael Ignatieff assured us in May 2004 that "we can confidently expect that terrorists will attempt to tamper with our election in November."[48] When nothing happened (a terrorist wearing kilts did show up to disrupt the marathon in

Athens briefly, but this, I should think, does not count), the argument was
floated that a taped encyclical issued by bin Laden in late October somehow
demonstrated that he was too weak to attack before the election and also that
he was marshalling his resources such that the several months *after* the election had now become especially dangerous.[49] A notable terrorist attack during that interval would generate hundreds of thousands of news items not to
mention a veritable paroxysm of breast-beating by the terrorism industry.
The absence of an attack during the same time would scarcely be noticed.

COSMIC ALARMISM

Members of the terrorism industry are truly virtuosic at pouring out, and poring
over, worst-case scenarios—or "worst-case fantasies," as Bernard Brodie once
labelled them in different context.[50] "Many academic terrorism analyses," notes
Bruce Hoffman, "are self-limited to mostly lurid hypotheses of worst-case scenarios, almost exclusively involving CBRN (chemical, biological, radiological,
or nuclear) weapons, as opposed to trying to understand why—with the exception of September 11—terrorists have only rarely realized their true killing
potential."[51] That is, if terrorism is so easy and terrorists so omni-competent,
why isn't there more of it? For example, why don't they snipe at people in
shopping centers, collapse tunnels, poison food, cut electrical lines, derail
trains, set forest fires, blow up oil pipelines, and cause massive traffic jams?

Retaining his worst-case perspective, however, Joshua Goldstein worries
about terrorists exploding nuclear weapons in the United States in a crowded
area and declares this to be "not impossible" or the likelihood "not negligible." Meanwhile, to generate alarm about such dangers and to reshape policy
to deal with them, Graham Allison's recent book opens by grimly recycling
Einstein's failed half-century-old prediction about all-out nuclear war: "Since
the advent of the Nuclear Age, everything has changed except our modes of
thinking and we thus drift toward unparalleled catastrophe." Both of these
members of the terrorism industry want to massively increase expenditures
to hedge against these "not impossible" scenarios.[52]

But there are, of course, all sorts of things that are "not impossible." Thus,
a colliding meteor or comet could destroy the earth; Tony Blair or Vladimir
Putin and their underlings could decide one morning to launch a few nuclear
weapons at Massachusetts; George Bush could decide to bomb Hollywood;
an underwater volcano could erupt to cause a civilization-ending tidal wave;
bin Laden could convert to Judaism, declare himself to be the Messiah, and
hire a group of Roman mafiosi to have himself publicly crucified.

That is, what we mostly get is fear-mongering, and much of it borders on
hysteria. Some prominent commentators, like David Gergen, have argued
that the United States has become "vulnerable," even "fragile."[53] Others like

Indiana senator Richard Lugar are given to proclaiming that terrorists armed with weapons of mass destruction present an "existential" threat to the United States, or even, in columnist Charles Krauthammer's view, to "civilization itself." Allison, too, thinks that nuclear terrorists could "destroy civilization as we know it," while Goldstein is convinced they could "destroy our society" and that a single small nuclear detonation in Manhattan would "overwhelm the nation." Michael Ignatieff warns that "a group of only a few individuals equipped with lethal technologies" threaten "the ascendancy of the modern state," and a recent best-selling book by a once-anonymous CIA official repeatedly assures us that our "survival" is at stake and that we are engaged in a "war to the death."

Apocalyptic alarmism by the terrorism industry reached a kind of pinnacle during the Orange Alert at the end of 2003. At the time Homeland Security czar Tom Ridge declared that "America is a country that will not be bent by terror. America is a country that will not be broken by fear." Meanwhile, however, General Richard Myers, chairman of the Joint Chiefs of Staff, was assuring a television audience that if terrorists were able to engineer a catastrophic event which killed 10,000 people, they would successfully "do away with our way of life."[54]

The sudden deaths of that many Americans—although representing less than four thousandths of 1 percent of the population—would indeed be horrifying and tragic, the greatest one-day disaster the country has suffered since the Civil War. But the only way it could "do away with our way of life" would be if we did that to ourselves in reaction. The process would presumably involve repealing the Bill of Rights, boarding up all churches, closing down all newspapers and media outlets, burning all books, abandoning English for North Korean, and refusing evermore to consume hamburgers.

Alarmist Ignatieff, who predicted terrorist events in connection with the 2004 elections with such assurance, is at least equally certain that "inexorably, terrorism, like war itself, is moving beyond the conventional to the apocalyptic."[55] And he patiently explains in some detail how we will destroy ourselves in response. Although Americans did graciously allow their leaders one fatal mistake in September 2001, they simply "will not forgive another one." If there are several large-scale attacks, he confidently predicts, the trust that binds the people to its leadership and to each other will crumble, and the "cowed populace" will demand that tyranny be imposed upon it, and quite possibly break itself into a collection of rampaging lynch mobs devoted to killing "former neighbors" and "onetime friends." The solution, he thinks, is to crimp civil liberties now in a desperate effort to prevent the attacks he is so confident will necessarily impel us to commit societal, cultural, economic, and political self-immolation.[56]

It seems, then, that it is not only the most-feared terrorists who are suicidal. Ultimately, the enemy, in fact, is us.

However, it does not seem unreasonable to point out that the United States regularly loses 40,000 lives each year in automobile accidents and still somehow manages to continue to exist. Equally, we should note that countries have endured massive, sudden catastrophes without collapsing: in 1990 and then again in 2003, for example, Iran suffered earthquakes that nearly instantly killed some 35,000 in each case, but the country clearly survived the disasters. They were major tragedies, of course, but they hardly proved to be "existential." In fact, there is extensive evidence that far the most common reaction to disaster is not self-destructive panic, but resourcefulness, civility, and mutual aid. The main concern would be that in the aftermath people would adopt skittish, overly risk-averse behavior that would magnify the impact of the terrorist attack, particularly economically. Most importantly in all this, public and private members of the terrorism industry must be able to restrain and contain any instinct to destroy their own societies in response should they ever be provoked.

All societies are "vulnerable" to tiny bands of suicidal fanatics in the sense that it is impossible to prevent every terrorist act. But the United States is hardly "vulnerable" in the sense that it can be toppled by dramatic acts of terrorist destruction, even extreme ones. In fact, the country can readily, if grimly, absorb that kind of damage—as it "absorbs" some 40,000 deaths each year from automobile accidents.

In 1999, two years before 9/11, the Gilmore Commission forcefully made a point they considered to be "self-evident," but one that nonetheless required "reiteration" because of "the rhetoric and hyperbole with which the threat of CBRN terrorism is frequently couched." The point was:

> As serious and potentially catastrophic as a domestic CBRN attack might prove, it is highly unlikely that it could ever completely undermine the national security, much less threaten the survival, of the United States as a nation. . . . To take any other position risks surrendering to the fear and intimidation that is precisely the terrorist's stock in trade.[57]

The fact that terrorists subsequently managed to ram airplanes into three buildings does not render this "self-evident" point less sound, and "reiteration" continues to be required.

TERRORISM, OVERREACTION, AND GLOBALIZATION

The process by which international economic interconnections and interactions are growing—lately labelled "globalization"—is a vast and unstoppable one. Unless international terrorists become *vastly* more effective than they are at present, terrorism will remain fundamentally a comparatively minor phenomenon and is unlikely, by itself, to alter this process very much.

However, the reaction—or overreaction—to terrorism could have appalling consequences. This is because it is carried out not by small bands of fanatical people, but by large states run by spooked leaders who find hysterical and sanctimonious overreaction, including even the launching of unnecessary and self-punishing wars, to be politically congenial, even necessary.

FASHIONING A TERRORISM POLICY

If the main cost of terrorism arises from the anguish and overreaction of the terrorized, it makes sense primarily to focus on this problem. Accordingly, policies could seek to reduce fear and anxiety as inexpensively as possible and to avoid or control overreaction at least as much as they attempt objectively to reduce the rather limited dangers terrorism is likely actually to pose. Where risks are real—as in the cases of smoking, obesity, alcoholism, and automobile driving—it makes sense to stoke fear: people should be *more* afraid, less complacent, and less in denial about these dangers than they are at present. However, where the real risks for any given individual are small—as with terrorism, shark attacks, and airplane flying—fear becomes the problem, and accordingly it makes policy sense to find ways to reduce it.[58] The communication of risk is a difficult and exasperating business.[59] But the constant untempered stoking of fear by politicians, bureaucrats, experts, and the media, however well received (or ignored) by the public, is on balance costly, enervating, potentially counterproductive, and unjustified by the facts.

Accordingly, there should be an effort by politicians, bureaucrats, officials, and the media to inform the public reasonably and realistically about the terrorist context instead of playing into the hands of terrorists by effectively seeking to terrify the public. That is, instead of inducing hysteria, which seems to be one of the terrorism industry's central goals, officials and the media should responsibly assess probabilities and put them in some sort of context rather than simply stressing extreme possibilities so much and so exclusively. What is needed, as one statistician suggests, is some sort of convincing, coherent, informed, and nuanced answer to a central question: "How worried should I be?" Instead, the message, as one concerned Homeland Security official puts it, is "Be scared. Be very, very scared. But go on with your lives."[60]

One element of a sensible policy approach for confronting terrorism might be to stress that any damage terrorists are able to accomplish likely can be absorbed, and that, while judicious protective and policing measures are sensible, extensive fear and anxiety over what at base could well prove to be a rather limited problem are misplaced, unjustified, and counterproductive. In risk analyst Howard Kunreuther's words, "More attention needs to be devoted to giving people perspective on the remote likelihood of the terrible consequences they imagine."[61] That would seem to be at least as important as boosting the sale of duct tape, issuing repeated and costly color-coded alerts based on vague and unspecific intelligence, and warning people to beware of Greeks, or just about anybody, bearing gifts.

For example, there is at present a great and understandable concern about what would happen if terrorists are able to shoot down an American airliner or two, perhaps with shoulder-fired missiles. Obviously, this would be a major tragedy in the first instance. But the ensuing public reaction to it could come close to destroying the industry. It would seem to be reasonable for those with that fear to consider the following: how many airliners would have to crash before flying becomes as dangerous as driving the same distance in an automobile? It turns out that someone has made that calculation. The conclusion is that there would have to be a set of 9/11 crashes every month for the risks to balance out.[62]

Also useful might be to reconsider the standards about what is harmful in some cases. The potential use of "dirty" bombs apparently formed the main concern during the Orange Alert at the end of 2003.[63] However, while a "dirty" bomb might raise radiation 25 percent over background levels in an area and therefore into a range the Environmental Protection Agency officially considers undesirable, there ought to be some discussion about whether that really constitutes "contamination" or indeed much of a danger given the somewhat arbitrary and exceedingly cautious levels declared to be acceptable by the EPA. In fact, since "dirty" bombs simply raise radiation levels somewhat above normal background levels in a small area, a common recommendation from nuclear scientists and engineers is that those exposed should calmly walk away. But this bit of advice has not been advanced prominently (or even, perhaps, at all) by those in charge. Effectively, therefore, they encourage panic, and, as one nuclear engineer points out, "if you keep telling them you expect them to panic, they will oblige you. And that's what we're doing."[64] By contrast, if trusted governmental officials can truthfully say that the contamination does not reach levels considered unsafe, undesirable negative reactions might be beneficially reduced and might far outweigh any risks involved.

In fact, the reduction of fear, anxiety, and overreaction is actually quite central to dealing with terrorism. Indeed, the inspiration of consequent overreaction seems central to bin Laden's strategy. As he put it mockingly in a videotaped message in 2004, it is "easy for us to provoke and bait. . . . All that we have to do is to send two mujahidin . . . to raise a piece of cloth on which is written al-Qaeda in order to make the generals race there to cause America to suffer human, economic, and political losses." His policy, he extravagantly believes, is one of "bleeding America to the point of bankruptcy," and it is one that depends on overreaction by the target: he triumphantly points to the fact that the 9/11 terrorist attacks cost al-Qaeda $500,000 while the attack and its aftermath inflicted, he claims, a cost of more than $500 billion on the United States.[65]

Since the creation of insecurity, fear, anxiety, hysteria, and overreaction is central for terrorists, they can be defeated simply by not becoming terrified and by resisting the temptation to overreact: as Friedman aptly puts it, "one way to disarm terrorists is to convince regular Americans to stop worrying about them." The 2001 anthrax attacks, Hoffman argues, suggest that "five persons dying in mysterious circumstances is quite effective at unnerving an entire nation."[66] To the degree that is true, policies for limiting terrorist damage should focus on such unwarranted reactions.

By contrast, if the more hysterical worst-case scenarios detailed in the previous section materialize after a terrorist attack, globalization would suffer as an attacked country dutifully destroys itself in response. However, as suggested there, the spectacular terrorist attacks these scenarios depend on are highly unlikely, and a country will usually be able to refrain from committing societal suicide even if they do come about. More generally, it should be pointed out that doing nothing (or at least refraining from overreacting) after a terrorist attack is not necessarily politically unacceptable. Although it is often argued that it is imperative that public officials "do something"— which usually means overreact—when a terrorist event takes place, there are many instances where no reaction took place and the officials did not suffer politically or otherwise. Ronald Reagan's response to a terrorist bomb in Lebanon in 1983 that killed 241 American marines was to make a few speeches and eventually pull the troops out. Bill Clinton responded similarly after an unacceptable loss of American lives in Somalia ten years later. Although there were the (apparently counterproductive) military retaliations after the U.S. embassy bombings in Africa in 1998 as noted earlier, there was no notable response to terrorist attacks on American targets in Saudi Arabia (Khobar Towers) in 1996 or to the bombing of the *U.S.S. Cole* in 2000. The response to the anthrax attacks of 2001 was the same as to terrorist attacks against the World Trade Center in 1993 and in Oklahoma City in 1995—the dedicated application of police work to try to apprehend the perpetrator— and this approach proved to be acceptable politically.

Extreme cases like 9/11 put this proposition to the greatest test, but it seems likely that even here a communicative leader could have pursued a more patient and gradual policy. The requirement to "do something" would need to be fulfilled, but a policy in agile coordination with other countries— almost all of them very eager to cooperate after the shock—stressing pressure on the Afghan regime and the application of policing and intelligence methods to shore up defenses and to go after al-Qaeda and its leadership could probably have been sold to the public, even without the invasion of Afghanistan and Iraq.

TRAVEL, TRADE, AND THE EXCHANGE OF PEOPLE

Historically, a common reaction to dramatic acts of terrorism has been ethnic or even racist in character: if the terrorists can be more or less identified with a specific racial or ethnic or religious or political group, all members of that group become suspect.[67] The hostility toward Arabs and Muslims in the United States and Europe has led to considerable restrictions on immigration and travel for members of those groups, something likely to hamper globalization a bit, but not by any means to destroy it.

Equally, American higher education has been hurt by overly zealous and often utterly incomprehensible restrictions on foreign students and colleagues who constitute important participants in the educational and research process. Some predict that the various 9/11-induced restrictions on visas that have constricted visits and residencies of scientists, engineers, and businesspeople so vital to the economy will dampen American economic growth in a few years' time.[68] However, while such developments may harm the American economy and its institutions of higher learning, the impact on globalization is likely to be minor since the travelers and visitors will go elsewhere as foreign educational institutions improve.

Globalism, by enhancing international travel and interconnectedness, may help to facilitate some international terrorism, as is often noted. However, it is not at all clear that things are better in this regard for international terrorists than they were before 1914 when the movement of peoples over international borders was substantially unregulated.

RUSSIA AND CHECHNYA

Most important for globalization and one of the key long-term goals of the West (in all probability vastly more consequential than dealing with terrorism) is to fully integrate Russia (and China), the losers of the Cold War, into the international community in the spectacularly successful manner by which the losers of World War II, Germany and Japan, were integrated after that conflict.

This crucial process certainly hasn't been helped by Russian reactions to terrorism. After a set of terrorist attacks in Russia in 1999, the country furiously launched itself into a massively destructive war against the homeland of the small groups which had apparently perpetrated the deeds, the tiny, impoverished, distant breakaway republic of Chechnya. The war has resulted in far more destruction of Russian (and, of course, Chechen) lives and property than the terrorists ever brought about.

In overall context, that conflict on the Russian fringe, however brutal, seems to have formed more of a distraction than a diversion from the globalization process. But it has been costly nonetheless, and it has formed a convenient pretext for some authoritarian maneuvering by Russia's president, Vladimir Putin, that could have broader international consequences.

AFGHANISTAN

The war in Afghanistan came almost entirely in reaction to the 9/11 terrorist attacks. The degree to which the venture reduced the threat from international terrorism to the American homeland is not clear: the number of such attacks in the three years since 9/11 has been zero, exactly the same as for the three years preceding the attack.

However, the Afghan war will probably actually help globalization at least in the long run by returning that country from its isolation under the Taliban to international normality and respectability. In a not entirely pleasant sense, globalization has also been enhanced by the increase in the drug trade that apparently has been facilitated by armed liberation. Beyond that and Afghan carpets, the country does not have much in the way of exports, but it may be able to play a role as a conduit for oil and gas products from the north and be entirely willing to do so.

On the other hand, the impact of the reactive war in Afghanistan has probably pushed neighboring Pakistan (a much more important country economically) toward becoming a political, security, and economic basket case. This development is unlikely to be good for globalization.

TERRORISM AND THE ROGUE STATE

In the post–Cold War era, special status was given to a newly identified category of "rogue states" as if this were a new problem in international affairs. Yet there were plenty of such states—"devils du jour," one might call them—during the Cold War such as Sukarno's Indonesia, Nasser's Egypt, Castro's Cuba, Qaddafi's Libya, Khomeini's Iran, and Noriega's Panama. Moreover, the "rogue state" label implies that they are too irrational to be deterred by policies designed to deal with "normal" countries, and it therefore leads to an extreme version of the security dilemma as weaponry that might be obtained by such states to deter an attack is almost automatically assumed to be designed for offensive purposes even though such use would be patently suicidal for the rogues and their regimes.

The rise of fears about international terrorism has vastly increased concerns about "rogue states" by enhancing the alarmist argument that nuclear weapons (or lesser "weapons of mass destruction") in the hands of such states are especially dangerous because they might palm the weapons off to terrorists who might then explode them in Israel, Europe, or the United States.

NORTH KOREA

Despite considerable evidence to the contrary,[69] the United States has consistently viewed North Korea as a continuing threat even though its neighbors, especially South Korea, do not. The United States has accordingly adopted an intensely hostile and threatening posture that only increases the North's frightened desire to build such weapons.

Some Americans even think that a war on the Korean peninsula is preferable to letting the North pursue a nuclear weapons program. In 1994, a U.S. National Intelligence Estimate concluded that there was "a better than even" chance that North Korea had the makings of a small nuclear bomb, a conclusion hotly contested by other American analysts.[70] This propelled the Clinton administration into moving toward war with the miserable North Korean regime to prevent or to halt its nuclear development.[71] A full-scale war on the peninsula, estimated the Pentagon, could kill 1,000,000 people including 80,000 to 100,000 Americans, cost over $100 billion, and do economic destruction on the order of a trillion dollars.[72] That crisis was defused by ex-President Jimmy Carter, who quickly worked out a deal whereby North Korea would accept international inspections to guarantee that it wasn't building nuclear weapons; in exchange it would graciously accept a bribe from the West: aid, including some high-tech reactors which were capable of producing plenty of energy, but no weapons-grade plutonium, as well as various promises about normalizing relations—promises that went substantially unfulfilled in the hope and expectation that the North Korean regime would soon collapse.[73]

The same threat-exaggerating, overreactive perspective toward the North Korean rogue continues to be embraced in the new century. Richard Perle, the prominent neoconservative and Defense Department adviser for the George W. Bush administration, has bluntly asserted that "the interests of the South Koreans are not at all identical to ours. They have an interest in doing everything possible to avoid military conflict, and it's understandable. Seoul is within artillery range of thousands of North Korean artillery tubes. They would much prefer to take a risk that North Korea will become not only a nuclear power, but the nuclear bread basket of the world, building and selling nuclear weapons, as they are now building and selling missile technology, and anything else they can lay their hands on. From the South Korean point of view, that is a lesser immediate threat than artillery landing on Seoul. So it's hardly surprising that the South Koreans are going to see this differently from the way we see it. But our president has, first and foremost, a commitment to the security of the United States."[74] Meanwhile, Graham Allison, an advisor to the opposition Democrats, has maintained the same essential view. Out of concerns about the potential for nuclear terrorism, he designates the North Korean problem a "supreme priority" and is prepared if necessary to confront that country (and presumably also Iran) to reduce the likelihood that his worst-case outcome will materialize. He does propose, however, that Seoul should be evacuated before the attack on the North is launched.[75]

IRAQ

Having worked themselves up during the 1990s, the Americans and the British went to war against Saddam Hussein's pathetic regime in Iraq in 2003 because, unlike all of Iraq's neighbors except Israel, their leaders imagined a "grave and gathering" threat to lurk there. Prominent fear-mongers, many of whom had previously been active in exaggerating the Soviet threat,[76] asserted that Saddam was planning to dominate the Middle East and that the country possessed weapons of mass destruction. Antiterrorism formed a central role in this battle cry.

When the U.S. invaded in 2003, Saddam's military—with which Middle East domination was presumably to be carried out—crumbled pathetically, incoherently, and predictably.[77] Moreover, post-war inspections revealed the pre-war fear to have been based more on selective perception, willful deception, and self-induced hysteria than on evidence.

THE POTENTIAL IMPACT ON GLOBALIZATION OF THE IRAQ SYNDROME

The unpleasant and costly results of America's war in Iraq, the most extensive, notable, and bloody overreaction to the events of 9/11, may be in the process of correcting the excesses inherent in the rogue state phenomenon. This corrective process is likely to have—indeed, already has had—significant repercussions in the country's foreign policy, and it may in various ways affect the process of globalization, mostly beneficially.

Since World War II, American foreign policy has endured, or wallowed in, several perspectives, often labelled "syndromes," that have been triggered by foreign policy debacles. One of these was the Vietnam Syndrome that began around 1975, and another was the Somalia Syndrome that began around 1992. It seems likely that the United States is currently in the process of embracing a third: the Iraq Syndrome. And indeed, policy in Iraq seems to be evolving in a manner familiar from Vietnam and Somalia: a combination of cut, run, and hope. Responsibility for policing the resistance is increasingly being handed over to a shaky, patched-together government, army, and police force; American tactics seem to be in the process of being shifted to reduce American casualties, and troops will probably gradually begin to be removed. Support for the locals will increasingly be limited to economic aid and encouraging words.[78]

As in Somalia and particularly Vietnam, there is no way to defeat the armed opponents at a tolerable cost in American lives: the insurgents are variously motivated, but they are likely, despite tactical setbacks, to be willing and able to continue their activities at least until the hated Americans leave. The removal of Saddam Hussein's regime remains an achievement. However, there has been a substantial downside to the war: military victory was achieved at the cost of creating chaos in the country, killing tens of thousands of Iraqis, and alienating many of the rest.[79] The notion that Iraq, without an effective army, ever posed much of a threat to anyone, even Israel, becomes highly questionable. Oil supplies from the country are likely to remain uncertain for years. International animosity to the United States generated by the venture remains high.

Indeed, the chief beneficiaries of the Iraq venture are the rogue/axis-of-evil states of Iran and North Korea. In part because of the American military and financial overextension in Iraq (and Afghanistan), the likelihood of any coherent application of military action or even of focused military threat against these two unpleasant entities has already substantially diminished, as it has against what at one time seemed to be the next dominoes in the Middle East: Syria especially, Saudi Arabia, Egypt, and Lebanon (all of which have a major incentive to make the American experience in Iraq as miserable as possible). Moreover, impressed by that war and by their designation, together with Iraq, as members of a diabolical "axis of evil" by the president of the United States, Iran and North Korea may have logically concluded that they need nuclear weapons to deter the crusading, out-of-control Americans from attacking them next. Although the American experience in Iraq may serve to alleviate some of their fears, the whole situation is likely to slow the process by which these two countries are brought back into the international community, and, to that degree, it will hamper their inclusion into an overarching globalization.

The war in Iraq will also probably prove encouraging to international terrorists because they will take even an orderly American retreat from the country as a great victory—even greater than the one against the Soviet Union in Afghanistan. Osama bin Laden's theory that the Americans can be defeated, or at least productively inconvenienced, by inflicting comparatively small, but continuously draining, casualties on them will achieve apparent confirmation, and a venture designed and sold in part as a blow against international terrorists will end up emboldening and energizing them. A comparison might be made with Israel's orderly, even overdue, withdrawal from Lebanon in 2000 that insurgents there took to be a great triumph for their terrorist tactics—and, most importantly, so did like-minded Palestinians who later escalated their efforts to use terrorism to destroy Israel itself. People like bin Laden believe that America invaded Iraq as part of its plan to control the oil in the Persian Gulf area. But the United States does not intend to do that (at least not in the direct sense bin Laden and others doubtless consider to be its goal), nor does it seek to destroy Islam as many others also bitterly assert. Thus just about any kind of American withdrawal will be seen by such people as a victory for the harassing terrorist insurgents, who, they will believe, are due primary credit for forcing the United States to leave without accomplishing what they take to be its key objectives.[80] Moreover, the insurgency in Iraq seems to have developed as something of a terrorist breeding and training experience.[81]

The consequences of the Iraq Syndrome on U.S. foreign policy could be considerable and damaging. Among the casualties are likely to be the Bush Doctrine, empire, unilateralism, preemption (or, actually, preventive war),[82] last-remaining-superpowerdom, and indispensable nationhood. Specifically, there will probably be notable declines in the acceptance of such notions as: the United States should take unilateral military action to correct situations or regimes it considers reprehensible but which present no very direct and very immediate threat to it; the United States should or can forcibly bring democracy to nations not now so blessed; the United States should embrace a mission (even a "crusade") to eliminate evil from the world; the United States has the duty to bring order to the Middle East; the United States can and should apply its military supremacy to straighten out lesser peoples even if a result of this policy becomes the establishment of something of a new American "empire"; the United States can or should use military force to make the Middle East safe for Israel; most people (particularly Arabs) only understand force; international cooperation is of only very limited value; having by far the largest defense budget in the world is necessary and mostly brings benefits; Europeans and other well-meaning foreigners are naive and decadent wimps.

The longer-term result of the war against Iraq on the United States, however, is likely to be to encourage it to become a more normal and cooperative, even humble, participant in the international arena and less of a rogue state—something that, presumably, will enhance the process of globalization. Moreover, although the tumult generated in the Middle East by American policy and by the war in Iraq presumably does not help facilitate the processes by which Middle East oil is supplied to the international market, any disruptions (at least outside Iraq) are likely to be minor and overwhelmed by the imperatives of the market. There is some evidence that hostility toward the United States inspired by American foreign policy arrogance has hampered the appeal of American products in many parts of the world. This has even led Coca-Cola to try to present itself as a local product in some areas, surely one of the more Herculean marketing endeavors of all time.[83] But thus far the effect on actual sales seems to be minor and is likely to be reversed if the U.S. pulls in its fangs. Moreover, if the effect of the war simply causes people to shift their preferences from American goods to European or Japanese ones, any resultant effect on globalization as a whole is, of course, obviated.

GLOBALIZATION AND THE "WAR" AGAINST TERRORISM

The extreme reaction by the United States government to 9/11 has made bin Laden into the most famous man on earth: as Seitz puts it, "the rhetoric of extinction . . . serves to inflate into satanic stature a merely evil man."[84] Moreover, the consequent heedless, violent, and unnecessary venture into Iraq inspired recruits from around the world into embracing his movement.

But any benefit to the radical Islamic movement may be temporary at best. As it continues to alienate the moderates (in part by attacking targets in mainstream Islamic countries), it is likely that Kepel's verdict will continue to hold: "their political project," he writes, "now has a track record showing that it banks on the future, but is mired in the past."[85]

Despite U.S. overreaction, including the costly war against Iraq, the campaign against terror appears generally to be going rather well. This is because, no matter how much they might disagree on other issues (most notably on America's war on Iraq), there is a compelling incentive for states—including Arab and Muslim ones, who are also being targeted—to cooperate to deal with this international threat. And it is methodical, persistent international policing of individuals and small groups that is most needed.[86]

CONCLUSIONS: TERRORISM AND GLOBALIZATION AND THE CREATION OF NEW STATES?

Two counterterrorism officials from the Clinton administration contend that a small nuclear detonation in the U.S. "would necessitate the suspension of civil liberties," halt or even reverse "the process of globalization," and "could be the defeat that precipitates America's decline," while a single explosion of any sort of weapon of mass destruction would "trigger an existential crisis for the United States and its allies."[87] On balance and by contrast, it seems likely that, despite such hysterical proclamations and despite the various overreactions to terrorism, globalization remains essentially on track. Moreover, a notable global impact of the spectacular terrorist acts of September 11, 2001, was to put international cooperation in policing and intelligence-sharing into high gear, something likely to enhance, not retard, globalization.

Hysteria and hysterical overreaction to terrorism are scarcely required, however, and they can be costly and counterproductive. There are uncertainties and risks out there, and plenty of dangers and threats. But these are unlikely to prove to be existential. The sky, as it happens, is not falling, nor is apocalypse creeping over the horizon. Perhaps we can relax a little.

The same is true for the prospect of creating new states. Where nationalist movements exist, there is the prospect of using terrorism to advance their political cause. In recent years, however, nations and to some degree even peoples have come increasingly to recognize that the use of terrorism defeats the objective, the attainment of political independence with recognized legitimacy conceded by the international community. Terrorism may not be as bad as many have made out, but that does not mean that nations regard it as an acceptable strategy of political advancement.

NOTES

1. See Walter Laqueur, *No End to War* (New York: Continuum, 2003).

2. See Gregg Easterbrook, "Term Limits: The Meaninglessness of WMD," *The New Republic* (Oct. 7, 2002).

3. On the rise of the sentiment that killing by gas is peculiarly wicked and immoral (as opposed to killing by bullets and shrapnel), see Frederic Brown, *Chemical Warfare: A Study in Restraints* (Princeton, NJ: Princeton University Press, 1968).

4. Matthew Meselson, "The Myth of Chemical Superweapons," *Bulletin of the Atomic Scientists* (April, 1991).

5. Thomas McNaugher, "Ballistic Missiles and Chemical Weapons," *International Security* (Fall, 1990).

6. Gilmore Commission (Advisory Panel to Assess Domestic Response Capabilities for Terrorism Involving Weapons of Mass Destruction), 1999, 28. Although gas was used extensively in World War I, it accounted for less than 1 percent of the battle deaths. In fact, on average it took over a ton of gas to produce a single fatality.

7. Russell Seitz, "Weaker Than We Think," *American Conservative* (Dec. 6, 2004).

8. Meselson, 1991. Don Terry, "Treating Anthrax Hoaxes with Costly Rubber Gloves," *New York Times* (Dec. 29, 1998).

9. Gilmore, 1999, 25.

10. George Christopher et al., "Biological Warfare," *JAMA* (Aug. 6, 1997).

11. Michael Ignatieff lives in dire fear that terrorists will in the future be able to acquire and use chemical, biological, or nuclear weapons, and he cheers himself up very slightly by issuing a preposterous comparison: "at least the terrorism we face uses conventional weaponry, available for over a hundred years." Michael Ignatieff, *The Lesser Evil* (Princeton, NJ: Princeton University Press, 2004), 62–63. But, of course, the same could be said for chemical and biological weaponry.

12. Gilmore, 1999, 25. David C. Rapoport, "Terrorists and Weapons of the Apocalypse," *National Security Studies Quarterly* (Summer, 1999), 57.

13. Gilmore, 1999, 38.

14. Gilmore, 1999, 31, emphasis in the original.

15. See Graham Allison, "How to Stop Nuclear Terror," *Foreign Affairs* (Jan.–Feb., 2004), 104.

16. Brian Jenkins, "International Terrorism: A New Mode of Conflict," in David Carlton and Carlo Schaerf, eds., *International Terrorism and World Security* (New York: Wiley, 1975), 33.

17. Norman J. Rabkin, "Combating Terrorism," United States General Accounting Office, GAO/T-NSIAD-00-145, 6 April 2000, pp. 4, 12.

18. Center for Nonproliferation Studies, "Suitcase Nukes: A Reassessment," Monterey Institute of International Studies (September, 2002), 4, 12.

19. Testimony before the Senate Select Committee on Intelligence, 6 October 2004. See also Seitz, 2004.

20. Allison, 2004, 97.

21. Joshua Goldstein, *The Real Price of War: How You Pay for the War on Terror* (New York: New York University Press, 2004), 128, 132. Allison, 2004, 15.

22. C. P. Snow, "The Moral Un-Neutrality of Science," *Science* (Jan. 27, 1961), emphasis in the original.

23. George Will, "Global Warming? Hot Air," *Washington Post* (Dec. 23, 2004).

24. Clark Chapman and Alan Harris, "A Skeptical Look at September 11th: How We Can Defeat Terrorism by Reacting to It More Rationally," *Skeptical Inquirer* (Sept.–Oct., 2002).

25. Gilles Kepel, *Jihad: The Trail of Political Islam* (Cambridge, MA: Harvard University Press, 2002), 19–20, 375–76.

26. Brian Ross, "Secret FBI Report Questions Al Qaeda Capabilities" (ABC News, March 9, 2005).

27. B. R. Myers, "Mother of All Mothers: The Leadership Secrets of Kim Jong Il," *Atlantic* (Sept., 2004), 142.

28. Charles Krauthammer, "Blissful Amnesia," *Washington Post* (July 9, 2004); Allison, 2004, 6.

29. Mark Mitchell, "The Impact of External Parties on Brand-Name Capital: The 1982 Tylenol Poisonings and Subsequent Cases," in James Flynn et al., *Risk, Media and Stigma: Understanding Public Challenges to Modern Science and Technology* (London: Earthscan, 2002).

30. On the preference of terrorists for weapons that they know and understand, see Rapoport, 1999, 51; Gilmore, 1999, 37.

31. Seitz, 2004. Willmott observes of the Japanese army in World War II that "not a single operation planned after the start of the war met with success" (H. P. Willmott, *Empires in the Balance* [Annapolis, MD: Naval Institute Press, 1982], 91).

32. Jason Burke, *Al Qaeda: Casting a Shadow of Terror* (New York: Tauris, 2003), 167–68; Kepel, 2002, 420 n. 50.

33. Benjamin Friedman, "Leap Before You Look: The Failures of Homeland Security," *Breakthroughs* (Spring, 2004), 35.

34. James Fallows, "Success without Victory," *Atlantic* (Jan.–Feb., 2005), 80–90.

35. *Financial Times* (14 September 2004), 8.

36. Dean Calbreath, "Attacks to Cost 1.6 Million Jobs," *San Diego Union-Tribune* (Jan. 12, 2002).

37. Roger Congleton, "Terrorism, Interest-Group Politics, and Public Policy," *Independent Review* (Summer, 2002), 62.

38. Jeffrey Rosen, *The Naked Crowd* (New York: Random House, 2004), 68.

39. Michael Sivak and Michael Flannagan, "Flying and Driving after the September 11 Attacks," *American Scientist* (Jan.–Feb., 2003).

40. See *Economist* (6–12 November 2004), 81–82. The wars have also, of course, been quite costly economically.

41. David Banks, "Statistics for Homeland Defense," *Chance* (Jan., 2002), 10.

42. Francis Clines, "Karl Rove's Campaign Strategy Seems Evident: It's the Terror, Stupid," *New York Times* (May 10, 2003), A28.

43. Office of Homeland Security, "The National Strategy for Homeland Security," July 2002.

44. Friedman, 2004, 33–34, 36. Rosen, 2004, 79.

45. Rosen, 2004, 222.

46. H. G. Wells, *The War That Will End War* (London: Duffield, 1914). H. G. Wells, *The Last Books of H. G. Wells* (London: H. G. Wells Society, 1968), 67.

47. See also Siobhan Gorman, "Fear Factor," *National Journal* (May 10, 2003), 1464.

48. Ignatieff, 2004a, 48.

49. Gorman, *National Journal* (November 20, 2004), 3534.

50. Bernard Brodie, "The Development of Nuclear Strategy," *International Security* (Spring, 1978), 68.

51. Bruce Hoffman, "Rethinking Terrorism and Counterterrorism since 9/11," *Studies in Conflict and Terrorism* 25 (2002), 311–12.

52. Goldstein, 2004, 128, 132. Allison, 2004, 1.

53. David Gergen, "A Fragile Time for Globalism," *US News and World Report* (Feb. 11, 2002).

54. Jennifer Kerr, "Terror Threat Level Raised to Orange," *Associated Press* (Dec. 21, 2003).

55. Michael Ignatieff, *The Lesser Evil: Political Ethics in an Age of Terror* (Princeton, NJ: Princeton University Press, 2004), 146.

56. Ignatieff, 2004a, 46–48.

57. Gilmore, 1999, 37.

58. For a more extensive discussion, see Mueller, "Why Isn't There More Violence?" *Security Studies* (Spring, 2004).

59. See Paul Slovic, "Informing and Educating the Public about Risk," *Risk Analysis* (1986).

60. Gorman, 2003, 1461–62.

61. Howard Kunreuther, "Risk Analysis and Risk Management in an Uncertain World," *Risk Analysis* (August, 2002), 663.

62. Sivak and Flannagan, 2003. More generally, they calculate that an American's chance of being killed in one non-stop airline flight is about one in 13 million (even putting the September 11 crashes into the mix), while to reach that same level of risk when driving on America's safest roads, rural interstate highways, one would have to travel a mere 11.2 miles.

63. Allison, 2004, 56–57.

64. Theodore Rockwell, "Radiation Chicken Little," *Washington Post* (Sept. 16, 2003). See also Allison, 2004, 8, 59, 220.

65. Full transcript of bin Laden's speech, algazeera.net, 30 October 2004.

66. Friedman, 2004, 32. Hoffman, 2002, 313.

67. The Jewish pogroms in Russia at the end of the 19th century, for instance, were rationalized in major part because Jews were notable in several terrorist movements at the time: David C. Rapoport, "Weapons of Minimum Destruction," *Journal of Terrorism and Political Violence* (August, 2004), 68; see also Ignatieff, 2004, 63.

68. Kenneth Rogoff, "The Cost of Living Dangerously," *Foreign Policy* (Nov. 2004).

69. See Leon Sigal, *Disarming Strangers: Nuclear Diplomacy with North Korea* (Princeton, NJ: Princeton University Press, 1998); Selig Harrison, *Korean Endgame* (Princeton, NJ: Princeton University Press, 2002).

70. Don Oberdorfer, *The Two Koreas* (New York: Basic Books, 2001), 307.

71. Oberdorfer, 2001, 308, 316.

72. Oberdorfer, 2001, 324; see also Harrison, 2002, 117–18.

73. Sigal, 1998, chs. 6–7; Harrison, 2002, ch. 18. Expect collapse: Harrison 2002.

74. Interview for Frontline, PBS, conducted March 27, 2003, http://www.pbs.org/wgbh/pages/frontline/shows/kim/interviews/perle.html.

75. Allison, 2004, 171.

76. On this issue, see Stefan Halper and Jonathan Clarke, *America Alone* (New York: Cambridge University Press, 2004).

77. Saddam was so afraid of his own army that he would not allow it to bring heavy weapons anywhere near Baghdad out of fear that regular troops might turn and use them against his government (Maggie O'Kane, "Saddam Wields Terror—and Feigns Respect," *Guardian* [Nov. 25, 1998]).

78. Essentially, the same policy was applied as well by the Soviet Union to its frustrating effort in Afghanistan. It withdrew in 1989 but continued its financial support of a government that eventually collapsed in 1992.

79. *Economist* (6–12 November 2004), 81–82.

80. Polls suggest that the percentage of Jordanians with a favorable opinion of the United States plunged after the invasion from 27 to 1. This surely suggests that the recruitment of terrorists would be easier there, although their focus is more likely to be Israel than the United States.

81. See Steven Miller in chapter 11.

82. On this point, see especially Jeffrey Record, *Dark Victory* (Annapolis, MD: Naval Institute Press, 2004), 34–39.

83. Dan Roberts and Gary Silverman, "Tarnished Image: Is the World Falling out of Love with US Brands?" *Financial Times* (Dec. 30, 2005).

84. Seitz, 2004.

85. Kepel, 2002, 371.

86. Actually, by some standards, it may all be nearly over. Stephen Flynn, like others in the terrorism industry, likes to begin articles with such dramatic lines as "the United States is living on borrowed time—and squandering it," and end them with "the entire nation . . . must be organized for the long, deadly struggle against terrorism." However, in mid-course he cheers up enough to supply a standard for "how much security is enough" and determines that to be when "the American people can conclude that a future attack on U.S. soil will be an exceptional event that does not require wholesale changes in how they go about their lives" (Stephen Flynn, "The Neglected Home Front," *Foreign Affairs* [Sept., 2004], 20, 33, 27). It seems reasonable to suggest that they can so conclude now, though that might require them to stop listening to the terrorism industry.

87. Daniel Benjamin and Steve Simon, *The Age of Sacred Terror* (New York: Random House, 2002), 398–99.

II

SPECIFIC OUTCOMES

5

Can China Be Effectively Punished through Global Economic Isolation?

Richard N. Cooper

With the end of the Cold War, and until 9/11/01, many academic and journalistic pundits averred that military power was no longer of great importance and that the future lay with economic power. The claim was made that the United States was an "economic superpower," and therefore would continue to be the world's dominant power in any case. Does this term mean anything other than "biggest national economy?" If so, what exactly does it mean? This chapter will discuss the concept of economic power, and then apply the concept to the proposal of John Mearsheimer that on strategic (balance of power) grounds the United States should take steps to slow down the economic growth of China. In doing so, the United States should attempt to limit "globalization" as it applies to China.

THE EVANESCENT CONCEPT OF ECONOMIC POWER

The dictionary defines "power" as "capability of producing an effect" or, what is probably more directly relevant for normal use in the international arena, "possession of controlling influence over others." Military power involves the capability to coerce a recalcitrant party. That possibility, combined with a perception that the possessor has the will to use it if necessary, is often sufficient to attain the desired effect. Economic power by analogy involves the capability decisively to punish (or to reward) another party, according to whether that party responds in the desired way, combined with a perception that the possessor has the will or political ability to use it if necessary.

Economic power in this sense surely exists. But apart from its possible connection to national military power through a country's tax base it is largely local, or ephemeral, or both. It is difficult to wield on a global scale. The basic reason is that the locus for most economic decision-making is households and firms, and is thus highly diffuse. Households rarely have enough wealth to influence national economic outcomes, and firms are subject to competitive pressures which penalize them, possibly severely, if they deviate too far from what the "market" will permit. The last decade has seen the failure of such large respected firms as the Bank of New England and Barings; and the humbling of huge global firms such as General Motors, IBM, and state-owned Crédit Lyonnais.

There are many large corporations in the world, and these corporations surely have "power" over their employees, some of their suppliers, and the towns in which they are resident. But this power is sharply limited both in scope and in time, largely because of the existence of effectively functioning markets, increasingly global in character, such that in anything but the short run individuals, suppliers, and even communities command a range of choice which sharply limits the leverage even of large corporations. In addition, most governments are much on the alert to abuse of corporate power over their employees, suppliers, and communities.

It is moreover a mistake to aggregate corporations by nationality, as is commonly done, especially with respect to Japan. National corporations are in fact separate entities, often in vigorous competition with one another, and they have great difficulty working together for common aims on a sustained basis without the strong encouragement and usually the coercive power of government. In short, they can sometimes become the instruments of effective national policy; they can rarely if ever exercise sustained leverage on their own.

American firms were demonized by some Europeans in the 1960s; Japanese firms were criticized by some Americans in the 1980s. It is true that firms from a particular country sometimes act in a parallel fashion, as when many leading Japanese banks internationalized their activities in the 1980s. However, that is generally not because their actions are coordinated, but because they are in vigorous competition with one another and each is reluctant to let any other get a major competitive edge in the presence of new opportunities, such as those opened by deregulation. Since they will be compared with leading competitors and judged by financial markets, initiative by one firm is quickly imitated by others. That way no one can achieve a striking advantage; and if the action was financially risky, like much lending to developing countries in the early 1980s, then all will experience similar losses.

Power is a relative concept; not everyone can have equal economic power. Equality violates the conditions for power. So if in fact economic capacity is highly diffuse, power is eroded. Widespread economic capacity, in a globally competitive environment, creates options for all parties. And the presence of

alternatives undermines the capacity of any one player to achieve its preferred ends, except through good performance in the eyes of its customers.

Can enterprises, the source of economic capability, be harnessed by governments, aggregating to national economic power? In at least one respect,
the answer is "yes": they can be levied with taxes, as can households.
The resulting revenues provide governments the wherewithal to carry out
national objectives. Total tax revenue is obviously related to size, larger
economies generating larger revenues. What is not so obvious, however, is
that it is also related to per capita income, with rich countries being able to
tax away a higher portion of income than poor ones do. The share of GDP
taken as total tax revenues generally rises from 10–20 percent in the poorest
countries to 20–30 percent in middle-income countries, to 30–50 percent in
the rich countries. Such revenues can help finance military expenditure, but
also foreign aid, diplomatic representation, and other sources of international
influence. The United States today enjoys enormous tax revenues, even
though (contrary to what many Americans think) Americans are taxed more
lightly than citizens in any of the other rich countries. Even Japan and
Switzerland tax their citizens more; France and Germany, not to mention the
Scandinavian countries, have much higher tax burdens.

What about the purchasing and selling activities of corporations? Could
Japan really reduce U.S. military power by holding back on the export of
semi-conductors (memory chips), as Shintaro Ishihara rashly suggested some
years ago in *The Japan That Can Say No*? Or could countries successfully close
markets to other countries, or threaten to, as a source of economic leverage?

The international community has rules, now embodied in the charter of
the World Trade Organization, which govern much of world trade. They generally prohibit closing markets to other members of the WTO except under
special circumstances, involving response to trade violations by trading partners, or the implementation of economic sanctions under United Nations
auspices. Any country closing markets therefore risks the general opprobrium of the international community, unless the reasons are clear and
acceptable. (These rules do not apply to the countries that are not members
of the WTO or its predecessor the General Agreement on Tariffs and Trade
[GATT], which included most of the Communist countries.)

An interesting example occurred involving an economic threat by China.
During the 1994 debate in the United States over whether MFN treatment of
China should be renewed, China threatened to deny orders to American
firms if the extension were not forthcoming. China quickly came to appreci-
ate that such a threat, unless sharply circumscribed (e.g. to procurement by
government agencies), would, if exercised, violate the rules of the WTO, for
membership in which China had applied. The threat thus complicated its
application, and was withdrawn.

No such rules exist for exports. Countries are free to restrict them, and routinely do so for potentially dangerous products, such as weapons or nuclear materials. But in fact most countries are still mercantilistic in outlook and strongly desire to build export markets, which are seen as vital to economic growth. They are in practice therefore hesitant to jeopardize such markets by restricting exports. That is especially true of Japan, whose sense of vulnerability remains high, especially after the two oil shocks of the 1970s. German law sharply circumscribes the ability of the German government to restrict exports.

Perhaps not surprisingly, it is the United States, more than any other country, which has attempted to herd American firms into support of national political objectives. U.S. law gives the president discretion to restrict exports for reasons of foreign policy, and such restrictions have been imposed from time to time. They can even involve the infamous extra-territorial reach to American-owned subsidiaries in other countries, a reach that has been vigorously contested by America's closest allies, especially Britain, as in the Soviet gas pipeline to Western Europe which the U.S. (unsuccessfully) objected to in 1982. The Helms-Burton Act to penalize foreign firms that deal with Cuba attracted similar opprobrium abroad.

If a country, for example the United States, dislikes the decisions by a foreign government, it has several ways to deal with it beyond diplomatic protest and short of military threats or action. It can try to:

1) *persuade* the government to change its decision, perhaps by revealing new information, or by successfully encouraging a re-examination of the government's preferences;

2) *induce* the country to change its decision by offering it something it considers desirable, contingent on the change, such as a formal agreement or economic assistance, thereby enlarging its menu of choice;

3) *threaten* action against the country if it does not change its decision, thereby altering the menu of choice of the foreign government for the worse by removing the status quo;

4) implicitly *accept* the decision, thereby deciding to live with it (but leaving our country in a less preferred position).

Power conveys the capability to use inducements as well as threats—this is perhaps implicit in Robert Dahl's celebrated and widely accepted definition of power: the ability to induce another party to do something it would not otherwise do. Economic power specifies economic instruments in the achievement of power. Some prefer to encompass by the term "power" all of the first three options listed above, introducing the notion of "soft power," where the offended country commands enough respect to get others to reconsider their preferences leading to the offending decision, or even to change the decision to acquire the respect of the powerful country, without expectation of either threats or inducements.

"Influence" and "inducement" do not have the connotation of coercion, which the word "power" has. And all these are different from "dominance." A country can be economically dominant without being powerful; the former implies that events within the country have great influence on other national economies, i.e. that there are large spillovers, e.g. from a recession. The latter implies a purposeful or willful action, not merely incidental spillovers. Of course, dominance can sometimes be translated into power and purposeful influence, on which more below.

"Economic leverage" can be exercised through inducements or sanctions, carrots or sticks. The principal inducements are financial grants or loans (e.g. foreign assistance or military aid), trade preferences (through government procurement or through tariff and non-tariff policies), and willingness to export military equipment (or occasionally other high-tech products not generally available). The principal sanctions involve partial or full embargo of exports to the target country, partial or full embargo of imports from the country, and freezing or confiscating assets owned by the country or its residents. If financial assistance is provided on a regular basis, cutting or eliminating expected assistance also represents a sanction. Leverage of course might also arise from the direct or implied threat of the introduction of sanctions; they may not actually have to be used.

ECONOMIC SANCTIONS

High hopes were once entertained for the efficacy of economic sanctions against internationally anti-social national behavior. In 1919 Woodrow Wilson said: "A nation boycotted is a nation that is in sight of surrender. Apply this economic, peaceful, silent, deadly remedy and there will be no need for force. It is a terrible remedy. It does not cost a life outside the nation boycotted, but it brings a pressure upon the nation which, in my judgment, no modern nation could resist."

The field of economic sanctions used to provide lots of grounds for more or less informed conjecture, usually based on a few examples, with much room for continuing disagreement on the question of efficacy. Thanks to Hufbauer, Schott, and Elliott (HSE) at the Institute for International Economics those days are now past with respect to economic sanctions. They have undertaken detailed study of 115 uses of economic sanctions (*Economic Sanctions Reconsidered*, 1985, revised edition 1990), including all those by major countries in the period 1950–1990, and have drawn various conclusions from their comprehensive survey. Their study does not cover the use of inducements, and only a few threats of sanctions that were not exercised, especially since some examples in the latter category are not publicly known.[1]

HSE draw an important distinction between whether the sanctions actually had discernible economic impact on the target country and whether they contributed to a desired change in government policy. The impact could be weak, in which case it is not likely to change policy. But even if it is strong, it may not change policy if the government leaders are impervious to the well-being of some or all of the population under their rule (Iraq under Saddam Hussein comes to mind), or if the sanctions themselves help to mobilize public sentiment against yielding to foreign pressure (Cuba in 1960 comes to mind, although extensive assistance from the USSR also weakened the material effect of the U.S. sanctions after the initial impact).

HSE are somewhat surprised by their findings: in about one-third of the cases they judge sanctions to have been successful, in that they made at least a modest contribution to attaining the goal desired by those imposing the sanctions, although possibly at some cost to those imposing the sanctions. The success ratio was highest (52 percent) when the goal was to destabilize the government; it was lowest (20 percent) when military impairment was sought.[2]

The HSE authors attempt to derive from their case studies circumstances under which economic sanctions are most likely to be effective. They judge that sanctions are most likely to be successful when: 1) the objective is modest and well specified; 2) the target country is in a weakened position at the outset; 3) economic relations with the target country are relatively great before imposition of the sanctions; 4) the sanctions are relatively heavy; 5) the duration of the sanctions is limited (i.e. the passage of time erodes their effectiveness); and 6) the impact on the target country's GDP is relatively high (2.4 percent for successes as against 1.0 percent for failures).

Somewhat surprisingly, two potentially important factors did not seem to be very important: 1) international cooperation was modestly higher in cases of failure than in successful cases, perhaps because the goals were more ambitious when international cooperation was involved; and 2) the cost to the country imposing the sanctions was only modestly higher in the failures than in the successes, although HSE caution against a government undertaking sanctions if the costs to its own public will badly erode public support.

The HSE study is impressive and carefully constructed. But the judgments expressed are inevitably subjective and not beyond challenge. For example, I would judge two of their cases (in both of which I had some involvement) quite differently from the way they do: British and UN sanctions against Rhodesia over the period 1965–79, and U.S. sanctions against the USSR in 1980, following the invasion of Afghanistan. HSE give the first case their second highest mark, and the second case the lowest mark. I consider the Rhodesia economic sanctions largely a failure, and the U.S. sanctions against the USSR a modest success. The difference hinges in the first case in differences in judgment about the role of the sanctions in bringing about eventual majority rule in Rhodesia (now Zimbabwe), the desired objective; and in the second on what the objective was. Without Portuguese and especially South African cooperation, economic sanctions against Rhodesia could not have been expected to be effective in squeezing Rhodesia significantly, and were not. GNP grew an average of 6 percent a year for a decade after the sanctions were imposed. The ultimate objective was achieved largely through prolonged civil war and exhaustion of the minority population, although after the withdrawal of Portuguese (1975) and South African (1976) support helped isolate the Rhodesian government, sanctions can be said to have played some role, but much less than HSE accord to them.

In the case of U.S. sanctions against the USSR in early 1980, in particular the embargo on sale of U.S. grain (with understandings from Australia, Canada, and the EC, but not from Argentina, that they would not make up the difference), there was no serious expectation that the USSR could be induced to withdraw from Afghanistan, or even that it would be hurt seriously beyond an impact effect in the spring of 1980 that hinged on bottlenecks in Soviet transportation. Rather, the real target was the nervous countries in southern Asia, whose sense of vulnerability would rise sharply (particularly after the Iranian Revolution and hostage crisis, which was contemporaneous) if the West, and the United States in particular, seemed to treat the Soviet invasion of Afghanistan with indifference. It was understood by U.S. officials that, short of war, U.S. sanctions could not greatly hurt the USSR (one consequence of having isolated that country economically for so many years), and that the damage of the grain embargo would be short-lived. But like withdrawal from the Moscow Olympics, it was a dramatic action. Ironically, loud protests by American farmers reinforced the fact that it was a difficult, serious action. Saudi Arabia, in particular, remained firmly in the western area of influence instead of drifting to a more neutral, standoffish position. In that respect the embargo was a success.

These examples illustrate how difficult it sometimes is to assess the efficacy of a given action, leaving the question of economic sanctions open to debate despite the careful work of Hufbauer, Schott, and Elliott. In any case, on the basis of their comprehensive survey, HSE find a sharp decline in the efficacy of U.S. sanctions: from 1945 to 1973 economic sanctions contributed to U.S. foreign policy objectives in 18 of 35 cases examined (51% success); in the period 1973–1990 sanctions failed to contribute to U.S. objectives in 38 of 46 cases examined (17% success).

The *threatened* use of sanctions is another issue: although HSE include a few such cases, they are often not made public. They remain implicit in the situation, however, and thus may influence the behavior of governments that feel structurally vulnerable. Japan's sense of vulnerability with respect to OPEC comes to mind. An interesting case was reported in the mid-1990s, when Japan was the only country to vote against establishment of an Antarctic sanctuary for whales in the deliberations of the International Whaling Commission. Several Caribbean countries abstained, allegedly to demonstrate quiet support for the Japanese position. Since these countries have no interest in whaling one way or another, their vote raises the question whether they felt vulnerable to a reduction or cutoff of Japanese foreign aid. Japan now offers the world's largest bilateral aid program; its size will lead actual and prospective recipients to be more sensitive to Japan's positions in international forums. This is not to suggest that Japan buys support explicitly but only that recipients may feel vulnerable to a cutoff of aid if Japan is displeased with the positions they take.

The use of inducements has not yet been systematically studied. There are, however, many examples, one of the best known of which is periodic U.S. negotiations with countries such as the Philippines and Greece over military base rights. The Philippines continued to raise the price to a point at which a deal could no longer be struck (complicated fortuitously by volcanic eruption that badly damaged Clark Air Field), and the U.S. withdrew from its naval base at Subic Bay. West Germany also allegedly used economic inducements in the 1960s and 1970s to dissuade countries from formally recognizing the DDR, and France from selling various high-technology products.

The European Community has used trade policy extensively to influence the broad political attachments of governments of countries around the Mediterranean and in central and eastern Europe, and the U.S. Caribbean Initiative of 1983 can be seen as an effort to stabilize that area politically and economically. These efforts, however, were designed to create broad prowestern attachments in the target political systems rather than to influence the behavior of foreign governments in specific ways.

The relative efficacy of leverage through inducements may well increase, but they will be seen less often because of the tight fiscal condition that exists in almost all the rich countries these days, and the shift in their attention from foreign to domestic concerns. Rapidly growing domestic entitlements will weaken their willingness to use financial inducements to foreigners.

The main point, however, is that economic power is generally weak and uncertain in its effects—it fails to meet the standard of producing a "controlling influence over others"—even when it is wielded by the state, and even when states collaborate in attempting to exercise it. One only has to think of Libya, Iraq, Serbia, and North Korea in a contemporary setting. In each case economic sanctions were applied, with varying degrees of pressure, in the first three instances under UN resolutions. Populations in all these countries suffered as a result of the sanctions, but except for Libya, they did not bring the desired political response. Leaders survived despite the sanctions, and the sanctions were eroded in various degrees. Arbitrageurs are omnipresent, ready to run risks for high rewards. The case of Serbia was complicated by the fact that Greece was somewhat sympathetic to Serbian objectives, if not to Serbian means, and a lively border trade occurred in petroleum, denial of which could have throttled the Serbian economy and military efforts, despite strong European Community support for the sanctions. But Brussels did not get the full cooperation of Athens; and in any case Athens would have had difficulty stopping all arbitrage even if it had wanted to.

There is an ever-present temptation, especially in the United States, to use economic leverage, especially trade sanctions, to influence the behavior of other countries. This instrument is seen as preferable to war, and more effective than diplomatic representations. It is built into the escalating sequence of discipline in the United Nations Charter. Its use, if not its success, has become more common with the political rapprochement between Russia and the United States, on the one hand, and with increasing regional disorder made possible in part by the disappearance of client state relationships, which provided some stability, with the ending of the Cold War.

But the increasing globalization of world markets is also likely to erode the effectiveness of trade sanctions as a source of leverage. There are today so many decision makers—individuals and enterprises—with options that governments can do no more than shape in broad terms the environment in which they function, and provide incentives to operate in desired ways.

SLOWING DOWN CHINA?

John Mearsheimer has reminded readers that traditional "realism" has not vanished in international relations, and has applied balance of power reasoning to the world of states roughly two decades from now.[3] Most of his analysis is applied to Europe, which will not concern us here, but he also addresses the future balance of power in Northeast Asia, with and without the presence of U.S. military forces there. His conclusion is that China will become the regional hegemon, and that without U.S. troops the Asian configuration will be unstable. He urges the United States to take steps to slow down China's growth, to postpone the rise of China as a regional power. This proposal is simply asserted, not developed. This section will address how such a proposal might be executed, with a view to testing the viability, in an operational context, of the notion of economic power. I will not address, except briefly at the end, whether the proposal has merit, i.e. whether it should govern U.S. policy; the focus rather will be on the feasibility of carrying it out.

The conclusion, in brief, is that the United States does not have the economic power to slow down China's growth, beyond a transition period of several years immediately following the introduction of such a policy. Moreover, the costs to the United States of introducing such a policy would be considerable, since transformation of the framework for international transactions would at a minimum introduce much uncertainty into the world economic order and at a maximum would alienate the United States not only from China but from many other countries as well.

But first it is worth commenting on Mearsheimer's conception of China's medium-term evolution, which can only be described as faulty, and on the realistic prospects of the Chinese economy over the next two decades.

Mearsheimer is concerned with the "latent power" of countries, which operationally he identifies as the Gross National Product (GNP) for countries of similar levels of economic and technological development, while putting some (unquantified) discount on the GNP of poorer and more technically backward countries.[4]

Mearsheimer, it should be clear, is concerned mainly with military capacity, including nuclear weapons, but in the long run, he argues, the interests of states drive them to develop their latent power into the required military capacity. Latent power is therefore the starting point. Here is the context he provides for China:

> China is the key to understanding the future distribution of power in Northeast Asia. It is clearly not a potential hegemon today, because it is not nearly as wealthy as Japan. But if China's economy continues expanding over the next two decades at or near the rate it has been growing since the early 1980s, China will surpass Japan as the wealthiest state in Asia. Indeed, because of the vast size of China's population, it has the potential to become much wealthier than Japan, and even wealthier than the United States.
>
> To illustrate China's potential, consider the following scenarios. Japan's per capita GNP is now more than 40 times greater than China's. If China modernizes to the point where it has about the same per capita GNP as South Korea does today, China would have a GNP of $10.66 trillion, substantially larger than Japan's $4.09 trillion economy. If China's per capita GNP grew to be just half of Japan's present per capita GNP, China would have a GNP of $20.04 trillion, which would make China almost five times as wealthy as Japan.[5]

It sounds easy for China to reach the standard of living of South Korea. But for China to attain South Korea's per capita GNP in twenty years, per capita GNP would have to grow by 12.5 percent a year, a figure hardly possible for a single year, and not remotely possible for twenty years in a row. To reach half of Japan's per capita income in twenty years, China's GNP would have to grow by more than 17 percent a year. Considering the huge obstacles and uncertainties China faces, these "scenarios" can only be considered fantasy. Mearsheimer also holds out the possibility of China's becoming more wealthy (i.e. having a higher GNP) than the United States. He neglects that as time goes on countries other than China are also likely to grow, even if less rapidly. The Council of Economic Advisers (2001) has suggested that for the next decade full employment growth for the United States is 3.4 percent a year. The World Bank (1997) has suggested that China's growth to 2020 might average 6.5 percent a year, a figure that others (e.g. RAND 2000) consider too high, and the World Bank itself envisions a slowdown in the decade 2010–2020. We can pose the following question: suppose China's GNP grows indefinitely by 3 percent a year more than the U.S. GNP: how long will it take for China's GNP to equal that of the United States, given their relative starting positions in 2001? The answer is 74 years, i.e. China's "wealth" will equal that of the United States in 2075—more than half a century beyond Mearsheimer's two-decade horizon.[6] And even then per capita income in China would be less than one quarter that in the United States, a feature that bears on potential tax revenues available to the central government of each country.

In fact, while it is possible, China will have great difficulty sustaining a 6.5 percent annual growth rate over the next two decades, much less beyond that. First, China faces a series of domestic challenges in order to sustain that high a growth rate. It must grow the private and township sectors enough to compensate for declining production in parts of the state-enterprise sector. It must reform and recapitalize the banking system, and build a viable financial system beyond banking. To close many loss-making state enterprises, it must create a social safety net (unemployment compensation, pensions, health care) for urban employees, financed by government. It must deal with rapid growth in need for water, sewage disposal, and new housing in urban areas. It must greatly improve agricultural productivity, partly through large and more efficient irrigation projects. Moreover, on current projections China will experience a sharp decline in population growth beyond 2020, as the one-child policy, introduced in 1980, begins to affect significantly the number of women of child-bearing age, especially in view of the marked bias during the past two decades toward birth of boys. However desirable population decline may be on other grounds, it will make sustaining future high growth in GNP more difficult.

A team at RAND, responding to a request by the Office of Net Assessment of the Defense Department, has recently published a study of various adverse scenarios, along with estimates of their negative impact on Chinese growth over the period 2005–2015.[7] The adversities cover a socially disruptive increase in unemployment, increased corruption, a major epidemic (focused on AIDS, written before SARS or Avian flu), failure to solve the emerging shortage of water in northern China, a major disruption to world oil supplies, a domestic financial crisis, a sharp decline in inward foreign direct investment, and a military conflict over Taiwan or elsewhere. Others are imaginable, e.g. a severe world recession. Each scenario has an adverse impact on Chinese growth ranging from 0.3 to 2.2 percent a year given the assumptions made in the study, lowering Chinese GDP by 3 to 24 percent by 2015 from an unspecified baseline. Of course, none of these adversities may eventuate, a possibility which the authors consider implausible. If one occurs, others may be triggered, at least in part, because of interdependencies among them.

Good luck as well as skillful management will be required for China to continue on a course of sustained growth.

What economic actions could the United States take to affect China's long-term growth, representing an exercise of U.S. economic power? (Note that of the adverse scenarios considered by the RAND team, the only one subject to possible U.S. action would be limitation of foreign direct investment [FDI], a topic taken up below.) The U.S. could think of reducing China's export growth by reducing American imports from China; reducing China's imports by restricting U.S. exports to China, especially high-technology exports but arguably also food and animal feed; reducing U.S. FDI in China (and incipient Chinese FDI in the United States); reducing other flows of U.S. capital to China; and reducing Chinese migration to the United States, especially students. Mearsheimer's argument presumes that United States strategy is to reduce the Chinese growth rate. Thus Washington would not be responding to some extremely provocative act by China, such as an unprovoked attack on Taiwan. This assumption assures that the United States would be acting alone, in pursuit of its strategic interests as Mearsheimer sees them, and that it would not have the cooperation of other countries, particularly Europe, in pursuing parallel actions.

Reducing Imports

The United States could reduce its imports from China in three ways: by reducing overall demand, by slowing U.S. growth; by restricting imports (or imports of China-relevant products) from the world; and by restricting imports from China on a discriminatory basis, all relative to prospects in the absence of these strategically motivated actions. At first glance it might seem as though greatly reducing China's exports to the United States would have a major impact on China's growth, since exports account for about a fifth of China's GDP and exports to the United States amount to about a quarter of China's exports, or 5 percent of GDP. However, exports are measured at gross value, not value-added in China, and many of China's exports involve processing imports, which come especially from Southeast Asia, Korea, Taiwan, and Japan. Total cessation of exports to the United States would thus have a much smaller impact on China's GDP than the 5 percent would suggest, and indeed would at least in the short run have a significant negative impact on China's overseas suppliers, some of which are U.S. allies.

The first of the three approaches, probably the most effective in terms of total value, would also be self-defeating. Maintaining American strategic superiority, one observes, involves enhancing, not retarding, U.S. growth. The second would be welcomed by certain U.S. firms producing the products in question; import protection is helpful to firms in direct competition with the imports. But it would reduce U.S. standards of living and would be harmful to firms, relative to their foreign competitors, that use Chinese products as inputs. Moreover, it would be not only resented but seriously challenged by all countries exporting such goods to the United States, as violation of their rights—and U.S. commitments—under the terms creating the World Trade Organization (WTO). Except under special circumstances, product by product, they would succeed in this challenge, so the United States would be faced with backing down on the import restrictions, or backing out of the accepted principles of international trade that the United States, in particular, has worked so hard to achieve over the past six decades.

Restricting imports from China on a discriminatory basis, again except under special circumstances, product by product, entails an analogous dilemma. Now that China has become a member of the WTO, subject both to its rights and obligations, a membership that followed especially intense negotiations with the United States, China could challenge widespread discriminatory restriction of imports from China, and would win the challenge. This would involve the United States reneging on a recent international commitment, unless the United States formally invoked the national security clause in WTO. Yet invocation of that clause without clear provocation by China would signal to the rest of the world a sudden unilateral change in the basic trade rules by the United States, unpersuasive to others, indeed potentially threatening to them.

Given China's heavy dependence on the American market, any sudden move by the United States to restrict imports from China would of course have a negative impact on the Chinese economy in the short to medium run. But in the longer run Chinese manufacturing would adjust to the diminished sales possibilities in the United States and would sell elsewhere—not perhaps in the same magnitude, given the size of the U.S. market, but enough to prevent stifling Chinese growth. Moreover, China now has foreign exchange reserves in excess of $700 billion, and therefore could continue to import critical products from abroad (e.g. oil) for a long time even after the loss of sales to the United States.

Recall also that the United States did embargo products from China during the period 1951–1972. Other countries continued to trade with China, however, and China's economic growth in 1952–1959 was over 6 percent a year, before it was disrupted by Mao's Great Leap Forward and slowed by the Cultural Revolution, both events internal to China.[8]

Cutting Exports

China might acquire some critical products from the United States, which the latter could restrict, thereby harming China. Curiously, restrictions on exports are not covered by the same tight and comprehensive international rules as are restrictions on imports, so exports could be restricted without violating the WTO. Indeed, exports of military equipment and so-called dual-use technology to China are *already* restricted, resulting in complaints by China. Dual-use technology includes equipment such as high-end computers, and in the view of the Defense Department has potential military as well as civilian uses. Exports to China (and indeed to most countries) require licenses from the Commerce Department, and exports to China operate under a special regime designed to inhibit any direct U.S. contribution, through exports, to enhancement of China's military capacity. U.S. industry chafes at the way these regulations are implemented, arguing that in many if not most cases they simply cause Americans to lose Chinese orders to foreign firms, mainly European and Japanese. The key point here is that U.S. firms rarely have a monopoly on modern technologies, and others are eager to sell where American firms are denied the sale. The United States has generally been unable to persuade its high-technology European and Japanese allies to forego the sales of such dual-use technology, except in limited areas (e.g. involving nuclear weapons or missile technology). This was a problem even with the Soviet Union during the height of the Cold War, when a procedure for vetting and challenging such sales was in place; it is even more difficult today. Tightening these U.S. restrictions or widening their coverage would have negligible effect on China's growth, and indeed might have some negative impact on U.S. growth, although probably small. The European Union has already served notice that it may resume selling military equipment to China.

China is increasingly dependent on imports of agricultural products, particularly feed grains, and must soon make some strategic decisions regarding its agricultural policy. The United States arguably could influence those decisions by restricting agricultural exports. There are two problems with this action: first, other agricultural exporters, especially Canada, Australia, Argentina, and the European Community, would be happy to take up any slack left by the United States. Second, American farmers would complain bitterly, as they did following President Carter's embargo on grain sales to the Soviet Union following that country's invasion of Afghanistan, an item that figured heavily in Ronald Reagan's presidential campaign the following fall, when he promised never, under any circumstances, to restrict exports of American farm products.

Reducing Foreign Direct Investment

As in the case of high-technology exports, the United States already has a procedure for vetting foreign direct investment in the United States, and for denying it if it might act as a vehicle for transferring sensitive technology abroad.[9] Chinese FDI in the United States is small. It is growing now, but tightening the regulations or even prohibiting it altogether would have a negligible impact on China's economic growth, and is likely to hurt the United States more than it hurts China, although again the impact would be small.

Foreign direct investment in China, in contrast, has been substantial, and has made a substantial contribution both to China's growth in exports and to its industrial technology. Indeed, during 2002 China was the largest recipient of FDI, and for previous years followed only the United States as a destination for FDI. The RAND team includes a sharp drop in FDI as one of their adverse scenarios for China. On their admittedly sketchy and uncertain calculations, China's growth would decline by 0.6–1.6 percent a year over the period 2005–2015 following a decline in FDI of $10 billion a year.[10] However, the relevant question for Mearsheimer is not the impact of a general decline in FDI, which would almost certainly occur as a result of perceptions of developments within China adverse for foreign investors. Rather, it is the impact of a policy-induced decline in American direct investment in China. The stock of U.S. FDI in China amounted to only $40 billion in 2005, only a small percentage of total FDI in China.

Thus the question becomes: how crucial is this U.S. FDI for China, and in its absence how much would FDI from other countries fill in behind it? With respect to two important sectors, automobiles and finance, in both of which U.S. firms have expressed interest, we can reasonably guess the answer: FDI has been controlled by the Chinese authorities, demand for it exceeds supply, and with U.S. restrictions the Chinese authorities could allow others in instead (but might choose not to, if they felt the gains were not sufficient). A general proposition, then, is that FDI from other countries would quickly fill in behind prohibited FDI from the United States, which Chinese authorities would certainly permit. Thus the impact of U.S. restrictions on Chinese growth would be small or negligible. U.S. firms wanting entry into the Chinese market, however, would complain bitterly that they were being penalized in favor of their global competitors by a misguided U.S. policy. (Some labor unions, in contrast, might favor the restrictions on FDI, as involving the "export of jobs," a controversial proposition, although their ire has been directed more at the much larger U.S. FDI in Mexico than in China.)

Cutting Capital Inflows

Restrictions on exports of capital other than FDI would have no impact whatever. China is a high saving country, not reliant on foreign capital per se. Indeed, it is a major exporter of capital, via its central bank's purchases of foreign exchange, held mainly in U.S. Treasury securities, while the United States has been a major importer of capital during the past two decades. The London-based financial market is worldwide in scope, and denial of U.S.-origin funds to China would result in modest rearrangement of flows.

U.S. votes against loans by the World Bank or the Asian Development Bank to China would not stop those loans unless the United States could garner sufficient support from other lending countries, which it could not do under the postulated circumstances.

Reducing Migration

Finally, the United States could attempt to restrict Chinese migration to the United States. Some of this migration is illegal and is subject to restriction now. U.S. authorities are likely to have as much, or as little, influence on that flow in the future as they have in the past, and in any case the influence on overall Chinese growth (as distinguished from the well-being of particular families or villages) would be negligible even if it were stopped altogether.

More serious in the long run might be denial of entry to Chinese students. They seek American education in large numbers—63,000 were studying in the United States in 2002. Those returning to China bring both technical knowledge and new ideas about how to organize and manage firms, and even society. Disadvantages of such a policy are that it would hurt American colleges and universities, just when especially public institutions are under heavy budgetary pressure; it would deny the U.S. economy the benefit of the many highly trained and diligent Chinese who one way or another end up staying in the United States; and it would weaken future American influence on the evolution of policy in China ("soft power," according to some) that is plausibly more favorable to the United States, just as U.S.-trained Mexican officials took a more confident and less hostile view of the United States when they came to power. Moreover, it does not sit well with America's self-image, fostered around the world, to deny access to American colleges and universities to qualified and eager prospective students, each wanting to improve his or her life chances. Moreover, in the aftermath of 9/11, Chinese student migration to the United States has already been curtailed.

CONCLUSIONS

The implicit assumption of those who expound on the economic power of the United States is that the U.S. government is a unitary actor that can mobilize at will the U.S. economy to pursue its foreign policy ends, much as it can instruct the U.S. ambassador to the United Nations what resolutions to table and how to vote at the UN. Nothing could be further from reality, even though some, like Mearsheimer, consider themselves "realists" when it comes to foreign policy and the interactions of states. Economic issues in a pluralistic society involve many interests, and in a democratic society agents will try to protect those interests. They will often be successful. The government, particularly a government that invokes the rule of law and the sanctity of private property, cannot ignore much less disregard those interests when framing foreign policy, except possibly in circumstances of extreme national emergency when calls to patriotism overwhelm these private interests.

Political constraints on actions by the political leadership blur the frequently made distinction between capability and willingness when it comes to the exercise of power, or leverage. A country may be technically capable of achieving a particular result, and the leadership may be willing to take a decision to that effect, but the political system may fail to support the leadership, making their willingness otiose. Thus I prefer to include the acceptability of the proposed exercise of power to the political system as part of its capability—if the constraints are effective, action cannot be taken—and apply the term "willingness" to the leadership. This is semantics again; the important point is to keep the concepts straight.

More specifically, the United States is not capable of exercising its "latent power" to slow China's growth for two quite different reasons. First, domestic economic interests translated into political constraints on actions will not allow it, absent some clear provocation. Second, the existence of world markets, ample competition with U.S. products, and an unwillingness of foreign governments to cooperate all undermine the effects of any U.S. action— assuming it could take action—beyond an immediate impact lasting at most a few years. In effect, pervasive globalization limits the United States (as well as China) in carrying out unilateral economic policies.

We turn, in conclusion, to the desirability of the proposal, as distinguished from its feasibility. There is no doubt that China is growing rapidly, and if well managed has the possibility of reaching the level of U.S. GNP, although decades later than Mearsheimer suggests. Moreover, nationalist sentiments in China are high, fed by years of teaching about the humiliations China experienced at the hands of foreigners. They are likely to be heightened further, not diminished, by Chinese economic success. They could at some point be mobilized demagogically. In addition, the surplus of young males creates a potentially explosive situation. The world, especially China's neighbors, thus relies on the good sense and political skills of China's leaders to maintain China on a stable, peaceful, growth-oriented path. As Joseph Nye has said somewhere, the best way to make an enemy of China is to treat it like one.

NOTES

1. Gary Hufbauer, Jeffrey Schott, and Kimberly Ann Elliott, *Economic Sanctions Reconsidered* (Washington, DC: Institute for International Economics, 1990).

2. HSE, 93.

3. John Mearsheimer, *The Tragedy of Great Power Politics* (New York: Norton, 2001), and "Great Power Politics in the 21st Century," *Foreign Affairs* (2001).

4. Mearsheimer, *Tragedy*, 63–67.

5. Mearsheimer, *Tragedy*, 397–98.

6. If China could grow 6 percent faster than the United States per year, this period would be shortened by 37 years.

7. See Charles Wolf, Jr., K. C. Yeh, Benjamin Zycher, Nicholas Eberstadt, and Sung Ho Lee, *Fault Lines in China's Terrain* (Santa Monica, CA: RAND, 2003).

8. Calculated from Angus Maddison, *Chinese Economic Performance in the Long Run* (Paris: OECD, 1998). 157. Official Chinese figures suggest a growth of 9.0% between 1952 and 1957. (Maddison, 160).

9. See Edward Graham and Paul Krugman, *Foreign Direct Investment in the United States* (Washington, DC: Institute for International Economics, 1995).

10. Wolf et al., 2003, 156.

6

Globalization, Terrorism, and the U.S. Relationship with Russia

Graham Allison

Following the September 11 attacks on America, the great power relationship between the United States and Russia changed significantly. Operational cooperation moved to a new level, facilitated by good personal chemistry between Presidents George W. Bush and Vladimir Putin, but driven by the common goal of fighting global terrorism. Using the Cold War hotline, Putin was the first world leader to reach Bush to offer his sympathies and pledge to stand with the U.S. against the terrorists. Recognizing that U.S. forces would go to alert status, Putin cancelled a Russian military exercise to avoid any possible confusion.[1] As National Security Advisor Condoleezza Rice noted, "If you think back 25 years ago, this would have been a spiral of alerts between two heavily armed, ideologically opposed camps." This was, in her view, "the crystallizing moment for the end of the Cold War."[2]

In a press conference immediately following the attacks on the World Trade Center, Putin proclaimed: "the entire international community should unite in the struggle against terrorism" because this is the single most "blatant challenge to humanity."[3] In the weeks that followed, Russia shared specific intelligence about Afghanistan, opened Russian airspace for humanitarian missions, encouraged Central Asian states to open their airspace to the U.S., and increased direct military assistance to the Northern Alliance.[4]

Following the brutal killing of Russian schoolchildren in Beslan, North Ossetia on September 3, 2004, President Bush vowed that the United States would stand "shoulder to shoulder" with Russia in the War on Terrorism. During an unexpected visit to the Russian Embassy in Washington, D.C., President Bush signed a book of condolences and expressed his "heartfelt sympathies for the victims and the families who suffered at the hands of the evil terrorists."[5] Through the lens of 9/11, the U.S. government's previous view of Chechens as "fighters" morphed into a recognition of such Chechens as "terrorists." In February 2003, three Chechen groups were officially placed on the U.S. State Department's list of international terrorist organizations. One month after the 9/11 assault, at the end of a summit at the Crawford ranch, Presidents Bush and Putin officially declared a "new relationship" between the United States and Russia.[6] Together, they identified the nexus of terrorists and weapons of mass destruction as the greatest threat to both nations. Together, they pledged "to keep the world's most dangerous technologies out of the hands of the world's most dangerous people."[7] Unfortunately, however, neither nation's deeds have matched either president's words.

A review of their governments' performance in meeting this challenge is unsettling:

- On the current Russian schedule of extending enhanced protection, thousands of potential "loose nukes" in Russia will remain vulnerable to theft until 2017.[8] Presidents Bush and Putin have acquiesced in this timetable, allowing obstacles and logjams within and between their own bureaucracies to determine the rate at which this job will be finished. As demonstrated in a recent Harvard report, fewer "near nukes" (fissile lumps of highly enriched uranium [HEU] or plutonium) were secured in Russia during the two years after 9/11 than in the two years before that assault.[9]
- Since January 2003, North Korea has withdrawn from the Nonproliferation Treaty; turned off the 24-hour-a-day video cameras that were watching their 8,000 fuel rods containing enough plutonium for six additional nuclear weapons; kicked out the IAEA inspectors; trucked the fuel rods off to reprocessing facilities; and reprocessed these rods to produce enough plutonium for six more nuclear weapons.
- While President Bush has been distracted by Iraq, Iran has rushed to complete construction of factories for producing HEU and plutonium. It now stands within months of completion of this infrastructure for its nuclear weapons program.

This chapter addresses the necessity for deeper cooperation between the United States and Russia to prevent nuclear terrorism and the proliferation of weapons of mass destruction; the ways in which this challenge is affected by ongoing processes of globalization; and the possible consequences of a serious global effort to prevent nuclear terrorism for globalization and national self-determination. Section one provides a basic framework for this discussion by briefly analyzing the negative consequences of globalization for the risk that international terrorists will acquire the world's most destructive weapons. Section two addresses the basic question of *who* could mount a nuclear terrorist attack on Russia. Section three addresses *what* weapons could be used in such an attack, as well as the immediate danger that Russia's loose nukes pose to the United States and the rest of the world. Section four stretches beyond these threats to a central but largely unrecognized truth: that nuclear terrorism is, in fact, *preventable*. Section five outlines a strategy and agenda of specific actions that could—if taken—essentially eliminate the risk of nuclear terrorism. The concluding section explores implications of an ambitious agenda for preventing nuclear terrorism for the prospects of groups seeking national self-determination.

GLOBALIZATION: THE INFRASTRUCTURE FOR TERRORISM[10]

Globalization is clearly the buzzword of the era. But we must understand that globalization is a conceptual construct, not a simple fact. As currently used, globalization is too often an ill-defined pointer to a disparate array of phenomena—frequently accompanied by heavy breathing that implies that behind these phenomena, or at their root, is some yet-to-be-discovered substance.

Operationally, globalization should be thought of in terms of *identifiable networks*.[11] Etymologically, networks are a conceptual extension of a simple object called a net, for example, a fishing net, in which connected strands cross at regular intervals. Using this metaphor, globalization can be defined as the creation or expansion of an identifiable network around the globe. A global network connects points and people around the globe on some specified dimension or medium.

Earlier discussions of growing global interconnectedness produced the concept of "interdependence," meaning, essentially, reciprocal dependences resulting from ties among different countries. Over time it became clear that interdependence captured only part of the story. Countries and actors in different countries are often interconnected on specific dimensions, and by virtue of this connectedness have reciprocal impacts on one another. But rarely are the effects of such interactions symmetrical. Relative power and influence are also defining factors in relationships among countries or actors in different countries.

Today, the most dangerous dimension of interconnectedness between individual actors across countries is the growth in size, influence, and destructive capacity of transnational terrorist organizations. Individual actors and groups, such as al-Qaeda, now wield the kind of destructive power that was previously preserved by states alone: the power to attack citizens across the globe with weapons of mass destruction, and cause losses many times worse than 9/11. According to the White House *National Security Strategy*, "the nature and motivations of these new adversaries, their determination to obtain destructive powers hitherto available only to the world's strongest states, and the greater likelihood that they will use weapons of mass destruction against us, make today's security environment more complex and dangerous."[12]

Global networks that create opportunities for fast and cheap transfer of capital, shipment of goods, and movement by people also, and inevitably, provide superhighways for those who would launder money, ship illegal immigrants, transport destructive materials, and bring terror to the homes and lives of Americans. As President Bush noted in the introduction to the *National Security Strategy*, "Now, shadowy networks of individuals can bring great chaos and suffering to our shores for less than it costs to purchase a single tank. Terrorists are organized to penetrate open societies and to turn the power of modern technologies against us."[13]

Unlike the two great adversaries of America in the 20th century—fascism and communism—terrorism is not an ideology in its own right. Terrorism is a tactic, not a cause. While terrorist groups exchange tactics, information, and resources, they are not united by a shared ideology or identity. Claims about "root causes" of terrorism frequently confuse more than clarify, because they seek commonalities between disparate terrorist groups that simply do not exist. The most commonly cited cause of terrorism, for example, is poverty. But as Alan B. Krueger of Princeton University has shown, "most terrorists are not motivated by . . . the hopelessness of poverty." Recently, he found that "only 13 percent of Palestinian suicide bombers are from impoverished families," corroborating other studies' conclusions that "terrorists are drawn from society's elites, not the dispossessed."[14]

Terrorism has been employed by an array of strategic actors, each with their own agenda. What most terrorist groups do have in common are substantive political claims that conflict with the contradictory political claims of more powerful actors. The weaker factions in such conflicts may turn to terrorism as a tactic or default response for promoting their claims. Nationalist self-determination movements, as in the Chechen case, often fit this model, since their opponents generally have a fundamental interest in maintaining control of the disputed territory, and wield greater conventional force through control of the state apparatus.

Today, dozens of terrorist groups have sufficient motive to use a nuclear weapon, several could potentially obtain nuclear means, and hundreds of opportunities exist for a group with means and motive to make the United States or Russia a victim of nuclear terrorism.[15] If they had one, terrorists would not find it difficult to sneak a nuclear device (such as a suitcase nuclear weapon) or nuclear fissile material into the United States via cargo containers in trucks, ships, or aircraft. Since Russia's land borders are nearly twice as long as America's, connecting it to more than a dozen other states, the opportunities for terrorists to smuggle a nuclear weapon into or out of Russia are even greater.[16]

In sum, globalization provides the infrastructure for terrorism because globalization multiplies networks that both enlarge destructive capacity and reduce barriers and borders to delivery. The combination of globalization and the revolution in information technology has empowered individuals and groups worldwide. Decreased transaction costs, lowered international barriers, and the increased global reach of non-state actors have enabled terrorist organizations to finance, coordinate, and execute attacks on a global scale, as Osama bin Laden did in attacking the World Trade Center, and operate via networks of semiautonomous cells, making their organizations much harder to infiltrate and destroy.

NUCLEAR TERRORISM:
HOW SERIOUS A THREAT TO RUSSIA?

The *National Security Concept of the Russian Federation* clearly identifies international terrorism as the greatest threat to Russia's national security.[17] The illegal drug trade and the diffusion of Islamic extremism in states along Russia's southern periphery threaten Russia's border and weaken its own security as well as the security of the Commonwealth of Independent States.[18] In addition, "frozen conflicts" in the former Soviet Union, including those in South Ossetia, Abkhazia, and Nagorno-Karabakh, provide feeding grounds for the extremism that fuels terrorism. In addition, Russia's proximity to the Middle East and South Asia increases concern about terrorist fallout from those regions.[19] Finally, Russia has been victimized repeatedly by terrorist attacks perpetrated by Chechen radical separatists, including, most recently, twin plane hijackings, a Moscow suicide bombing, and the school seizure in Beslan—all of which occurred within one week.[20]

As underscored by recent events, Russians are clearly more vulnerable to terrorist attacks today than they were when Putin came to power. Consider the evidence: almost half of all major terrorist attacks between 1995 and 2004 occurred in the first eight months of 2004.[21]

Chechen separatists have been engaged for more than a decade in a deadly fight for independence from Russia. This war for national self-determination, the bloodiest conflict in the former Soviet Union, has left more than 100,000 civilians dead and nearly half of the region's population homeless. The Chechens have proved a ready audience for Islamic extremism, particularly the militant Islam espoused by the late Ibn Al-Khattab, the Saudi Arabian–born self-proclaimed Commander of the Foreign Mujahedin in Chechnya. Khattab, who was first indoctrinated in Islamic jihad when he joined the fight against the Soviet Union in Afghanistan in the 1980s, gained notoriety and respect among Chechens for his warring skills and cruelty, leading to greater ties between the Chechen separatist movement and Islamic extremist organizations.

Chechen fighters have demonstrated imagination, organization, determination, and a willingness to sacrifice their own lives in the process in a series of terrorist attacks. On September 1, 2004, approximately 30 Islamic militants seized school No. 1 in Beslan and held over 1,000 hostages for nearly three days. The hostage-taking ended in the death of nearly 350 people—half of them young children. Chechen guerilla forces proved yet again their ability to unleash extreme violence and terror on unprepared civilian targets.

One week prior to the school seizure, two Chechen female suicide bombers—or "Black Widows"—bribed their way onto a pair of airplanes that later exploded simultaneously, killing a total of 90 people. Several days later, another Black Widow blew herself up outside a Moscow metro station, killing 10 people and injuring at least 30 others. Earlier, in October 2002, Chechen fighters exhibited their capacity for major operations deep inside Russia by taking over a theater in Moscow and holding over 800 hostages for three days before Russian Special Forces stormed the scene. The two hostage-taking offensives and the plane hijackings demonstrate the heightened sophistication and audacity of Chechen terror tactics, the details of which are further testimony to their ability to commit increasingly large-scale terrorist attacks on Russian soil.

Despite these threats, careful observers of the discussion in the Russian and American national security community note that Americans are more concerned about the threat of a nuclear terrorist attack than are Russians. Specifically, American experts have described more vividly potential nuclear terrorist attacks on U.S. soil than have Russians, at least in the writings and conversations that are publicly accessible. Why this is the case is a puzzle. No one doubts that Chechen fighters are serious, capable, determined adversaries whose objectives could be advanced by using nuclear weapons. If Chechnya succeeded in capturing, stealing, or buying a nuclear weapon (or material from which a weapon could be made), their first target would surely be Moscow, not New York or Washington, D.C.

To date, the only confirmed case of attempted nuclear terrorism occurred in Russia on November 23, 1995, when Chechen separatists put a crude bomb containing 70 pounds of a mixture of cesium-137 and dynamite in Moscow's Ismailovsky Park. The rebels decided not to detonate this "dirty bomb," but instead alerted a national television station to its location. This demonstration underscored Chechen insurgents' long-standing interest in all things nuclear.[22] As early as 1992, Chechnya's first rebel president, Dzhokhar Dudayev, began planning for nuclear terrorism, including a specific initiative to hijack a Russian nuclear submarine from the Pacific Fleet in the Far East.[23] The plan called for seven Slavic-looking Chechens to seize a submarine from the naval base near Vladivostok, attach explosive devices to the nuclear reactor section and to one of the nuclear-tipped missiles on board, and then demand withdrawal of Russian troops from Chechnya. After the plot was discovered, Russian authorities disparaged it, and yet it is a fact that the former chief of staff of the Chechen rebel army, Islam Khasukhanov, had once served as second-in-command of a Pacific Fleet nuclear submarine.[24]

For Movsar Barayev, the leader of the rebel unit that took 800 hostages only a few blocks from the Kremlin in October 2002, the Dubrovka Theater was his second-choice target. Initially, Barayev planned to seize the Kurchatov Institute, one of Russia's leading nuclear design centers, with 26 operating nuclear reactors and enough HEU to make dozens of nuclear bombs.[25] Though far from optimal, the security at Kurchatov proved formidable enough for Barayev to pass up the nuclear facility for a softer target.[26]

Chechen separatists have had a long-standing interest in acquiring nuclear weapons and material to use in their campaign against Russia. In addition to surveying Kurchatov, Chechen militants have conducted surveillance of the railway system and special trains designed for shipping nuclear weapons across Russia.[27] They also succeeded in acquiring radioactive materials from a Grozny nuclear waste plant in January 2000 and stealing radioactive metals—possibly including some plutonium—from the Volgodonskaya nuclear power station in the southern region of Rostov between July 2001 and July 2002.

Al-Qaeda and other Islamic extremist organizations are among Chechen militants' major sources of financial support. Al-Qaeda operatives were alleged to have negotiated with Chechen separatists in Russia to buy a nuclear warhead, which the Chechen warlord Shamil Basayev claimed to have acquired from Russian arsenals.[28] While the Chechens' target of choice for their first nuclear terrorist attack will surely be Moscow, if the Chechens are successful in acquiring several nuclear bombs, they could well arm their al-Qaeda brethren as well.

MISSILES, MATERIALS, AND ACCIDENTS

If a nuclear terrorist attack occurs, Russia will be the most probable source of the tools of destruction—not because the Russian government would intentionally sell or lose weapons or materials, but simply because Russia's eleven-time-zone expanse contains more nuclear weapons and materials than any other country in the world, much of it vulnerable to theft or sabotage. From outright nuclear theft and smuggling to more general problems of inadequate resources for nuclear security systems and low pay and morale for nuclear workers and military forces, alarming reports of nuclear insecurity in Russia continue to emerge. If we know about these lapses, terrorist groups—including Chechen militants—certainly know about them, too.

The collapse of the Soviet Union presented an enormous threat to nuclear security with the Soviets' arsenal spread across four separate states. Efforts to remove strategic nuclear weapons from Kazakhstan, Belarus, and Ukraine required intense Russian-American cooperation during a period of political and economic upheaval. The Soviet Ministry of Defense had to move 22,000 tactical nuclear weapons from newly emerging states of the former Soviet Union to Russia as the country was coming apart at the seams. Inflation had jumped to over 2,000 percent, fueling corruption and criminality throughout Russian society. In the slogan of that era, "Everything was for sale." In light of these realities, is it conceivable that all nuclear weapons were recovered without a single loss? In 1991, then U.S. Secretary of Defense Dick Cheney observed, "If the Soviets do an excellent job at retaining control over their stockpile of nuclear weapons—let's assume they've got 25,000 to 30,000; that's a ballpark figure—and they are 99 percent successful, that would mean you could still have as many as 250 that they were not able to control."[29]

To the world's great fortune, Russian professionals apparently succeeded in extracting and returning safely every last one of these warheads. What we know for certain is that not a single former Soviet nuclear weapon has been found in another country or in an international arms bazaar. This incredible result is testimony to the determined efforts of the Russian government, in particular the nuclear guardians in its Ministry of Defense and Ministry of Atomic Energy, supported by technical and economic assistance from the United States authorized by the Nunn–Lugar Cooperative Threat Reduction (CTR) initiative in 1991 and subsequent acts of Congress. Yet, although we have no proof that a Soviet nuclear weapon has reached an unintended destination, we cannot rule out this possibility. In his February 2005 testimony to Congress, CIA Director Porter Goss took the unprecedented step of reporting the intelligence community's best judgment of Russian loose nukes. In response to questions, he said, "There is sufficient material unaccounted for so that it would be possible for those with know-how to construct a nuclear weapon." Senator Jay Rockefeller followed up, asking, "Can you assure the American people that the material missing from Russian nuclear sites has not found its way into terrorist hands?" Goss could only reply, "No, I can't make that assurance."

Realistically, nuclear terrorists are most likely to use a small weapon stolen from the arsenal of one of the nuclear states, or an elementary nuclear bomb made from stolen HEU or plutonium. Of particular interest would be the former Soviet arsenal of tactical nuclear weapons, which was even larger and much more widely dispersed than the strategic nuclear forces. These bombs included suitcase nuclear devices; suitcase backpacks (*yadernyi ranets*), such as the Army's RA-155 and Navy's RA-115-01 (to be used underwater), which weighed as little as 65 pounds and could be detonated by one soldier, producing a yield of between 0.5 and 2 kilotons;[30] atomic landmines weighing 200 pounds; air-defense warheads; and 120-pound atomic artillery shells designed to destroy an enemy force at a 200-mile range.[31] The full extent of the Soviet tactical arsenal, however, remains shrouded in secrecy, particularly the existence and fate of special KGB suitcase nuclear weapons.

In 1997, Boris Yeltsin's Assistant for National Security Affairs, General Alexander Lebed, acknowledged that 84 of some 132 such weapons were not accounted for in Russia. These weapons are miniature nuclear devices (0.1 to 1 kilotons), small enough to fit into a suitcase carried by a single individual. The Russian government reacted to Lebed's claim in classic Soviet style, combining wholesale denial with efforts to discredit the messenger. In the days and months that followed, official Russian government spokesmen claimed that: (1) no such weapons ever existed; (2) any weapons of this sort had been destroyed; (3) all Russian weapons were secure and properly accounted for; and (4) it was inconceivable that the Russian government could lose a nuclear weapon.

The best evidence *against* Lebed's claim is the fact that no suitcase nuclear devices have been detonated, and none have been discovered to date. The best evidence *for* his claims combines the logic of Soviet war planning and the specificity of a number of the official denials. For example, just after Lebed's disclosure, the Operation Directorate of the GRU (Russian military intelligence) denied that "any 60 x 40 x 20 briefcases containing nuclear charges" existed. Americans can imagine a cagey spokesperson defending the truth of this statement with an explanation that it depends on the meaning of the word "existed"—or the fact that the weapons in question were a centimeter larger or smaller. In 2001, General Igor Valynkin, the commander of the organization that has physical control of all Ministry of Defense nuclear weapons, confirmed that the "RA-115" serial number cited by Lebed in the debate about suitcase nuclear weapons referred to a type of ammunition that had been in the Soviet arsenal, but, he said, had been eliminated.[32] In a March 2004 interview, Former Chief of Russia's Strategic Missile Troops General Staff Colonel-General Viktor Yesin stated "with 100-percent certainty" that the loss of a Soviet or Russian weapon was impossible. Yesin did note that it was conceivable that "mock-up" nuclear devices could have disappeared, and that "it is possible," in principle, to create "nuclear suitcases weighing 15–20 kilograms," but that such devices "would be so expensive that no state could afford them."[33]

In its campaign to discredit General Lebed's revelations, the Russian government insisted that the loss of a nuclear weapon was unthinkable. No responsible party could lose something so important. But to the contrary, there can be no doubt about the fact that enough nuclear material to build more than 20 nuclear weapons was lost in the transition from the Soviet Union to Russia. Indeed, over one thousand pounds of HEU was purchased by the U.S. government, removed from an unprotected site in Almaty, Kazakhstan, and is now securely stored in Oak Ridge, Tennessee. But, as former CIA director John Deutch observed, "It's not so much what I know that worries me, as what I know that I don't know."[34]

National security experts agree that the most likely way terrorists will obtain a nuclear bomb will involve not theft or purchase of a fully operational device, but purchase of fissile material from which they construct their own. Terrorists would find it easiest to steal fissile material because it is smaller, lighter, more abundant, and less protected than the weapons themselves. With about one hundred pounds of HEU, a crude gun-type nuclear device is simple to design, build, and detonate. In fact, two declassified U.S. government publications based on the work of Manhattan Project scientists and engineers in the 1940s, *The Los Alamos Primer: The First Lectures on How to Build an Atomic Bomb* and *Atomic Energy for Military Purposes*, offer instruction about how to build such a device. Furthermore, recent revelations about A. Q. Khan's nuclear network demonstrated that complete bomb designs are now available for sale on the black market.[35] An IAEA official who reviewed plans confiscated in Libya remarked to the journalist Seymour Hersh that the design in question was "a sweet little bomb" that would be "too big and too heavy for a Scud, but it'll go into a family car"—a "terrorist's dream."[36]

Supplies of HEU are extensive, and numerous instances of HEU smuggling have been documented. During the Cold War, the Soviet Union established a vast nuclear enterprise under its Ministry of Atomic Energy that employed more than a million people in ten "closed" cities requiring special entry and exit visas. The scientists and technicians in these cities designed and built weapons and produced uranium and plutonium not only for weapons but also for the fuel that powered the nation's fleet of nuclear-powered submarines and its nuclear power plants. U.S. experts have estimated that Russia possesses over 2 million pounds of weapons-usable material, or enough for more than 80,000 weapons.[37] Yet a dozen years after the dissolution of the Soviet Union, much of this vast stockpile remains dangerously insecure.

THE ULTIMATE PREVENTABLE CATASTROPHE

A basic examination of the "who" and "what" questions finds both supply and demand for nuclear terrorism in Russia. The unanswered questions are when and where buyers and sellers will come together, negotiate a deal, and strike. On the first day of the hostage crisis in Beslan, Putin recognized Chechen terrorists' prowess and responded by dispatching troops to guard Russia's notoriously undersecured nuclear facilities.[38] Despite past claims by Russian officials that all facilities are completely secure, Putin recognized that, whatever the security at these facilities was the day before the school seizure, it was inadequate the day after.

For the central but largely unrecognized truth remains that this ultimate catastrophe is preventable. All that Russia, the United States, and its allies have to do to avert nuclear terrorism is to keep terrorists from acquiring HEU or weapons-grade plutonium. This "all," of course, will involve a huge undertaking. But it is a finite challenge, subject to a finite response.

The world's stockpiles of nuclear weapons and weapons-usable material are vast, but not unlimited. Technologies for locking up highly dangerous or valuable items are well developed. The United States does not lose gold from Fort Knox, nor Russia treasures from the Kremlin Armory. Moreover, producing additional new fissile material requires large, complex, expensive, and visible facilities, leaving such enterprises vulnerable to interruption by a watchful, determined international community. Keeping nuclear weapons and materials out of the hands of the world's most dangerous people is thus a challenge to international will and determination, not to our technical capabilities.

BUILDING A GLOBAL ALLIANCE AGAINST NUCLEAR TERRORISM

The United States cannot undertake or sustain the war on nuclear terrorism unilaterally. Fortunately, it need not try. Today, all the Great Powers share vital national interests in the proposed campaign. Each has sufficient reason to fear nuclear weapons in the hands of terrorists, whether they are al-Qaeda, Jemaah Islamiya, or Hezbollah—organizations that are international in scope—or Chechens, Kashmiris, or Chinese Uighur separatists—national liberation groups which have used terrorist tactics to advance their cause. Each nation's best hope to achieve conditions essential for its security requires cooperation with the others. The Great Powers are therefore ripe for mobilization for a global concert—indeed, a Grand Alliance Against Nuclear Terrorism (GAANT). The mission of this alliance should be to minimize the risk of nuclear terrorism by taking every action physically, technically, and diplomatically possible to prevent nuclear weapons or materials from being acquired by terrorists.

Construction of this new alliance should begin with the United States and Russia. As creators of the nuclear world, the United States and Russia have a special responsibility to ensure that the world's arsenals of weapons and materials are contained and secured. Russia is also positioned to be America's closest ally in the ongoing War on Terrorism. As both countries favor the expansion of open trade, financial markets and other "globalized" trends, they will not "wish to see these disrupted by international terrorism."[39] Russia's key relationships in Europe, the Middle East, and Asia give it a geopolitical weight that far exceeds that of traditional U.S. allies. In addition, Russia's national interests are aligned with an international presumption against the creation of new states (beyond the exceptional cases of East Timor and the would-be Palestine), since Russia could find itself the victim of additional separatist movements that, as President Putin recently noted, would "mean for [Russia] the loss of huge territories, primarily in the south of the country, and could disorganize the entire state."[40]

President Bush's talking points in attempting to engage Putin as a full partner in this common cause should start by reflecting together on what would happen the day after a nuclear terrorist attack. How will these two presidents explain their acceptance of practices that left nuclear weapons less secure than gold in Fort Knox or the Kremlin Armory? If a state deliberately sold a nuclear weapon to terrorists who used it to attack the United States or Russia, how would either respond? For having harbored and protected al-Qaeda prior to the attack on the World Trade Center, President Bush declared war on the Taliban rulers of Afghanistan, and announced that any other regime that followed the Taliban's example would be treated likewise. What about a government that supplied a nuclear weapon to terrorists through distraction or neglect? If a weapon were stolen from Russia, or Pakistan, or the United States, who would be accountable? To whom? With what consequences? In the confrontation with the Soviet Union over missiles in Cuba in 1962, President Kennedy stated explicitly that "it shall be the policy of this nation to regard any nuclear missile launched from Cuba against any nation in the Western Hemisphere as an attack by the Soviet Union on the United States, requiring a full retaliatory response upon the Soviet Union."[41] Should some analogous principle of nuclear accountability be developed for terrorism?

A mutual commitment by Presidents Bush and Putin to do everything technically and physically possible to prevent theft of nuclear weapons and materials, and to demonstrate that progress to the other, would send a lightning bolt through both bureaucracies. A first step would be to develop a specific plan of action and sequence of performance-measurable milestones for securing all nuclear weapons, weapons-usable material, and know-how on the fastest possible timetable. This process would be overseen by a joint U.S.-Russian commission with high-level appointees (Howard Baker or Sam Nunn would be appropriate American examples) reporting back to the two presidents on a weekly basis.

One major product of this effort would be the establishment of a new "gold standard." The United States and Russia must devise a process by which each nation's methods of securing its own weapons and material are sufficiently transparent to give others confidence that their stockpiles cannot be used by terrorists. It would require states to build or strengthen their control systems, from stricter monitoring of personnel who have access to nuclear facilities, to electronic portal monitors that sound alarms if material is removed without authorization, to high-surveillance no-man zones surrounding the compound. It would also demand independent audits and tests of security systems led by retired nuclear guardians such as General Yevgeny Maslin (former commander of the 12th Main Directorate of the Russian Defense Ministry), General Eugene Habiger (former Commander-in-Chief of United States Strategic Command), and Siegfried Hecker (former director of

Los Alamos National Laboratory). Final certification would be sent to cabinet-level officials and ultimately the president of each nation.

Once the United States and Russia have demonstrably addressed nuclear risks within their own borders, the two presidents must then engage the leaders of other nuclear weapons states and secure the personal commitment of each to this enterprise.[42] Every nuclear power must commit to securing all weapons and materials in its territory to the new gold standard—and to certification by another member of the nuclear club as having done so. Were technical or financial assistance required to meet these standards, the United States would be forthcoming with help. The two presidents must use all their powers of persuasion and refuse to accept no for an answer.

CONCLUSION

The central conclusion of this essay is that ongoing forces of globalization will increase the risk of mega-terrorist attacks in capitals and key economic centers of major states, thus creating a powerful, shared interest in denying terrorists access to the most destructive technologies. If that shared interest is mobilized in a future alliance of governments, then this will have consequences for groups seeking independence from current states. The net of these implications for those attempting to realize their "right of national self-determination" will almost certainly be negative. As a result of this, the number of new national states will be fewer than would have occurred otherwise.

A comprehensive strategy for preventing nuclear terrorism will tilt the playing field against all acts of terror—no matter what their underlying cause or claim. Pursuit of this agenda will lower the tolerance threshold in the international community for groups that employ terrorist tactics to achieve independence.[43] The Bush administration's marked shift in its characterization of Chechen fighters as "terrorists" is suggestive. As a consequence of globalization, an increasing number of ethnic, tribal, or national groups may rise to the temptation to seek independence, and seek international assistance in this quest.[44] But if new global norms delegitimize and stigmatize movements that resort to terrorist tactics in pursuit of their aspirations, then this tactic will come to be seen as counterproductive. Advocates of national self-determination will thus have a diminished arsenal of instruments with which to pursue their goals.

Much as the prospect of an aggressive Soviet Union provided a powerful impetus for solidarity among NATO members, a common threat from nuclear bombs in the hands of terrorists should light a similar fire under countries to undertake the necessary cooperative effort to prevent this catastrophe. The fundamental truth is that the highest national security priorities of the United States and Russia converge much more than they conflict. President Putin recently noted that he is "sure that Russian-American relations during George Bush's second term of office will be as dynamic and fruitful" as the first due to the "long-term interests of our countries."[45] Presidents Bush and Putin should capitalize on their second terms by insisting on a maximum joint effort to achieve true security in their countries. Absent deeper, sustained cooperation between Washington and Moscow, efforts to prevent nuclear terrorism will be much more difficult.[46]

It can be argued that even if states band together to effectively deny terrorists nuclear weapons or the materials from which weapons can be made, such an alliance need not extend to specific terrorist tactics employed by groups that have plausible claims against oppressive regimes. If terrorist groups like al-Qaeda succeed in making credible the argument that they are only attacking targets in states whose actions attract such attention (for example, attacking countries whose troops are occupying Arab lands), then they may be able to drive a wedge between allies in the War on Terrorism. Even in that case, major powers would be wise to recognize their shared stakes in preventing any terrorists from acquiring the most destructive technologies. And that undertaking will impact negatively any and all groups that rely on terrorist tactics to advance their claims.

NOTES

1. Graham Allison and Andrei Kokoshin, "A U.S.-Russian Alliance against Megaterrorism," *Boston Globe* (16 November 2001).

2. As quoted in Allison and Kokoshin, *Boston Globe* (16 November 2001).

3. President Vladimir Putin, Kremlin News Conference (11 September 2001).

4. Commission on America's National Interests and Russia, Interim Report: "Advancing American Interests and the U.S.-Russian Relationship" (Washington, DC: Nixon Center, September 2003), 17.

5. President George Bush, Statement outside Russian Embassy (12 September 2004).

6. "Joint Statement by President Vladimir V. Putin of Russia and President George W. Bush of the USA on a New Relationship between Russia and the USA," Press Release, Ministry of Foreign Affairs of the Russian Federation (15 November 2001).

7. Ibid.

8. Matthew Bunn and Anthony Wier, *Securing the Bomb: An Agenda for Action* (Washington, DC: Nuclear Threat Initiative and the Project on Managing the Atom, Harvard University, May 2004).

9. Ibid.

10. This section draws on the argument in Graham Allison's "The Impact of Globalization on National and International Security," in *Governance in a Globalizing World*, ed. Joseph S. Nye and John D. Donahue (Cambridge, MA: Visions of Governance for the 21st Century, 2000).

11. For a more detailed study of the global network phenomenon, please see *Networks and Netwars: The Future of Terror, Crime and Militancy*, ed. John Arquilla and David Ronfeldt (Santa Monica, CA: RAND, 2001).

12. The White House, *The National Security Strategy of the United States of America* (17 September 2002).

13. President George W. Bush, Introduction to *The National Security Strategy of the United States of America* (17 September 2002).

14. Alan B. Krueger, "Cash rewards and poverty alone do not explain terrorism," *New York Times* (29 May 2003). Please also see Alan B. Krueger and Jitka Maleckova, "Education, Poverty, Political Violence, and Terrorism: Is There a Causal Connection?" *National Bureau of Economic Research Working Paper No. W9074*, July 2002.

15. Allison and Kokoshin, 41.

16. Ibid.

17. See the *Concept of National Security of the Russian Federation*, signed January 10, 2000. English translation from *Rossiiskaya Gazeta* (18 January 2000) available at http://www.nyu.edu/globalbeat/nuclear/Gazeta012400.html.

18. Allison and Kokoshin, 37.

19. Ibid.

20. These three terrorist attacks occurred between August 25 and September 1, 2004.

21. Seven out of seventeen attacks between 1995 and September 2004 (40%) occurred between February and September 2004.

22. For a detailed analysis of Chechen separatists' nuclear ambitions, see Simon Saradzhyan, "Russia: Grasping Reality of Nuclear Terror," BCSIA Discussion Paper 2003-02 (Kennedy School of Government, Harvard University, March 2003).

23. *BBC Monitoring* (5 February 2002).

24. *ITAR-TASS* (31 October 2002).

25. Bunn and Wier, 35.

26. Nabi Abdullaev, "Picture Emerges of How They Did It," *Moscow Times* (6 November 2002).

27. Simon Saradzhyan, "Russia: Grasping Reality of Nuclear Terror," BCSIA Discussion Paper 2003-2 (KSG, Harvard, March 2003).

28. Bill Keller, "Nuclear Nightmares," *New York Times Magazine* (26 May 2002); Mark Riebling and R. P. Eddy, "Jihad@Work," *National Review Online* (24 October 2002).

29. Interview on *Meet the Press* (15 December 1991).

30. Nikolai Sokov, "'Suitcase Nukes': Permanently Lost Luggage" (Center for Nonproliferation Studies, Monterey Institute of International Studies, February 13, 2004).

31. RANSAC, 3.

32. Dmitry Safonov, "Individualnaya Planirovka," *Izvestia* (27 October 2001).

33. "Could Al Qaeda Have a Bomb?" *Yezhnedelny zhurnal* (29 March 2004), 20–22.

34. Remarks made by former CIA director John Deutch at BCSIA Director's Seminar (17 March 1998).

35. Joby Warrick and Peter Slevin, "Probe of Libya Finds Nuclear Black Market," *Washington Post* (24 January 2004).

36. Seymour M. Hersh, "The Deal," *The New Yorker* (8 March 2004).

37. U.S. Department of Energy, *A Report Card on the Department of Energy's Non-proliferation Programs with Russia*, Howard Baker and Lloyd Cutler, Co-chairs of Russia Task Force (10 January 2001).

38. "Russia sends troops to guard nuclear sites," *Reuters* (1 September 2004).

39. Please see Richard Rosecrance and Arthur Stein in chapter 1.

40. President Vladimir Putin, "Interview with Director of News Programmes at Channel One Kirill Kleimenov, Chief Editor of the News Service at NTV Tatyana Mitkova, and Political Correspondent at Rossia Television Channel Nikolai Svanidze" (18 November 2004), available at http://www.kremlin.ru/eng/speeches/2004/11/18/1705_79606.shtml.

41. John F. Kennedy Library and Museum, "Radio and Television Reports to the American People on the Soviet Arms Buildup in Cuba," President John F. Kennedy, The White House (22 October 1962).

42. The gold standard should reach beyond nuclear weapons states to include non–nuclear weapons states, such as Japan or Germany, with significant stockpiles of weapons-usable materials related to their civilian nuclear programs.

43. In the wake of Beslan, the United Nations Security Council adopted Resolution 1566 on October 8, 2004, which unanimously calls on countries to prevent and punish "criminal acts, including against civilians, committed with the intent to cause death or serious bodily injury, or taking of hostages, with the purpose to provoke a state of terror in the general public or in a group of persons or particular persons, intimidate a population or compel a government or an international organization to do or to abstain from doing any act." However, while the UN has taken this step to encourage countries to prosecute and extradite those who participate in the planning of terrorist attacks, as well as those who support these schemes, it has no means of enforcement.

44. Please see Rosecrance and Stein.

45. As quoted in *Interfax* (3 December 2004).

46. See Christian Reus-Smit, *The Moral Purpose of the State* (Princeton, NJ: Princeton University Press, 1999), 154.

7

Globalization and the State in the Middle East: Iran, Turkey, Israel, and the Palestinians

Gitty M. Amini

GLOBALIZATION AND THE MIDDLE EAST

The most interesting aspect of Middle Eastern politics and economics is how different they are from other regions of the world.[1] There are no nuclear weapon states off the coast of Asia and only North Korea threatens to acquire a capability. In the Middle East there were nuclear weapons programs in Israel, Iraq, Iran, and Libya, and an initial start in Egypt, although only Israel's reached fruition. Still, Middle Eastern arms races, international tension, and global involvements have been far greater than those on the East Asian littoral. Why is that? Etel Solingen hypothesizes that globalization can create internationalizing coalitions which in addition to influencing economics can affect a country's nuclear strategy. East Asia's Association of Southeast Asian Nations (ASEAN) has provided a regional security blanket which allows each country to concentrate upon economics and world trade. In contrast, the Arab League has failed to provide comity among its own members, to say nothing of including Israel. While East Asian growth rates have burgeoned at 5 percent or more, Middle Eastern growth (unless stimulated by high oil prices) has foundered at 3 percent or less. Globalization has been embraced by few Middle Eastern countries and certainly not by oil producers.[2]

In fact, while globalization elsewhere has somewhat diminished a military nationalism, in the Middle East, the reaction against globalization has if anything heightened Arab and Muslim nationalism. While elsewhere the reaction to globalization has lessened the prospects of national self-determination, in the Middle East it has heightened assertive and expansionist nationalism. While elsewhere globalization focuses attention on the future, in the Arab world (in reaction) it has concentrated upon the Arab and Shiite past. Gamal

Abdul Nasser's Arab socialism was one negative reaction to the world econ-omy. Saddam Hussein's military expansion was another. In Iran and Saudi Arabia, Shiite and Wahhabist influences have focused on ancient or retro-grade interpretations of the Koran. Oil has facilitated and financed this atavis-tic perspective. But with oil "the gold of the 21st century," each regional country has sought to acquire more, even at the expense of its neighbors. This competition has been restrained in a degree by superpower involve-ment and also by the presence of a strong Israel. The failure to achieve Arab-Israeli peace has also diverted attention from internal economic devel-opment. The Palestinian Authority is a basket case in economic terms, and few other countries, though attracted by globalization, have been able to redevelop their economies to take advantage of it. Egypt, Jordan, and Turkey have sought to do so, but others, except perhaps for a reforming Libya, have cast globalization aside. In the Middle East, rejectionist nationalism has become the substitute for East Asian acceptance of globalization.

Three countries and their associated quandaries stand out as paradigmatic responses to the challenges of globalization. Turkey would like to be an "acceptor," if the European Union and the United States will agree. Iran, rein-fused with the power stemming from oil price increases, is a resolute rejector of globalization and its ancillary restraint on nuclear weapons. Like early modern Spain, however, Iran may find that too much reliance upon one product (gold or oil) will increase inflation and make transition to a modern economy difficult if not impossible. Finally, the Palestinians are caught in the middle, unsure which way to jump. Their means of getting power through terrorism has been discredited (though it has not been completely unsuccess-ful), but a transition to a modern economy apparently lies beyond their reach. The recent elections sanctifying Hamas as the residuary legatee of Yasir Arafat have made this transition even more difficult. The Palestinians may not be able to choose globalization even if they would like to.

This chapter will examine the role of the non-Arab states of Iran and Turkey and the future state of Palestine in the Middle Eastern region in terms of this choice. How have they each responded to the pressures of globalized trade? What is the status of the governments that rule these countries, and what will their futures hold? Even though Iran and Turkey are grappling with issues of nationalism, Islamism, and foreign pressure, it appears they will emerge largely intact as nation-states—Turkey because of the pressures of the European Union, keeping it on a narrow course; Iran because of pres-sures to denuclearize. Both will consolidate further under international stress, and there is little chance of ethnic disintegration in either case. In fact, despite fears about its Kurdish minority, Turkey is in a more stable position than Iran. The Islamic Republic of Iran faces much greater opposition abroad and some dissent at home. Its current conservative orientation may not stand the test of time, but regime change could mean peaceful electoral reform or (as in 1979) a violent coup. Most uncertain of the three is Palestine's future: will the Palestinians ever achieve statehood, and if they do, will they become a traditional state in the mold of the European model? The Palestinians may have to settle for less autonomy, independence, and territorial integrity than is commonly thought necessary for a nation-state.

Key to understanding each of these cases is the regime's acceptance or rejection of globalization and its associated political influence. Acceptors of globalization in a modern Western sense have been less nationalistic and more amenable to foreign influences. Rejectors like Iran, and to some degree the Palestinians (Syria could be added to this list as well), have been much more nationalistic and exclusivist in economic terms. It is perhaps not accidental that the one Arabian state in the Middle East which has been most comfortable with globalization is a country which did not opt for nuclear weapons: Egypt. Cairo held back when other Arabs—including Iran and Iraq—were considering nuclear possibilities. And it did so when its immediate neighbor, Israel, went nuclear. Globalist Turkey has also not proceeded in a nuclear direction, though Iran has done so. Thus far, the pressures of globalization have not begun to determine policy of the mullahs.

IRAN

The interesting question with respect to Iran is whether Iranian nationalism is consistent with internationalism or if it necessarily leads to the nation's marginalization. Will Iran be isolated from the international community or can it be co-opted? The United States, Europeans, Russians, and Chinese would like to bring Iran into the community of nations, but disagree on the best means to use. The most obvious manifestation of this disagreement comes in the arena of nuclear counter-proliferation. The West's effectiveness in securing Iran's cooperation on nuclear matters may be limited; the United States lacks leverage over Iran and only now has it begun to use the influence it possesses. Successful American persuasion will depend on the cooperation of many other actors. More interestingly, Iran has learned from its recent past, and has not only halted its voluntary isolation but has begun to use its participation in globalization processes to thwart the policies of the West. Iranian nationalism is beginning to emerge out of the previous Islamic isolation. Thus, globalization has altered Iran and has brought Teheran to a more nationalist policy, one which does not accept Western norms. The prospect of IAEA disapproval and Security Council sanctions, however, does concentrate the Iranian mind, and it may become a real factor influencing Iran's decisions.

Globalization and Iran

Iran's Islamic Republic has evolved in very complicated ways since the 1979 revolution, since the Reagan-era unilateral sanctions, and even since the secondary sanctions on third parties in the 1990s.[3] Iran's post-revolutionary decision to retreat from the global community has involved a significant economic price. Strict American bans on development aid and loans to Iran have starved it of foreign investment. This has had significant effects on Iran's infrastructure. Without sufficient investment capital, the nation's oil and natural gas productivity has continued to decline. Today, Iran is consistently producing 35 percent less crude oil than it did under the Shah.[4] Moreover, Iran has fallen behind in developing its industrial and manufacturing sector.[5] With a domestic consumer market that is rapidly expanding, Iran has been unable to satisfy the demands of its own population for consumer goods, let alone concentrate on exports. It requires foreign investment and expertise to improve and modernize its industry. Nor are these difficulties likely to be solved by higher oil prices. Money alone is not sufficient. The weaknesses in Iran's economy have had a direct impact on the overall prosperity of its population. Unemployment rates have risen along with inflation. Inflation rates for 2004–05 have been between 14 and 16 percent.[6] Considering Iran's population growth as a result of the baby boom of the 1980s, "the government must generate 800,000 jobs annually, but is only producing 400,000."[7] The younger generation of Iranians has become disillusioned and dissatisfied with the regime for its failures to provide adequate economic opportunities and growth. The regime has begun to feel the pressure to provide tangible benefits to its population or face the consequences. Higher oil prices, of course, may permit government subsidies to unemployed workers, but they will not solve overall structural problems.

Ironically, these woes have not led to the liberalization of Iranian domestic politics, despite the failures of the mullahs. Since the landslide election of reformist Mohammad Khatami in 1997 and reelection in 2001,[8] the voting public has become disillusioned with the liberal reformist movement. The conservative clerical establishment has benefited from the demise of the reformists. Their dominance over the unelected branches of the government, such as the judiciary, the security forces, and the Guardian Council, has enabled Islamists to block almost all of the reformist agenda and to manipulate the most recent elections for Iran's parliament, the Majlis. However, this temporary move to the right may portend hidden troubles for the conservatives. With the election of Mahmoud Ahmadinejad, the June 2005 presidential election returned the hard-line conservatives to executive power, but voter turnout was so low as to raise questions about the legitimacy of the result. In municipal elections held in February 2003, turnout in the major urban areas was as low as 12 percent.[9] In the February 2004 parliamentary elections, turnout in the urban areas was in the high 20s to low 30s, which represented a significant drop since the previous national elections.[10] In the June 2005 elections, the conservatives garnered seats in the Majlis and gained the presidency, but still find themselves without the backing of the population. So far, the conservative clique has been adept at resisting popular pressure to liberalize, but it remains to be seen if it can continue such a policy. President Mahmoud Ahmadinejad, however, has appeased popular critics with his new and more intensive brand of Iranian nationalism, some of it dedicated to nuclear independence.

The country's economic woes, however, have not made Iranians more amenable to U.S. positions on regional or arms control issues. While American culture remains popular among ordinary citizens, U.S. policies with respect to Israel, Iraq, Afghanistan, and Iran's nuclear program are controversial and unpopular. Iranian nationalism has been strengthened by the drastic regional shifts that have occurred in the last five years. The invasions of Afghanistan and Iraq by the United States have been a double-edged sword for Iran. Regimes hostile to Teheran were eliminated: both the Taliban and Saddam Hussein were no friends of Iran. Yet, the occupation of Iran's neighbors by the United States means that it is encircled by the so-called "global hegemon." This siege mentality has translated into widespread support for policies that defy the U.S. and assert Iran's independence. On the other hand, the prospect of a Shiite-led regime in Baghdad could make the U.S. invasion's effects more palatable.

> Without doubt, acquisition of nuclear weapons is supported by the clergy and the ordinary man on the street. The Iranian sees it as a symbol of national pride, of power commensurate with their nation's status as a major regional power, an ancient, 5,000-year-old civilisational entity. The more Israel threatens a strike against Iran's nuclear facilities, the more powerful the ruling elite becomes. Public opinion, however inimical to the clergy, only consolidates behind them.[11]

The depth of support for the nuclear policy crosses ideological, class, and political categories. Even if George W. Bush's policy of regime change in Iran were successful, it might not alter Iran's nuclear ambitions, its opposition to Israel, or its efforts to influence the politics of its immediate neighbors.

Thus, Iran's nationalism may cause it to engage with the world, rather than retreat. Even though the current spike in nationalism may seem to augur a period of defiance and isolation, recent Iranian overtures to nations and international institutions temper this conclusion. Ayatollah Ruhollah Khomeini's isolation from the world taught Iran that international activism is in its interests. Rather than conceding to American and European demands on terrorism, human rights, and nuclear proliferation, Iran may be entering the international trading community on its own terms. Recent maneuvers by Iran to establish gas and oil contracts with Pakistan, India, and China, show that

Iran has learned to build alternative coalitions to counteract western influ-ence. Iran had been trying for years to negotiate separate agreements with India and Pakistan for a natural gas pipeline that would serve both nations, but with little cooperation between the South Asia rivals there was little suc-cess. Now it would appear that Pakistan has agreed to guarantee the flow of gas through its territory. In October 2004, China's Sinopec Group signed a $70 billion deal with Iran, in which Sinopec will buy 250 million tons of liq-uefied natural gas, develop the Yadavaran field, and China would be guaran-teed 150,000 barrels of Iranian crude oil per day for 25 years.[12] This is not a new strategy for Iran. For example, in the 1990s Iran had struck a $3 billion deal with Australia's BHP to construct a natural gas pipeline from Iran to Pak-istan and India.[13] BHP backed out of the deal in 1996 after the United States threatened to impose secondary sanctions on corporations doing business with Iran. But Iran's attempts may have more success this time around. Unin-tended consequences of the Iraq war have pushed together two unlikely allies. Iran and Turkey have had a turbulent past marked by differences of opinion on most issues,[14] yet their common interest in preventing the cre-ation of an independent Kurdistan has enabled them to patch up relations. In addition, changes in the international energy market may make Iran's current overtures to foreign investors more sanction-proof than they were in the 1990s. The increased demand for oil and natural gas and the perceived long-term tightening of supplies mean that many states are more interested in securing future supply lines. The economic growth of India and China has led them to seek energy supplies from Iran. Teheran has used these overtures to broaden its political appeal and gain support at the United Nations and elsewhere.

Nuclear Dispute: Iran and the U.S.

As mentioned above, the United States has imposed sanctions in some form since the 1979 Islamic Revolution. The stated goals at various times have been to demand the freedom of the American embassy hostages, to thwart Iran's support of terrorism, to encourage its adherence to human rights standards, to encourage its support for the Israeli-Palestinian peace process, or to hasten the demise of the conservative regime. Despite varia-tions in the Iranian response, the United States has not altered its approach except to increase the level of punishments under what was initially the "dual containment policy." Thus, it has not been clear to Iran that the U.S. will ease the sanctions regime if Iran behaves well. This has made Teheran question American sincerity.

Yet the Bush Administration appears unwilling to consider the types of influence it can most readily and effectively wield against Iran. Until recently, the United States was determined to adhere to coercive options without emphasizing the associated inducements that must go along with any influence strategy. The president and his advisers stressed threats and punishments if Iran proceeds with her nuclear program. Early in George W. Bush's tenure, there were unabashed references to the goal of regime change in Iran. The famous 2001 State of the Union targeted Iran as part of the "axis of evil." Despite a recent retreat from language advocating direct American involvement in the change of regime, U.S. officials have continued to call for a dramatic change in Iranian leadership. Now the U.S. is appealing to Iranians to act on their own, calling on opposition forces or reformist political parties to take the action the United States is not willing to take itself. In his February 2005 State of the Union address, Bush said, "To the Iranian people, I say tonight: As you stand for your own liberty, America stands with you."[15] To further the impression that the U.S. is committed to the overthrow of the mullahs (though not necessarily through an American invasion), the White House did not contradict reports that American commandos had been conducting covert missions in Iranian territory since the summer of 2004.[16]

Strategies of invasion or revolution, however, do not address the immediate problem of Iran's nuclear ambitions. Long-term political transformation will not come soon enough to halt Iran's progress on uranium-enrichment, nor the advancements in its missile program. As an alternative to regime change, the United States has recently shifted its rhetoric to more limited threats of military action. For example, Vice President Dick Cheney has publicly hinted that Israel might be prepared to take unilateral action, as it did in 1981 against Iraq's Osirak nuclear reactor. Neither the President nor Secretary of State Condoleezza Rice has "taken any options off the table."[17] Yet, will the "Osirak option" solve the proliferation problem? Most analysts of the Iranian program do not think that bombing known reactors or enrichment facilities is a guarantee of success now. Iran has dispersed its nuclear programs to a number of locations and is believed to have hardened many of these sites. The well-known centers are at Natanz, Isfahan, Bushehr, and Arak, but there are believed to be at least a dozen other sites as well.[18] An Osirak-style strike would temporarily disrupt Iran's progress but would not halt it entirely; Iran has the technical knowledge and resources to repair and restart its nuclear buildup, just as Iraq did.

So what should the United States, Britain, France, Germany, and the others do to address the problem of Iran's proliferation? As Secretary Rice has said, they need to keep *all* options on the table. This means that Washington should bargain with Iran and that both the U.S. and the Europeans should not be timid in their threats. Some have suggested that the United States is playing the role of the "bad cop" while the Europeans are the "good cop." The U.S. supplies the threat of military action or invasion if Iran persists while the Europeans offer the carrots of trade and aid as rewards if Iran complies. The problem is that each cop needs full credibility. For the Europeans to succeed, the United States has to participate in the inducements package that is offered as it is now doing in accepting the Russian offer to enrich Iranian nuclear fuel. Similarly, for the American threats to have effect on Teheran, the Europeans must be willing to refer the matter to the UN Security Council and take further harsh decisions if need be. But Iran has not been impressed with either side's credibility. Iran views the Europeans as weak and pliable.[19] Iran also expects the U.S. to come up with a strong inducements package.[20] Since Iran feels it has the advantage of time and the technicalities of the NPT on its side, the West needs to become more adept at both the positive and negative sides of the influence equation.

Conclusions on Iran

Iran has reentered the international arena with a forceful and domestically persuasive argument against the big powers. It has been significantly affected by hegemonic trade pressures and has decided to join the global oil economy rather than retreat from it. However, this decision does not change matters internally where hardliners govern with popular support. Rather, Iran is using its potential power as an energy provider to South and East Asia to counterbalance American and European pressure. If the goal of the West is to alter the Islamic Republic's behavior rather than seek the demise of the Islamic regime, then it needs to emphasize a more effective policy of persuasion. This would involve clearer expectations of needed change in Iran's behavior, assurances regarding the incremental lifting of Western punishments in the event of Iranian cooperation, and the realistic possibility that Iran will be welcomed into the community of nations once it has reformed. The U.S. needs a strategy like that which succeeded with Libya. In short, the European approach of engagement will work only if the United States also accepts it and participates. This strategy will almost certainly need Russian as well as European assistance. And it may not work at all.

TURKEY

Much like its neighbor Iran, the Republic of Turkey finds itself at a crossroads. It is on the verge of becoming incorporated into Europe through its possible accession to the European Union (EU). But while this lofty goal would obviously be beneficial for Turkey's economic outlook, it comes at a domestically inconvenient time. Also surprising is Turkey's recent difficulty with its long-time ally, the United States. Turkey's complicated juggling act, balancing its domestic, regional, and global interests, has become much more uncertain lately. Whether this will have any effect on the stability of the Erdogan government, tip the scales toward either the secularists or the

Islamists, or influence the prospects for an independent Kurdistan, all remain to be seen.

Turkey and the EU

The conventional wisdom about Turkey's unique position in the Middle East is that it can act as a bulwark of secularized Muslim democracy against a sea of authoritarianism and Islamism. Moreover, Turkey's accession to the European Union would strengthen Turkey's domestic political structure and bring such riches to its economy as to create a model for other Middle Eastern nations. How realistic are such prospects?

The first issue is whether Turkey is really a liberal, secular state or if it has created an elaborate façade as part of its bid to gain European acceptance. The history of modern Turkey is steeped in the personal commitment of its founder, Mustafa Kemal or Atatürk, to secularism, westernization, and modernization. There is no doubt that from 1923 to the 1990s Turkey followed a strictly republican, nationalist, and secular model, eschewing Islamism.

> By virtually every measure, that vision of a unitary state bonded by civic loyalty has been a remarkable success. A modern bureaucracy, a Western legal system, progressive national education, and all the trappings of a modern state are the progeny of a revolution that arguably redrew the boundary between Europe and the Middle East. Kemalism has been especially emancipating for women, who have enjoyed full civil rights since 1934.[21]

But this success came at a high price. To achieve this outcome, Turkey homogenized its culture, sublimating differences to the litmus test of Turkish nationalism. This meant that ethnic differences were suppressed, Islam was reinterpreted to meet the civic needs of the republican government, and the civil rights of minorities and dissenters were disregarded. For example, a 1983 national law prohibiting the instruction of children in any language other than Turkish still has lingering impact on public education despite its recent repeal.[22] As a consequence, in the Kurdish-majority regions of East and Southeast Turkey, students—especially native speakers of Kurdish—have been underperforming and failing at much higher rates than in the Turkish-majority regions of the nation.[23] Naturally, such practices led to higher rates of unemployment, inadequate economic opportunities, greater popular discontent, and thus to increased legitimacy for the Kurdish separatist movement. As can be seen, it is too simplistic to hold up Turkey as a model of Middle Eastern liberalism.

It is possible that EU membership will enable secular democracy to triumph over authoritarianism and Islamism and bring in economic globalization as well. For example, Turkey has been forced to repeal the law banning minority languages to conform to the standards of human rights required by the European Union. But such small triumphs in tolerance and liberalism are overshadowed by the effects of these forced measures: while the linguistic minorities may be pleased, it has renewed tensions between minorities and the majority Turks. Thus, the introduction of liberal democratic principles such as civil rights and local self-determination has eroded the authoritarian control of the Kemalists. It would appear that Turkey has paradoxically combined authoritarianism with secularism and democracy with Islamism and ethnic nationalism.

As formal negotiations on EU accession begin, Turkey seems as conflicted as ever over its ethnic and religious identity. In fact, the prospect of the "Europeanization" of Turkey has caused a backlash from both Islamist and ultra-nationalist camps. The EU's demands as well as its continued waffling over whether a majority-Muslim state should be admitted have raised domestic concerns in Turkey. Kemalists and Islamists are united in being offended by the French and German implications that they are not good enough to join the club. After all, Turkey's application has been 43 years[24] in the offing and Turkey's participation in NATO seemed perfectly appropriate when its strategic contribution was needed during the Cold War.[25] Moreover, the conditions Turkey must meet before admission, as laid out in the 1993 Copenhagen European Council, have brought out the nationalistic side of the Kemalists who chafe at letting important national decisions be made in Brussels.

Besides having some paradoxical effects on the Kemalist position, EU accession may also have strengthened the hand of the Islamists at the expense of the Kemalists. Perhaps as an accident of timing, the EU's requirements for greater civil rights for minorities and greater civilian control over the military have caused a shift in the power dynamics between the civilian politicians (who are currently "progressive" Islamists) and the military establishment (who are mostly Kemalists). From 1923 to 1997, Turkey's secularism and nationalism were made possible by the guardianship of the military establishment, which stepped in to enforce Atatürk's secular vision when necessary. "On four occasions since Turkey's founding, the military has displaced politicians who challenged its power or deviated from Atatürk's ideology."[26] Each time it has handed power back to civilian authorities once stability was restored, but this interposition suggested that Turkish secular republicanism was not viable without the strong-arm backing of the Turkish Armed Forces (TAF). The 1990s brought the weaknesses of the Kemalist approach to the fore. During that decade "nine different coalition governments ruled Turkey."[27] From this period of turmoil, the Justice and Development Party (AKP), led by Recep Tayyip Erdogan, has emerged as a dominating movement which combined moderate Islam with a commitment to democracy and reform. The AKP's overwhelming victory in November 2003 parliamentary elections means that Turkey has a single-party government of Islamists, not secular republicans. During this same period, the Kemalist generals in the TAF have found themselves under pressure not just to accept the Erdogan regime, but to vest it with greater power of oversight over them. Naturally, this does not please them. So far, Erdogan has been able to avoid any direct showdown with the TAF and strengthen his own position, much of it thanks to the influence of the EU and of the United States.

The possibility of joining the European Union has had some surprising and paradoxical effects. The European requirement of respect for human and civil rights has made Turkey a less stable place. Kurdish separatist and Islamist elements have asserted themselves after the lifting of these authoritarian measures. But the trends are not all negative. The Islamists, too, have had to reform themselves to achieve EU compliance. Erdogan and the AKP have moderated their rhetoric and some of their policies in order to placate the military and the Europeans. This raises the possibility that one can combine moderate political Islam and democracy in a Middle Eastern state. But it remains to be seen whether the AKP's nods to modernity and liberalism will become entrenched in Turkey after it is admitted to the European Union. The success of globalization strategies after this point will clearly be determinative.

Turkey and the United States

During the Cold War, Turkey and the United States enjoyed a strong alliance: Turkey was the occasion for the Truman Doctrine, and Turkey has been a longstanding member of NATO. But, in the last four years, the relationship has become troubled. Much of the tension arises from their differences of opinion on the future of Iraq, especially with regard to the Kurdish minority in Northern Iraq. The situation reached its nadir on March 1, 2003 when the Turkish parliament refused to support the American invasion of Iraq. Yet, despite some acrimony, the overall state of the alliance remains much as before. Each side needs the other, and there is little danger of their mutual dependence diminishing. The relationship does, necessarily, become more complex. The United States will have to decide whether it is willing to keep an ally that will, on occasion, go its own way.

The 1991–92 Gulf War created fissures in U.S.-Turkey relations that are still evident today. Turkey's interests could not allow it to be enthusiastic about the U.S. plans with regard to its neighbor to the south. "Turkey suffered drastic economic losses after the 1991 Gulf War due to the collapse of trade with Iraq"[28] and due to the burden of caring for the influx of Kurdish refugees.[29] In addition, despite differences of opinion with Saddam Hussein on many matters, Turkey did share Iraq's concerns over their respective Kurdish minorities. The defeat of Saddam Hussein in 1991 and the U.S.'s commitment to protecting Iraqi minority groups through the imposition of no-fly zones have been troubling for Turkey. Under the protection of the U.S. no-fly zone in northern Iraq, the Iraqi Kurds expanded their power and developed much regional autonomy that emboldened Kurds not just in Iraq, but also in Turkey, Iran, and Syria.

Turkey's skepticism of the American position in the 1990s should have prepared the Bush Administration for the diplomatic wrangling which would inevitably come with plans for an invasion of Iraq in 2003. On the American side, Deputy Secretary of Defense Paul Wolfowitz offered Turkey a $24 billion aid package in exchange for use of Turkish military bases and airspace.[30] The Turks had asked for up to $92 billion, and perhaps the March 1 parliamentary vote was an attempt to up the ante.[31] If so, the gamble failed. The United States had to forego access to Iraq through Turkish land and turned instead to the Iraqi Kurds to provide tactical assistance during the war. At the time, many saw this as a disastrous outcome for Ankara. It had damaged its relations with the U.S. and had allowed the Iraqi Kurds to fill the vacuum and to occupy oil-rich Kirkuk and Mosul. However, with 90 percent of the Turkish population opposing the war, it was difficult to see the AKP government doing otherwise. Moreover, the move strengthened Erdogan's position as an independent leader and increased his credibility among his neighbors in the region. The immediate fallout, however, was not good. The July 4, 2003 Sulaymaniya Incident—when Americans arrested eleven Turkish Special Forces troops and accused them of plotting the assassination of the mayor of Kirkuk—may be seen as a consequence of the cooling relationship between Turkey and the U.S.[32] This was interpreted as a sharp message from the U.S. that Turkey's presence in northern Iraq would not be tolerated even though their troops had operated there in the past with American blessing. Despite these differences, the U.S.-Turkish alliance remains intact. Turkey is still a member of NATO, has continued to allow U.S. military overflights of territory, and shares intelligence with the U.S. on Syria, Iran, and other states.

While the bilateral relationship with the U.S. is ongoing, Turkey has created some backstops to strengthen its position. American actions in Iraq have been seen by Turks to give impetus to the Kurdish drive for independence and to lend credibility to calls for the creation of an independent state of Kurdistan to be carved out of parts of Turkey, Iraq, Iran, Syria, and Armenia. To counter this perceived threat to its territorial integrity, Ankara has reached across to Iran, Syria, Russia, and Saudi Arabia—neighbors with whom it had little in common in the past.[33] In the past, Turkey has disagreed with Iran and Syria on policy issues such as Israel, support of Islamic militancy, and local water rights. However, the emergence of common interests on trade, the Kurdish problem, and defense cooperation has enabled closer ties. Thus, Turkey has broadened its international reach and has tried to diversify its dependence on others. This has meant a reduction in the overall influence of the West and an expanded role by other countries.

Conclusions on Turkey

U.S. and EU policies have had mixed strategic consequences for Turkey. The EU's demands for political reform and economic liberalization have empowered the nationalist and the Islamist interests within Turkey. Likewise, the American war in Iraq has caused Turkey to draw closer to non-western countries. Neither of these necessarily forebodes negative outcomes. For example, the moderation of the public stance of the devoutly Muslim Prime Minister Erdogan may provide a positive role model for "pragmatic" or moderate Islamists in other Muslim nations. Similarly, Turkey's recent coziness with Syria and Iran may provide the United States with new avenues of dialogue within which the U.S. can influence these "rogue" states. Turkey is in no danger of turning against the West; however, this case shows the variety of outcomes that are possible when following a policy of active internationalism. The West may have to come to terms with the fact that it will have allies and partners that do not agree with the western take on every issue every time. The long-term payoff for Turkey, of course, is inclusion within EU globalization structures.

A PALESTINIAN STATE?

In the 1990s, prior to the start of the latest intifada, optimistic assessments of the creation of a Palestinian state led to various conclusions about what that state would look like. In many ways, the Oslo peace process rested on the traditional view of the nation-state. The assumptions built into the Oslo-Wye process (still included in the language of the current Road Map/Saudi Initiative processes) involved political authority, territorial contiguity, and economic viability. For example, the creation of the Palestinian Authority as a proto-state was thought to be an important precursor to eventual full-fledged statehood. The idea was that a nation-state could be created if there was a legitimate, authoritative government in power. However, this view ignores the economic dependence of the Palestinians on the Israeli economy and on international donors. Moreover, it overlooks the reluctance of Israelis to hand over control of the skies and waters bordering the Gaza Strip and West Bank to the Palestinians. If a future state of Palestine is inseparable from Israel in terms of economics, security, and foreign policy, can it really be a full-fledged state?[34] Palestine would be circumscribed by its dependence on Israel, but that is not essentially different from other states bound up in the toils of globalization.

Since the breakdown of the Oslo process in 2000, the vision of a peaceful settlement of the conflict and the creation of a separate Palestinian entity has faded but not vanished. Israeli reactions to the second intifada, including the closure of its borders and its unilateral withdrawal from Gaza, have raised questions about a negotiated settlement that would lead to Palestinian independence. Rather than showing how a future Palestine may survive without Israel, the uncertainty following upon acts of violence and the economic decline of both Palestine and Israel in the past five years seem to underscore their dependence upon one another. The death of Yasir Arafat and the dedicated work of Mahmoud Abbas have not been sufficient to overcome the electoral success of Hamas—which has at least temporarily sidelined the peace process.

If a Palestinian state is ever created, it will have qualified sovereignty. What would such a state look like? It will not be a nation-state in the traditional sense: with a contiguous territory and completely autonomous political authority over an ethnically-distinct population. It will have two different political enclaves: Gaza and the West Bank. Its provinces could be linked together along lines of a Swiss canton system; they could be confederated with Jordan; there could be a Belgian-style union with separate legislatures. In addition the two provinces could be joined via "the Arc" proposal for a superhighway linking Gaza and the West Bank, which is RAND's model of infrastructure and economic development.

Links with Jordan

Jordan's central role in Israeli-Palestinian relations, its proximity, and its population demographics have always made it a de facto representative of the interests of Palestinians. Israel's reluctance to negotiate with the PLO and other organizations it considered terrorists made it difficult to negotiate directly with Palestinian leaders within the West Bank and Gaza. Instead, Israel preferred to partner with the more moderate and credible Hashemite Kings of Jordan, Hussein and now Abdullah. On Jordan's side, there was little doubt that King Hussein's active role in the peace process was linked to his desire to maintain influence on the occupied territories.

However, since the creation of the Palestinian Authority (PA) in 1994, full Jordanian-Palestinian integration is no longer possible. The quasi-governmental role envisioned for the PA in the West Bank and Gaza dictated that Palestine would evolve into a political entity separate from Jordan.[35] And Jordan's authorities acknowledged Palestinian independence.

A Federal System?

Various other possibilities have been discussed including a canton system like Switzerland or the duopoly in Belgium of the Walloon and Flemish communities. The Swiss system depended upon "everyone being a minority" at least in some respect—language, religion, or class-basis. When the Swiss civil

war occurred in 1847, the Catholic cantons were overwhelmed by more liberal Protestant elements supporting the center. Since then, Swiss neutrality
has obviated participation in European wars which have involved one or
more of their linguistic groups—French, German, or Italian. The four parties
in the cantons have been also represented at the center. In Belgium, the
government has balanced between the separate linguistic communities, initially favoring the depressed Flemish against the Walloons (French) and
then changing sides as Flemish communities gained economic and political
strength. While tensions remain, the center in Brussels has maintained a tolerable cohesion. In Palestine, a central government would find its military
options limited by agreements with Israel, and it would have to make sure
that Jewish communities in the West Bank receive adequate treatment. It
would have to coordinate outposts in Gaza as well as the West Bank. For a
long time a Palestinian state will depend upon both Israel and international
donors for its economic sustenance. Israeli cooperation in turn will hinge on
the PA controlling terrorism. A common labor market, with Arabs working in
Israel, cannot function if open borders foster terrorism. This puts an incredible burden on the PA in terms of its relations with Hamas, a past proponent
of terrorism. The Palestinian elections in February, 2006, which Hamas won,
intensified the issue and raised the question whether funds would be cut off
as Hamas assumed the reins of power.

The RAND Model[36]

Proposed by a team of analysts at the non-partisan think tank, this plan side-
steps the political dimensions of the Israeli-Palestinian problem and instead
addresses the economics and infrastructure of nation-building. The theory is
that regardless of the exact outlines of the final political settlement, the status
of Jerusalem, whether the Israeli settlements will be dissolved, and where the
exact borders between Israel and Palestine will be, a future Palestine will need
economic development to sustain itself. In order to assure the success of such
a state, it will be necessary to get a head start on integrating the noncontiguous
territories of the West Bank and Gaza through a unified communication and
transportation system, called "the Arc." This massive superhighway network
would link Gaza's main urban centers with the highest density Palestinian centers in the eastern West Bank, necessarily traversing Israeli territory through the
southern Negev. In addition, the RAND plan involves other infrastructure projects to ensure viability, such as proposals for health care, security, education,
local transportation, housing, and water systems.

"The Arc" appears to be the leading plan among the international community for renewing progress along the road to Palestinian statehood. In addition to receiving high profile acceptance outside the region, it has been
officially endorsed by both sides in the dispute. Following this plan, the

authorities could begin working on economic integration between Gaza and the West Bank without waiting until the final status issues are resolved. It is impossible to envision a Palestine lasting very long if it cannot feed, house, or employ its population. To function reasonably well, matters of local governance, national security, and economic growth have to be dealt with before the political issues of borders and capitals are ironed out.

Yet, while it may be tempting to think that an economic approach is the answer for now, this plan makes political assumptions that are not validated in practice. For example, the Arc's design specifically ignores Israeli population centers in the West Bank since their final status is not known. However, this has aroused suspicion from the Palestinians who charge that by *avoiding* such disputed territory, the plan in essence *sanctions* the annexation of such territories by Israel. To portray independent Palestine as a nation without East Jerusalem seems unthinkable, yet its status is not specified in the plan. Thus, the plan's strengths may ultimately turn out to be sources of weakness. It may prove the adage that nothing is apolitical in this conflict. The RAND plan also does not address the political indeterminacy which Hamas's victory has caused.

Conclusions on Palestine

The Al Aqsa Intifada has actually had two seemingly contradictory effects on the prospects of a Palestinian state. On the one hand, it has set back the progress that the proto-state and population were making. It has cost many lives, jobs, and has tarnished the reputation of the Palestinian Authority. On the other hand, it has proven to the world that a negotiated peace and the establishment of a Palestinian state are necessary for peace and stability in the region. Therefore, while the task may have become more difficult, the international community and the two sides may now be more prepared to see it to a conclusion.

Still, the changing global economy and the setbacks of the last six years will have a real impact on the kind of state that will emerge. The Palestinians may have to get used to a national government with less than complete autonomy. After all, in this age of increasing economic and political integration, autarky is neither possible nor advisable. Certainly a Palestinian government will have to accept restrictions on the types of weapons it can deploy within its territories.

OVERALL CONCLUSIONS

In all three cases, the influence or rejection of globalization is at work in the outcomes we observe. Turkey has largely embraced a Western form of globalization which will link it increasingly with Europe and the United States. Iran has had the liberty to reject Western-style economic openness because its oil revenues have provided a cushion. They do not, however, solve the structural, technological, nor educational problems of its economy. Like early modern Spain, Iran and Saudi Arabia can prosper on revenues from key minerals (gold or oil) but that will not ensure their economic future. Such infusions raise prices and diminish the competitiveness of other products, leading ultimately to stagnation.

In addition, the examples of Iran and Turkey illustrate the complexity of international influence. American sanctions on Iran have had measurable economic effects and may have contributed to the weakening of the Islamic regime. However, this damage has not appreciably altered Iran's government or its foreign policy behavior. The U.S. has little to show for its twenty-seven years of threats and punishments. Instead, Iran has continued to flout American demands and even to step up defiant activities, especially in the pursuit of nuclear energy. Moreover, the conservative Islamic establishment has not shown signs of demise. Iran has learned a lesson about the drawbacks of isolationism. Rather than be co-opted by the West, however, Iran has begun to take advantage of its energy reserves to establish trade and strategic ties with its neighbors to the east. This approach has proven popular with much of Iranian society and may save the current regime, at least for a time. It appeals to Iranian nationalism and promises to improve Iran's economic prospects. The United States must consider alternative means of influence on Iran besides threat-based strategies. Like its concessions on North Korea, Washington will have to think of inducements, not just punishments.

Similarly, the West must come to recognize that its relationship with Turkey has matured and become more complex. Turkey's entrance into the international economy has offered an energetic work force and manufacturing possibilities for Western nations. At the same time, Turkey has surprised the West by shifting from secularism to Islamism and by becoming more amenable to engagement with its Muslim neighbors while at the same time asking to be accepted as a charter member of the European Union. Success in its bid to enter the European Union is likely but not guaranteed. In addition, Turkey's military alliance with the United States has undergone strain over Iraq. However, the West recognizes that Turkey still provides the nexus between the West and the Middle East, which the West could use to advantage. A European-oriented Turkey might still improve its connections with its southern neighbors. The EU and U.S. will have to tolerate a moderate Islamism in Turkey since it may provide an alternative to secularism for the Muslim world. The Erdogan experiment of the last several years suggests that political Islam may, in fact, be compatible with globalization.

The Israeli-Palestinian issue is still not settled, but the Israeli evacuation of Gaza leaves the PA in charge there. How much longer can Tel Aviv stay in the

West Bank? The Palestinian Authority is the residuary legatee in both sectors, and the only question is whether it will manage them competently over the long term. The newly elected Hamas will have to change its charter to make possible ultimate negotiations with Tel Aviv for an independent state. Israel could well reject this prospect and opt instead for the Fence and reliance on Israel's Defense Forces to keep terrorism within limits. But fencing off the West Bank can only lead to economic strangulation of the Arab population living there. It would hurt Israel as well. Polls indicate that the Palestinian population strongly favors a halt to violence within society. They voted, however, to seat Hamas at the center of power, and this leaves Palestinian legitimacy very much in question.

THE MIDDLE EAST AS A WHOLE

Globalization has frayed the ties of traditionalism in the Middle East. Unlike the situation in East Asia, however, no Arab regime has been successful in embracing it. Yet none have been able to ignore it. Globalization has probably stimulated terrorism directed against Western-oriented regimes. It has also caused traditional regimes to reemphasize nationalism in face of Western influences. No new states, however, with the possible exception of the Palestinians, look as if they may be created. Iraq, under U.S. and coalition occupation, of course remains an uncertainty. (See chapter 11.) Possibly a Shiite regime will reach an agreement with the Kurds and Sunnis. But this could fail. Iraqi federalism, therefore, could lead to the ultimate creation of three Iraqi states, though the international community will continue to resist this outcome.

NOTES

1. See for instance Etel Solingen, *Nuclear Claimants: Contrasting Trajectories in East Asia and the Middle East* (Cambridge: Cambridge University Press, 2006).

2. Since oil is such a large percentage of world trade, this conclusion may seem paradoxical. But it is precisely the concentration upon oil (one of the key products of the factor of land) that allows oil producers to slight industrialization, commercial capital, and educated labor. Land has been exploited, but capital and labor—the key elements in globalization—have been almost wholly neglected in Middle Eastern development.

3. Presidents Ronald Reagan and Bill Clinton signed a number of executive orders (Executive Orders 12613, 12959). These presidential directives ended all direct government assistance to Iran, barred the use of American funds for development projects by international aid agencies, NGOs, banks, or investors, and sanctioned various forms of private trade with Iranian interests. In 1996 Congress passed the Iran-Libya

Sanctions Act, which sanctioned foreign companies for investing over $20 million in Iran's energy sector.

4. In 1974 Iran produced 6 million barrels of crude oil per day but since 1979 has not exceeded 3.9 million barrels per day as an annual average. See U.S. Department of Energy statistics: www.eia.doe.gov.

5. See Bijan Khajehpour, "Iran's Economy: Twenty Years after the Islamic Revolution," in *Iran at the Crossroads*, ed. John L. Esposito and R. K. Ramazani (New York: Palgrave, 2001), 93–122.

6. This is the range of figures released by the Central Bank of Iran for 2004 and 2005. For example, inflation for the eleven months preceding February 2005 has been reported as 15.1 percent. See Iran News Agency.

7. Sanam Vakil, "Iran: The Gridlock between Demography and Democracy," *SAIS Review*, vol. 24, no. 2 (Summer 2004), 47.

8. Khatami was elected with 69 percent of the popular vote in 1997, and was reelected with 77 percent of the vote in 2001.

9. Modher Amin, "Analysis: Iran Voting, A Legitimacy Test?" United Press International, November 20, 2003.

10. "Iranian Cabinet Evaluates Low Turnout," Deutsche Presse-Agentur, February 23, 2004.

11. Neena Gopal, "Will Iran Be Next?" *Financial Times*, January 16, 2005.

12. "China to Cooperate with Iran in Oil," Iranian News Agency, December 27, 2004.

13. From the United States Energy Information Administration, Department of Energy. www.eia.doe.gov.

14. For example, until recently Turkey has been staunchly secular and hostile toward Iran's Islamic theocracy. In return, Iran has been appalled by Turkey's ongoing close association with Israel.

15. "US policy is not to change Iran regime," Agence France Presse, February 4, 2005.

16. Robert Collier, "Tough U.S. Stance on Iran Brings Echoes of Iraq Debate," *San Francisco Chronicle*, February 9, 2005, A-16.

17. Tod Robberson, "Rice: Iran Attack Not in Plan," *Dallas Morning News*, February 5, 2005.

18. These sites include locations at Parachin, Qazvin, Saghand, Yazd, Fasa, Darkhovin, Bonab, Tabriz, Karaj, Moa'allem, Kalaych, Chalus, and Neka. See Neena Gopal, "Will Iran Be Next?" *Financial Times*, January 16, 2005.

19. "Does Europe Need a Guardian?" *Keyhan*, March 16, 2005, translated and reported by BBC Worldwide Monitoring, March 19, 2005.

20. "The outlook for the future of Iran-America relations: A new initiative at the boiling point," *E'temad* website, February 9, 2005, translated and reported by BBC Worldwide Monitoring, February 9, 2005.

21. Thomas W. Smith, "Civic Nationalism and Ethnocultural Justice in Turkey," *Human Rights Quarterly*, vol. 27, no. 2 (May 2005), 437.

22. Ismet Sahin and Yener Gulmez, "Social Sources of Failure in Education: The Case in East and Southeast Turkey," *Social Indicators Research*, vol. 49, no. 1, p. 85.

23. Ibid., 83.

24. Turkey didn't apply for full membership until 1987, but had signed an Association Agreement with the European Community in 1963. David L. Phillips, "Turkey's Dreams of Accession," *Foreign Affairs*, vol. 83, no. 5 (September 2004), 92.

25. Hasan Kosebalaban, "Turkey's EU Membership: A Clash of Security Cultures," *Middle East Policy*, vol. 9, no. 2 (June 2002), 130.

26. Phillips, 87.

27. Ibid., 91.

28. Thalif Deen, "Iraq: UN Sees Massive Damage to Mideast Economies," *Global Information Network*, April 16, 2003, p. 1.

29. Turkey and Iran bore the brunt of the 2 million refugees that fled as a result of the 1991–92 Gulf War. Ahmed Ferhadi, "The Kurds in Iraq, Iran and Turkey: Three Kurdish Perspectives," *Washington Report on Middle Eastern Affairs*, vol. 11, no. 1 (June 30, 1992), 40.

30. Michael M. Gunter, "The U.S.-Turkish Alliance in Disarray," *World Affairs*, vol. 167, no. 3 (Winter 2005), 119.

31. Ibid., 119.

32. Yigal Schleifer, "Relations with U.S. Hit Lowest Point Yet," *Toronto Star*, July 20, 2003, p. F3.

33. James C. Helicke, "Turkey Pushes for Closer Ties in Mideast," Associated Press, January 17, 2004.

34. Of course Canada is a state dependent on its southern neighbor for defense as well as trade and, to some degree, economic growth.

35. See Hillel Frisch, "Jordan and the Palestinian Authority: Did Better Fences Make Better Neighbors?" *The Middle East Journal*, vol. 58, no. 1 (Winter 2005), 52–71.

36. See the RAND Palestinian State Study Team's *Building a Successful Palestinian State* (Santa Monica, CA: RAND Corporation, 2005); and Doug Suisman et al., *A Formal Structure for a Palestinian State* (Santa Monica, CA: RAND Corporation, 2005).

8

The Failure of Chechen Separatism

John Reppert and Alexei Shevchenko

CHECHNYA AND GLOBALIZATION

The prospects for independence of nationalist movements which reject globalization are quite poor. Such movements do not engender support from the international community, and they are particularly isolated if the metropole which surrounds them also embraces globalization. In this respect Chechnya faces problems even greater than those of the Palestinians who might, under appropriate circumstances, like to become a modern state.

The prospects for Chechen independence have if anything worsened in the past several years. Chechnya is in fact rapidly becoming a failed state-territory, with criminal elements and social disorganization preponderating in society. This does not mean that Russian policy has succeeded. The prevention of Chechnya's secession is at best only a partial victory for the Russian leadership. With the spread of conflict into neighboring regions of the North Caucasus, particularly Dagestan,[1] President Putin's repeated assurances of "stabilization" of the situation in the breakaway republic pose unanswered questions. According to one recent analysis of the Chechen situation, Chechnya has not returned to the status of one of the provinces of the Russian Federation; it is rather an occupied territory where the Constitution does not apply and the laws are not even enforced. For a long time it had been an isolated black hole, but now it is rather the eye of the storm in the North Caucasus.[2] A Russian grant of independence for Grozny is now even less likely than before.

The decade-long predicament in Chechnya has led to tens of thousands of civilian and military casualties on both sides, forced Moscow to permanently deploy 100,000 military, police, and security troops in the region and to spend billions of dollars on the war effort.[3] The failure there raised the threat of terrorism in Moscow and other Russian cities. The Kremlin has been unable to integrate the breakaway republic economically and politically. As noted by Richard Rosecrance and Arthur Stein, globalization and economic interdependence provide metropolitan powers with an option of buying off dissident provinces and thus getting them to remain in the fold. But such tactics have not yet been used in Chechnya. Up to now, the Putin regime has preferred "sticks" to "carrots" in dealing with the Chechen separatists.

Nonetheless, independence remains unlikely and for three reasons. First, the international environment has changed in ways that make global support for Chechen independence/autonomy even less likely. Second, the Chechen-Russian relationship has soured and shifted in ways that strengthen Moscow's hand. Third, events within Chechnya have produced a reduced likelihood of enhanced status for Chechnya, other than firmly in Russia's orbit. Despite each of these changes, the armed struggle in Chechnya goes on with mounting Russian and Chechen casualties.

Several interrelated factors account for this outcome. The first one is the inability of the Chechen elite to develop an effective, unified political leadership with which Russia might negotiate. The Chechen state has failed. In addition, Russian leaders have used the Chechen crisis—recently augmented by the attack on Beslan—to ensure their political power and survival. In the short term at least, it has been useful to them.

CRIMINALIZATION AND COLLAPSE OF THE CHECHEN STATE

The crisis of the Chechen state was undoubtedly aggravated and accelerated by a protracted destructive military conflict with Russia. However, internal politics also help to explain failure. Chechen elites are unable to establish a strong and effective regime capable of legitimate rule which exercises an effective monopoly on armed force, demonstrates a commitment to developing the Chechen economy, and is willing to engage in productive negotiations with Moscow.

The chaos in Chechnya can be attributed to structural characteristics of the Chechen society based on the strong clan (*teip*) system as well as the long-term tradition of defying central control inherent in the Chechen warrior-political culture. Chechnya functioned as "a working anarchy ruled by an unsuccessful dictatorship."[4] Most of the Chechen ruling elite never came close to becoming Olsonian "stationary bandits." Instead they approximated the unambiguously predatory "roving" bandits, willing to expropriate resources from the population. The dominance of warlords in the Chechen politics and economics and their "violent neo-patrimonial" patterns of behavior[5] contributed to a rapid derationalization of the Chechen society, a substantial weakening of social institutions and resources,[6] catastrophic de-urbanization, and economic collapse. "Criminal entrepreneurship" flourished, and the breakdown of the legal system was the result.

Unable to arrest the internal economic crisis since the early 1990s (see below), the Chechen roving elites increasingly relied on illegal markets for economic survival. The institutional vacuum in the post-Soviet period was quickly filled by a black market economy rapidly transforming the republic into a paradigmatic criminal state. The "criminal formula" used by Chechen leaders included several ingredients. One was illegal money from the Chechen mafia operating outside the republic. The Chechen mafia burgeoned when controls over black market activities under Brezhnev were loosened, and by the late 1980s, it emerged as one of the most powerful criminal groups in the Soviet Union, monopolizing control over sales of automobiles, the drug trade, and the hotel business.[7] Moscow-based Chechen gangsters sent a large part of their profits home to be shared among their clans.

Due to mafia activities in 1992–1993 Chechnya emerged as the major center of counterfeit money and financial fraud in the former Soviet territory. In 1993 alone, Chechnya produced more than half of the counterfeit bonds seized on Russian territory.[8] A series of major bank frauds in Moscow by the Chechen gangs in 1992–1993 involving promissory notes from the Russian Central Bank netted around $500 million (this sum amounting to a third of the credit line the IMF granted to Russia for that year) much of which was channeled back to Chechnya. As the father of the Chechen independence, Dudaev, boasted in one of his interviews, "We sent you (Russians) useless slips of paper and instead got back bags of cash."[9]

Another source of criminalization was the Chechen elite's systematic plunder of the only two functioning sectors of the economy (accounting for more than two-thirds of Chechen republic revenues)—oil extraction and refining. With the lessening of oil extraction in Chechnya, incoming Russian oil played an enormous role in stimulating corruption. At the initial stage of Dudaev's regime, Russian economic pressure was limited to an extremely ineffective trade blockade coupled with the cutting off of central subsidies to Chechnya. However, since Grozny was at the center of a major pipeline network connecting Kazakhstan, Siberia, Baku, and the Black Sea port of Novorossiysk and since Chechnya traditionally supplied the rest of the North Caucasus with fuel, Moscow continued to allow Chechnya to import Russian oil for processing at local plants. Russia also allowed the reexporting of the refined product right up until the outbreak of the first Chechen war at the end of 1994.

In 1991–1994 Chechnya exported at least 20 million tons of oil to international markets with $300 million in profits from oil going to the Chechen government. This did not show on the official receipts.[10] In addition, oil was often simply siphoned from Chechen pipelines and stolen by numerous

Chechen "businessmen." Over half a million tons of oil extracted each year from Chechnya were illegally turned into low-grade petrol at thousands of homemade microrefineries.[11] It is also widely documented that top officials of the Dudaev regime openly embezzled oil revenues.[12] Towards the end of that regime, attempts to control oil trade and distribution were essentially abandoned with oil sector bureaucrats involved in stealing. On top of this, Dudaev's inability to exercise effective authority over his compatriots was accompanied by criminal violence and banditry such as attacks on passenger trains. By the summer of 1994, hijackings and kidnappings spread into Russian territory, fuelling a Russian outcry that became an important justification for the initiation of the first Chechen war.

Two rounds of protracted armed conflict with Russia followed, and the criminalization and progressive weakening of the Chechen state coincided with the rise of radical Wahhabi Islamic groups who were committed to creating a "North Caucasus Caliphate" between the Black Sea and the Caspian.

Elected in 1997 after the first Chechen war, President Maskhadov pursued a strategy of appeasement of the radical warlords and their terrorist allies. He could not, however, control the situation. In April 1997 he appointed one of the most influential radicals—Shamil' Basaev, who became one of the most notorious Chechen field commanders who purveyed mass murder as a tactic—to the post of the first prime minister with the responsibility for the oil sector, a move that dramatically enhanced the radicals' economic base and political clout. By February 1999 Maskhadov had essentially lost control over Chechen politics, a fact demonstrated by his consent to the suspension of the Chechen parliament, and the formation of an alternative governing structure—the Islamic Council (Shura)—with Basaev as its head. He also accepted an official transition to Shariah law, sanctioning mutilations for crimes and public hangings throughout Chechnya.[13] By the fall of 1999, two years after de facto independence from Moscow, Chechnya played host to kidnappings, the slave trade, and massive trafficking in weapons, drugs, and stolen goods.[14] Finally, in August–September 1999 forces of Chechen militants and fundamentalist Wahhabi Muslims under command of Basaev and Khattab (an Arab mercenary based in Chechnya) crossed the Dagestan border and clashed with Dagestani and Russian Interior Ministry troops. The incursion into Dagestan coincided with the "Russian 9/11"—a wave of terrorist attacks by Chechen separatists which targeted apartment buildings in Buinaksk (Dagestan), Moscow, and Volgodonsk (Russia), killing some 300 people.[15]

The initial Russian response to this military incursion was more limited than in the first war. However, open warfare soon broke out throughout Chechnya, thousands of deaths were recorded, and hundreds of thousands of residents were displaced from their homes. Grozny was devastated once again, and the U.S. and European nations resumed political pressure to settle the conflict through negotiations. After 9/11, however, American policy changed, and the "war on terrorism" focused all American energies. The Chechens were now seen as representatives of the terrorist threat.

President Putin swiftly and decisively moved Russia into full-fledged support for the war on terrorism and included Chechnya within it. Russia provided practical assistance to the United States that went beyond verbal assurances, and in particular offered intelligence on Afghanistan welcomed by American officials and the military. Members of the European Union also jumped on board and found themselves allied with Russia and Pakistan, two countries that had recently been the focus of criticism for their internal policies.

THE FAILURE OF INTEGRATION

Moscow's perennial obsession with the security and military dimensions of the Chechen crisis was coupled with a persistent disregard of the severe economic and political plight of the region, leading to the absence of even a semblance of coherent strategy for Chechnya's reintegration in 1991–2004.

Moscow failed to provide economic incentives for Dudaev's regime in the early 1990s. Chechnya's drive for independence from Russia occurred under extremely unfavorable economic circumstances. By the end of the Soviet rule, Chechnya was one of the poorest regions in Russia, the situation aggravated by the high birthrate leading to thousands of unemployed young men. By the mid-1980s, unemployment had become chronic, and by 1992 the unemployment rate in the region was nearing 40 percent. In 1991 oil extraction—the key industry of the republic—dropped to just 4 million tons from the peak of 21 million two decades previously. In addition, due to the legacy of heightened integration and centralization of the Soviet system, Chechnya was by no means ready to become an independent economic entity, since around 75 percent of its products were dependent on deliveries from Russia and other countries of the former Soviet Union.[16]

After nationalists took power in September–October of 1991, economic decline dramatically accelerated, leading to a full-blown economic crisis due to the collapse of Soviet rule and Dudaev's inability to govern the economy and political system. The new rulers immediately demonstrated a general economic incompetence that compounded other hardships.[17]

Initially, the economic crisis in Chechnya seemed to provide Moscow with significant leverage on the secessionist province. Chechen leaders' attempts to find a way out of the economic impasse through cooperation with Russia were reflected in Dudaev's July 1992 proposal that Moscow grant Chechnya control of its oil exports in return for a Chechen payment of transit fees for use of Russian pipelines. However, Dudaev's initiative was rebuffed.[18] Moscow also did not endorse Dudaev's summer 1993 attempts to bring foreign investment to Chechnya through the United Nations Industrial Development Organization (UNIDO).[19] When Dudaev fell in 1993, Yeltsin claimed that he did not see "a place for the Chechen republic outside the single economic, political and legal space" of the CIS.[20]

Russian authorities also dismissed a strategy of transforming the northern part of Chechnya (the Nadterechnyi district controlled since 1994 by the pro-Moscow opposition to Dudaev) into a showcase of successful integration with Russia by allocating money from the federal budget to pay salaries and by investing in the local economy. Such a plan, advocated by Emil Payin, head of the presidential advisory group on Chechnya, had been designed to influence the Chechen population through positive incentives and lead them to reject independence and poverty in favor of reunification with Russia.[21] Later, during both of the Chechen wars, Moscow failed to make use of economic aid to win over the civilian population and instead opted to treat the residents of Chechnya as criminals.

Moscow's record in providing economic incentives to Dudaev's successor, Aslan Maskhadov, during 1996–99 was only marginally better. If Moscow's unwillingness to bolster the unpredictable Dudaev regime can be easily understood, its indifference and hostility to the legitimately elected Maskhadov who pushed for normalization of economic relations with Russia was definitely a major mistake. It contributed to the quick descent of Chechnya's de facto independence into a full-blown anarchy by 1999 with the growing influence of radical Islam groups within Chechnya.

In May 1997 Maskhadov signed a number of economic agreements with Russia, and the then Russian Security Council Secretary Rybkin was willing to give Grozny a share of tariff revenues from oil exports going through Chechnya—essentially resurrecting Dudaev's 1992 proposal. In July of 1997 Azerbaijani President Aliev signed an agreement in Moscow allowing the shipment of Caspian oil through Chechnya with the support of British Petroleum. In October 1997 the Chechen government signed an agreement with potential British investors to restore the Chechen oil complex, and in April 1998 Maskhadov gained the support of all of the leaders of the North Caucasus republics as well as Georgia and Azerbaijan for the common oil market project.

However, the period of high hopes for Chechnya's quick integration into the regional system of oil production—the cornerstone of Maskhadov's vision for the future of his country's economy—lasted only a short time. Plans for transshipments of oil across Chechnya were killed by Russian-Chechen disagreements over transit fees. As a result of these disagreements in September 1997, Moscow announced plans to construct a new pipeline across Dagestan to North Ossetia, threatening to cut Chechnya out of Russian deals involving Caspian oil. In March of 1999, in an attempt to pressure Moscow, the Maskhadov government halted the shipment of Azerbaijani oil through the Chechen sector of the Baku-Grozny-Novorossiisk pipeline, a move that disrupted economic talks with the Kremlin. At the same time Western governments' enthusiasm for economic operations involving Chechnya was once again undermined by a spate of kidnappings of Western citizens organized by factions opposing Maskhadov.[22] In addition, most of the funds allocated by Moscow to improve economic and social conditions in Chechnya never reached the republic but instead were embezzled by the Russian bureaucracy. To make matters worse, Russian authorities did not attempt to crack down on the activities of the Chechen mafia groups in Moscow and other major cities that served as an important economic base for Islamic militants opposing Maskhadov. In early 1999 both Alexander Lebed, the former Russian security councilor who worked out an agreement ending the first war, and the presidential envoy to Chechnya, Valentin Vlasov, accused the Yeltsin government of not providing enough economic and political support to Maskhadov and warned of the tragic consequences of Maskhadov's possible loss of power to his radical opposition.[23] Lebed and Vlasov's fears became reality in a matter of months when Maskhadov condoned Basaev's incursion into Dagestan.

With the start of Putin's Chechenization policy in 2000, Moscow finally attempted to bolster the position of Akhmad Kadyrov—its chosen candidate for Chechen leadership—by providing full political support. However, as in the case of his predecessors, the Kremlin did not seem to care much about Kadyrov's economic record. For 2000–2004, Moscow allocated only 62 billion rubles ($2 billion) for the restoration of Chechnya. By contrast, the Russian government spent nearly 40 billion rubles on the sumptuous celebration of the 300th anniversary of the founding of St. Petersburg—Putin's native city.[24] Moreover, only a small fraction of the sum allocated for Chechnya actually reached the Chechen treasury.[25] Chechnya's unemployment rate currently still remains the highest among Russia's regions. For example, in the spring of 2005, according to official statistics, around 70 percent of working-age Chechens were unemployed. In today's Chechnya and in today's North Caucasus there are few employment opportunities aside from pervasively corrupt law enforcement organs, the narcotics trade, terrorism, and war.[26]

Under such circumstances there is little wonder that Kadyrov was widely perceived as a corrupt and self-serving puppet of Moscow. His ruthlessness and reliance on death squad tactics did not eliminate but rather stimulated resistance to his rule. The recent dramatic upsurge of fragmented unorganized violence and terrorist activities within Chechnya is largely motivated by families taking revenge on the regime for the murder of close relatives by Kadyrov's private army.

RUSSIAN POLITICS AND THE INSTRUMENTAL
USE OF THE CHECHEN CONFLICT

The circumstances behind the outbreak of the second Chechen war strongly suggest that the Russian political and economic elite used the Chechen conflict to ensure their political and economic power. Chechen rebel incursions in Dagestan coincided with the power transition in Moscow orchestrated by the representative of Yeltsin's inner circle. Having selected Vladimir Putin as their guarantor of personal safety, Yeltsin's entourage bolstered the new leader's popularity by escalating the Chechen conflict. The image of Russia's new head of the government (Putin was confirmed by the Duma as Prime Minister on August 16, 1999) played on the pervasive feelings of fear and vulnerability of the Russian public in the wake of the Dagestan incursion. It portrayed the youthful and vigorous Putin as a "strong hand" committed to "defending the population from bandits" by tough and uncompromising measures.

On September 30, 1999, federal troops entered Chechnya to conduct "antiterrorist operations." The plan was to move the Russian army to the Terek River to create a buffer zone between the pro-Russian and separatist regions of Chechnya while launching surgical strikes on terrorist bases.

However, Putin and his supporters evidently could not resist the temptation to cross the Terek and unleash a large-scale war with mass bombings of the Chechen territory. As Putin's popularity ratings skyrocketed at home, Russian military actions led to thousands of Chechen casualties among civilians and the creation of tens of thousands of new refugees. Despite the unfolding humanitarian catastrophe, the second Chechen war became a focal point for the consolidation of Russian society behind Putin's regime, paving the way for his confident performance in the winter 1999 parliamentary elections and easy victory in the March 2000 presidential marathon. He did this despite the lack of a coherent political and economic program.[27]

Since 2000 Chechnya was repeatedly used as a justification for Putin's centralization of the state power in Russia. Most visibly, the Beslan tragedy in September 2004 provided Putin an opportunity for advancing his long-discussed proposal on stopping regional elections and introducing the system of presidential appointment of regional governors.

CONCLUSION: REINTEGRATION?

Putin's landslide reelection to a second term in March 2004 and Kadyrov's assassination in May of 2004 inaugurated important changes in Moscow's policies in Chechnya. Putin's tough approach to the Chechen crisis was instrumental in his rise and consolidation of power. Now, however, continuing Russian military losses together with the prospect of terrorist acts in Moscow and other major cities prompt Putin and his inner circle to search for a less conflictual solution in Chechnya. The assassination of Kadyrov served as a key indicator that the policy of "Chechenization"—based on a reliable proxy government in the region associated with a reduction in Russian forces—is unlikely to work if Chechen economic problems are not addressed.

During his secret visit to Grozny in the wake of Kadyrov's assassination, Putin was reportedly shocked by the scale of destruction after a decade of war.[28] Shortly afterwards he called for a "radical modernization" of the Kremlin's policy in the North Caucasus, centering his attention on the collapsed economy of the region, unemployment, and poverty as conditions conducive to the spread of radical Islam.[29] Putin's belated attention to the depth of the regional economic and social crisis was influenced by the grim assessment of his representative, Dimitri Kozak, of the situation there.

Kozak's working group's summer 2005 "Report on the Situation in the Republic of Dagestan and Measures for Its Stabilization" presented a stark portrayal of economic negligence and desperation in the North Caucasus. Despite the fact that federal budget assistance to the Southern Federal District has increased 3.4 times and regional consolidated budgets have grown 2.6 times in recent years, the gross domestic product of the region failed to increase. It remained at half the national average while unemployment dramatically rose. According to estimates of the Kozak commission, criminalization of the district remains unusually high with around 26 percent of the economy belonging to the "shadow criminal sector."[30] The report especially pointed to Dagestan as a potential fertile ground for another Caucasus war, arguing that the republic's unresolved socioeconomic and political difficulties (high unemployment, corruption, inefficiency of state power, and rising Islamic radicalism) created major problems. He observed that "further ignoring the problems and attempts to drive them deep down by force could lead to an uncontrolled chain of events whose logical results will be open social, interethnic and religious conflicts in Dagestan."[31] Chechnya's problems were beginning to spill over to its neighbors.

While Putin is now paying attention, Moscow's strategy of reintegrating Chechnya and the North Caucasus into Russia is still not clearly defined. On the one hand, as Putin has repeatedly stated, Moscow is committed to signing a long-awaited agreement with Chechnya on the division of powers between the federal and local authorities, providing the republic "with a large degree of autonomy."[32] However, in the summer of 2005 negotiations between Moscow and Kadyrov's successor, Alu Alkhanov, failed to reach an agreement on Chechen demands for exclusive control over its natural resources for a decade.[33] While the details of tensions between Moscow and Alkhanov's regime have not emerged at the time of writing, disagreements are likely, due to Moscow's fears that Grozny's formal control over oil would create new opportunities for corruption and embezzlement among the Chechen elite and complicit federal officials.[34]

With negotiations deadlocked, the Kremlin was seriously deliberating imposition of direct presidential rule over the North Caucasus. One of Kozak's suggestions was that the autonomy of Russian regions should depend upon their degree of independence from federal subsidies or, as he put it, "whoever gives money should administer it. If you want to avoid restrictions, you must start earning and create a tax base." Kozak recommended that the Russian parliament pass legislation taking most economic powers from those regions which depend upon Moscow for 70–80 percent of their revenues (including Chechnya, Dagestan, Ingushetia, Kabardino-Balkaria, and Karachaevo-Cherkessiya).[35] One of his hopes was that centralization would limit the embezzlement of public funds, bribe-taking, and corruption otherwise rampant in the region.[36] Kozak's North Caucasus plan also seemed to dovetail with the logic of Putin's recent "power for development" idea based on transferring 100 federal powers to the governors of Russia's regions as a reward for the creation of successful socioeconomic programs.

In view of his doubts about Chechnya's new leadership and their ability to bring fragmented political forces together and considering Chechnya's persistent record as a "black hole" for Russian budgetary transfers, Putin may well favor direct presidential rule over Chechnya and the rest of the Caucasus. He needs to achieve one strategic goal: diffusing the threat of economic and political collapse in the North Caucasus by massive investment aimed at a rapid and visible rise of the population's living standards.[37] However, in order to fulfill this vital task, Putin and his team will need to rely not only on the federal bureaucracy but also on the support of the Russian business elite. If organized and managed wisely, a large-scale project restoring a vital part of the Russian Federation to normal economic growth might also become a model for a long-term economic and social recovery of other underdeveloped Russian regions.

RUSSIAN ASPIRATIONS

Over the longer term, Russian policy aims to assure the continued viability of the Russian Federation within its current borders, ruling out independence for any part of the North Caucasus region. Second, Putin seeks to remove Chechnya from the list of problematic relationships Russia has had with the European Union and the United States. The steps he put in place for the referendum in Chechnya and the amnesty act which he guided through the Duma move in the right direction to achieve this goal. The shift from military to political solutions also adds credibility to the process both domestically and internationally. While centuries-long conflicts seldom lend themselves to a single outcome, the motivation of the Russian Government and the change in both the international situation (favoring the struggle against terrorism) and the conditions within Chechnya all contribute to aligning the stars toward an eventual and sustainable peace between Russia and Chechnya.

The Chechen case serves as an interesting counterpoint to the typical effects of globalization on national self-determination. In one sense Chechnya rejects Moscow-style globalization and wishes to go on its own. In another way, however, Chechen elites have used criminal globalization networks to carry on their struggle for autonomy. Like the Mafia in other countries, Chechens are well schooled in globalization's techniques. To the degree that they also have penetrated Russian networks, Chechens may even prefer their ability to meddle and intervene in Russian society to fully acknowledged international independence and a smaller field of operation.

NOTES

1. "Putin Calls for Bolstering Southern Border," *Chechnya Weekly* (The Jamestown Foundation), vol. 6, no. 28 (July 20, 2005). It should be noted that the participants in recent terrorist acts are no longer exclusively Chechens. For example, the hostage-takers in Beslan included Ingush and residents of other regions of the North Caucasus. Ingush extremists were also a driving force behind a murderous raid on the Ingushetian city of Nazran in June 2004.

2. Pavel K. Bayev, "As Chechnya Braces for New Violence, Putin Retreats into Denial," *Chechnya Weekly*, vol. 6, no. 14 (April 6, 2005).

3. According to some recent attempts to calculate the cost of the Chechen war, Russia spends annually at least $1–1.5 billion on military operations. See Andrei Arkhipov, "What the War in Chechnya Costs Russia," *Zhurnalist*, no. 7, 2005.

4. Georgi M. Derluginian, "Ethnofederalism and Ethonationalism in the Separatist Politics of Chechnya and Tatarstan: Sources or Resources?" *International Journal of Public Administration*, vol. 22, no. 9–10 (1999), 1417. Quoted in Matthew Evangelista, *The Chechen Wars: Will Russia Go the Way of the Soviet Union?* (Washington, DC: Brookings Institution Press, 2002), 29.

5. Georgi Derluginian, "The Structures of Chechnya's Quagmire," PONARS Policy Memo 309 (November 2003).

6. This is one of the central conclusions of an influential ethnographic study of the Chechen crisis. See Valery Tishkov, *Obshestvo v Vooruzhennom Konflikte. Etnografiya Chechenskoi Voiny* [*Society in Armed Conflict: Ethnography of the Chechen War*] (Moscow: Nauka, 2001), 51–56.

7. For an overview of the Chechen mafia activities in Moscow see Paul Klebnikov, *Godfather of the Kremlin: Boris Berezovski and the Looting of Russia* (New York: Harcourt, Inc., 2000), 13–15.

8. Emil' Payin and Arkadii Popov, "Russian Politics in Chechnya," *Izvestiya*, 8 February 1995, p. 4.

9. For the results of the recently finished investigation of the notorious "Chechen avizo" fraud see www.compromat.ru/main/checha/avizo.htm.

10. Anatol Lieven, *Chechnya: Tombstone of Russian Power* (New Haven: Yale University Press, 1998), 74–75.

11. "The Lost Cause of the Caucasus—Russia and Chechnya," *The Economist*, November 2, 2002.

12. See John B. Dunlop, *Russia Confronts Chechnya: Roots of a Separatist Conflict* (Cambridge: Cambridge University Press, 1998), 128–34.

13. Evangelista, *The Chechen Wars*, 49, 56–59.

14. Ariel Cohen, "After Maskhadov: Islamist Terrorism Threatens North Caucasus and Russia," *Backgrounder* (The Heritage Foundation), no. 1838, April 1, 2005.

15. The Prosecutor-General's Office of Russia has completed the investigation into the explosions of apartment blocks in Moscow and Volgodonsk in September 1999. The investigation found out that Arab militants Khattab and Amu Umar were the organizers of the terrorist acts. *Ria-Novosti*, April 30, 2003.

16. See Dunlop, *Russia Confronts Chechnya*, 85–88; and Evangelista, *The Chechen Wars*, 20–21.

17. For example, after liberalization of prices in Russia in January 1992 Dudaev opted to retain price controls, despite the fact that Chechnya remained in the ruble zone. As a result, most of the local products wound up being resold outside the Chechen borders, leading immediately to almost universal shortages within the republic.

18. Yurii M. Baturin, et al., *Epokha Yeltsina: Ocherki Politicheskoi Istorii [The Yeltsin Epoch: Sketches of a Political History]* (Moscow: Vagrius, 2001), 588–89.

19. Taimaz Abubakarov, *Rezhim Dzhokhara Dudaeva: Pravda I Vymysel. Zapiski Dudaevskogo Ministra Ekonomiki I Finansov [The Regime of Dzhokhar Dudaev: Truth and Myths. Notes of Dudaev's Minister of Economics and Finance]* (Moscow: INSAN, 1998), 28.

20. Quoted in Gall and de Waal, *Chechnya: Calamity in the Caucasus* (New York: New York University Press, 1998), 121–22.

21. See Emil' A. Payin and Arkady A. Popov, "Chechnya," in Jeremy Azrael and Emil' Payin, eds., *U.S. and Russian Policymaking with Respect to the Use of Force* (Santa Monica, CA: RAND, 1996), 22–23.

22. Evangelista, *The Chechen Wars*, 51–56.

23. *RFE/RL Newsline*, vol. 3, no. 9, part 1, 14 January 1999, and no. 11, part 1, 18 January 1999.

24. John B. Dunlop, "Why Chechenization Will Likely Fail," *Chechnya Weekly*, vol. 6, no. 10 (March 9, 2005).

25. Robert Bruce Ware, "The Caucasian Vortex," *RFE/RL Newsline*, August 26, 2004.

26. Ibid.

27. For the detailed account of Putin's ascent see Lilia Shevtsova, *Putin's Russia* (Washington, DC: Carnegie Endowment for International Peace, 2005).

28. Russian Economic Development and Trade Minister Gref who accompanied Putin compared Grozny's main square to "a set from a Hollywood movie."

29. Liz Fuller and Julie Corwin, "Putin Reinvents the North Caucasus Wheel," *RFE/RL Newsline,* September 15, 2004.

30. *Chechnya Weekly* (The Jamestown Foundation), vol. 6, no. 24 (June 22, 2005).

31. "Dagestan: Can the Center Hold?" *Chechnya Weekly* (Jamestown Foundation), vol. 6, no. 27 (July 14, 2005); Shaun Walker, "Dagestan on the Edge? Growth in Vio-

lence and Instability in Southern Russian Republic," *Russia Profile* (www.russiaprofile.org), August 2, 2005.

32. *Kremlin Ru*, April 25, 2005.

33. *Kommersant*, June 7, 2005, quoted in *Chechnya Weekly*, vol. 6, no. 22 (June 8, 2005). In the spring of 2005 Alu Alkhanov complained that the Russian-state-owned oil company Rosneft was blocking the construction of a large oil-refining plant, which is widely viewed as one of the necessary immediate steps to lifting Chechnya's economy from crisis. John B. Dunlop, "Putin's Upbeat Message in Chechnya Contradicted by Realities on the Ground," *Chechnya Weekly*, vol. 6, no. 21 (June 1, 2005). On Chechnya's earlier economic demands see Liz Fuller, "Chechnya Spells Out Demands to Moscow," *RFE/RL Newsline*, January 27, 2005.

34. "Power Delimitation Treaty: A License to Steal?" *Chechnya Weekly*, vol. 6, no. 7 (February 16, 2005).

35. Yekaterina Grigorieva, Georgi Ilichev, Igor Naydenov, and Natalya Ratiani, "How the Vertical Hierarchy Was Tempered: President's Plenipotentiary Representative Dmitriy Kozak Introduces 'External Management' in Bankrupt Regions," *Izvestiya*, July 20, 2005.

36. *Gazeta.ru*, July 19, 2005.

37. Large-scale projects aimed at restoring Chechnya's destroyed infrastructure provide an obvious immediate opportunity for significantly lowering the unemployment rate.

9

The Status Quo in Kashmir?

Deepak Lal

The Kashmir dispute has led to three wars between India and Pakistan, a dangerous standoff between nuclear armed adversaries in 2002, and the spread of terrorism in both Kashmir and India. It is as old as the creation of the two successor states of India and Pakistan after the end of the British Raj in the subcontinent. To understand the seemingly intractable nature of the dispute and how it now might be solved, it is important to see its historical origins in the botched partition of British India, the twists and turns over the succeeding half a century in the Indo-Pak relationship, as well as the missed opportunities for a settlement in the aftermath of the Bangladesh war in 1971. This immediately follows. The next part of the chapter shows how a combination of Saudi-financed fundamentalism and the ham-fisted attempt to control the domestic politics of Kashmir by Indira Gandhi and her son Rajiv in the 1980s led to a "nationalist" insurrection, aided and abetted by both local Islamists and fundamentalist terrorists who infiltrated Kashmir and India. The final part of the chapter discusses how with the changed geopolitical situation in Central Asia and Afghanistan a solution might finally be found to this dispute.

THE HISTORY OF KASHMIR

With the opening of the British archives for the period covered by the transfer of power to the newly created dominions of India and Pakistan in 1947, a clear picture has emerged of the events which led to the Kashmir dispute.[1] In discussing these, certain aspects of the strategic importance of Kashmir and its unique culture need to be borne in mind.

The state of Jammu and Kashmir was one of the 556 princely states indirectly ruled by the British Raj. It consists of three distinct areas. A large Muslim majority area in the west, at the center of which the valley of Kashmir is located, is the most important. The Hindu-dominated area of Jammu in the south, and the predominantly Buddhist area to the west of Ladakh make up the total. Situated as it is on the borders of Afghanistan, China, and Tibet, and the vast plains of Central Asia to the north, Kashmir has always been of strategic interest to any power which maintained an empire on the Indo-Gangetic plain. The Kashmir valley itself is protected by high mountain ranges, and the passes through them are easily guarded. Also given the severity of winter at these high altitudes, the snows have often saved the valley from various intruders through its history. This relatively impregnable geography has allowed a distinctive cultural form called Kashmiriyat to develop.

The Kashmir valley, which had been predominantly Hindu, was converted to Sufi Islam in the 14th century. The syncretic Hindu-Muslim culture which resulted was a mixture of mystical Hindu Vedantism and Islamic Sufism. The concept of Kashmiriyat stresses the commonality between the Hindus and Muslims of the valley, as "there was enough in common between Vedantism and Sufism—the unity of the Divine, equality, rejection of both the ego and materialism, as well as idolatry—to make this possible."[2] Kashmiriyat is thus a culture of synthesis, understanding, and humanism. Thus whenever fundamentalists of either religion, supported by one of Kashmir's changing rulers, have sought to enforce their habits of the heart on the people, the Kashmiris have rebelled. Also, tellingly, Kashmir was the only part of India with a mixed Hindu-Muslim population which did not see communal rioting during the 1947 partition of the subcontinent.

Kashmir was incorporated into the Mogul empire by the Emperor Akbar in 1586. With the disintegration of the Mogul empire, it was briefly independent but was conquered in 1819 by the Sikh maharaja Ranjit Singh, who had established his kingdom in the Punjab. By the early 19th century the British had conquered much of northern India. In 1846 they divested Kashmir from the Sikh kingdom with the help of a Kashmiri Hindu called Gulab Singh. They then sold Kashmir to Gulab Singh for 7.5 million rupees. This created the Dogra state of Kashmir, ruled indirectly by the British, which was to last till the granting of Indian independence in 1947.

The rise of the freedom movement in India, during the early part of the 20th century, also spread to Kashmir. Its chief spokesman and icon was Sheikh Abdullah. His grandfather was a Hindu, a Brahmin Kashmiri Pandit. The family had converted to Islam in 1776 under the influence of a Sufi saint. Abdullah was thus the embodiment of Kashmiriyat. He converted the sectarian Muslim Conference, which sought democratization of the rule of the Hindu Dogra dynasty, into a more broad-based National Conference. This nationalist party, unlike its predecessor, allowed anyone to join, "irrespective of their caste, creed or religion."

The National Conference joined the Indian nationalist struggle spearheaded by the Congress party in India. Abdullah did not support the "two-nation" theory propounded by the Muslim League led by Ali Jinnah. He had formed a personal link with the Kashmiri Pandit, Jawaharlal Nehru, being attracted by his aim of creating a secular, socialist, independent India. Abdullah was to play a major role in the various twists and turns in the subsequent Kashmir dispute.

The dispute arose as soon as the British announced in early 1947 that they would depart on 15 August 1947 and be succeeded by the two successor states of India and Pakistan. As they would no longer be able to support the various Indian princes who owed allegiance to the Crown, they advised them to accede to whichever of the successor states they wished—it being recognized that territorial contiguity and the wishes of their subjects should be determining factors. They also instructed a British judge Sir Cyril Radcliffe to draw up the boundary between the two successor states in six weeks (between 8 July and 16 August 1947). Both decisions were to be the source of the Kashmir dispute.

Most of the princely states acceded to one or the other state because of their territorial contiguity and the religious propinquity of both the population and the rulers to one or the other of the successor states. There were exceptions. Junagadh, in Gujarat, which was one of the patchwork princely states surrounded by neighbors who had acceded to India, and which like Hyderabad in central India had a predominantly Hindu population but a Muslim ruler, and Kashmir, which was also contiguous with both India and Pakistan and which had a Hindu ruler and a predominantly Muslim population. On 15 August 1947 the Nawab of Junagadh announced that he had decided to accede to Pakistan. The Indians proposed that, as the population was primarily non-Muslim, the people's views should be ascertained in regard to the accession. There was no response from Pakistan, which waited till 13 September to inform India that it had accepted Junagadh's accession. This led to mass protest movements in Junagadh and the neighboring princely states, whose rulers had acceded to India. They demanded armed action from India. Rather foolishly the Nawab of Junagadh then occupied two areas in adjoining princely states which had acceded to India, but over which the Nawab claimed suzerainty. This led to the Indian government sending a small force to restore Indian civil administration in these two areas. Meanwhile the agitation in Junagadh became uncontrollable and the Nawab fled to Karachi, and his Dewan (Prime Minister) asked India to also take over the administration of Junagadh. Thus Junagadh was incorporated into the Indian Union. Pakistan has always seen this as an illegitimate action, particularly because in Kashmir, a Hindu ruler's accession despite a majority Muslim population was not allowed to be overturned.

The Hindu Maharaja of Kashmir, Hari Singh, had played a waiting game and had not acceded to either of the two successor states at the date of partition. He hoped to create an independent kingdom. He had imprisoned Sheikh Abdullah on the eve of the transfer of power by the Raj, because of the agitation he had launched for democratic rights in Kashmir. By September 1947 the Maharaja had realized the impracticability of an independent Kashmir, and decided to offer accession to India on the condition that he not be asked to immediately institute the democratic reforms demanded by Abdullah and his National Conference. Under pressure from India he did release Abdullah from prison but dragged his feet on granting democratic rights and thus handing power to Abdullah. The impasse over accession continued till the end of October.

On 21 October Pakistan, suspecting that the Maharaja was likely to accede to India, decided to take Kashmir by force. But there was a problem. As part of the partition of the subcontinent, the armed forces were divided among the two successor states, which included British officers on both sides. One of the primary purposes of Lord Mountbatten, who with the ending of his Viceroyalty became the Governor General of India, was to prevent open war between the two successor states, as that would have put the British officers in the armies of both countries in the invidious position of fighting each other. Not being able openly to use his armed forces, Jinnah personally authorized a plan to launch "a clandestine invasion by a force composed of Pathan (Afghan) tribesmen, ex-servicemen and soldiers on leave."[3] With the raiders at the gates of Srinagar, the Maharaja, Hari Singh, appealed to the Indian government for military help. But he was told this could not be provided till he had acceded to India. This was duly done on 26 October with the Maharaja agreeing to Sheikh Abdullah forming an interim government. The Indian government also agreed that once law and order had been restored, the will of the people would be ascertained about the accession. The Indians then airlifted a battalion to Srinagar, and the first Indo-Pak war began. It ended with the cease-fire, in which Pakistani forces obtained a substantial chunk of the western part of the state contiguous to its borders. This cease-fire line has been the de facto border in Kashmir between India and Pakistan ever since.

PAKISTAN'S VERSION

Against this historically validated account, Pakistan has maintained that there was a spontaneous uprising in Kashmir because of the Hindu maharaja's policies of "ethnic cleansing." This, and Kashmir's accession to India, inflamed Pathan tribesmen who came to the assistance of their coreligionists. It has also claimed that the accession to India was illegal, and due to a plot by India which was aided and abetted by Lord Mountbatten to tie Kashmir to India and prevent its accession to Pakistan. The evidence for this is claimed to be provided by the award of three small areas in the Gurdaspur district of Punjab by the Radcliffe Boundary Commission to India, despite the fact that Gurdaspur had a small Muslim majority and the interim boundary in the Punjab had placed it in Pakistan. The granting of this area to India allowed a land link to Kashmir which made its accession to India possible. Whether Mountbatten influenced Sir Cyril Radcliffe to grant Gurdaspur to India under prodding from Nehru still remains disputed, as Radcliffe left no notes and never spoke about the matter. But, from a note left by his secretary Christopher Beaumont and published in 1992, there is some circumstantial evidence that Mountbatten might have influenced Sir Cyril's decision.

BRITISH REVISIONS

But the Pakistani claim that there was a British plot to give Kashmir to India to prevent the southward expansion of the Soviet Union through Central Asia turns out to be the exact opposite of the truth. This has now been revealed by British official documents. The protection of the northern borders of Kashmir had been a part of the geostrategic objectives of the Raj since the days of the 19th century Great Game. It sought to deny an expansionist Russian empire access to a warm water port in the Arabian Sea. But the rise of air power changed the geostrategic picture. Whereas, previously, the threat from the North from Russia was a few months' march away, with the rise of air power it was only a matter of a few hours. With Britain's 1947 decision to leave India, Palmerston's Forward Policy—to protect the Indian empire from threats from the north and the west—lost much of its relevance. But London still had important strategic interests in the Indian Ocean and in the Gulf and Iran, particularly because of oil, the new fuel on which Western prosperity increasingly depended. Thus from 1946, when the Defense Council prepared a note for Attlee on Britain's strategic interests in the subcontinent, a note which was used to brief Mountbatten when he was sent out as India's last Viceroy, it is clear that "Britain's strategic interests in 'the Indian ocean and neighbouring area' would be served . . . if the treaty (with the successor government) allowed the British 'to move formations and units, particularly air units, into India at short notice.'"[4] With the recognition that India could not be kept united after the failure of the Cabinet mission, the British felt that this strategic objective might not be met, particularly as they felt that the Indian National Congress which was to come to power in New Delhi would be hostile to this aim.

In 1945 Lord Archibald Wavell produced a "breakdown plan" which proposed that "if an interim government could not be formed, the British should abandon the Congress-dominated provinces and move British government and personnel to the Muslim-dominated ones in the north east and north west of the country."[5] A variant of this Wavell plan, which required close military links with Pakistan, was the only one available after a unitary India proved impossible to maintain. "With the empire gone, Britain's interests in the neighborhood centered around the protection of its sphere of influence from Egypt to Iran. That coincided with the incipient American desire to create a 'cordon sanitaire' around the Soviet Union, which flowered into the pacts of encirclement signed by the USA in the early fifties. But the achievement of both these goals required bolstering Pakistan and absorbing Kashmir into the dominion. Kashmir was to have been the eastern end of a crescent that stretched from NATO to the roof of the Himalayas."[6]

By contrast, once India was partitioned, the shield provided by the Himalayas for the earlier Indian empires became irrelevant. This shield had already been breached with the creation of Pakistan. The enemy now was well within the gates. It was the Indo-Pak border which became the first and last line of strategic defense. This explains why India, and in particular the powerful Indian home minister Sardar Patel, was at best lukewarm about the accession of Kashmir to India. It was no longer strategically important for India. Nor was India itself seen as being of strategic importance by the West, particularly when it veered towards a deepening military and economic relationship with the Soviet Union.

Pakistan, by contrast, was seen as an essential strategic ally by the West in providing the bases for the exertion of air power in the region to contain Soviet Russia, as well as to protect the vital oil supplies of the Middle East. This explains why with Pakistan's 1955 signing of the Baghdad Pact, allowing the Peshawar airbase for U2 espionage flights, as well as a base to dislodge the Soviet Union from Afghanistan in exchange for military and economic aid, Pakistan has been of much greater strategic importance to the West than has India, a factor reinforced both by Nehru's admiration for the forced industrialization of the Soviet Union and by the West's subsequent close relationship with the enemy of its enemy.

In this tangled story, the big mistake made by Nehru was to take Mountbatten's advice, and that of Noel-Baker, the British Secretary of the Commonwealth Relations Office, to raise the issue of the Pakistani invasion at the United Nations in January 1948. After the military stalemate on the ground in Kashmir in the winter of 1947, India wanted to extend the war directly to the Pakistani heartland by crossing the international border in Punjab, where with its military superiority it could easily have defeated the "aggressor." Given Mountbatten's desire to prevent an inter-dominion conflict, in which British officers commanding the rival armies would have been involved, he suggested that, instead, the Indians should take their case to the United Nations. Here the UN decided to treat the countries on a par, and resolved that once the Pakistani raiders had vacated the one-third of Kashmir they had occupied, a plebiscite should be held to ascertain the people's will about accession. Because the occupied territory was never vacated, India has argued that there can be no plebiscite. This mistake in taking the issue to the UN has meant that, subsequently, India has refused any attempt to internationalize the dispute.

DE FACTO DIVISION

The most important long-term outcome of the first Indo-Pak war was that the cease-fire line established on January 1, 1949, has subsequently held for over fifty years as the de facto border in Kashmir, through subsequent periods of war and peace. This de facto extension of its borders has been of strategic importance for Pakistan. If the whole of Kashmir had gone to India, the essential rail and road link between its two major cities of Lahore and Rawalpindi would have been under threat. Also, with undivided Kashmir having a border contiguous with Afghanistan to the north, India could have intervened to prevent Pakistan from pacifying the tribes in the always unruly North-West Frontier Province. But Pakistan has not been satisfied with these strategic gains. Its domestic politics have pressed it to continue attempts to secure the Kashmir valley. With the West's strategic interest in propping up Pakistan, India has been unable to settle the dispute by force of arms, a route further blocked once the two countries became nuclear powers in the 1990s. Nor has the West, until recently, been willing to put pressure on Pakistan to settle the dispute, by recognizing the 1949 cease-fire line as both the de facto as well as de jure border between the two countries. This may now be changing. Meanwhile, given its past experience with the United Nations, India has continued to resist any international mediation in the dispute.

There was, however, one moment in the last fifty years when India could have in effect converted this de facto into a de jure border, putting an end to the issue. This occurred after the Bangladesh war fought by India and Pakistan in 1971. At the conclusion of the war, and with the Indian detachment from Pakistan of its eastern province into the new state of Bangladesh, India had captured a large number of Pakistani soldiers and also territory across the international border. Zulfiqar Bhutto, who had become President of Pakistan, met Indira Gandhi in Simla to conclude an agreement and to settle the issue of Pakistani prisoners of war, as well as the territory India had acquired in the now truncated Pakistan. In exchange for the POWs and Pakistani territory India could have insisted on the cease-fire line becoming the international border. But Indira Gandhi let Bhutto off the hook, and the Simla Agreement which she concluded with Bhutto merely converted the cease-fire line into what is called today the "line of control" (LOC). India returned the Pakistani POWs and Pakistani territory, and both countries agreed to deal with Kashmir on a bilateral basis.

This agreement has puzzled many. But we now know what transpired, from a two-part article published in *The Times of India* in April 1995 by Mrs. Gandhi's economic advisor, and subsequently the head of the Prime Minister's Office, Prof. P. N. Dhar, who was present at the Simla meeting. The full account is now set out in his memoirs.[7] The Indians sought and got Bhutto to agree, after a near breakdown to the talks, that "the Indian proposal [to settle the Kashmir dispute] was the only feasible one."[8] "The transformation of the cease-fire line into the line of control was the core of the Indian solution to the Kashmir problem. The de facto line of control was meant to be upgraded to the level of a de jure border."[9] But Bhutto was adamant that he could not agree to incorporate this into the written Simla Agreement because of the imperatives of domestic Pakistani politics. Dhar writes:

> Bhutto was personally inclined to accept the status quo as a permanent solution of the Kashmir problem. However he had several constraints in this regard which he spelt out as follows: (a) His political enemies at home, especially the army bosses, would denounce him for surrendering what many in Pakistan considered their vital national interest. This would endanger the democratic set-up which had emerged after fourteen years of army rule. In this context, Bhutto repeatedly talked about his fear of what he called the Lahore lobby, though he never clearly explained what it was. (b) He was anxious to obtain the support of all political elements in Pakistan in favor of any agreement that might emerge at Simla.[10]

The Indian side, in particular the then head of the PMO, P. N. Haksar, was sympathetic to Bhutto's claim that a formal acceptance of the status quo would nurture a revanchist ideology in Pakistan, and as with the Versailles Treaty would be looked upon as the imposition of harsh terms by the victors which could lead to another war. "Mrs. Gandhi herself was worried that a formal withdrawal of the Indian claim on Pakistan-occupied Kashmir could create political trouble for her. She agreed that the solution should not be recorded in the agreement for the reasons advanced by Bhutto, but it should be implemented gradually, as he had suggested."[11]

That this account of the secret verbal agreement is true is shown by a report filed by the *New York Times* correspondent James P. Sterba within hours of the signing of the Simla Agreement. Sterba, who was close to the Pakistani delegation and was briefed by them, wrote:

> President Bhutto, Pakistan's first civilian leader in fourteen years, came to Simla ready to compromise. According to sources close to him, he was willing to forsake

the Indian-held two-thirds of Kashmir that contains four-fifths of the population and the prized valley called the "Vale," and agree that a ceasefire line to be negotiated would gradually become the border between the two countries. The key word is "gradually." . . . President Bhutto wants a softening of the ceasefire line with trade and travel across it and a secret agreement with Mrs. Gandhi that a formally recognized border would emerge after a few years, during which he would condition his people to it without riots and an overthrow of his government.[12]

When Dhar revealed the secret verbal agreement in 1995, there was a furious Pakistani response. "About the only person in authority who did not respond was Pakistan's Prime Minister, Benazir Bhutto." She was with her father in Simla and must have known about the text.

But this secret agreement depended upon both the protagonists remaining in power. Bhutto was deposed by his army chief Zia-ul-Haq (who subsequently hanged him), while Mrs. Gandhi lost the election which ended the Emergency in 1977. Thus the foolish Indian gamble on settling the dispute with the unwritten part of the Simla Agreement failed. But it still offers the only viable solution to the long-standing and continuing Kashmir dispute.

DOMESTIC POLITICS

Domestic politics in both Kashmir and Pakistan were to complicate the picture even further in the 1980s, laying the ground for the bloody insurrection aided and abetted by army-backed infiltrators from Pakistan (as in 1947). It began in Kashmir in 1989, and still engulfs the state, while raising the danger of a nuclear war between India and Pakistan. Central to this is the story of Sheikh Abdullah, as well as one of the consequences of the OPEC coup in raising oil prices in 1973.

In his accession agreement Maharaja Hari Singh had inserted a clause which in effect gave Kashmir considerable autonomy. It was to be governed by the Jammu and Kashmir Act of 1939, with Delhi's jurisdiction extending only to external affairs, defense, and communications. Sheikh Abdullah too agreed that Kashmir should continue to be ruled by its own laws, but these should be devised by a new Kashmiri Constituent Assembly. The special status of Kashmir, granting it considerable autonomy within the Indian Union, was confirmed by Article 370 of the Constitution of India. This special status for Kashmir had been a bone of contention with the Hindu nationalist party, the Jan Sangh, and its descendant, the current Bhartiya Janata Party (BJP).

By 1949, after meeting various Western ambassadors, Sheikh Abdullah formed the impression that the West would support an independent Kashmir. He then began a tussle with New Delhi, wanting it to stick by the strict terms of the letter of accession, against the Indian desire to integrate Kashmir further into its secular democracy. In July 1953 he made a speech advocating independence for Kashmir. This was too much for Nehru, who put his old friend in jail. In January 1957 Kashmir approved its own Constitution, which among other things ratified the accession of Kashmir to India, and as far as India was concerned ended all discussions about the plebiscite that India had offered in the past. But Abdullah claimed that the Kashmiri Constituent Assembly no longer represented the will of the people. Thus the demand for a plebiscite was even more justified. Freed in 1964, he began to toy with the idea of a confederation between India, Pakistan, and an independent Kashmir. Nehru seemed to be attracted by the proposal, but Pakistan would have nothing to do with it. After Nehru's death, Abdullah was reported to have met Chou En-lai to further his plan for Kashmiri independence. The outcry caused by this hobnobbing with India's enemy, China, which had inflicted a humiliating defeat in 1962, led Nehru's successor Shastri to arrest Abdullah once again in 1965. He was to remain in jail till the end of the Bangladesh war in 1971. The Indian victory convinced Abdullah that he could no longer get much joy from Pakistan. He gave up his demand for a plebiscite and accepted the ratification of the accession by the Kashmir Constituent Assembly. In the subsequent elections in 1977, notable for being free and fair, he won handsomely against the Congress and the extremist Hindu and Muslim parties. But by 1982 he was dead.

The politics of Kashmir in the 1980s is one of rigged elections, with the Congress party attempting to gain control over the State, splits within the National Conference, corruption, and misgovernment. But there was a darker cloud which had been gathering on the horizon since the OPEC oil price coup of 1973. The massive rise in oil prices brought untold wealth to Saudi Arabia—the home of the virulent Islam of the Wahhabis. They began spending part of their newfound wealth on promoting their version of Islam. A fundamentalist Islamic group "the Jamat-I-Islami" was able to set up about 600 madrasas (religious schools) in Kashmir with the help of Saudi and Gulf money. These new institutions were staffed with trained cadres of the Jamat from UP and Bihar, whose goal was to produce a new generation of Kashmiri Muslims who would forsake the more tolerant version of their forefathers' religion and minimize attachment to a Kashmir identity. Sure of the success of his efforts, the Amir of the Jamat-I-Islami of Kashmir told an Indian journalist in 1973: "we will produce a generation of New Muslims in Kashmir in fifteen years."[13] And they did.

GROWTH OF ISLAMIC MILITANCY

The strength of the growing Islamic militants, who demanded the separation of an "Islamic" Kashmir from a "Hindu" India, was shown in May 1989, when their call for a boycott was widely obeyed. The inroads they had made into Kashmir were further shown by the massive implicit endorsement of the militants in the elections of November 1989, which they asked the electorate to boycott. Only 5 percent voted. After having capitulated to the demands of the militants who had kidnapped the daughter of the Indian home minister, Mufti Mohammed Sayeed, the most powerful Kashmiri Muslim in independent India's history, the Indian government decided that it was time to get tough with the militants. On the night of January 18, 1990, Indian paramilitary forces began the most intense house-to-house search seen in Srinagar. Till then support for the separatists demanding independence was implicit not explicit. The heavy-handed searches ordered by the new Governor of Kashmir, Jagmohan, changed that.

First, frightened, and then discovering the courage of desperation, the people began pouring out into the streets that day. The most startling presence was that of women, old, middle-aged, young. The administration got completely unnerved and gave orders to fire. The number is disputed, but there is no doubt that paramilitary bullets left more than fifty dead. . . . 19 January became the catalyst which propelled [the demand for independence] into a mass upsurge. Young men from hundreds of homes crossed over into Pak-occupied Kashmir to receive training in insurrection. Benazir Bhutto, her support base wiped out by malfeasance and misrule, desperate to save herself, whipped out the Kashmir card. . . . Pakistan came out in open support of secession, and for the first time did not need to involve its regular troops in the confrontation. In Srinagar, each mosque became a citadel of fervour; the khutba became a sermon in secession.[14]

A long period of protest, violence, repression, and curfew followed, with the nationalist fire being fueled by cross-border Islamist terrorists, for whom Kashmir had become as much an Islamic cause as Bosnia, Chechnya, and Afghanistan. The terrorism, much of it masterminded and funded by the Pakistani intelligence services, spilled over into India, with the most audacious of the terrorist attacks being the failed attempt to wipe out virtually the entire Indian political class in the attack on the Indian parliament in December 1991. This led to the tense confrontation between the two countries with full mobilization of their forces on the borders, which only came to an end after some nuclear saber-rattling in June 2002.

TOWARD A SETTLEMENT?

The subsequent state elections in Kashmir held in 2003 were the fairest and cleanest after 1975. The large turnout despite the militants' demands for a boycott showed that perhaps the militant tide had turned. The elections returned the same Mufti Mohammed Sayeed as Chief Minister, whose daughter's kidnapping had led to the series of events which caused the 1989 insurrection. He won on a platform of reconciliation. Together, with the announcement of talks between India's Hindu hard-line BJP Home Minister, L. K. Advani, and the various moderate secessionist groups in the valley gathered in the umbrella party the Hurriyat, there is some hope that the Indian government will be able to find a political solution to pacify the valley.

Furthermore, the cease-fire recently announced along the LOC by the two countries, following Prime Minister Vajpayee's reopening of the peace process with Pakistan, suggests that there might also be some hope for a settlement of the long-standing Kashmir dispute.

What form is a solution likely to take? Some alternatives can be ruled out. Both India and Pakistan have denied independence for Kashmir, if for no other reason that this would strengthen the demands from other secessionist movements in their multiethnic countries. Nor is it conceivable that either side would agree to the territory occupied by the other to be ceded to the other. Domestic politics in both countries would not countenance such an outcome, given the enduring passions that the dispute has engendered from the time both countries gained their independence. With both sides armed with nuclear weapons, an armed conflict to settle the dispute is also ruled out. As the last confrontation in 2002 showed, the balance of terror provided by nuclear weapons has endured. As nuclear powers, the two countries which had fought three previous wars have not since converted their continuing cold war into a hot one. The only remaining alternatives are a formal recognition of the Line of Control as the international border, or a continuing stalemate, with an armed truce, broken ever so often, along what has been the de facto border since 1949.

There are some straws in the wind which suggest that the stalemate along the LOC might be converted into a final agreement making its status de jure. The crucial changes are the demise of the Soviet Union, and geostrategic developments since 9/11. As we have seen, the strategic importance of Pakistan to the West was in providing bases against the "evil empire." This ended with the collapse of the Soviet Union. A relative decline of Western interest in Pakistan followed, which had the unfortunate effect of allowing it to deteriorate both economically and politically. With the "war on terror" launched after 9/11, the U.S. can now project its power in Central Asia and the Middle East from bases in Afghanistan and Central Asia. But with General Musharaff's joining the "war on terror" in the American Afghan campaign against Osama bin Laden, for the time being the U.S. and its allies need whatever help the general can give. But can they force him to call off the Pakistani-sponsored terrorists who have entered Kashmir and India since the 1990s, and reach a settlement by converting the LOC into the de jure border?

Selig Harrison has reported that both the U.S. and China put pressure on General Musharaff to stop Pakistani-sponsored insurgent groups based in

Kashmir and Afghanistan from providing training and help to the regrouping Taliban in Afghanistan and the Uighur separatists fighting Chinese rule in Sinkiang (Xinjiang). This was why he declared a unilateral cease-fire along the LOC in response to the Indian government's peace proposals in October.[15] Similarly Russia too is threatened by Islamist terrorists, many of whom trained in the Wahhabi madrasas in Pakistan. With this pressure from the major powers in the region, there is some hope that beginning with the cease-fire, a final settlement between the two countries will be possible to convert the LOC into the de jure border.

But this would mean that Pakistan would finally have to abandon its claim to the Kashmir valley. This poses a danger to the general given the spread of Islamists in Pakistan, since President Zia after the loss of Bangladesh exploded the "two-nation" theory on which Pakistani identity was based, and sought to find an alternative identity as an Islamic country. The Islamists look upon the liberation of Kashmir as part of their jihad. The general could contemplate an agreement to recognize the LOC as the de jure border only if he turned his back on domestic jihadis. But if Pakistan wishes to move back from the danger of becoming a failed state, controlling the jihadis and ultimately recognizing the LOC are logical steps. Whether the general has the will and means to do so remains an open question.

The *Financial Times* recently reported:

> Gen. Musharaff has given increasingly clear signs that he understands the connection between the jihadi groups that operate in Kashmir, and which are still allegedly sponsored by the Pakistan army, and his growing domestic problem with Islamist violence—not least the attempts on his life. Yet US officials believe Gen Musharaff still shows some reluctance to tackle the Islamist groups head-on in spite of the most recent crackdown, launched in November 2003. Likewise US officials continue to praise Pakistan's co-operation with the US in the war on terror in the border areas with Afghanistan. But many privately doubt whether it is whole-hearted. "Gen. Musharaff is riding two horses at once and shows no inclination to dismount either," says one former ambassador to Islamabad. "But the US cannot contemplate a breach with Gen. Musharaff—that would leave everybody in a miserable situation, including us."[16]

This does not augur well for the future.

Selig Harrison observes that the United States retains great leverage over Pakistan through economic and military aid. However, "it would be the ultimate folly to pour new military hardware into Pakistan if it continues to support the Kashmir insurgency, risking another war with India that could all too easily go nuclear."[17]

Settling the Kashmir dispute will also meet resistance from the Pakistani army as it removes one of the prime justifications the military has used for its enormous budgets. But against this is the 9/11 precedent: when placed between a rock and a hard place, the general wisely chose the U.S. against the jihadis. Perhaps if U.S. (and Chinese) pressure continues, he and his military may be willing to swallow the bitter pill, move decisively against his jihadis, and accept the LOC as the final settlement of the Kashmir dispute.

Meanwhile, India has to complete the process it has begun of talking to the moderate insurgent groups in the umbrella Hurriyat in Kashmir, offering them greater autonomy and the prospect of prosperity in the large and growing common market of the Indian Union. That it is willing to accept the LOC as the final border is shown by the Indians' building a 304-mile fence to block infiltration along a crucial part of the LOC on the mountain passes. It has proceeded slowly in the face of occasional Pakistani artillery barrages. The cease-fire along the LOC should allow this $2.4 billion project to proceed more swiftly, while the ending of the cover that the artillery shelling by the Pakistanis gave to the infiltrators should also make their entry into Kashmir more difficult.

CONCLUSIONS

India and Pakistan are recent converts to economic globalization, and their nuclear standoff facilitates agreement on other issues. Meanwhile, Islamist rejectors of globalization incubate in Pakistan and on the frontiers of Afghanistan. As the "war on terror" proceeds, however, governments are impelled to act to end strife on their frontiers and to contain terrorist Islamic movements. In conclusion, an important by-product of the "war on terror" might thus be that the long-standing Indo-Pak dispute over Kashmir is resolved with a compromise on all three sides, by accepting the LOC as the international border between India and Pakistan. The LOC might become like the line dividing East and West Berlin. Sustained by nuclear deterrence on both sides, it could not be modified short of a complete collapse of one party or the other. Such a collapse is unlikely. If such a compromise is not reached, there will be a continuing stalemate which could—particularly if there is an Islamist takeover in Pakistan—produce a nuclear crisis on the subcontinent.

NOTES

1. The best accounts of this are provided by C. Dasgupta, *War and Diplomacy in Kashmir, 1947–48* (New Delhi: Sage Publications, 2002), and P. S. Jha, *Kashmir 1947—Rival Versions of History* (Oxford: Oxford University Press, 1995).

2. M. K. Akhbar, *Kashmir—Behind the Vale* (New Delhi: Roli Books, 2002), 6.

3. Dasgupta, 9. Colonel Akbar Khan, the director of weapons and equipment in the Pakistani army, was put in charge of the operation, and has left a valuable

account (A. Khan, *Raiders in Kashmir—the Story of the Kashmir War, 1947–48* (Karachi: Pak Publishers, 1970) of the role played by senior military officers supervised by Pakistani politicians in this "invasion."

4. Jha, 85–86.

5. Ibid.

6. Jha, 87.

7. P. N. Dhar, *Indira Gandhi, the 'Emergency', and Indian Democracy* (Oxford: Oxford University Press, 2000).

8. Quoted in Dhar, 193.

9. Dhar, 192.

10. Dhar, 190.

11. Dhar, 194.

12. James Sterba, "The Simla Agreement—Behind the Progress Reports There Is the Possibility of a Secret Agreement," *New York Times* (July 3, 1972).

13. Dhar, 220–21.

14. Akhbar, 218–19.

15. See Selig Harrison, "Shoring Up the Kashmir Truce," *Financial Times*, Dec. 10, 2003.

16. "Nuclear neighbours take the initiative to tackle problems as region drops down US agenda," *Financial Times*, Dec. 17, 2003, p. 10.

17. Ibid.

10

Global Incentives and Local Responses to Self-determination: An Application to Aceh

Etel Solingen

INTERNATIONALIZATION: DOMESTIC IMPLICATIONS AND REGIONAL EFFECTS

Internationalization or globalization involves the expansion of global markets, institutions, and certain norms, a process progressively reducing the purely domestic aspects of politics everywhere.[1] But domestic responses to globalization are not uniform. Perhaps there have been fewer barriers to international flows of goods, capital, and ideas in recent years, but this does not mean global convergence, at least in the short run.

The acceptance of globalization or internationalization depends upon domestic coalitions, some of which are endangered by new values and external influences. Uncertainty about the likely impact of internationalization leaves people unable to predict where they will come out at the end of the process. Table 10.1 depicts a political landscape out of which politicians must craft coalitions under global conditions. Constituencies are aggregated according to their positions vis-à-vis international security regimes on the one hand, and the global political economy on the other.[2]

Domestic constituencies may have varying levels of commitment to support or reject a particular cluster of security or economic regimes, feeling strongly about a certain issue but less so about others.[3] For instance, in quadrangle I (northwestern corner) we find strong support for both clusters (economics and security), as is often the case for many European countries, Australia, or Singapore. At the opposite southeastern corner in quadrangle IV, leaders and constituencies oppose economic and security cooperation, as is mostly true in the cases of North Korea, Syria, or Iran.

Table 10.1.   Internationalization of Security and Economy

		Economy	
		Positive	Negative
Security	Positive	I. Openness—security and economy	II. Hybrid outcome
	Negative	III. Hybrid outcome	IV. Backlash coalitions

There are different responses to globalization or internationalization.[4] Internationalizing coalitions aggregate preferences concentrated in quadrangle I. They are driven by dynamic sectors favoring openness among business, labor, or symbolic analysts in private or public institutions. They also include consumers of imported products, state agencies that benefit from economic openness, and others. The armed forces join these coalitions when openness does not threaten them financially or institutionally or when a political entrepreneur succeeds in purging tendencies toward expansive military-industrial complexes that could threaten the economic fundamentals of an internationalizing strategy. In contrast, backlash coalitions are deeply rooted in quadrangle IV which aggregates societal groups and institutions threatened by internationalization—such as private and state-owned enterprises and banks, labor employed in uncompetitive sectors, state employees, and agencies dealing with capital controls or import licensing. The military and its associated industrial complex often join this coalition given the prospects of diminished resources accompanying economic reform and increased openness, at least in the short and medium term. Civic-nationalist, ethnic, and religious movements and leaders likely to be undermined by global forces also defy what they regard as "Western-inspired" regimes and institutions. Hybrid coalitions bridge the gap in quadrangles II and III, some favoring economic linkages but denying security ties with other nations. Still others favor security ties, but hesitate on economic linkages. Uncertainty about the likely impact of internationalization can lead to high concentrations in quadrangles II and III.

Given this landscape, politicians can engage in "positive logrolling" between those who feel positive about one cluster but are opposed to the other. One example is an alliance between economic nationalists who may be opposed to international security regimes and opponents of international security regimes who are supportive of economic regimes or cooperation.[5]

On the basis of the nature and strength of the coalition they fashion, politicians advance "grand strategies" that link effects across the domestic extraction and allocation of resources, regional relations, and global regimes.[6] These grand strategies tend to follow three ideal-typical forms. The synergies sought by internationalizing grand strategies, pivoted on macroeconomic stability, involve: (a) Adjusting domestic political economies in an internationalizing direction; (b) Safeguarding access to global markets, capital, investments, and technology; and (c) Preserving a stable and cooperative regional environment to enable (a) and (b). Hence, they oppose unrestrained military allocations, budget deficits, unproductive investment, currency instability and unpredictability, and negative conditions for foreign investment. Backlash grand strategies maintain an alternative set of synergies that leads them to: (a) Resist external pressures for liberalization and intrusions on sovereignty; (b) Undermine internationalizing adversaries and their beneficiaries at home and abroad; (c) Conserve and foment regional competition that validates (a) and (b), i.e., their domestic allocation of resources and their international policies. Hybrid grand strategies occur in the two other ideal-types and are less coherent and synergistic across the three domains.

The strength of a coalition relative to its domestic challengers can lead to pure or diluted versions of grand strategies, the latter evident in coalitions located in quadrangles II and III. Sometimes these hybrid coalitions will seek to court competing constituencies in I or IV at different points in time. Coalitions are also constrained externally by regional coalitional balances of power. Reflecting the identity and strength of competing coalitions in neighboring states, these balances can lead to three main types of regional orders.

Internationalizing orders are heavily populated with their coalitional namesakes and are expected to develop into "zones of stable peace." Domestic considerations drive economic rationalization—and military downsizing—as much as external factors, acting as tacit self-binding commitments. Hence these regional orders offer both strong guarantees against militarized strategies and strong inducements to tame territorial, ethno-confessional, and other disputes. Trading and virtual states[7] thrive under this coalitional configuration. Backlash orders are prone to become "war zones," where most states in the region are ruled by backlash politicians whose power derives from an emphasis on self-reliance, military prowess, sovereignty, and national or confessional purity. Power balancing and competitive mechanisms are active here, against both internationalizing and backlash coalitions across the border. Military-industrial and ancillary scientific-technological constituencies loom large in these orders, foiling collective security arrangements that threaten their existence. Mixed orders reflect coalitional competition at the regional level between internationalizing and backlash coalitions. This creates open-ended regional orders that elude extensive cooperation or warfare, as long as coalitional stalemates linger domestically and regionally, and are not overwhelmed by either ideal-type.

Qualitative and quantitative studies along these lines provide preliminary support for the relationship between coalitional composition and behavior and policies. Internationalizing coalitions deepen trade openness, increase exports, invite foreign investments, contain military-industrial complexes, instigate fewer international crises, abstain from weapons of mass destruction, uphold international economic and security regimes, and labor toward regional cooperative orders that buttress those objectives. In contrast, back-lash coalitions have diminished trade openness and exports, restricted foreign investment, fostered military industries including weapons of mass destruction complexes, defied international regimes, aggravated civic-nationalist, religious, or ethnic cross-border tensions, and initiated international crises. The behavior of hybrids straddles both categories, irregularly striving for economic openness, smaller military complexes, sometimes initiating international crisis, and sometimes cooperating regionally and internationally, but neither forcefully nor coherently.

AN APPLICATION: THE CASE OF ACEH

Indonesia's conflict with Aceh is reported to have not only displaced hundreds of thousands of people but also caused 12,000 mostly civilian casualties over the last two decades. Although this is several times the number of casualties for well-reported cases such as Israel/Palestine, this conflict has gained far less attention despite Aceh's important strategic position at the entrance to the Malacca straits, a vital waterway for oil routes between East Asia and the Persian Gulf.[8] Control over Aceh's natural resources (oil and natural gas fields) is at the heart of violent encounters between Jakarta and Aceh, a province of 4.1 million people. Aceh's gas amounts to about 3 percent of Indonesia's GDP. Furthermore, the Indonesian leadership fears demonstration effects from separatist efforts that might unravel the country as a whole, particularly after East Timor. Some have also traced the rift as one between radical Islamist secessionists in Aceh and a modernizing government in Jakarta. However, a systematic examination of the demand and supply dimensions of self-determination along the lines outlined above offers a more complete understanding of the forces at work than do any of these partial accounts.

DEMAND SIDE: ACEH

Aceh's separatist movement had been active since Indonesia achieved independence in 1948. In 1953, under *ulama* leader Daud Beureueh, the Acehnese demanded the establishment of an Islamic republic and launched an armed rebellion against Sukarno. In time, economic and educational changes under Suharto's New Order created new, more secular constituencies in Aceh who, from their new administrative and academic positions, began challenging the *ulama*'s objectives against ties with Jakarta.[9] By the 1970s, this cleavage between Aceh's "technocrats" coopted by the New Order and the local *ulama* had become significant. A third group emerged that challenged the technocrats' entrenched control of important positions and their alliance with Golkar (Suharto's party) while demanding a devolution of Aceh's resources by Jakarta. This group found common ground with Aceh's Islamists although some among the latter developed ties with Golkar as well, particularly in the 1970s. In 1976, a small group of these professionals launched "Aceh Merdeka" (Free Aceh or GAM) seeking an alliance with *ulama* from the 1950s rebellion and demanding independence. Aceh got provincial status instead, but GAM leader Hassan de Tiro continued to insist on an independent Islamic state from his exile in Sweden. Following a relatively dormant period, the return of several hundred Libyan-trained radicals to Aceh reignited GAM activities in 1989, initiating a decade of Indonesian control of Aceh as a Military Operation Area.[10] The professionals that created the GAM gained support for the rebellion from farmers adversely affected by the fall of clove prices and by the crackdown on marijuana production, from unemployed workers displaced by an influx of non-Acehnese into the new industrial enclaves in Aceh, and from some Islamist groups.[11]

The GAM widened its popular support significantly only after East Timor in 1999, when mass demonstrations demanding a referendum on independence in November 1999 were attended by over 500,000 people.[12] The GAM's political machine collected taxes and appeared to draw considerable backing among some community, religious, and political officials, as well as arms and drug dealers, people-smugglers, and others involved in piracy, extortion, and other illicit businesses.[13] The GAM sought and obtained economic and military assistance from backlash sources in Iran and Libya as well as from neighboring movements in Southeast Asia that challenged their own (internationalizing) ruling coalitions. Islamists in Southern Malaysia, the Thai Pattani United Liberation Organization (PULO), and Acehnese businessmen in southern Thailand and Malaysia reportedly provided support to Acehnese separatists.[14] The GAM's insurgency was estimated at 3,000–4,000 men engaged in guerrilla warfare, sometimes involving atrocities against civilians but also retaining popular support in light of an even worse human rights record by the Indonesian military. The GAM's attacks on Exxon-Mobil's Arun natural gas facilities gained it considerable support as well, given widespread Acehnese frustration at the perceived collusion between Indonesia and Exxon-Mobil, the main agent of globalization in the region.[15] The GAM controlled about 80 percent of Aceh's territory until the June 2003 onslaught by the Indonesian military that followed the unraveling of a two-year peace process.

The GAM's leadership was split following a succession rift in the late 1990s.[16] On the one hand, the Aceh/Sumatra National Liberation Front (ASNLF) was led by Hasan di Tiro, exiled in Sweden and revered as Father of the Nation (*Wali Negara*). This faction denounced compromise, dominated Aceh's military forces, and demanded full independence despite intermittent tactical acceptance of autonomy as a step toward independence.[17]

This militant wing was able to set the tone, depicting Indonesia as "proxies of imperialist Western governments," directly denouncing Western media, Western business corporations, and Western governments "smugly calling themselves 'democracies.'"[18] On the other hand, the MP-GAM (*Majelis Pemerintahan—Gerakan Aceh Merdeka*, or Free Aceh Movement Government council) was led by Teungku Don Zulfahri, exiled in Malaysia and backed by a breakaway faction expelled by de Tiro and led by Husaini Hasan (exiled in Sweden), Daud Paneuek, and Zulfahri.[19] This faction claimed to be more "Islamic" and accused de Tiro of secularism. Some were more willing to accept autonomy and to entertain links with elements in the Indonesian military and with Acehnese businessmen (*Kelompok Aceh Sepakat*). The armed faction of the MP-GAM was led by Maulida, whose rivals are considered to be subordinated to Indonesia's special military forces (Kopassus). All of this suggests a far more complex and fluid political background than the one often posited by explanations based on "identity clash" (or Islam versus modernism). Beyond cleavages between these two main groups there were rogue groups engaged in criminal activities operating within the GAM.[20]

Both groups claimed to represent the GAM, a fact that raised difficulties during the 2002 negotiations on special autonomy (the Cessation of Hostilities Agreement). This agreement would allow Aceh to implement Islamic laws (*Saryiah*) and to field their own candidates in direct elections for provincial officials. Some local religious, economic, and educational leaders encouraged the émigrés to agree to the terms of the Agreement coordinated by the Henri Dunant Center in Geneva. The émigré leadership appeared to heed their demands but local field commanders opposed it, particularly rogue elements that stood to lose from the interruption of certain economic and criminal activities.[21] The GAM's commander Tengku Syafei was killed in early 2002 and ensuing atrocities by GAM militants eventually resulted in some erosion in popular support. Even after the agreement was negotiated in late 2002, the chief rebel negotiator Sofyan Ibrahim Tiba asserted maximalist claims that "Indonesia must give Aceh its sovereignty" and "Aceh will eventually be independent."[22] The Swedish government arrested GAM's exiled leaders in June 2004 on grounds of committing grave breaches of international law.

Aceh's governors have been appointed by, and remain accountable to, the regional parliament. Islamist parties and Golkar attracted about half of the vote each in the early 1970s, but the United Development Party (PPP) of former Indonesian vice-president Haz grew stronger since. Although the Acehnese public has been divided over autonomy versus independence, a poll by the International Crisis Group found that a majority of the Acehnese favored independence in 2002.[23] The special autonomy law that allowed a high percentage of Aceh's revenues to remain there has largely benefited Acehnese provincial officials reportedly responsible for missing and misspent funds, cronyism, illegal logging, and smuggling.[24] *In other words, the struggle for those revenues is not merely between metropole and province, as the simple distributional explanation would have it, but within the latter as well.*

On December 27, 2004 Aceh was the epicenter of one of the worst natural disasters in history, as a consequence of a tsunami that originated near Sumatra's coast. The death toll was estimated at 150,000 dead and the general devastation was unprecedented.

SUPPLY SIDE: JAKARTA

Prior to 1965, President Sukarno presided over a backlash coalition that led a wider array of Indonesian political forces to its independence. This coalition backed up Sukarno's hyper-nationalist agenda in economics and security. Acehnese discontent rose in the early 1950s under Sukarno,[25] who sought to tighten Jakarta's control over separatist units such as Aceh. Between 1950 and 1953 Jakarta appointed non-Acehnese (mostly Javanese) to key administrative positions in Aceh, imposed a ban on Aceh's direct trading with Malaya and Singapore, disbanded the Acehnese army, allowed gambling and beer drinking, and starved Aceh of resources. *Ulama* Daud Beureueh launched an armed rebellion in 1953 in response. Sukarno's regional and global policies followed backlash lines as well, condemning the global economy, removing Indonesia from the UN, and engaging Indonesia in a military confrontation (*konfrontasi*) against Malaysia in the early 1960s. In many ways this conjuncture of forces resembles the conditions of quadrangle IV in Table 10.1 above. Sukarno's coalition was not constrained by the regional or international environment in its approach to Aceh. Despite granting Aceh a limited recognition of some religious prerogatives in principle (1959), tensions with Jakarta remained.

After a coup that ruthlessly repressed pro-Sukarno forces, the Communist Party (PKI), and Islamic contenders, General Suharto organized a new coalition in the late 1960s that would rule Indonesia until 1997. The pivotal partners in Suharto's New Order (*Orde Baru*) coalition were his party (Golkar), the armed forces, a small group of industrial entrepreneurs and bankers (mostly ethnic Chinese), key state bureaucracies coordinating integration with the global economy, and, during the latter part of his tenure, some *pribumi* (native Indonesian) economic groups with ties to the Indonesian Muslim Intellectual Association (ICMI). Suharto's coalition thus presided over a relatively more open and deregulated economy that coexisted with a more closed crony system.[26] Yet this coalition had come a long way, particularly by the 1980s, in erasing Sukarno's backlash policies by launching an export-led strategy of integration into the global economy; seeking U.S., Japanese, and other Western trade and investment partners; applying IMF stabilization plans; reducing state enterprises; and deepening regional cooperation.[27] The liberalization of the banking sector allowed industrial barons to further their economic reach. Sukarno also replaced Suharto's *konfrontasi* (of Malaysia) with support for regional cooperation and for the creation of the Association of Southeast Asian States (ASEAN) in 1967.

Although Suharto's strategy benefited primarily his own coalition, in time he was able to co-opt growing segments of Indonesian society through economic growth. Indonesia's average trade openness—imports plus exports as percentage of GDP—under Sukarno had been about 21 percent, declining to 18 percent between 1960 and 1965.[28] Immediately after Suharto's coup, trade openness jumped from as low as 10 percent in 1964 to about 33 percent (of a $6 billion GDP) in 1966. By the late 1970s it climbed to over 50 percent of a GDP of $78 billion in 1980. Net foreign direct investment inflows grew tenfold between 1970 and 1989. Although Suharto rejected Acehnese aspirations for independence, he also reversed many of Sukarno's positions and granted Aceh provincial status after 1976, in the very early stages of an internationalizing shift that peaked after the 1980s.

Acehnese entrepreneurs sought links with multinational corporations in the 1970s, when Suharto was beginning to allow foreign investment in extractive industries. However, the New Order regime was suspicious of Aceh, where opponents of Golkar would regularly prevail in elections, and the military was wary of separatist movements. The regime thus imposed its own arrangements between multinationals (including Exxon-Mobil) and Suharto's private and public economic allies, excluding the Acehnese from most of these profitable arrangements.[29] Revenues from oil, fertilizers, paper, palm oil, cocoa, rubber, coconut, fishing, and other sectors ended up largely in Jakarta. Aceh got a standard baseline regional budget from the metropole even though Aceh was among the poorest of the eight provinces in Sumatra.[30] Suharto allowed extensive repression by the military in 1986 after a renewal of Aceh's rebellion in 1983, but also sought a strategy of reconciliation and co-optation. He appointed Ibrahim Hasan, an Acehnese economist who crafted a coalition between local Islamist leaders that no longer saw Golkar as anti-Islamist and secular leaders that sought to increase Aceh's share of its resources.[31] In the 1987 elections, the strategy yielded a small electoral majority for Golkar and an even greater one in 1992. This cooperative period coincided with a more advanced phase in Suharto's internationalizing strategy, involving financial liberalization, but this cooperation unraveled as well.

In the aftermath of the 1997 crisis Suharto was replaced by B. J. Habibie, his vice president and first Indonesian Muslim Intellectual Association (ICMI) chair. In his short and ineffectual presidency, Habibie, himself a long-standing proponent of economic nationalist-populism and Islamism, presided over a disjointed economic program. Habibie also appointed high-ranking military officers to important positions, officers who had played important roles in repressing Aceh. Indonesia's economy contracted by 14 percent in 1998 and pressures for elections built up. Acehnese calls for a referendum grew in tandem with calls for boycotting Indonesia's general elections. The People's Consultative Assembly gathered in 1999 in Indonesia's first free and fair elections since 1955, getting Sukarno's daughter Megawati Sukarnoputri's Democratic Party-Struggle the largest majority (34 percent) but less than the total won by Muslim-affiliated parties.[32] A compromise in October 1999 brought Abdurrahman Wahid—who led the largest Muslim organization Nahdlatul Ulama, with 35 million members—to the presidency. Wahid relied initially on a grand coalition backed by key political actors, business, and a military under pressure to reform after East Timor, reflecting Wahid's main objective of achieving national reconciliation.[33] Wahid himself acknowledged his cabinet reflected "horse trading," but he did attempt to override economic nationalist and populist ministers, demanding implementation of IMF commitments, economic restructuring, and privatization.[34] However, the coalition's heterogeneity and weakness doomed Wahid's efforts to restore political and economic stability and to prevent further centrifugal forces in Aceh and West Papua (Irian Jaya) from pressing for independence from Indonesia.

An odd array of oppositional forces exacerbated economic, political, and ethnic tensions without leading to the emergence of a viable alternative coalition.[35] The opposition included Suharto's old allies, industrialists hurt by economic restructuring, moderate Islamists favoring state enterprises as a way to foster a (protected) *pribumi* business class à la Malaysia, radical Islamist groups (such as the Laskar Jihad, which opposed both the IMF and communism while radicalizing Maluku's Muslims), and segments of the military resentful of its institutional decline. These largely backlash constituencies challenged Wahid's heroic efforts to stabilize the economy, develop democratic institutions, reconstitute civil-military relations, and relieve ethno-religious tensions. Assembly President Amien Rais (PAN—National Mandate Party) rejected Wahid's efforts to maintain the separation of state and Islam, a policy that Wahid believed would prevent an Algerian-style dilemma between military and theocratic options. Rais also challenged Wahid's efforts to reform the economy along "Western" lines to restore international investors' confidence. IMF prescriptions during the 1997 crisis had inflicted unnecessary economic and social damage, buttressing anti-globalization groups. General Wiranto, the former armed forces chief, mobilized opposition against Wahid after he suspended Wiranto from his cabinet position pending the completion of a probe into military-induced violence in East Timor.[36] Clearly, if Wahid had any intention to promote an internationalizing strategy, the nature of the opposition and the fragility of his own power base stood in the way.

Meanwhile, ethnic and religious clashes in West Kalimantan, Batam, and Maluku flared up and Chinese-Muslim and Christian-Muslim relations remained tense. The military pressed for the imposition of martial law and

strongly opposed a referendum in Aceh in 1999.[37] Notwithstanding this formidable opposition, Wahid offered Aceh greater autonomy in 1999, in the
midst of an effort to restore confidence, stability, foreign investment, and
democratization. In early 2001 Wahid steered a law granting special autonomy to Aceh through the parliament, a measure that would enable Aceh to
implement its own laws based on *Saryiah* (Islamic law) and to retain 70 percent of its revenues. Wahid's policy, which he labelled "liberal autonomy,"
came under pressure to suppress militant separatists in West Papua. Yet
Wahid's PKB party remained more inclined to negotiate with the GAM and to
allow a referendum that had the potential of leading to independence.
Unsurprisingly, the stepped-up military campaign against Wahid ended with
the latter's resignation in July 2001, after he became embroiled in an
impeachment process.

The Wahid was succeeded by his vice president Megawati Sukarnoputri, whose
coalition was similarly weak and under pressure from backlash constituencies resistant to economic reform and foreign investment and from her vice
president Hamzah Haz and his Islamist constituencies (United Development
Party—PPP) including their allies in Aceh. As a result of pressures from the
Islamist flank Megawati refused to dissolve paramilitary groups associated
with Islamist parties, to acknowledge the existence of al-Qaeda connections
in Indonesia, or to promote anti-terrorist legislation.[38] Vice President Haz
denied any connections between radical Indonesian Islamists (including
Jemaah Islamyiah) and terrorist activities. Islamist parties also opposed
Megawati's effort to bring Indonesia's policy closer to the U.S. after 9/11. Support for militant Islam had developed deep roots in the late Suharto period
and particularly during Habibie's rule.

The 2002 terrorist massacre at Bali forced a reconsideration, leading to more
forceful legal steps against cleric Abu Bakar Bashir, head of Jemaah Islamyiah,
and associated terrorist networks including some reportedly related to al-
Qaeda.[39] Megawati specifically linked the economics and security dimensions
of terrorism in an apparent effort to garner enough domestic support for anti-
terrorist legislation. While opposing the war in Afghanistan, she highlighted
that "terrorism has created widespread fear and has subsequently caused the
drastic plunge in international economy activity, the foundation of human
prosperity."[40] On the economic front, Megawati developed a stronger relationship with the IMF, adopting fiscal austerity and allowing price increases in
fuel, electricity, and other services. Her efforts to revive cooperation with the
IMF and foreign investment are evident in her address to the People's Consultative Assembly: "We have to amend our image as to reconfirm that Indonesia
is not a high-risk country in terms of politics, economics, and security. In this
way, it is to be hoped that investors would be more interested in investing in
Indonesia. . . . Apart from this safe environment, the investors also need certainty in the rules of the game. It is against this backdrop that I have directed
the economic ministers to implement policies that are coherent and transpar-

ent to avoid any confusion among business operators."[41] Megawati's coalition also allowed foreign investors into areas previously dominated by state enterprises, such as the purchase by a Singaporean firm of 42 percent of the telephone company Indosat. The World Bank's lead economist praised Indonesia's fiscal consolidation and the reduction in its budget deficit under Megawati. Nonetheless, despite signs of economic recovery and growing exports (albeit declining high-tech exports), instability kept foreign investors away, particularly as China provided the economic conditions, political stability, and receptivity to investments that Indonesia lacked.[42]

On separatism, Megawati endorsed Wahid's policies initially, rejecting the independence option in her first state of the nation address, but offering Aceh and West Papua special autonomy. This meant granting Aceh 70 percent of oil and gas revenues for eight years and allowing it to base its legal system on *Saryiah*.[43] In September 2001 Megawati visited Aceh and movingly apologized to the Acehnese for their past suffering. On January 1, 2002 the special autonomy law was to come into effect but was largely rejected in Aceh as an imposition by Jakarta.[44] For two years (2001–2002) Megawati had encouraged Indonesia's unprecedented participation in negotiations with the GAM mediated by a private NGO, the Henri Dunant Center, and supported by all major donors. Clearly, Megawati's coalition included some political forces that were highly aware of Aceh's potential for burdening the coalition's task of economic and political reform and for undermining international support for that agenda.

At the same time, the fragility of Megawati's coalition made it highly responsive to pressures from the military which demanded to prosecute the war against the GAM more vigorously. The role of the military (Tentara Nasional Indonesia, TNI) deserves particular scrutiny in the context of decisions related to Aceh. The armed forces have benefited from their presence in Aceh, allowing them to maintain their constitutional status as the protector of national security assets but also to protect related special economic interests (including drug trafficking and timber exploitation). The TNI leadership thus pressured Megawati for a military offensive and found her far more receptive than Wahid had been (after all, the military had removed Megawati's father from power!). In a speech to the People's Consultative Assembly in early August 2002, Megawati proclaimed that her government would restore peace "by crushing the armed separatist movement." Since Megawati assumed office in July 2001, the TNI heightened its military presence in Aceh and by the summer of 2002 Megawati endorsed an ultimatum to the GAM to accept the government's terms by December 31, 2002.[45] The presumed violation by GAM militants of the stipulations of the agreement mediated by the Henri Dunant Center in December 2002—primarily the reported inability to disarm GAM militants—provided additional ammunition for TNI to launch the May–June 2003 offensive. TNI also used claims that the GAM had links to al-Qaeda through Jemaah Islamyiah.[46]

Aceh thus provides a microcosm for the dilemmas facing the TNI and their mixed incentives regarding an internationalizing strategy. To the extent the latter threatens them financially or institutionally the TNI has worked against politicians seeking to advance such strategies. However, segments of the military are also beneficiaries of ties to multinational corporations, sometimes more legal (providing security services), sometimes less so. At the very least, internal divisions within TNI may have been a major contributor to the hybrid character and weakness of ruling coalitions in the metropole.[47] Successive leaders, authoritarian and democratic, have refrained from (Suharto) or failed to (Wahid) counter military-industrial activities that threaten the economic and political fundamentals of an internationalizing strategy. Pressures to act forcefully against Aceh rebels also came from Megawati's party and from Golkar.[48]

The Islamist movement together with segments of labor excluded from the benefits of internationalization also provided barriers to further openness. Together they oppose privatization, deregulation, and globalization, either on material or normative grounds. Islamists also rebuff the regional and international campaign against terrorism. Yielding to these particular demands, the government weakens even further the appeal to an already moribund flow of foreign investment. China and other Southeast Asian states provide better economic incentives and more forceful commitments to stability and anti-terrorism. Wide segments of her Islamist opposition regarded Megawati's policies vis-à-vis Aceh as wrong-headed. The Muslim community in Aceh also selected prominent leaders such as Syafi'i Ma'arif, former deputy chief of Nahdlatul Ulama Ali Yafie, Muslim scholar Nurcholis Madjid, former foreign minister Ali Alatas, and former home affairs minister Surjadi Soedirdja as mediators in the dialogue sponsored by the Henri Dunant Center.[49] These leaders, as well as Islamist PAN leader Amien Rais, condemned any military operations in Aceh— blaming the last three civilian presidents for favoring this approach, and calling for an internationally supervised referendum on autonomy vs. independence. Megawati consistently rejected a referendum opposed by the military, PDIP, and Golkar.[50] Vice President Haz and his Islamist party (PPP), who had provided political protection for radical Islamist groups, attacked Golkar's dominance in Aceh, which he considered a natural heartland of PPP. Golkar had been able to co-opt some Acehnese economic and business leaders and even grass-roots Muslim constituencies.[51] Clearly, the diverse and sometimes overlapping cleavages within the metropole on economic and security issues cast their shadow on Aceh's internal political landscape.

The 2004 elections replaced Megawati by a landslide with Susilo Bambang Yudhoyono, a former general who became Indonesia's first directly elected president. Yudhoyono committed himself to stimulate the economy and uproot corruption and terrorism, in line with an internationalizing agenda. Yudhoyono, as Megawati's former security minister, was also instrumental in arranging for a truce with the GAM in December 2003. A secular figure, Yudhoyono came under pressure from the Assembly's leader Hidayat Nur Wahid, founder of the new conservative Islamist Justice Party for Prosperity, which advocates changing Indonesia's constitution to implant an Islamist state. Yudhoyono had to replace his initial choice for finance minister, the former director for Asia-Pacific at the IMF in Washington, D.C. The tsunami disaster strained even further the already dismal social situation of Aceh. Yudhoyono immediately declared another cease-fire in ongoing military activities against Acehnese separatists and ordered the military to help provide relief day and night, pledging Indonesia's obligation to save each and every life.

SUPPLY SIDE: INTERNATIONAL AND REGIONAL RESPONSES

How have global structures—markets, power, norms, and institutions— affected Aceh's demand for self-determination and the metropole's response? According to Alesina and Spolaore, the more open an international economic order, the greater the incentives of subnational economic units to secede from extant states.[52] Some historical data may provide warrant for this hypothesis but more contemporary cases suggest that the results are now different. Purely economic incentives are usually modified by political constraints, both on the supply side and on the demand side. In a particular period, expected economic rationality leading to smaller state size and supporting secession may no longer hold. Of particular importance on the supply side of the story is that the last decade has seen a decline in tolerance for secessionist claims or "external self-determination." It has also witnessed a greater endorsement of demands for equality in linguistic, cultural, educational, and other representational and participatory rights.[53] These philosophical and theoretical trends have made significant inroads in international organizations and in the associated activities of NGOs, including formulations by former OSCE High Commissioner on National Minorities Max van der Stoel and by experts who drafted the Lund Recommendations (the Effective Participation of National Minorities in Public Life—September 1999).[54]

These general trends cast their shadow on the case at hand. International support for GAM separatism has been quite weak, perhaps strengthening groups in Aceh that favored negotiations with Indonesia over autonomy in the process mediated by the Henri Dunant Center in 2002. Other NGOs in Aceh have sought to protect civilians against human rights violations blamed on the Indonesian military. International NGOs have also worked to strengthen the hands of their NGO allies in Aceh who, in turn, advocated a referendum and called for monitoring human rights violations by international NGOs, including Amnesty International and Asia Watch.[55] The Washington-based International Labor Rights Fund took Exxon to a U.S. court accusing it of complicity with the Indonesian military on severe human rights violations.

Human rights groups had asked Exxon-Mobil to cease its operations until its security would not require TNI protection. In 2001, Amnesty International called on the ASEAN Regional Forum, the most inclusive security institution in the Asia-Pacific, to address grave violations of human rights in Aceh. This institution, however, like ASEAN (which spearheaded it) is predicated on the concept of nonintervention and constitutes a dialogue forum rather than a conflict resolution mechanism.

Indonesia's role as the largest producer of liquefied natural gas is an important determinant of incentives and constraints faced by Indonesia, Aceh, and outside actors respectively. Aceh's gas fields continue to account for over one-third of Indonesia's gas exports and for state revenues of $100 million per month. Exxon-Mobil ceased operations temporarily in 2001 but was pressured by Jakarta and Petramina—the state oil company—to resume them. Indonesia's major economic partners were also negatively affected by discontinuities in supply of natural gas. (Exxon-Mobil exports its liquid natural gas to Japan and South Korea.) These countries responded to Aceh's separatist demands by asserting the territorial integrity of Indonesia while calling for the protection of human rights in Aceh. The U.S., the EU, and Japan do not support Acehnese independence. Indeed, not a single country in the world seems to support the GAM's demand for Acehnese independence.[56]

In a visit to Indonesia, retired General Anthony Zinni, a mediator for the Henri Dunant Center, pressured Susilo Bambang Yudhoyono for continuous dialogue rather than the imposition of martial law. At a White House meeting in 2001, immediately after 9/11, Presidents Bush and Megawati Sukarnoputri discussed Aceh and Irian Jaya and agreed on the need for a peaceful resolution of separatist demands. Megawati committed herself to enhance dialogue and reconciliation, and President Bush emphasized his firm support for Indonesia's territorial integrity: "The U.S. does not support secessionist aspirations in these areas or elsewhere."[57] Bush also approved $400 million to promote trade and investment, especially in oil and gas, as well as $100 million in additional benefits to Indonesia under the Generalized System of Preferences. Megawati was also encouraged to improve counter-terrorism measures and to promote military and economic reforms and the rule of law. The U.S. later resumed limited military aid to the Indonesian military for its anti-terrorist campaign in the face of strong opposition in the U.S. Congress. Although Indonesia was considering a request to the United Nations to include GAM in its list of terrorist organizations,[58] the U.S. refused to do so and continued to support the Geneva dialogue.

Indonesia's largest foreign donor, Japan, also rebuffs independence-seeking groups although it opposes Indonesia's military suppression of Aceh and seeks to help Jakarta become more attentive to some of the claims of separatist movements.[59] In a statement during an ASEAN 10 Plus 10 Meeting, Japan's Minister of Foreign Affairs Yoehi Kono stated: "With respect to provincial problems such as the situation in Aceh and Irian Jaya, Japan supports the territorial integrity of Indonesia and intends to support the current government indirectly in solving these problems."[60] Even in the midst of its own economic crisis, Japan provided over $700 million in economic and social assistance to Aceh by 2002, emphasizing the need for a truly democratic mechanism that reflects the aspirations of the Aceh people. Tokyo also organized a meeting to coordinate economic aid to Aceh and mediated the May 2003 efforts to save the agreement negotiated in late 2002. Indonesia's political stability as well as free and unimpeded maritime traffic in that area is of utmost concern to Japan, which imports virtually all its oil resources via the Straits of Malacca. Japan pledged the highest initial amount ($500 million) to victims of the December 2004 tsunami, including Aceh.

China, which is casting an ever more important role for itself in all of Southeast Asia, signed the 2000 Shanghai Cooperation Organization Pact on Striking at Terrorism, Separatism, and Extremism, a clear warning signal to any such movements in the region. The United States, Japan, the EU, and the World Bank cosponsored a Preparatory Conference on Peace and Reconstruction in Aceh in December 2002, as the Cessation of Hostilities Agreement signed earlier that month between the Government of Indonesia and the Free Aceh Movement appeared to be holding.[61] They also organized a visit to Aceh in January 2003 to assess Aceh's development needs directly. Under Wahid, World Bank President James Wolfenson specifically linked financial support for Indonesia to its ability to control the military in the aftermath of East Timor.

A previous section explained how the institutional characteristics of ASEAN and the background leading to its emergence led to a policy of upholding each member's territorial integrity and abstaining from intervening in the domestic affairs of fellow member states. ASEAN leaders possessed strong incentives to coordinate this policy to avoid retaliatory support for separatist movements in their own territory. Thus, such movements were never aided by neighboring ruling coalitions, maintaining mutual protection of their respective national sovereignties. Justifying this hands-off approach as applied to Aceh, ASEAN's secretary-general Rodolfo Severino of the Philippines proclaimed in 1999: "ASEAN's relevance does not hinge on a specific problem that at this point is still a matter internal to Indonesia."[62] ASEAN states enhanced their border security to stem arms smuggling to Acehnese rebels, particularly from southern Thailand and Mindanao (Philippines), and have explicitly vowed to deny separatist movements such as Aceh's any protection in their territory.[63]

Militant movements such as the GAM find even less receptivity in the post-9/11 environment, and ASEAN states quietly but strongly support U.S. military aid to Indonesia to put it down. Furthermore, some ASEAN states (the Philippines in particular) are interested in uninterrupted supply of oil and gas from Aceh and Irian Jaya. Leaders of Indonesia, the Philippines, Malaysia, Singapore, and Thailand signed agreements covering energy, tourism, fisheries, and investment. The energy agreements would speed up the development of an ASEAN natural gas grid, the supply of Indonesian coal from East Kalimantan and South Sumatra for power generation in the Philippines, and supplies of liquefied natural gas from Indonesia's Tangguh gas field in Irian Jaya.[64] A Thai general headed teams of monitors from Thailand and Philippines that Indonesia had agreed to allow into Aceh following the December 2002 agreement.

The Agreement between the Indonesian government and the GAM negotiated in late 2002 unraveled by mid-2003, leading to a full-scale campaign by the Indonesian military and the declaration of martial law in May 2003. Indonesian officials blamed the GAM for refusing to comply with the terms of the agreement to surrender their weapons. A senior adviser to Megawati, Rizal Mallarangeng, argued that the U.S. war against terrorism had helped Jakarta justify a military operation and that the campaign was "the only way."[65] However, according to leading Indonesian scholar Jusuf Wanandi, the military onslaught on Aceh should not be traced to such external factors but rather to the strong support for a military solution across Indonesia's public opinion. Indeed, Mallarangeng himself acknowledged that the Aceh campaign would "help lift" Megawati's sagging popularity. The U.S. and all major powers, argues Wanandi, have been at the forefront of a political solution and only a convergence between international pressure and an internal realization of the futility of force will allow such a solution to last.

In 2003 arsonists destroyed 200 schools during the first few days of military operations, with each side blaming the other, and 48,000 residents were displaced.[66] Despite warnings against human rights abuses, external responses were subdued. Australia now works closely with Indonesia on anti-terrorism and did not interrupt its cooperation with Indonesia's special military forces. Even as the military campaign unfolded in June 2003, Megawati visited Japan as a state guest of Emperor Akihito and Prime Minister Koizumi, the first such visit for an Indonesian president since 1968. The situation has not changed under General Yudhoyono.

CONCLUSIONS

In sum, the international and regional context has provided no support for Aceh's separatist movement even if it has pressed Indonesia to respect Acehnese human rights. Yet a fragile ruling coalition in Indonesia succumbed to a military solution after failed negotiations in 2003, just as nationalistic themes in economics and security had become more central to the 2004 presidential elections. These themes included confronting the International Monetary Fund, precluding foreign firms from acquiring Indonesian government companies, and toughening up measures against separatist movements.[67]

The East Timor experience helps explain Indonesia's fear of disintegration from the vantage point of a unified state (the "national security" hypothesis), but only to some extent. After all, very few states have disappeared in recent decades, with Yugoslavia, Czechoslovakia, and the former Soviet Union providing the only frequently cited cases.[68] Furthermore, Jakarta's responses to Acehnese demands for self-determination have not been uniform over time, fluctuating between utter neglect, repression, some predisposition to accept a referendum under Wahid (even after East Timor!), participation in serious mediation efforts, and outright military action. *Clearly, more than the logic of "national interest" seems to be at work in producing such variation in policies.* On the one hand, the composition and fragility of ruling coalitions in the metropole may explain the relative and varying receptivity to outside inducements and injunctions.[69] On the other hand, the external perception of both a weak ruling coalition in Indonesia (including fears of its potential decomposition into a full-fledged backlash central government) and backlash forces at work within the GAM may explain the outside world's tepid response to Indonesia's military onslaught in Aceh in 2003. Internationalizing forces at the global level have little incentive to either rescue the GAM or undermine even further the fragile succession of ruling coalitions in Indonesia.

Over 40 percent of Acehnese were classified as poor, and unemployment was high prior to the late December 2004 tsunami. The effects of the tidal inundation were horrifying, but they only added to Aceh's problems. In its aftermath, General Yudhoyono called for a permanent end to the rebellion, acceptance of the conditions of autonomy offered in 2001, and a joint international effort to reconstruct Aceh. Whether or not the prospects for Aceh independence will change in the aftermath of this human catastrophe, Indonesia's responses will come under tighter scrutiny from an international audience than ever before. This does not mean, however, that Aceh will be given independence. Some form of autonomy is far more likely to result.

In the net, internationalizing forces—whether brought by international capitalism or disastrous weather and sea conditions—have largely told the tale in recent Indonesian experience. GAM and some Acehnese activists have propounded independence, but the government's response has been serially to emphasize both the carrot, and finally the stick, with, to this point, apparent success.

NOTES

1. See Etel Solingen, *Regional Orders at Century's Dawn* (Princeton, NJ: Princeton University Press, 1998).

2. This modal landscape was inspired by Hirschman's (1963:285–91) discussion of a parliamentary debate over economic reform. For further elaboration, see Solingen (2001), from which this brief discussion borrows.

3. Although this discussion approaches security in a more general, classical sense, one may restrict it to international regimes dealing specifically with self-determination.

4. Notice that these coalitions span state institutions and societal actors, which differentiates this particular coalitional characterization from others focusing on purely economic societal agents.

5. On this classical convergence between economic-nationalists and security-nationalists, see Gilpin (1987).

6. For a more detailed understanding of these coalitions and their grand strategy, see Solingen (1998). On the domestic sources of grand strategy more generally, see Rosecrance and Stein (1993).

7. See R. Rosecrance, *The Rise of the Trading State* (New York: Basic Books, 1986), and Rosecrance, *The Rise of the Virtual State* (New York: Basic Books, 1999).

8. On casualties, see "Déjà vu in Indonesia" (editorial), *The Japan Times*, July 7, 2003:16; Richel Langit, "Aceh Rebels Lose the Plot and the War," *Asia Times*, Nov. 18, 2002; and Paddock (2003). Up to 7,000 may have been killed between 1989 and 1998, and thousands were raped and tortured according to some human rights organizations (Shiraishi 2000). The GAM places the number of deaths between 1989 and 1998 at 25,000, acehnet.tripod.com/why.ht.

9. On historical divisions within Aceh between the traditional territorial chiefs (*uleebalang*) and a reformist *ulama* (religious leaders) on the one hand, and among religious leaders with different occupational interests and competing attitudes towards Saryiah on the other, see David Brown, *The State and Ethnic Politics in Southeast Asia* (New York: Routledge, 1994), 137–38, who also discusses the implications of these cleavages for relations with the metropole in the post-independence decades.

10. "Indonesia's war that won't go away." Comment by Sidney Jones in *The Observer Online* crisisweb.org/projects/showreport.cfm?reportid=72, 2002.

11. See Brown (1994).

12. Data on the GAM is sketchy. This section builds largely on reports by Uchida (1999), Larry Niksch, "Indonesian Separatist Movement in ACEH," CRS Report for Congress: Congressional Research Service, Library of Congress, 2002; Gerry Van Klinken, "What Is the Free Aceh Movement?" *Inside Indonesia Digest* 89 (Nov. 25, 1999); Langit (2002), STRATFOR (2002), McCulloch (2002), and several websites claiming to represent or portray different groups under the GAM.

13. Langit (2002); STRATFOR (2002). On the lucrative marijuana trade among elements of the GAM and the Indonesian military, see Peter Searle, "Ethno-Religious Conflicts: Rise or Decline? Recent Developments in Southeast Asia," *Contemporary Southeast Asia* (April, 2002).

14. Searle (2002).

15. Niksch (2002).

16. Van Klinken (1999).

17. On De Tiro's personal business grievance about losing a bid to the Bechtel corporation to build one of the natural gas pipelines, and on probable GAM efforts to extract protection money from the plant itself, see Ross (2003).

18. De Tiro, in http://acehnet.tripod.com/asnlf.htm.

19. Husaini attended an International Forum on Aceh in Washington D.C. (April 1999) as the leader of the Aceh Liberation Front.

20. Van Klinken (1999).

21. Langit (2002).

22. Michael Casey, "Aceh's Hopes for Permanent Peace under Strain," *The Japan Times*, March 21, 2003.

23. http://acehnet.tripod.com/asnlf.htm. Searle (2002) estimates the Acehnese are seriously divided on the merits of each alternative.

24. "Indonesia's war that won't go away" and "The key step for peace is ending corruption," comments by Sidney Jones in *The Observer Online*, crisisweb.org/projects/showreport.cfm?reportid=72 2002.

25. Jusuf Wanandi, "Regional Perspective on Asia Pacific Security: A Southeast Asian View" (Singapore, May 31, 2003—The Second International Institute of Strategic Studies, Asia Security Conference).

26. Samuel Kim, "East Asia and Globalization: Challenges and Responses," *Asian Perspective* (Dec. 1999).

27. MacIntyre (1994); Solingen (1999 and 2004). On the muted quality of Indonesian nationalism since the mid-1960s for reasons of political economy and regional cooperative security, see Leifer (2000).

28. Data on trade openness for 1950–1992 is from Heston and Summers (1991, 1995), supplemented for 1992–1996 by *World Development Indicators* (1998:310) and *World Development Reports* (1991 through 1997). All data on exports is from *World Tables* (1980, 1995), supplemented for 1992–1996 by *World Development Report* (1991–1997) and *World Development Indicators* (1998:188–89). All data on FDI is from *World Tables* (1980, 1995), supplemented for 1992–1996 by *World Development Report* (1991–1997) and *World Development Indicators* (1998:334).

29. Sylvia Tiwon, Northeast Asia Peace and Security Network Special Report, East Timor (Sept. 21, 1999).

30. Ross (2003) reports that Aceh's poverty rates in the 1970s and 1980s were the worst in Indonesia.

31. Brown (1994).

32. Golkar, Suharto's former party, got 20 percent of the votes, Abdurrahman Wahid's National Awakening Party (PKB) 16 percent, the Islamic party PPP 11 percent, and Amien Rais's PAN 7 percent of the vote. The 500-member Assembly also included 200 representatives from "functional groups" (religious, ethnic) and, notably, the military (38 members).

33. Soesastro (1999); Harymurti (1999); Murphy (1999); Solingen (2004). On the unwieldy and cleavaged nature of this coalition, see Shiraishi (2000).

34. "Wahid Prods Ministers to Fulfil IMF Obligations," *Jakarta Kompas*, June 28, 2000 (*FBIS-EAS*-2000-0628); *Far Eastern Economic Review*, April 6, 2000, p. 64, and April 13, 2000, p. 5; *Asiaweek*, April 21, 2000, p. 19. See also Murphy (1999:256). Wahid's own Coordinating Minister for Finance and Economy Kwik Kian Gie and Minister of State-owned Enterprises Laksamana Sukardi (from Megawati's party) were advancing populist policies.

35. Seth Mydans, "Indonesia Recoils at Uncurbed Island Killings," *New York Times*, June 28, 2000.

36. On the military's internal reform process and plots to oust Wahid, see "General Criticises Military Leadership," *Jakarta Kompas*, December 15, 1999 (*FBIS-EAS*-1999-1215), and "Defense Minister Says He Has Asked Wiranto to Resign," Hong Kong, *AFP*, February 4, 2000 (FBIS-EAS-2000-0204).

37. In the words of military spokesman Major General Sudrajat: "The demand for a referendum is not realistic. . . . Aceh is a part of Indonesia. So Aceh is managed by Acehnese people together with the Indonesian people. . . . That's why the demand for a referendum is not realistic and . . . separatism is unconstitutional. . . . A referendum on autonomy is fine . . . but a referendum on independence—no, because it will lead to a Balkanisation process. Yesterday, Timor; today Aceh; tomorrow Irian Jaya and the day after tomorrow Kalimantan" (Uchida 1999).

38. Suryadinata (2002a and b) defined Megawati's government as a "nationalist-Islamist coalition," and considered moderate Islamism as remaining weak in Indonesia, at least until early 2003.

39. *The Asian Wall Street Journal*, January 13, 2003:A10; Leheny (2003).

40. Jakarta TVRI 1 Television (November 1, 2001).

41. Jakarta TVRI 1 Television (November 1, 2001).

42. Sadanand Dhume, "Calling the IMF," *Far Eastern Economic Review*, Jan. 23, 2003:18. Foreign investment had already declined from $34 billion in 1997 to $9 billion in 2001 (*Far Eastern Economic Review*, December 12, 2002:19).

43. Searle (2002).

44. Lesley McCulloch, "Power before Peace in Aceh," *Asia Times*, March 2, 2002.

45. In July 2002, there were about 30,000 troops and police in Aceh, and TNI was reportedly pressing for at least an additional 3,000–4,000 troops (Niksch 2002).

46. William Furney, "Swede Span Soon Forgotten," *Daily Yomiuri*, June 13, 2003.

47. On cleavages within the military, see Shiraishi (2000).

48. *Global News Wire* (2003); Uchida (1999).

49. *The Jakarta Post*, August 21, 2002; Uchida (1999).

50. Alwi Shihab of the Islamist reform party PKB and a foreign minister under Wahid also feared a referendum could lead to the potential breakup of Indonesia.

51. Laksamana.net. 2003. April 20–29, 2003.

52. Alberto Alesina and Enrico Spolaore, "On the Number and Size of Nations," NBER Working Paper, March 1995.

53. External self-determination implies that each ethnic group would have the right to establish its own sovereign state. For some of the theoretical foundation for this thinking about external vs. internal self-determination, see Tomuschat, Sellers, Hannum. For more legalistic perspectives, see Lapidot (1992) and Koskenniemi (1994).

54. Stoel and speeches available on the OSCE website (www.osce.org/hcnm); I thank Anne Marie Gardner for introducing me to these sources.

55. SIRA (2000); Global Policy Forum/Forum Asia (2003).

56. On Megawati's own awareness that nearly all UN members endorse Indonesia's territorial integrity, see her address to the People's Consultative Assembly (November 1, 2001), Jakarta TVRI 1 Television (Nov. 1, 2001). The GAM leadership is also aware of its own weak international status. Addressing the massive demand for a referendum by the Acehnese in 1999, the Executive Council of the GAM raised a rhetorical question: "What has the world done so far since [1999] to respond to Acehnese demands? NOTHING! The world today is full of hypocrites and cool-blooded killers," acehnet.tripod.com/why.ht. A GAM commander defected on the eve of the 2003 Indonesian military offensive concluding that "Aceh did not have the international support needed to gain independence" (BBC News, news.bbc.co.uk/go/pr/fr/-/2/hi/asia-pacific/3026225.stm).

57. http://www.whitehouse.gov/news/releases/2001/09/20010919–5.html.

58. Furney (2003)

59. MOFA (2000); Personal interviews (Tokyo, June 2003).

60. July 28, 2000 http://www.mofa.go.jp.

61. The text of the Agreement can be found at www.usip.org/library/pa/aceh.

62. "Asean defends hands-off policy on Aceh," Indian Express, Reuters, Tuesday, November 23, 1999.

63. Thailand's Thaksin Shinawatra, revealing that Thailand and Indonesia agreed to exchange more intelligence on terrorism, added: "We will respect the rights and the territory of Indonesia. . . . No-one would be allowed to use Thailand as a base for separatist activities, especially groups operating in Aceh and Irian Jaya." *Bangkok Post*, "Indonesian leaders discuss anti-terrorism, fisheries, trade cooperation," January 22, 2002 (Internet Version WNC ASEAN). Malaysia's Prime Minister Mahathir Mohamad refused to grant asylum to a separatist leader of the Moro National Liberation Front (Philippines) and had him arrested in 2001 (Kirk 2001).

64. *Philippine Daily Inquirer* (Manila), November 14, 2001, "Arroyo, Megawati agree to work more closely to fight terrorism." Internet Version, WNC ASEAN.

65. Jane Perlez, "Indonesia Says It Will Press Attacks on Separatists in Sumatra," *New York Times*, May 23, 2003:A11.

66. "Déjà vu in Indonesia" (editorial), *The Japan Times*, July 7, 2003:16.

67. Jones (2003). Speaker of the Assembly Amien Rais went as far as proposing to cut diplomatic relations with Sweden unless it agrees to expatriate GAM leaders back to Indonesia. As for the IMF, senior economic minister Dorodjatum Kuntjoro-Jatki declared in July 2003 that Indonesia will not seek new IMF funding once it repays a $10 billion outstanding loan.

68. Migdal (2002) identifies three factors that explain why states have largely stayed intact: a global legal, normative, and political environment empowering states over centrifugal forces; the organizational imperatives of states and the exchange of citizens' loyalty for public goods or private rents; and people's "naturalization" of states as the most legitimate unit even when they fail in the provision of goods. Evangelista's (2002) findings suggest the Russian Republic is not likely to disintegrate as the Soviet Union did, nor will other ethnic republics follow the Chechen example.

69. The U.S., other powers, international institutions, and NGOs were able to persuade Megawati to accept the Henri Dunant mediated agreement in late 2002. A much less receptive neighboring backlash regime in Myanmar/Burma has used only brutal force and repression to effectively subjugate ethnic rebel groups such as the Christian Karens.

11

Mired in Mesopotamia?
The Iraq War
and American Interests

Steven E. Miller

It is now incontrovertibly clear that the Bush Administration seriously miscalculated the costs and benefits associated with its invasion of Iraq. Its determination to fight this easily avoidable war of choice was predicated on an interlocking set of optimistic assessments about the likely course and consequences of the conflict.[1]

It anticipated a quick, cheap win, a swift turnover to a stable and friendly Iraqi government, a brief stay for American forces in Iraq, and wide regional and international benefits from a successful intervention. According to numerous accounts, the Bush Administration expected that by August of 2003 U.S. forces would be largely extricated from Iraq.[2] It further expected that this decisive display of American power would cow other hostile powers, improve Washington's ability to coerce other rogue states in the region (notably Iraq's neighbors, Iran and Syria), and produce positive, reformist ripple effects throughout the Middle East. The Bush Administration firmly believed that much would be gained at modest cost.

Some portions of the Bush vision have come to pass and some of its aims may yet be achieved. Saddam's regime has been destroyed; Iraq has a real chance to build a better future; there have been some reformist developments in the region. But more than two and a half years after the invasion, large numbers of American forces remain in Iraq, losses mount week after week, and no end is in sight. Post-Saddam Iraq has become an unstable, violent, corrupt, deeply troubled place. The Bush Administration finds itself confronted with a tenacious and resilient insurgency and a political scene in Iraq that is less controllable and more complex than anticipated. All-out civil war has so far been avoided and some political and economic progress has been evident, but political momentum in Iraq has been halting and fragile; despite relentless pressure from Washington, relations among important political forces in Iraq are tense and antagonistic, and domestic power seems to be devolving to Islamist groups and religious figures whom the U.S. government views with suspicion.[3] Long after Washington expected to be able to withdraw from Iraq, the costs mount, the troubles persist, and crucial outcomes remain uncertain.

A big success cheaply achieved would have been an unambiguous triumph for the Bush Administration, particularly if it brought all the benefits which proponents of the war envisioned. It is far more difficult to appraise the messy reality that has actually materialized in Iraq since the U.S. invasion in March of 2003—particularly given the uncertainties in assessing the true character of that reality.[4] The Bush Administration underestimated the costs and overstated the gains of its Iraq policy, but it is still possible (indeed, many still argue) that the benefits will ultimately exceed the costs. Most observers' reaction to the war depends on whether or not they supported the Bush Administration and the launching of war in the first place. Supporters of the intervention grasp at every indication of progress in Iraq as evidence that U.S. policy will succeed and that the war was worthwhile. But it would be a hugely bankrupt policy that inflicted such substantial costs and problems for so long without producing any visible benefit. Conversely, opponents of Bush and the war are preoccupied with the ever-mounting costs and difficulties of the American presence in Iraq and often fail to credit the aims achieved and the progress made. All ambitious policies, especially those that entail the use of force, have costs: the existence of painful difficulties does not in itself demonstrate that the costs of the war exceed the benefits.

Not surprisingly, those directly responsible for a war that has taken many thousands of American, coalition, and Iraqi lives and has consumed more than $200 billion of American taxpayer money continue to insist that the war was necessary and that the results are positive, despite the ongoing trouble in Iraq. President Bush remains unapologetic and assertive in proclaiming the war was correct and that the outcome will be satisfactory—the U.S. will "prevail."[5] The public debate, however, is highly polarized even on the most basic judgments. For example, are we winning or losing in Iraq? On one side are those who believe that the United States is winning or that it will eventually win. Some argue, indeed, that the United States has already won or that the insurgents cannot possibly win.[6] In contrast are those who judge that the United States is losing in Iraq, has already lost, or that it cannot possibly win.[7] At some level, of course, this debate cannot be resolved in the midst of an ongoing intervention. As Condoleezza Rice suggested at her confirmation hearings in January 2005, it is too early to pass firm or final judgment on the war because the outcomes in Iraq are not yet clear. Signs of progress today could turn into success in the future (Rice did not add the opposite proposition but of course it is equally true that troubles today could be a mere prelude to disaster ahead).

Rice is correct, of course, that subsequent developments in Iraq will affect how Bush's policy is viewed in the future. If the eventual result in Iraq is congenial (that is, a reasonably stable, democratic, and friendly state emerges), the Bush intervention in Iraq will be viewed more favorably than if Iraq experiences a protracted period of violence and instability or descends into civil war or ends up governed by an unfriendly regime. It is incorrect, however, to suggest that interim assessment is neither possible nor desirable. On the contrary, wise policymaking should be based on a continuous honest audit of the costs and benefits of the chosen course of action. Furthermore, assessment of the intervention in Iraq should not be cast narrowly in terms of possible outcomes in Iraq. Though the public debate has become preoccupied with success or failure against the insurgency and success or failure in the democratization of Iraq, the essential question is not what ultimately happens in Iraq—though clearly that matters—but the aggregate impact of Bush's Iraq policy on American interests.

In this wider context, the proper question is not success or failure in Iraq per se, but rather what benefit to American interests at what costs. The analysis that follows suggests that the benefits of the Iraq intervention have been more modest than advertised while a comprehensive reckoning of the costs indicates that the United States has paid an enormous price for these modest benefits. Even if developments in Iraq turn out well, the net impact on American interests is arguably negative. If Iraq turns out badly, the United States will have paid a very high price in terms of America's net international position in order to produce a disaster.

SHRINKING BENEFITS (OR, THE DISAPPEARING RATIONALES)

Even a very costly policy can be justified if the aims are worthy, substantial, achievable, and achieved. In the case of Iraq, however, the benefits have turned out to be more limited than anticipated by proponents of the war. Indeed, each of the three primary rationales for the war—the gains to be achieved, the interests advanced—has proven in the event to be less worthwhile, or less real than advertised. Some gains have of course been made—above all the removal of a brutal tyrant—but overall the benefits have been small and the impacts on American interests modest or negative. This is because the imminently threatening weapons of mass destruction (WMD) were never found, the al-Qaeda connection did not exist, and democracy for Iraq has proven to be both elusive and an unreliable promoter of American interests.

No Weapons of Mass Destruction

The case for war against Iraq rested heavily on the perception that Saddam Hussein possessed weapons of mass destruction in contravention of both Iraq's international legal obligations and the UN resolutions associated with the termination of the 1991 Gulf War.[8] In particular, the Bush Administration asserted that Iraq was aggressively and successfully pursuing nuclear weapons. The prospect of Saddam Hussein armed with weapons of mass destruction was almost uniformly regarded as highly undesirable. The Bush Administration went further, insisting that the imminent threat posed by Saddam's WMD programs was intolerable and needed to be eliminated by force of arms. In the run-up to war, this was the primary rationale for invasion.

However, when UN inspectors went into Iraq in the period before the war, they found no nuclear, biological, or chemical weapons, nor evidence of active WMD programs. When U.S. forces rolled into Iraq they went looking at the sites the Bush Administration had loudly and confidently proclaimed to be WMD facilities, but they found no nuclear, biological, or chemical weapons. After Saddam's regime had fallen, the search for Iraq's WMD fell to the special Iraq Survey Group (ISG) which had no other purpose than to discover Iraq's WMD. More than a year of intensive investigation yielded the conclusion that there were no weapons of mass destruction.[9] The Bush Administration wanted very badly to find conclusive evidence of Saddam's active and imminently threatening WMD programs and tried very hard to discover such evidence in order to validate the assumption that supported the case for war.[10] Instead, as David Kay, the first head of the ISG, bluntly put it in prominent testimony before the Senate Armed Services Committee, "It turns out we were all wrong."[11]

Iraq had once had active WMD programs, including a nuclear weapons development program that was surprisingly advanced when discovered after the first Gulf War. This was proven conclusively by the inspections undertaken by the UN Special Commission (UNSCOM) during the course of the 1990s. Nor does there seem to be any doubt that Saddam Hussein had an appetite for WMD—perhaps especially for nuclear weapons. But the UN destroyed that program as a consequence of the first Gulf War. On the basis of the extensive evidence gathered so far, it appears that Iraq simply had not made any meaningful progress toward acquisition of nuclear weapons or other WMD after the UN inspectors were withdrawn in December 1998.

Given Saddam's obvious desire for nuclear weapons, Iraq would remain a nonproliferation worry so long as he remained in power. With Saddam's regime eliminated, Iraq is no longer a proliferation concern. This is a plus for the Bush policy. Nevertheless, there is no indication that Saddam was close to obtaining nuclear weapons or that his nuclear weapons program had any significant momentum, and no suggestion in the evidence gathered since the invasion that Saddam possessed a significant operational capability to use chemical or biological weapons. Thus, the Bush Administration initiated war with Iraq in large measure to eliminate an imminent WMD threat that simply did not exist.

No Link to al-Qaeda?

In the aftermath of the 9/11 attacks, it was clear that the United States was going to pursue and strike back at the terrorist organization that perpetrated the attack. The Bush Administration also understandably and correctly proclaimed a policy of holding accountable any state sponsors allied and providing support to members of the al-Qaeda consortium. Al-Qaeda was threatening enough in its own right, but al-Qaeda backed by the resources of a state represented an even more formidable danger—a combination the Bush Administration deemed intolerable. This policy led directly to the war in Afghanistan against a Taliban regime both closely allied with and providing bases and support to al-Qaeda. The war in Afghanistan commanded wide international support and was willingly endorsed by America's allies, some of whom volunteered to participate in the war effort, because the ties between the Taliban and al-Qaeda were clear and substantial.

From the earliest moments after the 9/11 attacks, however, the Bush Administration harbored suspicions that Baghdad was involved and contemplated using force against Iraq, a possibility that was set aside when President Bush decided that Afghanistan must be addressed first.[12] Once the Taliban was driven from power in Afghanistan, Iraq reemerged at the top of the Bush Administration's agenda, and the period from the spring of 2002 until the invasion on March 19, 2003 appears in retrospect to have been one long inexorable movement toward war. Both before and after the invasion, President Bush frequently represented the war in Iraq as a key element of the post-9/11 war on terrorism—indeed, he has described it as the central battleground of the American fight against terrorism. Because it assumed that Iraq possessed or was aggressively seeking WMD and might share them with terrorists, the Bush Administration viewed the Iraq campaign as imperative.

If there were clear evidence of substantial ties between Saddam Hussein and al-Qaeda, the war in Iraq, like that in Afghanistan, would have attracted wide support. However, though the case for war often implied such a connection, no evidence suggests that Iraq was in any way involved in 9/11. The Bush Administration eventually conceded this.[13] There is still no significant evidence demonstrating a link between Saddam Hussein and Osama bin Laden.[14] Saddam's Iraq, like many Arab and Islamic countries, viewed the Palestinian cause with great sympathy and gave tangible support to Palestinian groups regarded as terrorist by the United States though not in much of the Arab world. Those Palestinian groups, however, were not the target of the U.S. war against terrorists with "global reach"—that is, those who had struck the United States on 9/11 and might strike it again.

In short, the Bush Administration made the war against Iraq one of the centerpieces of its strategic response to 9/11 though there is nothing substantial that connects Iraq to either 9/11 or the organization that perpetrated it. Ironically, since the coalition invasion in March of 2003, Iraq has become a center of terrorist activity and a haven for violent jihadists from throughout the greater Middle East. It is the Bush Administration's war against terrorism that turned Iraq into a terrorist hot spot.

Bringing Democracy to Iraq (and to the Middle East)

As the other two primary rationales for war in Iraq faded, the Bush Administration has increasingly emphasized the democratization of Iraq as the driving objective of American policy. President Bush has repeatedly asserted that the United States is bringing freedom to Iraq and suggests or implies that so doing will advance U.S. interests in the war against terrorism by pacifying Iraq and promoting desirable reform throughout the Middle East. The President's determination to "stay the course" in Iraq is driven largely by the belief that perseverance by the United States will produce the desired democratic result in Iraq. Unfortunately, nearly three years of American presence in Iraq has not yielded any confidence that the outcome will conform to Washington's preferences. Worse, even if the Bush Administration succeeds in bringing democracy to Iraq, it is questionable whether that success will include the anticipated benefits for American interests and the war on terrorism. The Bush Administration's democratization policy, like its broader case for the Iraq war, is based on a set of dubious assumptions.

First, indications of progress notwithstanding, the objective of producing a stable democracy in Iraq may not be feasible. Quite apart from the serious difficulties still evident in Iraq, the record of externally imposed democratization or that democracy is a reliable consequence of the use of force is not heartening. The United States has been in the business of promoting democracy around the world at least since the time of Woodrow Wilson, and democracy promotion was a major element in the foreign policies of Presidents Carter, Reagan, and Clinton. If Washington knew how to successfully "export" democracy, the world today would be overwhelmingly democratic. As Robert Jervis has written, for example, as a general proposition "there is no reason to expect the United States to be able to make most countries democratic even if it were to bend all its efforts to this end," while history suggests that in Iraq "it is hard to believe that the near future will see a full-fledged democracy in that country, with extensive rule of law, open competition, a free press, and checks and balances."[15]

Those who wish to suggest that in Iraq there are hopeful signs of democratic progress will point to the successful transfer of sovereignty in the spring of 2004, the emergence of political parties in Iraq, the Iraqi elections of January 2005, and the ongoing process of writing and ratifying the new Iraqi constitution. These are indeed components of the complex reality in Iraq—and one can only hope that these are harbingers of things to come. But the dominant reality in Iraq today is internal strife and hardship. Iraq now does not possess anything remotely resembling a normal or stable social, economic, or political life. Rather, it is a violent, bloody, lawless, dangerous land in which the existing authorities have not come close to satisfying one of the minimum criteria for political order: establishing a monopoly on the use of force within the borders of the state. In Iraq today, kidnappings and murders are endemic.[16] Assassinations are common.[17] Iraqi political figures are particular targets. Those who work for or cooperate with American forces and authorities jeopardize their lives. Attacks against Iraqi police and security forces are frequent; several hundred are killed monthly, nearly 2,000 in the first nine months of 2005.[18] Insurgent attacks occur daily, killing Americans but far more Iraqis, including many innocent civilians. It is not unusual for daily losses among Iraqis to number in the hundreds. Gangs and private militias control significant areas within Iraq and in places are more effective providers of public goods—trash pickup, traffic control, public safety, than the official authorities. Corruption appears to be widespread. Sectarian violence among Iraq's major religious groupings, particularly between the Shia and the Sunni, appears to be escalating rather than abating. Alongside the persistent, routine, daily violence, the long-suffering Iraqi population continues to experience regular deprivations involving basic necessities of life: water supplies are subject to prolonged interruptions; electricity cannot be counted on for more than a few hours a day in Baghdad; gasoline is in short supply.[19]

Perhaps all this trouble represents nothing more than a temporary detour on the road to democracy, just the sensational underside of the transformation of Iraq. But it may instead represent a breakdown of political order so deep that democracy is unattainable on any timeline or at any price that the U.S. government and public should be willing to pay. The Bush Administration has paid a heavy price in pursuit of an untenable objective.

Second and even more vexing, if Bush actually succeeded in promoting democracy in Iraq, would this also promote America's regional and international interests? In a bitter irony, democracy in Iraq is bringing to power governments unfriendly towards the United States. The political process which the Bush Administration unleashed in Iraq has produced a situation in which the single most influential political figure in Iraq is an ayatollah with an Iranian passport—the formidable Ayatollah Sistani. The Iraqi elections of January 2005 in which the Bush Administration takes understandable pride, have brought to the fore Islamist Shiite parties whose ideologies and aims seem far different from those of the United States. The two parties most empowered so far by the electoral process in Iraq are the Supreme Council for the Islamic Revolution in Iraq (SCIRI) and the Dawa party, which is devoted to promoting Sharia (Islamist) law in Iraq. Though Secretary of Defense Rumsfeld has insisted that the United States did not fight a war in Iraq in order to create an Islamic republic, these parties seem quite likely to desire just such a state. As one close observer of the Iraqi scene, Peter Galbraith, has written, "It may be the ultimate irony that the United States, which, among other reasons, invaded Iraq to help bring liberal democracy to the Middle East, will play a decisive role in establishing its second Shiite Islamic state."[20] The United States may prefer a secular democratic state with civil rights for women and respect for minority rights, but to date the political situation disfavors such equality and has produced disaffection among Iraq's minorities, above all the Sunnis. The internal character of the emerging "democratic" Iraq appears significantly different from that which Washington envisioned when it invaded Iraq.

Even more troubling for American interests is the likely external orientation of the emerging Iraqi government, which is unlikely to favor American bases in Iraq or a protracted American presence. Indeed, the Shiite clerics who are now dominating Iraq's post-intervention politics do not favor the United States in general: "None of Iraq's leading Shiite clerics is friendly to the United States. . . . None seem to trust the United States or assume that the United States has a benevolent agenda in the region. The ouster of Saddam thus earned the United States surprisingly little credit with a clerical leadership that suffered unspeakable oppression under the ousted tyrant."[21]

The future Iraqi government also may not be favorably disposed toward Israel. Those Iraqi factions who distrust the United States are unlikely to be warm towards Washington's Israeli ally. But even those Iraqi political forces favorably inclined toward the United States may share the deep dislike of Israel so common in the Islamic world.

Even more problematic, a democratic Iraq ruled by Shiite parties may have better relations with Washington's enemies than with Washington. The new Iraqi government is reconstituting affinity with Iran, America's largest and most worrisome rival in the region. As Mark Danner explains, "A truly democratic Iraq was always likely to be an Iraq led not only by Shia, who are the majority of Iraqis, but by those Shia parties that are largest and best organized—the Supreme Council for the Islamic Revolution in Iraq and the Dawa Islamic Party—which happen to be those blessed by the religious authorities and nurtured in Iran."[22]

There are many indications that this emerging rapprochement between Iraq and Iran should worry Washington. Elected Iraqi leaders have made pilgrimages to Teheran. A substantial Iran-Iraq pipeline deal has already been signed. There have reportedly been discussions between the emerging Iraqi government and Iran about joint training of military forces. In the complex relationships within Islam, the Shiite regimes in Teheran and Baghdad are Shiite brethren. Thus, the Bush invasion of Iraq not only provided Teheran a major strategic gain by eliminating Iran's mortal enemy, Saddam Hussein, but also created the opportunity for Iran to forge close ties with its Shiite neighbor. So long as U.S. relations with Iran remain deeply hostile, this can hardly be regarded as a plus for the United States.

In a number of specific respects, therefore, a "democratic" Iraq is problematic for Washington. The overriding premise of the Bush policy that a democratic Iraq will be a tame and congenial international actor and a benign factor within its region thus turns out to be a questionable premise.

The premise that Iraq will be a benign regional factor is based on the proposition that democracies do not fight each other—the so-called democratic peace hypothesis. But Iraq's situation does not meet the conditions of this logic. First, while it seems that mature democracies do not fight each other, democratizing states turn out to be quite force-prone. As the most extensive analysis of the question concludes, "transitions to democracy often give rise to war rather than peace."[23] A democratizing Iraq could easily be a reckless and aggressive regional actor—leaders in new democracies often resort to virulent nationalism and assertive external policies to promote cohesion within. Second, while it may be true that mature democracies do not war against one another, many of Iraq's neighbors and rivals are not democratic. Nothing in the democratic peace notion suggests that a single democratic state in a largely nondemocratic region will bring peace and stability. (In the Middle East, the presence of Israel, a democracy surrounded by hostile nondemocracies, surely demonstrates the point.)

Finally, in the context of the war on terror, it is necessary to ask whether democracy is an effective antidote to terrorism. The Bush policy asserts that the "expansion of freedom" and the spread of democracy will diminish or eliminate the threat of terrorism. As one observer has commented, "Democracy has become George W. Bush's reflexive answer to terrorism."[24] Unfortunately, considerable evidence suggests that democracy is not a reliable answer to terrorist threat, either for Iraq or countries like Iran which are hesitantly seeking to democratize in the greater Middle East.

THE CONSEQUENCES

Mounting Costs: Growing Pain for Limited Gain

Thus the benefit side of the ledger has been meager, but the cost side is even worse. The obvious costs are painful enough: more than 2,000 American lives lost and more than $200 billion of American taxpayer dollars spent. These costs continue to grow daily. But to these negatives we must add a disturbing array of political, reputational, and military costs, as well as adverse consequences for the war against terrorism. The United States has paid a high price for its limited gains in Iraq.

Diplomatic Consequences: Damaging America's International Position

In the immediate aftermath of the attacks on September 11, 2001, the United States had the support and sympathy of nearly the entire world. Washington's NATO allies quickly and without hesitation invoked for the first time the famous Article V of the North Atlantic Treaty: an attack on one is an attack on all. The mood in Europe was captured by a headline in the French newspaper, *Le Monde*, which famously proclaimed, "We are all Americans now." Indeed, not only America's friends and allies, but also its rivals and adversaries responded to 9/11 with surprising generosity and expressions of willingness to help in the war against terrorists. Washington's relations with China warmed considerably after a frigid first few months at the outset of the Bush Administration. The government of Iran offered immediate expressions of condolence, condemned the attacks, and indicated a willingness to cooperate with U.S. anti-terror efforts. Remarkably, the attacks of 9/11 provoked a global alignment against terrorism and gave Washington an opportunity to fashion a cooperative international endeavor against al-Qaeda and its terrorist cells. This unprecedented global support was a tremendous potential asset for the United States in the post-9/11 environment.

By March 2003, a scant eighteen months later, the Bush Administration's drive toward war with Iraq had left the great global coalition in tatters. The United States remorselessly pursued a policy opposed by rivals and allies alike. When the Bush Administration sought from the UN Security Council a resolution authorizing the use of force against Iraq, even two of Washington's long close allies, France and Germany, not only opposed the Bush initiative but worked actively to subvert American policy. China and Russia adamantly opposed Bush's resolution, and Moscow threatened to use its veto. The world saw the spectacle of the American Secretary of State begging the members of the Security Council for votes but failing to get them. Despite strenuous efforts to prod, persuade, bully, and bribe, in the end Washington could muster only four votes including its own and Britain's, thus meeting a stinging defeat. The process damaged many important relationships with developing nations as well as with allies.

In short, within eighteen months the United States squandered the near total support that existed after 9/11 and found itself meeting bitter opposition from much of the world. This was a stunning reversal of fortune. In March 2003, in his resignation speech from the pro-Bush Blair government, British Minister Robin Cook registered this point:

History will be astonished at the diplomatic miscalculations that led so quickly to the disintegration of that powerful coalition. . . . Our interests are best protected not by unilateral action but by multilateral agreement and a world order governed by rules. Yet tonight the international partnerships most important to us are weakened: the European Union is divided; the Security Council is in stalemate. Those are heavy casualties of a war in which a shot has yet to be fired.[25]

Reputational Consequences

Damaging America's Reputation for Power

Many advocates of the war in Iraq were motivated in part by a concern that America's vast power was not influential enough internationally and that restraint in the use of its power diminished the impact of American primacy. William Kristol commented that in the Middle East there was "a lack of awe for the U.S." and "an absence of respect that fostered contempt."[26] A triumphant use of force in Iraq would display both Washington's willingness to employ it, and its effectiveness. This would bolster America's reputation for power around the world, causing allies to be more respectful, opponents to be more compliant. The Bush Administration believed an impressive victory in Iraq would show America's superiority,

Thirty-one months later, however, the ongoing intervention in Iraq has had nearly the opposite effect on America's reputation for power. Although the U.S. military performed impressively in some respects, particularly in its dramatic dash to Baghdad and rapid defeat of Saddam's Baathist regime in Iraq, the main effect of the Iraq campaign has been to reveal "the limitations and inadequacies of American (military) power."[27]

The war has had at least four damaging consequences for global perceptions of U.S. power. First, the aura of invincibility is gone. For more than two years the mightiest military ever seen, a half-trillion-dollar-a-year behemoth, has been mired in the desert sands of Mesopotamia—stymied by relatively small numbers of lightly armed insurgents. The Bush Administration has had a big part in eroding the image of American power by its insistence for many months that the insurgency was the work of a mere 5,000 Baathist "bitter-enders." In other words, America's half-trillion-dollar-per-annum war machine and its 150,000 well-armed and well-trained forces are thwarted by a relative handful of Baathist thugs. While high-tech warfare against the United States is doubtless futile in the face of U.S. superiority, what Iraq has shown is how effective asymmetric warfare is against the muscle-bound superpower. According to the Bush Administration's own reckoning, tiny adversary forces can operate surprisingly well against forward-deployed U.S. military forces— not a message Washington wished to broadcast to the world.

Second, the United States has strained to maintain its deployments in Iraq. With the current size and character of the all-volunteer force, Washington's ability to deploy combat forces overseas to hostile environments is limited. The Bush Administration has been able to sustain force levels in Iraq only by drawing heavily on reserve and National Guard units. It has required regular Army and Marine contingents to accept repeated postings to Iraq. Forces for a large-scale escalation of the U.S. military presence in Iraq have simply not been available. Should another large-scale military crisis arise while the United States is still heavily engaged in Iraq, it is hard to say how Washington would find sufficient ground forces to cope with it. In short, Iraq has shown that the shortage of manpower in its combat ground force units significantly constrains America's expensive, capital-intensive, high-tech military.[28] This realization must be a relief to Washington's enemies around the world.

Third, by committing so much of its military power against Iraq, the Bush Administration has reduced its ability to threaten or sustain coercive pressure against other adversaries. Washington no longer enjoys the strategic value of uncommitted power. Uncommitted forces would be available for use against Iran, North Korea, or another adversary, and all serious opponents would worry that the forces might be concentrated against them. Once forces are mobilized for a particular scenario, however, their coercive potential becomes limited. For example, commenting on the U.S. involvement in the 1970 crisis in Jordan, Alan Henrikson observes that "the power that was held in reserve was the more effective and the power that was locally deployed became a potential reflector of weakness and cause of embarrassment."[29] So in Iraq, adversaries have had more license and room for maneuver. Thus, as America's leaders and American forces became engaged with Iraq, North Korea undertook a brazen series of moves to flout Washington—throwing out IAEA inspectors, restarting its plutonium production program, withdrawing from the NPT, while declaring itself to possess nuclear weapons. Preoccupied with Iraq and knowing that the U.S. military was tied down in Iraq, President Bush was left lamely to insist that North Korea's nuclear misbehavior did not constitute a crisis.

Not only does the Iraq war restrict the coercive potential of American power, sapping the credibility of future threats, it hampers Washington's ability to cope with other opponents. As Stanley Kober notes, "We are now encountering such difficulty [in Iraq] that even if we are able to achieve victory in some local sense, nobody will believe that we would willingly undertake such an effort again elsewhere."[30] And as Israeli scholar Barry Rubin adds: "Those who argue, in the words of Ayatollah Ruhollah Khomeini two decades ago, that the US cannot do a 'damn thing' are having that feeling reinforced today. The Iraq war's outcome has undermined the credibility of US power no matter how long American forces remain in Iraq. Indeed, one could argue that the longer they remain, the worse the problem will become."[31] Thus, instead of repairing America's reputation for power, the intervention in Iraq has undermined it.

Finally, Iraq has shown that the United States cannot convert its military superiority into desired political outcomes. Since the U.S. military arrived in Baghdad, very little has gone as Washington wished. The U.S. could not maintain public order. Iraq did not welcome Washington's favorite Iraqi exiles as the country's new leaders. The mullahs and ayatollahs emerged as the most influential political actors. The U.S. has been unable to suppress the violent insurgency. Most crucial, the political outcome in Iraq remains in doubt and appears unlikely to reflect Washington's preferences.

Damaging America's Moral Standing

Concern about the impact of unfortunate American behavior and policies that appear to approve, tolerate, or condone it, is voiced most passionately not by critics but by ardent conservative supporters of the war. Senator John McCain, for example, led the charge in the U.S. Senate to pass an amendment that explicitly prohibits the use of cruel, inhumane, or degrading treatment of detainees by U.S. forces. McCain offered an eloquent justification for holding the United States to high standards:

> I hold no brief for the prisoners. I do hold a brief for the reputation of the United States of America. We are Americans, and we hold ourselves to humane standards of treatment of people no matter how evil or terrible they may be. To do otherwise undermines our security, but it also undermines our greatness as a nation. . . . We stand for something more in the world—a moral mission, one of freedom and democracy and human rights at home and abroad. . . . These are the values that distinguish us from our enemies.

McCain's broadest reason why such considerations matter for U.S. interests concerns success in the war against terrorism. As he vigorously expressed it, "Prisoner abuses exact on us a terrible toll in the war of ideas, because inevitably these abuses become public. When they do, the cruel actions of a few darken the reputation of our country in the eyes of millions. American values should win against all others in any war of ideas, and we can't let prisoner abuse tarnish our image."[32] Similarly, conservative journalist Andrew Sullivan, a strong and unwavering supporter of the war in Iraq, has been relentlessly outspoken about the effect on U.S. interests of the protracted prisoner abuse scandal: "The prevalence of brutality and inhumanity among American interrogators has robbed the United States of the high ground it desperately needs to maintain in order to win. What better weapon for Al Qaeda than the news that an inmate at Guantanamo was wrapped in an Israeli flag or that prisoners at Abu Ghraib were raped?"[33]

Sullivan has extensively documented the Bush Administration's convoluted legal justifications for torture: he is convinced the highest levels of the

U.S. government blessed a policy of promoting torture. Regarding these policies and actions as a major betrayal of the war effort, Sullivan suggests that
the Bush Administration's "immoral, feckless, and inhumane" conduct of the
war has brought "profound moral disgrace" to the United States.[34]

Although McCain's Senate amendment prohibiting mistreatment of prisoners seeks to help improve America's moral standing, it will probably not
repair the damage to America's moral reputation in the international arena.
The deeds are done, the photos distributed, the revelatory reports published, the feeble rationalizations widely spread. Further evidence of mis-
deeds continues to arise. Strikingly, while a few lowly soldiers have been
punished, no important person in the higher chain of command has been
held accountable or faced serious penalty. The Bush Administration continues to insist that its approach is appropriate and justified. Indeed, the Bush
Administration strenuously opposed the McCain amendment and threatened
to veto it.[35] If official policy continues to defend and excuse what much of
the world regards as reprehensible, no amount of Congressional action or
journalists' outrage will restore America's moral standing. The U.S. has
already damaged its reputation on the world stage.

The sober message of *Financial Times* columnist Philip Stephens illus-
trates how erosion of America's moral reputation affects how others perceive
and respond to the U.S. and its policy:

> Guantanamo, and secret facilities elsewhere, were established to put suspects
> beyond the reach of the US constitution. The dispatch (known as rendition) of
> alleged terrorists to regimes practiced in torture and the clandestine activities of the
> CIA have the same purpose. In the eyes of much of the rest of the world the effect
> has been to rob the US of the moral high ground, to demean its democracy and to
> undermine its mission of spreading freedom. I have heard American friends say
> such draconian measures are proportionate to the threat. But I am not sure they
> appreciate how badly America's standing and influence has been tarnished.[36]

America's ability to convey its message of human rights and democratization and to justify war in terms of those worthy ends fails when American
behavior is incompatible with the values it professes to be championing.
Thus, columnist Nat Hentoff, after reciting a substantial list of documented
cases of American abuse of detainees, asks incredulously, "All this in further-
ance of spreading freedom and democracy throughout the world?"[37] In short,
America has lost the moral high ground. This is a cost—intangible, unmea-
surable, but real—of the war of choice in Iraq.

Damaging America's Political Attractiveness

The invasion of Iraq has had devastating consequences for American popularity around the world. As poll after poll shows, favorable views of the

United States have fallen to shocking lows. Anti-Americanism is deeper and broader than at any time in modern history, and though most acute in the Muslim world, the phenomenon spans the globe.[38]

Military Consequences

Vulnerable Flank

The Bush Administration complains about the opportunity it has created for America's rivals in the region, Iran and Syria, to cause problems, deploring any Iraq-Iran detente, and alleging that Iran is arming insurgents with powerful bombs.[39]

Damaging U.S. Ground Forces

Though the invasion was meant to display the scope of American military power, the protracted struggle in Iraq has shown the limits of America's ability to deploy ground forces overseas. We and the world have discovered that the U.S. military's all-volunteer force is too small to sustain needed overseas combat deployments without imposing great stress on the Army, Marines, and their Reserve and Guard components. Struggling to preserve inadequate deployments, the U.S. lacks forces to escalate its presence without expanding the military overall. American soldiers are suffering repeated prolonged tours of hazardous duty in Iraq, raising grave concerns that the U.S. ground forces are wearing thin.

How serious is this problem? In testimony before the Senate Foreign Relations Committee, retired U.S. Army General Barry McCaffrey warned that Iraq is causing the U.S. military to head toward a "meltdown."[40] Mackubin Thomas Owens believes that U.S. ground forces are "being stretched to near the breaking point."[41] Retired Lieutenant General Marc Cisneros believes that unless the U.S. changes course in Iraq "the damage will go deeper than it did in Vietnam"[42]—a shocking thought given that it took the U.S. military many years to recover from the traumas imposed by Vietnam. Former National Security Council staff member Richard Clarke reports growing alarm in the American officer corps that "the American military has been seriously damaged" and summarizes the evil which the protracted U.S. presence and the insurgency have caused:

One victim of this slow bleeding in Iraq is the American military as an institution. . . . The National Guard . . . is in tatters. Re-enlistments are down, training for domestic support missions is spotty at best, equipment is battered and many units are either in Iraq or on their way to or from it. Now the rot is beginning to spread into the regular Army. Recruiters are coming up dry. . . . With almost every unit in the Army on the conveyor belt into and out of Iraq, few units are really combat ready for other missions.[43]

There may be disagreement about how severe the problems are, but defense correspondent Fred Kaplan concludes that "the war in Iraq is wrecking the US Army."[44] He sees an increasingly serious problem with recruitment and retention. As an important RAND study concluded in the summer of 2005, "Deployments to Iraq and Afghanistan have stretched the US Army so thin that its ability to retain and recruit soldiers is threatened."[45] It is not surprising that the Army's recruitment problems have been described as "desperate"[46] because the Army has been missing monthly recruitment goals, is unlikely to meet annual targets despite a lowering of standards and increase in benefits for enlisting personnel. Even applications to the U.S. military academies have dropped significantly.[47] It is questionable whether the U.S. military can now preserve existing force levels.

The implications of this problem for U.S. military policy are huge. "Enormous strain is now being imposed on U.S. soldiers and marines by the Iraq mission and other responsibilities. Alas, there is little prospect that these strains will fade away anytime soon." The top priority for defense planners today is thus to avoid breaking the American ground forces by driving out good people who decide that they are no longer willing to endure the excessive pace of deployment after deployment.[48] It will, it appears, be a significant challenge just to preserve the existing size and quality of U.S. ground forces.

Iraq has also voraciously consumed equipment and logistics. Some equipment, of course, is directly destroyed. But much more equipment is simply worn out by intense use: the demands of the Iraq war greatly reduce the service life of weapons. This has caused equipment to be drawn from U.S. forces all over the world and resulted in a global maintenance issue for the U.S. military. For example, the General Accounting Office found in the fall of 2004 that 50–80 percent of the equipment with U.S. forces in Korea was not mission-capable.[49] The Iraq war therefore will leave not only a legacy of manpower issues, but the need for major capital reinvestment in military equipment. It will take years to recover from the drain on U.S. capabilities which the Iraq war has caused.

IRAQ AND THE WAR ON TERRORISM

President Bush has repeatedly described Iraq as the central battlefield in the war on terror. But Iraq is a net liability in the war on terrorism. Even if it has imposed some attrition on attacking jihadist groups and pulled terrorists to Iraq in lieu of other targets, the war in Iraq is fueling the hatred that provokes terrorism in the first place, inspiring more people to join the ranks of terrorism, and serving as a training ground for a transnational collection of Islamist terrorists. The Iraqi insurgents' success in prolonging the insurgency and tying down and draining American forces may raise their esteem in the eyes of Arab publics. More broadly, the war in Iraq has had a negative impact on America's ability to prosecute an effective anti-terror policy.

Impact on the Battle for Hearts and Minds

Combating terrorism is as much a political as a military struggle. The primary objective of anti-terrorist strategies and policies must be to minimize the appeal of terrorist ideologies and reduce the motivation to engage in terrorist acts. As Daniel Pipes has written, "The true enemy in the war on terror is the belief system that motivates the use of terrorism." This "political-ideological dimension . . . is the vital battleground."[50] Even the Bush Administration is aware of this need. As Secretary of State Condoleezza Rice put it, "To win the war on terror, we must win a war of ideas."[51] Accordingly, one must assess the impact of all major components of the war on terrorism including Iraq on this essential "war of ideas."

To put it mildly, Iraq fares poorly as a proving ground for ideas to combat terrorism. Most of the world opposed the U.S. invasion; its ongoing presence is deeply unpopular in the Arab world. The Iraq intervention appears to confirm many of Osama bin Laden's claims about the United States. Washington has repeatedly protested that its intentions are benign, but the Iraq intervention gives radical Islamist polemicists continuing ammunition for their assertions that the United States wishes to dominate Arab lands, covets the region's oil, despoils Islamic holy sites, and is indifferent to the loss of Muslim lives and the suffering of Muslim populations. By its actions in Iraq, the United States appears to have evoked a colonial past widely despised throughout the region. Rashad Khalidi asks, for example, "whether by invading, occupying, and imposing a new regime in Iraq, the United States may be stepping, intentionally or not, into the boots of the old Western colonial powers, and even worse, may be doing so in a region that within living memory concluded a lengthy struggle to expel their hated occupations."[52] The loss of innocent life—that is inevitable in a military operation and may especially accompany urban counterinsurgency operations—produces tragic deaths and pain. The horrible imagery of such tragedies is regularly on display across the Arab world, making the United States seem culpable for unspeakable cruelties and for bringing suffering and death to blameless civilians. That women and children, the elderly and the infirm, are among the victims of Iraq's violence only intensifies the impact of these negative consequences. The scandals involving torture at Abu Ghraib and Guantanamo only reinforce such imagery and its effect.

In short, America's invasion of Iraq is highly detrimental to the Arab and Islamic worlds that America must win to its side if the battle against terrorism is ever to succeed. When asked about the impact of the U.S. invasion, Syria's

Sheik Ahmad Hassoun (Grand Mufti of Aleppo) answered, "The United States will lose not only Iraq but the Islamic world with its current policy."[53] The course of America's Iraq policy gives reason to think such an assessment may be correct. Certainly the evidence shows that America's invasion and continuing presence in Iraq represent a devastating setback for the United States in the fundamentally important battle to win hearts and minds in the Islamic world.

Does Iraq Strengthen the Terrorists?

In a prescient essay published just before the invasion of Iraq, Israeli scholar Avishai Margalit warned that Iraq was the wrong war to fight because it represented exactly the sort of overreaction bin Laden was hoping to provoke. The effect of such a war, Margalit argued, would be increasingly to radicalize the populations that bin Laden was seeking to influence and from which his organization would draw its recruits. As Margalit explained: "Radical Islam is and should be regarded as the enemy. And fighting Saddam Hussein will greatly help this enemy rather than set him back. This will be true even if the war is successful, let alone if it turns out to be unsuccessful."[54]

Three years into Bush's Iraq intervention, it appears that Margalit was correct. The insurgents replenish their manpower despite efforts by the U.S. military to reduce their number. As the Bush Administration complains, foreign jihadis from throughout the region are pouring into Iraq by the hundreds, intensifying the difficulties of U.S. forces. Borders with Syria, Iran, and even Saudi Arabia are not secured. Iraq is undergoing an unprecedented epidemic of suicide bombings, directed against both Americans and Iraqis. There is apparently no shortage of insurgents willing to sacrifice themselves in such bombings. The almost daily casualties among American forces in Iraq, so ghastly and tragic from the American point of view, are a sign of skill, effectiveness, and success for the insurgents and a point of pride for their propaganda to promote. The insurgent attacks have become more sophisticated, suggesting that the forces opposing the United States are learning as a consequence of the Iraq experience.

In short, Iraq appears both to have given the radical Islamist enemy a significant propaganda victory and increased the size, skill, and motivation of the forces opposed to the United States. Many fear that the war in Iraq has been counterproductive in its effects on the war against terrorism. Philip Stephens of the *Financial Times*, writing in the aftermath of the July 2005 terrorist attacks in London, has summarized an increasingly common perception: "The present insurgency serves both as recruiting agent and training ground for Al Qaeda's war against the west. Whatever one thinks of the original decision to remove Mr. Hussein, the hubris that preceded the invasion and the negligence that has followed it have given strength and succour to the Islamists."[55] In sum, "Iraq is now a bloody playground for existing groups of Islamist terrorists—and probably a breeding ground for new ones."[56]

As a battleground in the war on terrorism as Bush has many times insisted, Iraq has many advantages for the al-Qaeda enemy. The Bush Administration and other supporters of the war will say it is better to meet al-Qaeda in Iraq than on the streets of America's cities. But al-Qaeda's high level of global terrorist activities since the invasion show that Iraq has not deprived bin Laden's affiliates of the ability to conduct terror strikes around the world. Attacks from Bali to Madrid, Istanbul to London, show that the war in Iraq far from inhibits further attack on a global scale. The United States has had the good luck to escape attack since 9/11, but there is no reason to think that war in Iraq is the reason for this good fortune, nor is there any reason to think that Iraq has made the United States immune from attack.

CONCLUSIONS

It is impossible to judge an event except in historical perspective. Nearly two hundred years after the events, Chairman Mao Zedong was not ready to say that the French Revolution of 1789 had been a success: he was still awaiting a final historical verdict. The invasion and occupation of Iraq by the United States and a few allies several years ago certainly cannot yet be called definitively a success or failure. Yet historians and policy analysts have to make proximate judgments, if only because they seek to discern trends or to influence policy in a more enlightened manner. The reasons for invading Baghdad that the United States officially propounded in January–March 2003 did not require this invasion, and it was not a success. No weapons of mass destruction were ever found. Later, the Administration argued that removing Saddam Hussein from power was a justification for the war. This removal was certainly a success, but one still does not know what the ultimate fate of Saddam will be, though presumably he will not be Iraq's next elected leader.

If the Iraq operation is listed as a part of a long-term campaign to bring democracy to the Middle East, the verdict remains uncertain because the prospects for Iraqi democracy remain tenuous. And even if the Iraqi population rallies to the support of a particular government, the result may not be wholly benign. The German population for a considerable period and on the basis of elections held in 1933 did support the National Socialist German Workers Party and its leader, Adolf Hitler. A popularly elected Shiite regime in Baghdad might concert with Islamic elements in Iran and elsewhere in ways that would be inimical to U.S. and Western policy.

If the objective was to gain support for American policy and to wage the "war on terrorism" on an international basis, the invasion has not been a short-term success. The numbers of terrorists and candidate suicide bombers rallying to the Islamic and anti-Western cause have certainly not declined since March 2003 and appear to have multiplied. Diplomatically, the United States has never been so isolated except perhaps during the deepening failure of the Vietnam War in the mid to late 1960s. Despite large defense expenditures, the American military has never been under such strain, with recruitment lagging behind retirements. Despite what commanders and troops have learned as a result of plunging into Iraq, the military has not demonstrated a capacity to handle insurgent wars in enemy terrain with open borders to sanctuary areas such as those in Iran or Syria. More than two thousand U.S. military deaths have not made Iraq or even the streets of Baghdad secure. While Europe, China, and Russia have not yet become "balancers" against the United States and its deemed hegemonic aspirations, they (with the partial exception of Britain) certainly have not become devotees of American foreign policy. Many of these nations would rather see the U.S. stumble than succeed with a policy of intervention into the affairs of other countries, great and small. The consequences of the Iraq war have demonstrably reduced American ability to threaten intervention in other contexts, like Iran and North Korea. America's moral standing—which influences the recruitment of terrorists—has continued to diminish.

This book has investigated the likelihood of new nationalist self-determination movements emerging in the context of globalization and Great Power policy. In the net, Great Power policy has not generally been supportive of the creation of new, fledgling nationalist states except in cases where a previous empire has collapsed. More often, it has favored their retention within the metropole, assuming that the metropole respects and even rewards the discontented group. U.S. intervention in Iraq has provoked a form of counter-nationalism in the Middle East. It appears in Iran, Syria, and to some degree even in Egypt. It is possible that the proposed Constitution in Iraq will lead to a satisfactory and balanced federalism including Kurdish, Sunni, and Shiite regions. But it is also possible that the center will not hold and federalism will lead to separation of the provinces. In that case, the United States and its supporters, without recognizing it, will have paid the ultimate tribute in acknowledging that Saddam Hussein did what they have been unable to do—hold the country together.

NOTES

1. I have examined the Bush case for war at length in Steven E. Miller, "Gambling on War: Force, Order, and the Implications of Attacking Iraq." In Carl Kaysen, Martin B. Malin, Steven E. Miller, William D. Nordhaus, and John D. Steinbruner, *War with Iraq: Costs, Consequences, and Alternatives* (Cambridge, MA: American Academy of Arts and Sciences, 2002).

2. See, for example, George Packer, "Letter from Baghdad: War after the War," *The New Yorker*, November 24, 2003, pp. 4–6 of web version as available at www.newyorker.com. Packer reports that both the U.S military and the U.S. civilian team, headed by Jake Garner, entered Iraq with instructions to plan on departure by August 2003. See also Larry Diamond, *Squandered Victory: The American Occupation and the Bungled Effort to Bring Democracy to Iraq* (New York: Henry Holt, 2005), 32–33, which describes the intention to hand over power to an Iraqi government (probably led by Iraqi exiles) and to withdraw in August. David L. Phillips, *Losing Iraq: Inside the Postwar Reconstruction Fiasco* (New York: Westview Press, 2005), 129, reports that the Garner mission was meant to operate for only three months. Fred Kaplan, in "The Dumbing-Down of the US Army," *Slate*, October 4, 2005, says there is now "overwhelming evidence" that the Bush Administration failed to engage in planning for post-war Iraq because "George W. Bush, Dick Cheney, Donald Rumsfeld & Co. persuaded themselves that their favored Iraqi exiles would quickly form a new government and that most American troops would be home by late summer 2003."

3. All-out civil war has been avoided but the growing sectarian violence already may amount to a low-grade civil war. As the estimable John Burns, Baghdad correspondent for the *New York Times*, has reported, "Events are pointing more than ever to the possibility that the nightmare could come true. . . . Many Iraqis are saying that the civil war has already begun." John Burns, "If It's Civil War, Do We Know It?" *New York Times,* July 24, 2005.

4. As one expert has emphatically stated, "No foreigner really knows what is going on in Iraq." From the excellent essay by Rory Stewart, "Degrees of Not Knowing," *London Review of Books*, March 31, 2005, p. 3 of web version.

5. See, among countless examples, Edwin Chen, "President Says War Was Right," *Los Angeles Times*, August 3, 2004.

6. Michael Graham, "Handing over the Mic," *National Review Online*, July 21, 2005. Visits Iraq. Finds troops upbeat. Concludes mainstream media preoccupied with bad news because they believe the war was a terrible mistake.

7. See, for example, Stanley Kober, "Implications of the Iraq War," Center for a Realistic Foreign Policy, October 1, 2004, who writes that "the war in Iraq has already been lost in the strategic sense" (p. 3 of web version).

8. As Hans Blix writes in his firsthand account of the UN effort to find weapons of mass destruction in Iraq, "The invasion of Iraq was about weapons of mass destruction." Hans Blix, *Disarming Iraq: The Search for Weapons of Mass Destruction* (London: Bloomsbury, 2004), 266.

9. The search by the Iraq Survey Group was ended in September of 2004, at which time it issued a final report. As the letter of transmittal from ISG's Executive Director, Charles Duelfer stated, there were lots of reasons to be suspicious of Saddam Hussein but the weapons "were not there." See *The Iraq Survey Group Final Report*, September 30, 2004 as available at www.globalsecurity.org.

10. Again, Blix offers a revealing comment, observing that "the US had become frantic—but also not very successful—about finding convincing evidence of Iraqi guilt." Blix, *Disarming Iraq*, 6.

11. "Transcript: David Kay at Senate Hearing," available at CNN.com, January 28, 2004.

12. President Bush's immediate suspicion, even on September 11, 2001, that Iraq was involved is described in Richard A. Clarke, *Against All Enemies: Inside America's War on Terror* (New York: Free Press, 2004). The Bush Administration's almost instant consideration of war against Iraq in response to 9/11 is reported in detail in Bob Woodward, *Bush at War* (New York: Simon and Schuster, 2002), 49, 83–85.

13. See, for example, Rebecca Christie, "US Rumsfeld Concedes No WMDs or Sept. 11 Ties in Iraq," *Wall Street Journal*, September 17, 2004.

14. For the argument that there is evidence of ties between Saddam and al-Qaeda, consult the work of Michael Ledeen, available on the website of the American Enterprise Institute. Ledeen sees an extensive interconnected terrorist threat (now centered in Iran) and believes that a comprehensive assault on both terrorists and their state sponsors is essential. He writes, for example, "We are at war with a series of terrorist groups, supported by a group of nations, and it makes no sense to distinguish between them." Michael Ledeen, "Coalition of Evil: The Big Picture of Our War," *National Review Online*, July 27, 2005.

15. Robert Jervis, *American Foreign Policy in a New Era* (New York: Routledge, 2005), 132.

16. See illustratively Anthony Lloyd, "Iraq's Relentless Tide of Murder," *London Times*, September 30, 2005. As Lloyd emphasizes, rampant murder in Iraq is not only due to sectarian violence but reflects a pervasive collapse of order. "Tribal feuds, revenge killings of Saddam-era officials and their families, mafia wars, and the constant killing by insurgents of anyone working for the coalition or security forces, all contribute to the toll."

17. As one example among many, see Andy Mosher and Omar Fekeiki, "Two Sunni Members of Constitution Panel Are Slain in Baghdad," *Washington Post*, July 20, 2005.

18. The losses among Iraqi police and security forces are tabulated in Iraq Coalition Casualty Count, available at http://icasualties.org/oif/.

19. The inconveniences of ordinary life in Baghdad are often recounted in the weblog "Baghdad Burning," available at http://riverbendblog.blogspot.com/, written by a young Iraqi woman.

20. Peter W. Galbraith, "Iraq: Bush's Islamic Republic," *The New York Review of Books*, August 11, 2005, p. 8.

21. W. Andrew Terrill, *The United States and Iraq's Shiite Clergy: Partners or Adversaries?* (Strategic Studies Institute, U.S. Army War College, February 2004), v–vi.

22. Mark Danner, "Taking Stock of the Forever War," *New York Times Magazine*, September 11, 2005, p. 53.

23. Edward D. Mansfield and Jack Snyder, *Electing to Fight: Why Emerging Democracies Go to War* (Cambridge: MIT Press, 2005), 2.

24. J. Peter Scoblic, "Moral Hazard: How Conservatism Leaves Us Vulnerable to Nuclear Terrorism," *The New Republic Online*, July 29, 2005, p. 1.

25. Speech by British Minister Robin Cook, March 2003, as available at the "Today in Iraq" website at http://dailywarnews.blogspot.com. When Cook died unexpectedly in August 2005, his obituary noted that this speech "was given the only standing ovation ever recorded in the Commons." "Robin Cook," *The Economist*, August 13, 2005, p. 75.

26. Khalidi recounts this story in *Resurrecting Empire*, 6, drawing on an account reported in the *Financial Times*.

27. Danner, "Taking Stock of the Forever War," 87.

28. For discussion of the strengths and limits of U.S. military power, see Barry R. Posen, "Command of the Commons: The Military Foundations of US Hegemony," *International Security*, vol. 28, no. 1 (Summer 2003), 5–46. Posen's analysis makes clear that in what he calls the "contested zones," in which U.S. high-tech advantages are irrelevant or neutralized, U.S. military forces will face much more difficult challenges.

29. Alan K. Henrikson, "The Emanation of Power," *International Security*, vol. 6, no. 1 (Summer 1981), 161.

30. Kober, "Implications of the Iraq War," 3, 5. Kober concludes, "Rather than demonstrating the invincibility of American military power, Iraq is demonstrating its limitations and vulnerabilities."

31. Barry Rubin, "War Against America," *Jerusalem Post*, August 30, 2004, as quoted in Kober, "Implications of the Iraq War," 4–5.

32. "McCain Statement on Detainee Amendments," October 5, 2005, as available on the website of Senator John McCain at http://mccain.senate.gov.

33. Andrew Sullivan, "Atrocities in Plain Sight," *New York Times Book Review*, January 23, 2005. Sullivan, an articulate and thoughtful supporter of the war, explains his continuing belief that the war is justified and still deserves support in his essay "Still Pro-War despite the Flaws," July 2, 2005, as available at his (always interesting) weblog, www.Andrewsullivan.com.

34. These quotes are taken from postings for October 6, 2005 on Sullivan's website, www.andrewsullivan.com.

35. The Bush Administration's unwavering opposition continued even after the Senate vote. See for example Brian Knowlton, "Bush Repeats Threat to Veto Torture Curb," *International Herald Tribune*, October 7, 2005.

36. Stephens as quoted by Nat Hentoff in "Facts and Documentation," *Washington Times*, June 13, 2005.

37. Nat Hentoff, "Whitewashing Rumsfeld," *The Village Voice*, April 4, 2005.

38. Lionel Barber, "America's Soft Power Needs Hard Work," *Financial Times*, July 22, 2005.

39. See, for example, Anne Gearan, "Syria Urged to Close Its Borders to Terrorists," *Boston Globe*, May 17, 2005; Robert Scheer, "Iraq's Dangerous New Friend," *Los Angeles Times*, July 19, 2005; "Iran Shipping Iraqi Rebels Powerful Bombs, NBC Says," *Washington Times*, August 5, 2005; Edward Wong, "Iraq Dances with Iran While America Seethes," *New York Times*, July 31, 2005.

40. "Iraq War Prospects Are Bleak: Ex-Officer," *Arizona Daily Star*, July 19, 2005.

41. From an analysis by an outspoken supporter of the war, Mackubin Thomas Owens, "Will This War Ruin the Army?" *New York Post*, July 19, 2005.

42. Quoted in Joseph Galloway, "Army Lowers Standards and Increases Bonuses But Still May Fall Short of Recruiting Goal," *Knight Ridder*, June 13, 2005, as available at news.yahoo.com.

43. Richard A. Clarke, "War and Weakness," *New York Times Magazine*, June 19, 2005.

44. Kaplan, "The Dumbing-Down of the US Army," 1.

45. As summarized in Guy Taylor, "Army Stretched Thin, Report Says," *Washington Times*, July 14, 2005.

46. Bob Herbert, "They Won't Go," *New York Times*, June 13, 2005.

47. Brian MacQuarrie, "Fewer Applying to US Military Academies," *Boston Globe*, June 13, 2005.

48. Michael E. O'Hanlon, "US Defense Strategy after Saddam," The Letort Papers, U.S. Army War College, July 2005, p. 14.

49. See Ann Scott Tyson, "Disrepair Cited in US Arms," *Washington Post*, October 5, 2005.

50. Daniel Pipes, "Defeating Militants and Winning Moderates: Reconceptualizing the War on Terror," *Australian Army Journal*, vol. II, no. 2 (Autumn 2005), 183, 186. Similarly, Steven Metz suggests that in fighting insurgency "the most decisive battle space is the psychological. . . . Insurgency is not won by killing insurgents, not won by seizing territory. It's won by altering the psychological factors that are most relevant." Metz is quoted in Mark Danner, "Iraq: The Real War," *New York Review of Books*, April 28, 2005, p. 41.

51. As quoted in David Kaplan, Aamir Latif, Kevin Whitelaw, and Julian Barnes, "Hearts, Minds, and Dollars," *US News and World Report*, April 5, 2005, p. 6 of web version. The same story quotes unnamed people from lower in the foreign policy bureaucracy complaining that the senior figures in the Bush Administration voice the rhetoric of the war of ideas without acting as if they really believe it.

52. Khalidi, *Resurrecting Empire*, 8.

53. As quoted in Stephen Glain, "Syria at a Crossroads," *Smithsonian*, July 2005, p. 72.

54. Avishai Margalit, "The Wrong War," *New York Review of Books*, March 13, 2003, p. 5.

55. Philip Stephens, "The Need to End Terror in Iraq," *Financial Times*, July 11, 2005.

56. Timothy Garton Ash, "The Great Powers of Europe, Redefined," *New York Times*, December 17, 2004.

12

Sustainable Peace Agreements in the Age of International Institutions: The Case of Cyprus

Barbara Koremenos

Globalization is generally defined as an increase in cross-border mobility of goods, services, capital, and people; broader transnational communications; and a fragmentation of production across borders. Beyond just increased flows, though, globalization also entails strengthened international institutions. Governance activities that once were the sole province of individual governments are now undertaken by groups of states or autonomous nongovernmental organizations. The European Union (EU) is widely considered to be the strongest such institution. This volume takes a varied look at how globalization affects the likelihood of state integration. In this chapter, I observe how globalization manifested through a strong international institution can influence state integration. Specifically, I look at the case of Cyprus and argue that the EU has the potential to accomplish what several third-party states could not: unite Cyprus under an ethnically neutral government.

Indeed, the EU may be an ideal candidate to foster unification: it has an interest in stabilizing the region; it commands enough power and legitimacy to effect change; and it is generally neutral with respect to Greek Cypriots and Turkish Cypriots. The EU can ensure that group rights are guaranteed, thereby precluding the need for destabilizing power-sharing arrangements based on ethnicity. Moreover, joining the EU may encourage Cypriots to adopt a more "European" identity, instead of one based on ethnicity, and to form political coalitions that cut across ethnic boundaries. Hence the European Union has the potential to remove several barriers to Cypriot unification.

A HISTORY OF DIVISION

The history of a unified Cyprus is not an encouraging one. Cyprus has a record of imperial domination, having been held in a subservient status by a number of powers. Especially consequential were three centuries of Ottoman rule, beginning in 1571, during which a minority Turkish population was imposed on an indigenous Greek population. Interestingly, the Turkish conquest in the 16th century helped preserve Hellenic-Byzantine culture because the Turks relied on the political and administrative expertise of their conquered subjects to maintain and rule the population of Cyprus. For example, the Sultan elevated the archbishop to the status of Ethnarch, national leader of the Greek population, and made him responsible for all Orthodox Christians. The Church collected state taxes and officially represented the Greeks in Constantinople. Hence under the Turks, the Church enjoyed unprecedented secular and spiritual powers.[1]

Nonetheless, by the 19th century, the special privileges and authority of the archbishop undermined the power of the local Turkish hierarchy. Many higher clergy, including the archbishop, were massacred for allegedly planning an overthrow. In the ensuing years, the power of the archbishop was curtailed. At the same time, however—and not surprisingly—the legitimacy of the archbishop and the Church as the guardians of the Greek Cypriots was strengthened; for the Greeks, the Church symbolized resistance to Turkish rule.[2]

In 1878, the British took control of Cyprus. The British were unwilling to recognize the archbishop as the political representative of the Greek Cypriots. Consequently, they further exacerbated Greek and Turkish Cypriot animosity and distrust by allocating regional power to the Turkish minority against the Greek Cypriot majority. Such an arrangement also brought about an antagonistic relation between Britain and the Greek Cypriots. The erosion of the traditional religious authority set the stage for an intense anti-British movement and also contributed greatly to the movement of "Enosis" or union with Greece.[3]

In 1955, a Church-supported war against the British began under George Grivas, who was closely tied to Archbishop Makarios. The final result in 1959, however, was to grant the feuding principality independence instead of union with Greece. The Cypriots "received" a new constitution, with Britain, Greece, and Turkey as the "guarantors" of the new state and of each group's ethnic rights.

In 1974, following a coup attempt by the military dictatorship of Greece and an invasion by Turkey, the Republic of Cyprus collapsed after fourteen years of turbulent independence. Although many factors combined to bring about this collapse, two causes in particular stand out: the rigidity built into the 1960 Constitution and the interference by Cyprus's supposedly neutral guarantors, Turkey and Greece.

CONSTITUTIONAL RIGIDITY

The Constitution of 1960 was partially responsible for the collapse of the first (and only) Cyprus Republic because it created an unworkable government and cemented rigidity into governance institutions. Instead of uniting the government and its people under a neutral Cypriot nationality, the Constitution of 1960 "recognized and perpetuated the historic separateness of the two ethnic communities of the island" by institutionalizing separatism and preventing the revision of traditions that kept the two communities apart.[4] For example, the Constitution of 1960 called for a presidency and legislature that were divided along cultural lines. There were to be a Greek Cypriot president and a Turkish Cypriot vice president. The legislature was made up of 70 percent Greek Cypriots and 30 percent Turkish Cypriots. Additionally, this divided government would be elected by a divided electorate, because the Constitution defined what it meant to be a Greek or Turkish Cypriot and mandated that only Greek Cypriots could vote for "Greek positions" and only Turkish Cypriots could vote for "Turkish positions." This arrangement was made to guarantee the political rights of Turkish Cypriots in the Constitution; in essence, to ensure group rights over individual rights.[5] Indeed, most efforts to end civil wars focus on this arrangement in order to bring opposing sides to the bargaining table and get them to agree on a Constitution.

An alternative governance arrangement would have put aside ethnic divisions to focus instead on individual rights and allow proportional representation.[6] This was not pursued, however, out of a Turkish Cypriot desire for political security. As Barbara Walter has argued, short-term security concerns often lead parties to negotiate an institutional arrangement that provides political certainty for the future.[7] This desire for security "arises most clearly over constitutional design issues relating to the nature of individual and group political representation and participation."[8] Thus, constitutionally mandated power sharing is one possible arrangement that will guarantee security and reassure the minority. In Cyprus, Turkish Cypriots feared Greek Cypriot dominance and so sought security in the form of guaranteed, explicit power-sharing.

However, this power-sharing arrangement not only hampered government operations but also created overly rigid governance institutions. Because both the president and vice president had the right to veto each other's executive orders, and because, in order to pass legislation, a majority was needed from both the Greek and Turkish Cypriot houses, the government was weak. Moreover, the excessive rigidity was destabilizing, because it undermined the creation of long-term institutions[9] and also encouraged reneging. As Rothchild argues, democratic institutions for the long run must be based on notions of individual rights and proportional representation. He cites Jack Snyder on the importance "of a dense web of such ethnic-blind institutions [as the highly professionalized civil service, police, armed forces, and courts] to serve as the basis for a civil nationalism that is based not on the coexistence of ethnic groups but on civil rights and duties of individuals."[10] These long-term institutions could not be developed in Cyprus because of an overwhelming focus on ethnicity and because of the identity politics that flowed from that focus. Additionally, an overly rigid agreement can encourage reneging over the long term. As I have argued elsewhere,[11] most efforts at international cooperation are heavily conditioned by the relative bargaining power of the states involved, but often states expect their bargaining power to change over time. Unpredictable changes may leave states in a situation of being bound to agreements whose division of gains no longer reflects their relative bargaining power. In particular, if their power has risen, states might go so far as to renege (or cheat) on an agreement whose gains have become too small relative to their bargaining power. I show how institutional flexibility can help solve this problem.

When the context is a peace agreement, sustainable cooperation is particularly critical because reneging on the terms usually implies another war.[12] Can peace agreements be designed in such a way that they can potentially survive changes in bargaining power? Since the central issue of many peace agreements is territory, and since we obviously cannot divide and redivide territory, flexibility in peace agreements seems irrelevant. Nonetheless, peace agreements are also about control—control of political institutions and control of the military, for example—and this control can be made flexible. For Cyprus, flexibility could have been built into the Cypriot Constitution to reflect population changes in governance institutions. However, the Constitution defined ethnic identity and created a government divided according to percentages. Of course, both identity and relative population levels can change, but the Cypriot Constitution did not provide for that. And, as evidenced by Lebanon, a rigid governance structure cannot evolve peacefully into a flexible one, since the losers will not accept it.[13]

In Cyprus, a growing Turkish population began to demand more while the Greek population struggled to remain in control. Thus, the rigid governance structures set up in the Constitution of 1960 engendered instability and contributed to the collapse of a unified Cyprus in 1974.

NON-NEUTRAL GUARANTORS

The text of the Constitution of 1960, as significant as it is, does not tell us the whole story of the collapse of the Cypriot Republic. Although the Constitution does not mention the role of Greece, Turkey, or other nations in relation to the Republic of Cyprus, the fact that it was drafted by "legal advisers who were Greek and Turkish nationals, since the British authorities had no representatives on the commission and the Cypriots were comparatively inexperienced in such matters" does suggest that Greece and Turkey were influential in an unofficial manner.[14] That is, in drafting the Constitution of 1960, Greece and Turkey, adamant about protecting their own interests on the island, created a state that reflected more of a compromise on how to divide Cyprus under cultural grounds rather than how to unite Cyprus under a single Cypriot banner.

Moreover, Greece and Turkey failed to exert the pressure that was essential to get Greek and Turkish Cypriots to unite under a single Cypriot identity. Rather, Athens and Ankara seemed to be the force that pulled and further segregated Greek and Turkish Cypriots away from each other. Evidence for this claim is suggested by the Treaty of Guarantee, signed along with the Constitution of 1960. Although most of the treaty affirms Cyprus's independence and sovereignty and prohibits Greece and Turkey from undertaking any political or economic unions with the island, the fourth article states:

> In the event of a breach of the provisions of the present Treaty, Greece, Turkey, and the United Kingdom undertake to consult together with respect to the representations or measure necessary to ensure observance of those provisions. In so far as common or concerted action may not prove possible, each of the three guaranteeing Powers reserves the right to take action with the sole aim of establishing the state of affairs created by the present Treaty.

The fourth article of the Treaty of Guarantee is significant because it gives Turkey, Greece, and the UK the right to take unilateral action in Cyprus in the event that the situation in the island is not, in their respective view, "acceptable." For Greece, it legitimized Greek interference in the internal affairs of the Republic, and, for Turkey, it legitimized the Turkish invasion of Northern Cyprus. Thus, the Treaty of Guarantee undermined, rather then protected, Cyprus's sovereignty and independence as laid out in the Constitution, and it reflected the powerful influence that Greece and Turkey had on the Republic and its eventual collapse.

Internal affairs within both states and the context of the Cold War also helped to perpetuate hostility between the two nations and to cause them to interfere destructively in the newly formed Republic of Cyprus. Although Greece was usually cooperative with respect to Cyprus before the Cold War, after the Cold War began, Greece wanted to annex Cyprus because it feared that a divided Cyprus would allow Turkey to get increased support from NATO and the United States. A fortified, NATO-backed Turkey would mean that Greece's nearest enemy could obtain a military advantage.[15] Therefore, Greece, especially during the dictatorship of Papadopoulos and later Ioannides, tended to interfere whenever peace accords were being brokered between the Greek and Turkish Cypriots. For example, in 1968 when Greek and Turkish Cypriot leaders seemed near agreement,

Papadopoulos "upstaged the Cypriot statesmen and destroyed a possible settlement in secret talks with Turkish Prime Minister Suleyman Demirel. By demanding union with Greece and other tough concessions, Papadopoulos forced Demirel to reject his proposals, and the hope of a peaceful settlement negotiated by the two Cypriot communities collapsed."[16] Greece also interfered in Greek Cypriot politics whenever it feared a link between the Greek Cypriots and communism. For example, from 1970 to 1974 Papadopoulos and Ioannides unleashed three assassination attempts against Makarios because they feared that he was negotiating with the Greek communist party, AKEL. Finally, in 1974 Greece backed a coup led by Nikos Samson, which drove Makarios out of office and began a reign of an even more extremist, anti-Turkish, pro-annexation regime. For its part, Turkey reacted to Greek hostility by invading Northern Cyprus. Turkey defended its action by alluding to the fourth article in the Treaty of Guarantee that allowed it to take unilateral action to restore the "state of affairs created by the Treaty."

Other actors relevant to the Cyprus problem were the United States and NATO. Unlike Greece and Turkey, the relatively neutral U.S. was not involved enough to create a positive change in the escalating problems that beset Cyprus. The U.S., with its concentration on communist containment, indulged in Realpolitik in respect of Cyprus. That is, instead of focusing on changing the distribution of power within Cyprus, U.S. leaders were more interested in ratifying the "existing distribution of power."[17] This suggests that the U.S. took the cultural divisions and mistrust between Greek and Turkish Cypriots as a given and worked out plans that maintained these divisions rather than changed them. Therefore, during the drafting of the Constitution of 1960, the U.S. did not pressure Turkey and Greece to come up with a Constitution that would unify the population of Cyprus, but rather approved a Constitution that maintained the status quo. The only pressure the U.S. did exert was when it realized that the Greek Cypriot leader Makarios was uniting with the Greek communist party AKEL. Not realizing that Makarios's real intentions for allying with AKEL were to mobilize political support for annexation, the U.S. became a staunch ally of Turkey. The U.S. pressured Greece to accept the Acheson-Ball plan, calling for the partition of Cyprus into two parts, with each part annexed by Greece and Turkey, respectively. This plan would give the U.S. and NATO control over Cyprus because it would be part of two NATO member states. The plan, however, ran contrary to the views of the Greek Cypriots, and they became not only more staunchly anti-Turkish, but anti-American as well. Although the Acheson-Ball plan was flatly rejected, many analysts suggest that the U.S. allowed Turkey to invade Northern Cyprus in 1974 because this action was in line with its design to stop the communist takeover of Cyprus.[18]

Finally, the UN played a very minor role in the Cyprus conflict—minor because of the UN's relative powerlessness. Many resolutions were passed in the UN, including General Assembly Resolution No. 3212 calling for the withdrawal of foreign armed forces from Cyprus, but all were ignored by either Greece or Turkey. Thus, unlike the U.S., although the UN was interested in pressuring the two parties to negotiate an agreement, it lacked the power to make this happen.

External parties thus heavily influenced Cypriot affairs and caused increased instability on the island. Even though Greece, Turkey, and the United Kingdom were supposed to act as neutral guarantors of group rights, both Greece and Turkey ended up undermining rather than guaranteeing stability. The UK took an entirely hands-off approach. The United States could have acted as a guarantor, but it was distracted by other events. In sum, the possible state guarantors were either non-neutral or preoccupied with other interests, while the possible non-state guarantor—the UN—was too weak to make much of a difference.

OTHER IDIOSYNCRATIC FACTORS

Besides the structural problems of the new government and the interference of external parties, another factor that led to the collapse of the Cypriot Republic was the fact that the Constitution of 1960 did nothing to discourage the identification of the government with Greek Cypriot culture. From the start, the organization of the new republic conformed to the broader historical/cultural institution of the Greek Cypriots. Continuing the tradition of allocating political leadership to the Greek Cypriot archbishop, Makarios was elected president of the new republic. The integration of church and state was a basic assumption of the Greek Cypriots, so deeply ingrained that it rendered other alternatives or strategies virtually unimaginable. In other words, the Greek Church culture served as Meyer and Rowan's "institutional rules which function as myths depicting various formal structures as rational means to the attainment of desirable ends."[19] Accordingly, Makarios ruled his country much more like a religious leader than a president, invoking his religious status and thereby transcending any political differences among (Greek Cypriot) people.

Given Cyprus's turbulent history and the tensions between the two ethnic groups on the island (80 percent Greek; 18 percent Turkish), such a basis may have been what Cyprus needed "to get on its feet." According to Meyer and Rowan, "dependence on externally fixed institutions reduces turbulence and maintains stability."[20] Makarios, by ruling like an Ethnarch while he was president, was, in a sense, reinforcing the stories and myths about how Cyprus survived in the past.

There was one great complication, however, in the case of Cyprus: the myths were valid only for the Greek Cypriots. Although Makarios was democratically elected, as Oriana Fallaci points out, "he gets those votes thanks to his relationship with heaven. For the peasants of Cyprus, voting for him is almost a sacrament. While handing in their ballots with his name, even the communists make the sign of the cross."[21] Thus, the legitimacy of Makarios's election to the presidency by a "majority vote" was compromised in the eyes of the Turkish minority, who viewed his election more as a confirmation of traditional Greek Cypriot traditions than a true affirmation of Makarios's political leadership. Acting on this suspicion, the Turks used their veto power to prevent the adoption of many of the acts that Makarios and the Greek legislative majority introduced. Thus given the nature of the Constitution and the two very different ethnic groups governed by it, the Greek Church culture which the government tried to instill not only constrained the new government, it paralyzed it.

Makarios was in a position to at least try to cultivate, in Weberian terms, a legal-rational authority and thereby foster the growth of functional institutional structures in the government. On the one hand, it is easy to see that Makarios was caught in a "catch-22" situation. For Cyprus to survive, Makarios, the ultimate insider, needed to surmount his own culture and change those features that alienated the Turkish Cypriots. At the same time, he needed the depth of vision to know what kinds of changes would be accepted by Greek Cypriots. He had to be sure that what he was selling would fit in with the other deep cultural assumptions of the Greek Cypriots. As if the intercommunal tensions on Cyprus were not enough, Makarios also had to keep the island in a precarious balance between the rival powers of Greece and Turkey, both of which, in their interests, encouraged still further divisions between the two ethnic communities.

Since part of Cyprus's problem stemmed from the nature of its imposed Constitution, in 1964 Makarios sought to introduce structural changes in the government in order to put an end to the paralysis. Makarios submitted thirteen amendments to the Constitution for the Turkish Cypriot vice president's consideration. The adoption of these amendments would have ended the separate political existence of the two communities while preserving wider privileges for the Turkish Cypriot minority. Specifically, Makarios wanted to strip both the president and vice president of their veto powers and to claim majority rights for the Greek Cypriots. Makarios also circulated the amendments among the three guarantor nations. Before the Turkish Cypriot vice president could reply, the government of Turkey rejected the proposals. In turn, Makarios stated "that the revision of the constitution of the Republic was an exclusively internal affair of Cyprus and that the circulation of these proposals to the three governments concerned was only 'to keep them informed' and not in expectation of either a positive or negative reply."[22] Nonetheless, Makarios's response did not work to ease the situation. Incited by Turkey, the Turkish Cypriots withdrew from the government, and within days, violence erupted between the two parties.

THE SITUATION TODAY

Despite this gloomy history, the situation in Cyprus today is much more encouraging. First, there has been a renewed push for unification on the island, due to the pressures of globalization. Second, an increasingly powerful European Union may finally become a truly neutral guarantor, which will allow for flexible political institutions by reassuring the Turkish minority without resorting to rigid power-sharing arrangements. The EU can also stifle the negative influences of Greece, a member, and Turkey, a potential member. Third, the EU can provide many new issues for Cypriots to argue about, which will enable the development of cross-cutting cleavages, relieve ethnic division, and help foster a new European identity.

GLOBALIZATION PRESSURES

Globalization has put pressure on Cypriots to give unification another try. The effect of globalization within a divided state, or a state that is dealing with a strong separatist movement, varies according to the dynamics of the internal and external pressures on the state. Rosecrance and Stein (this volume) argue, for example, that although Spain has a strong, centralized government that has been able in the past to quell the separatist Basque movement by either force or economic concessions, the introduction of globalization to Spain, especially after the 1992 Olympic games held in Barcelona, has led the Basques to call more urgently for independence. This is because after the 1992 Olympics, Barcelona and the entire Basque region gained more from globalization than from the traditional economic concessions offered by the Spanish central government.

However, within Cyprus, the globalization effect is different. Unlike Spain, Cyprus's lack of a strong centralized leadership allowed the differences between Greek and Turkish Cypriots to issue in civil war and effectively to divide the state. Now the unrecognized Turkish Cyprus is a poor country, and its political situation has left it out of the benefits of globalization. Thus, unlike the Basques, there is pressure for the Turkish Cypriots to unify with the Greek Cypriots so they can "break into" and reap the benefits of globalization, rather than "break out" of the country.

Indeed unification is likely to occur in Cyprus because, according to Rosecrance and Stein (this volume), there are four factors that indicate a strong likelihood of integration: (1) there is a high state of globalization; (2) metropolitan policy advocates globalization; (3) international policy advocates globalization; (4) the dissident group is satisfied with globalization. Cyprus meets all these requirements. With Greek Cyprus joining the EU, Cyprus will continue to reap the benefits of a high state of globalization. Cyprus is

situated in a world where there is a strong international preference for globalization. Moreover, there is pressure from the international community for
Cyprus to unite. According to Rosecrance and Stein, the international community, perceiving civil war and the terrorist activities perpetuated by separatist movements as a source of unnecessary disruption and interruption in
the region, "inveigh against independence of dissenting regions" and put
pressure on divided states to unify. Thus, added global pressure from the UN,
the EU, and the U.S. is another indication that Cyprus should unite.

Moreover, there is internal pressure, even from dissenting Greek and Turkish Cypriot groups, for Cyprus to take part in and reap the benefits of globalization. Rosecrance and Stein state that "the amount of literacy, infant
mortality, and years of schooling would presumably also affect the country's
reception of globalization." In Cyprus, the Greek Cypriots' higher literacy
rate, advanced education system, and low infant mortality rate would suggest
they are more in favor of globalization than are the Turkish Cypriots, who
have a less advanced educational system, lower literacy rate, and a higher
infant mortality. However, both the Greek and the Turkish Cypriots are in
favor of globalization. The Greek Cypriots are in favor of globalization
because the globalization they have already experienced in the last few years
has advanced their economic and social system greatly, and has improved
their standard of living. Although the Turkish Cypriots are behind the Greeks
in their economic and social development, their awareness of the stark difference between their standard of living and that of the Greek Cypriots, and
their dissatisfaction with their own condition, make them more ready to unite
with the Greek Cypriots so that they can also partake from the benefits of
globalization. Indeed, according to one EU survey of the Turkish Cypriot
population, "nine in ten adults and teenagers (88%) think that membership in
the European Union would be a 'good thing,' and only 9% have the opposite
opinion; and 89% claim that Turkish Cypriots would benefit from EU membership, while 91% of the respondents would expect personal benefits from
the Cypriot accession to the EU."[23] This broad popular support bodes well for
unification over the long run.

THE EU AS A NEUTRAL GUARANTOR

The EU can succeed in guaranteeing group rights where other actors have
failed. Why? First, it is truly neutral. Unlike Turkey or Greece, the EU does
not have security interests in Cyprus and has no reason to support one side
at the expense of the other. In addition to its neutrality, the EU is a potent
force in the area. The UN, though also genuinely neutral, failed to be an
effective guarantor for Cyprus during its original unification because it

lacked sufficient power resources. The EU is not only a more cohesive and tighter community, but also can offer real inducements to achieve compliance—and can effect costly punishments—for Greece, Cyprus, and, eventually, Turkey. Moreover, the EU has already had an effect on the fate of Cyprus: Turkey's desperate need to be part of the EU prompted it to exert pressure on the Turkish Cypriot leadership to negotiate with the Greek Cypriots.

Cypriots from both ethnic groups understand that the EU would provide the protection and assurances that each side needs in order to continue to form a single state. For the Turkish Cypriot minority, it would guarantee protection from any potential abuses suffered from the Greek Cypriot majority. For the Greek Cypriots, a unified state with membership in the EU would guarantee that Turkey will never invade Cyprus again or provide arms to Turkish Cypriots. These guarantees mean that the new Constitution can incorporate the necessary flexibility to make it robust over the long term; rigid power-sharing is no longer necessary to guarantee group rights. The trade-off between getting to an agreement in the first place and its long-term sustainability thus disappears.

THE EU AND NEW IDEAS, COALITIONS, AND IDENTITIES

Beyond guaranteeing minority rights, the EU can also introduce new issues for Cypriots to debate and discuss. Many of these issues will be economic or political, and they may bring about cross-cutting coalitions that will undermine traditional ethnic divisions. For example, Greek and Turkish Cypriot political elites may come together to lobby for increased development aid. Business unions may form to take advantage of lower trade barriers and potential economies of scale. NGOs may recruit members from both sides of the island in order to get their issue on the national or European agenda. In this way, a new Cypriot identity may emerge as actors seek to define the national interest and to profit from membership in the EU.[24]

Moreover, entrance into the EU may create feelings of a larger "European" identity among Cypriots. Although these cosmopolitan feelings are more common among elites than among "regular" Europeans, they still influence politics and policy choices.

In any case, Cypriot identity is subject to change. The admission to the European Union gives Cypriots many new issues to argue about, and new coalitions that cut across traditional ethnic divisions may emerge. There will be increased competition for the loyalties of Cypriots, and ethnic identity may become less important. These new loyalties will help ease ethnic tension and increase the likelihood of a successful reunification.

Chapter 12

CONCLUSIONS

Recent events in Cyprus appear to question these conclusions about Cypriot unification. Undoubtedly, the Greek Cypriot rejection of the unification referendum casts doubt on the whole unification enterprise. Indeed, over 75 percent of Greek Cypriots voted against the UN-sponsored Annan plan.[25] In my opinion, one of the main causes of this failed referendum was Greek Cypriot President Tassos Papadopoulos's frequent use of overblown rhetoric to push his views, such as when he told citizens in a television address: "I call on you to reject the Annan plan. I call on you to say a resounding no on April 24. I call upon you to defend your dignity, your history and what is right. I urge you to defend the Republic of Cyprus, saying no to its abolition."[26] Speeches like this clearly did not help the cause of unification. Kofi Annan, in explaining the failure of the resolution to the UN Security Council in 2004, put the blame squarely on Papadopoulos for not adequately explaining the plan to his citizens.[27] This overwhelming rejection makes the task of unification more difficult.

However, a deeper and longer-term view reveals cause for hope. Most importantly, a large majority of Turkish Cypriots voted in favor of the unification plan, signaling their support of a flexible constitution. Indeed, Turkish Cypriots have come to trust the European Union as guaranteeing their minority rights. Moreover, it is unlikely that mistrust of Turkish Cypriots dictated the Greek Cypriot vote. Rather, Greek Cypriots viewed the Annan plan—creating a federation with a rotating presidency—as not representing enough in a bargaining sense, and voted it down in the hope of getting more concessions in later rounds of bargaining. This is evidenced by Papadopoulos's balking at requests to change the Annan plan; he used bargaining tactics to extract greater demands. This fundamental shift away from mistrust makes a compromise solution much more possible. Another cause for optimism is that Greek Cypriot President Papadopoulos has toned down his rhetoric significantly. In October 2004 he argued against the idea that the possibility of settlement died with the rejection of the Annan plan.[28] More recently, in February 2005, he stated: "Our wish is for the resumption of Cyprus settlement talks as soon as possible under the auspices of the UN, with a more active involvement from the EU and within the framework of the Annan plan."[29] This encouraging speech has been accompanied by pacifying moves by Turkey and Greece. Turkey officially recognized Cyprus as an EU member in December 2004, and on March 29, 2005 Greece came out supporting new unification talks. Greek Foreign Minister Petros Molyviatis stated: "We expressed the view that there is a convergence now of views to the effect that we should restart the process of reunifying the island on the basis of the secretary general's plan. And we should make sure that this time there is no failure. We cannot afford another failure."[30] With Turkey and Greece, along with the EU, pushing for new talks, and with Cypriots letting go of their old mistrust, unification remains a real possibility.

I thus maintain my optimism, especially since the European Union can do what other third parties could not do before. Specifically, the EU helps to ameliorate both internal and external barriers to Cypriot unification. By acting as a strong, credible, and neutral guarantor of group rights, the EU removes the need for rigid power-sharing arrangements to be built into the constitution. Instead, a new government can be formed around individual rights, based on proportional representation, which is flexible enough to encourage long-term institutional development and discourage reneging. Additionally, the EU may make Cypriots base their identity more on issues and less on ethnicity. Moreover, the EU can prevent another Greek or Turkish intervention in Cyprus, since it can punish either state in the case of noncompliance. The presence of a strong international institution—the EU—makes unification possible, if Cypriots so desire.

NOTES

1. Sir G. Hill, *History of Cyprus*, vol. 4 (Cambridge: Cambridge University Press, 1952).

2. Kyriacos Markides, "Social Change and the Rise and Decline of Social Movements: The Case of Cyprus," *American Ethnologist*, May, 1975.

3. Ibid.

4. T. W. Adams, "The First Republic of Cyprus: A Review of an Unworkable Constitution," *Western Political Quarterly*, vol. 19 (1966).

5. Arendt Lijphart, *Democracy in Plural Societies* (New Haven, CT: Yale University Press, 1977).

6. Donald Horowitz, "Electoral Systems: A Primer for Decision Makers," *Journal of Democracy*, no 4 (2003).

7. Barbara Walter, "Designing Transitions from Civil War: Demobilization, Democratization, and Commitments to Peace," *International Security*, Jan. 1999.

8. Donald Rothchild, "Implementation and Its Effects on Building and Sustaining Peace: The Effects of Changing Structures of Incentives," in S. Stedman, D. Rothchild, and E. Cousins, eds., *Ending Civil Wars* (Boulder, CO: Lynne Riener, 2002).

9. Rothchild, "Implementation."

10. See Rothchild, "Implementation," and Jack Snyder, *From Voting to Violence* (New York: Norton, 2000).

11. Barbara Koremenos, "Can Cooperation Survive Changes in Bargaining Power? The Case of Coffee," *Journal of Legal Studies*, vol. 31 (2002).

12. This statement is borne out empirically; theoretically, it begs the question that has engaged scholars like James Fearon ("Rationalist Explanations for War," *International Organization*, Fall, 1995): Why do states fight costly wars as opposed to negotiating?

13. Lebanon's 1943 pact between Maronites and Muslims created an ethnically divided government which handed out administrative positions based on a rigid

formula. In the 1960s, when the heretofore-weaker Muslim population became wealthier and more educated, it mobilized to demand a greater role in government. Even a reform-minded Maronite president, however, could not meet Muslim expectations. Additionally, these reforms alienated and angered many Maronites, who feared a loss of power and a challenge to their identity. Rising tensions, and increasingly radicalized mobilizations, led to a collapse of the political system and a sixteen-year civil war beginning in 1975.

14. Adams, "First Republic."

15. Glen Camp, "Greek-Turkish Conflict over Cyprus," *Political Science Quarterly*, Jan. 1980.

16. Ibid., 51.

17. Ibid., 44.

18. Ibid., passim.

19. J. Meyer and B. Rowan, "Institutionalized Organizations: Formal Structure as Myth and Ceremony," *American Journal of Sociology*, 1977.

20. Ibid., 348.

21. Oriana Fallaci, *Interview with History* (New York: Liveright, 1974).

22. P. N. Vanezis, *Makarios: Pragmatism v. Idealism* (London: Abelard-Schuman, 1974), 120.

23. European Commission Directorate General Press and Communication, "Public Opinion Survey of Northern Cyprus," European Union.

24. Even the debate about whether to join the EU or not stimulates the formation of new coalitions and lobby groups.

25. BBC, April 25, 2004.

26. Niels Kadritzke, "Cyprus: Saying 'No' to the Future," *Le Monde diplomatique*, May, 2004.

27. BBC, June 3, 2004.

28. *Financial Times*, Oct. 27, 2004.

29. *SE Times*, March 29, 2005.

30. Ibid.

13

The Never-Ending Story: Quebec and the Question of National Self-determination

Alan S. Alexandroff

QUEBEC IN THE CONTEXT OF GLOBALIZATION

French Canada and particularly Quebec resides in a unique situation demographically and ideologically, relative to the rest of the country. The French immigrants (*seigneurs* and *habitants*) established the birthright to an autonomous though not independent Canada as early as mid-seventeenth century. They arrived first and created the initial settlements. Though numerically they were ultimately overwhelmed by English and/or American migrants in the 18th and 19th centuries, they are in a sense the originators of the Canadian myth—of the humane society. As the inheritors of the foundational past, French Canadians view English Canadians as latecomers or parvenus whose continuing loyalty to England (after the American Revolution) smacked of internationalism and diluted devotion to "la patrie."[1] For a while at least, the English were the liberals, politically and ideologically speaking, while French absolutism still reverberated in Quebec and elsewhere. Only much later did rural French areas become modernized and industrialized through strong state and provincial incentives until industrial Montreal became the economic equal of commercial Toronto. Thus the French ability to speak for the Canadian nation was certainly the equal in ideological terms of English Canada. When one assesses French demands for statehood or independence, it is important to remember the historic centrality of French experience.

Thus, it is perhaps not surprising that Quebec has not yet fully acquiesced in its provincial status within a Canadian society dominated by Ontario and the western provinces. One very interesting outcome in Canada, however, is that both French and English provinces now embrace globalization and the influence of the international economy. Quebec's hesitancy in remaining a province is not based on rejection of such influences. Rather, Quebec questions whether it will be a fully equal partner in the enjoyment of globalization within Canada or had better seek its economic and political future outside. Ideally, of course, Quebecois would like "to have their cake and eat it too," by remaining within Canadian economic space, enjoying the common currency and the market, while still opting to join NAFTA as an independent and equal political unit. They have not fully embraced the possibility that they may have to make a choice between them, or that NAFTA may not be available if they secede from the Canadian federation.

But the perhaps surprising and distinct feature of Quebec's desire for self-determination is that the Canadian federal government has not yet been able definitively to reassure Quebecois that they will do better staying within the Canada unit. Because of the similarity of French and English Canada's acceptance of globalization, Quebec might be expected to reject self-determination and independence. According to this view Ottawa's effort to buy off nationalist dissent should be successful. In addition international opinion has become less supportive of self-determination for Quebec.[2] In Quebec's case, the United States, Canada's closest and most influential ally, has remained unsympathetic to Quebecers' consideration of sovereignty. Even France, the state most willing to endorse Quebec's sovereignty, has turned ambivalent to the prospect of an independent Quebec. How then is it that demands for self-determination continue to reverberate?

THE PARADOX OF QUEBEC NATIONAL SELF-DETERMINATION

In 2005, Quebecers were observing the tenth anniversary of the Second Referendum in which they voted 50.6 percent against sovereignty by only the slimmest of margins. There continue to be political parties provincially (the Parti Quebecois) and federally (the Bloc Quebecois) dedicated to the independence of Quebec. The existence of both political parties can be explained partly by the continuing mobilization of nationalist sentiment by political elites. Though the best days of the national self-determination movement may have passed (including two unsuccessful referendums),[3] Quebec elites still cling to the nationalist dream. Nationalists generally favor self-determination. Public opinion polling shows that there has been, and continues to be, strong sentiment in the province favoring independence. But it is difficult to understand how sentiment supporting Quebec's independence could remain as high as it has over the last decade since the failed Second Referendum. Recently, Quebecers were asked whether they felt more sovereigntist or more federalist over the past ten years. The answer showed that 60 percent of those questioned had not changed their views.[4] How do we explain this continuity in face of globalization and the efforts of the Ottawa government to diminish provincial sentiment?

In the winter and spring of 2005, Canada, but particularly Quebec, was riveted by the work of the Gomery Commission which examined federal spending in the province. In this inquiry advertising executives were called to testify before Justice John H. Gomery. Only a year earlier (and before the release of the Auditor General's Annual Report[5] that had raised the alarm over federal sponsorship spending in Quebec), analysts examining the Quebec political scene had concluded that there might be a lessening of support for sovereignty in Quebec.[6] But the so-called "sponsorship scandal" appeared to turn the fortunes of sovereigntists around.[7] The Gomery testimony created public anger in Quebec towards federalists and federalist parties, principally the Liberal Party and its Ottawa regime. The Paul Martin Liberals saw Liberal (and unionist) fortunes in Quebec diminish. In the 2004 federal election, the prospects of the sovereigntist Bloc went from good to better. In the final tally the BQ raised its profile and secured 54 seats, a substantial increase from the 38 it had held after the 2000 election. And in the province, the PQ, after being driven from office by provincial Liberals, saw its fortunes improve. The new provincial Liberal government under Premier Jean Charest found itself unpopular as a result of a variety of policy decisions. By the summer of 2005 the PQ had completed a platform which adopted a plan that called for a referendum "as soon as possible." This, of course, would wait for a PQ victory in Quebec.

In the midst of these changes, pollsters also noted a growing support for sovereignty. As revealed by Rhéal Séguin of the Toronto *Globe and Mail* (reporting on a Léger Marketing survey conducted for the paper and for Montreal's *Le Devoir*) 54 percent of Quebecers favored sovereignty, the highest level of support since 1998.[8] This surge in support was apparently due to "the sponsorship scandal."[9] The Léger study also indicated that 76 percent of voters felt betrayed by the actions of the former prime minister, Jean Chrétien, and the Liberal Party of Canada after the 1995 referendum on sovereignty. According to pollster Jean-Marc Léger, the federal sponsorship program—involving grants to Quebec—had initially helped to "undermine support for sovereignty" between 1997 and 2002, but new revelations of mismanagement and perhaps corruption led to growing support for the cause of sovereignty. While spring 2005 polling seemed to indicate that sovereignty was "on the ropes," it was resuscitated by the scandal and the revelations that taxpayers' money had been used to sustain federal party donations to Quebec.

THE CONTINUING DRAMA

Yet polling data that POLLARA has gathered over the last ten years do not fully support a resurgence of sovereignty claims. First, all polling data need to be interpreted in the context of the framing of the question. This is a central issue in the referendum question itself. The following is the question that was posed to Quebecers in the First Referendum in 1980:

The Government of Quebec has made public its proposal to negotiate a new agreement with the rest of Canada, based on the equality of nations; this agreement would enable Quebec to acquire the exclusive power to make its laws, administer its taxes and establish relations abroad—in other words, sovereignty—and at the same time to maintain with Canada an economic association including common currency; any change in political status resulting from these negotiations will be submitted to the people through a referendum; on these terms, do you agree to give the Government of Quebec the mandate to negotiate the proposed agreement between Quebec and Canada?

This referendum question went down to defeat with 59.5 percent of Quebecers voting No and 40.4 percent voting Yes. By the Second Referendum the language had been tightened, though it remained a sovereignty-association question. The 1995 Referendum read:

Do you agree that Quebec should become sovereign, after having made a formal offer to Canada for a new Economic and Political Partnership, within the scope of the Bill respecting the future of Quebec and the agreement signed on June 12, 1995?[10]

As mentioned above, this question elicited significantly more support with 49.4 percent of Quebec voters voting Yes, thus barely rejecting the sovereignty-association proposal.

Indeed the wording of the question has been a major issue for the federal government and the Quebec government, since the framing of the question directly impacts the result. Stéphen Dion, the author of the *Clarity Act* (Canada), has strongly favored a clear-cut question in any subsequent referendum. The PQ has suggested that the next referendum question be about declaring independence for Quebec. And Stéphen Dion, still a federal Liberal Minister, has been even more direct, suggesting a question like: "Do you want Quebec to stop being part of Canada and to become an independent country?"[11] Nothing short of this, he believed, would put the choices squarely. Such a question might be harder even for nationalist Quebecois to accept.

That the framing of the question can be very important in the result has been established by the Strategic Counsel and its chairman, Allen Gregg.[12] As noted in figure 13.1, when Quebecers are asked their opinion over self-determination and specifically asked to support or reject it based on the 1995 Second Referendum question, Quebecers in October expressed 48 percent support for "sovereignty."

However, when Quebecers are asked a more direct question—in which the words "secession" and "independence" are used—as identified in figure 13.2, those favoring sovereignty drop to 43 percent with a majority failing to support independence. Another important factor in the outcome is the particular character of leadership of the Yes and No camps.[13] Some leaders have been more effective than others.

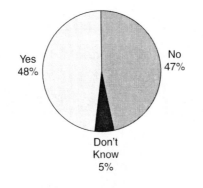

Figure 13.1. *Would Quebecers vote Yes to a referendum using the same question as in 1995?**
Source: The Strategic Counsel
*"Quebec Referendum Ten Years After," *The Globe and Mail* (October 22, 2005), p. A12.

The apparent recent surge in support for sovereignty was underscored in the English media. However, though it represented an increase, it was often unclear how to assess those numbers in the larger framework of support, or lack of support, for self-determination.

The quarterly polling of POLLARA on the question of self-determination helps us to unravel these issues. The virtue of the data is evident, beginning with the question asked. Unlike many other polling studies, this data set—outlined in figure 13.3—tracks opinion in Quebec and indeed in the rest of Canada with a so-called hard question. In this quarterly survey, the question is about independence and not about sovereignty-association or any aspect

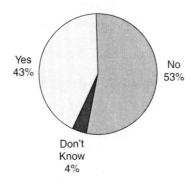

Figure 13.2. *Would Quebecers support seceding from Canada to become an independent country?**
Source: The Strategic Counsel
*"Quebec Referendum Ten Years After," *The Globe and Mail* (October 22, 2005), p. A12.

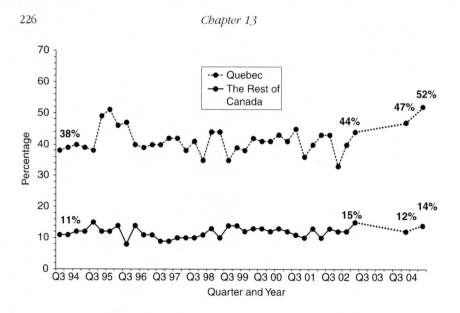

Figure 13.3. **Favoring Independence** (% strongly or somewhat favoring independence) *Question: Do you strongly favor, somewhat favor, somewhat oppose or strongly oppose the independence of Quebec?*
*POLLARA normally polled a sample 1,661 Canadians and within that 300 Quebecers

of partnership with Canada. It is the prospect of partnership with the rest of Canada that usually makes sovereignty for Quebecers easier to accept.

As is apparent from figure 13.3 and the solid line, support for independence has been consistently high through the ten years since the Second Referendum. Indeed, support for independence has remained in the high 30s or above during much of this extended period. There was only one period other than the most recent time period in which sentiment climbed above 50 percent in Quebec—that was immediately after the Second Referendum. The relatively high and continuing support for independence over this period questions the effectiveness of statements and actions by government and federalist leaders.

Figure 13.4 tracks the time frame of the independence question. This question asks those polled whether they anticipate Quebec will become independent within a three-year period. As is evident from the public opinion data, Quebecers' expectations of independence rose dramatically in the period just following the Second Referendum. Yet from just below 60 percent, expectations dropped to the teens in the early 2000s, though support followed no such trend.

It would seem that elite policies and community opinion—against independence—have had an impact on expectations in Quebec. These expectations may have been influenced by the view that sovereignty had become a

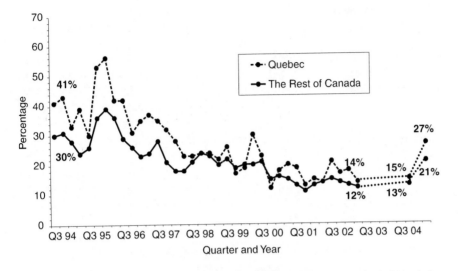

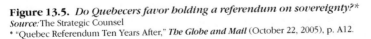

Figure 13.4. Perceived Likelihood of Quebec Independence (% who believe independence is very or somewhat likely within 3 years)
Question: Would you say it is very likely or somewhat likely, somewhat unlikely or very unlikely that Quebec will become independent within the next three years?

fading issue in Quebec. And, as we have seen earlier, opinion results are often dependent on the nature of the question asked. So in a question posed by the Strategic Counsel in October 2005 (figure 13.5), which asks whether Quebecers want to hold another referendum, Quebecers basically are split on the prospect of another debate and vote.

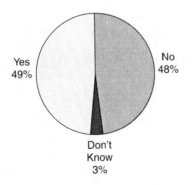

Figure 13.5. *Do Quebecers favor holding a referendum on sovereignty?** *
Source: The Strategic Counsel
* "Quebec Referendum Ten Years After," *The Globe and Mail* (October 22, 2005), p. A12.

STILL A "WITHIN CANADA" DEBATE IN QUEBEC

How can this persistently high level of support for independence be understood in the context of Quebec and globalization, or is it perhaps an artifact of the view that sovereignty will in fact not be achieved (therefore, there is no problem in siding with the independence side)? If Quebec is an example of the effect of globalization on sentiment for national-self determination, one might have expected an even less favorable attitude toward self-determination. In order to delve further into this question, we went into the field, "armed" with our question on independence and then executed a follow-on question. In December 2004, with a sample size in Quebec of 753, we asked the interviewers to ask a follow-up question of those who expressed support for independence.[14] Those individuals were asked to choose among reasons for their support. These included:

1. They want Quebec to exist as an independent country;
2. They want autonomy through a separate Quebec nation that is not formally independent from Canada; or
3. They want Quebec to obtain additional power in the Canadian federal system.

Figure 13.6 sets out the responses of those favoring independence. Of the 47 percent of Quebecers that expressed support for independence, 30 percent of them indicated that their support was based on their desire for an independent country. Twenty-six percent wanted an autonomous Quebec but

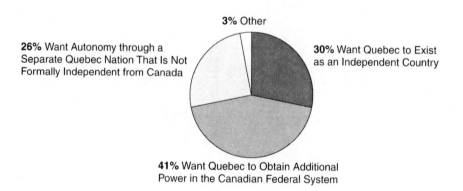

3% Other

26% Want Autonomy through a Separate Quebec Nation That Is Not Formally Independent from Canada

30% Want Quebec to Exist as an Independent Country

41% Want Quebec to Obtain Additional Power in the Canadian Federal System

Figure 13.6. *Question: Which of these 3 views best describes your own main reason for supporting independence?*

not an independent one. Finally, and significantly, 41 percent wanted to obtain additional power for Quebec within the Canadian federal system.

This result is very revealing. As the section title suggests, though there is persistent support for independence, Quebecers' attitudes endorse a continuing "within Canada" option. Even those who express support for independence still expect a non-independence outcome. Thus, even current sentiment for independence by Quebecers (which may reflect anger over the sponsorship scandal implicating federalists and the Liberal Party in Quebec) probably does not mean support for an independent country. PQ leaders in Quebec have to remain careful not to misinterpret these results for their own partisan advantage.

Rhéal Séguin argued the following: "Support for sovereignty appears to be more a reflection of Quebecers' anger toward the federal government than a deep-seated desire to achieve political independence."[15] Polling numbers from Léger Marketing back this up in suggesting that Quebecers express confidence in the possibility of renewed federalism in which Quebec would have its "rightful place in Canada," at the 48 percent level.[16]

"TOUGH LOVE" FROM THE METROPOLE

Following the near loss of the Second Referendum, the Liberal Chrétien government was suddenly galvanized into action. Chrétien devised a sponsorship program in Quebec to ameliorate provincial discontent, but after the scandals, this effort has come back to haunt federalists in Quebec.[17] In addition, the Chrétien government referred to the highest court in the land, the Canadian Supreme Court, to determine the legality of secession following a referendum on sovereignty. While the court did not accept a unilateral declaration of independence by Quebec, it suggested that a clear majority vote in Quebec on a clear question would constitute a moral obligation on the part of Canada to negotiate with a Quebec government over the country's future. In turn this led the federal government to propose the Clarity Act (Canada).[18] The act was intended to achieve two objectives: to force a "clear" question to be posed in any future referendum, thereby avoiding the partnership language and instead raising the issue of the independence of the province from Canada. It was also designed to prevent a mere 50 percent plus one outcome from triggering the automatic independence of Quebec. The legislation in fact directed that Canada's Parliament—thirty days after a Quebec government tabled a referendum question—pass a resolution determining whether the question posed by the Quebec government was sufficiently clear. Failing acceptance of the resolution question, the Canadian government would refuse to negotiate over independence following a Yes vote in

Quebec. Secondly. Canada would refuse to negotiate if Canada's Parliament passed a resolution that determined the Yes vote failed to represent "a clear expression of a will by a clear majority" that the province should become independent.

The federal strategy was designed to strip the sovereigntists of ambiguous questions, forcing the use of harder independence language. It was also designed to ensure that the achievement of independence would require more than just a 50-percent majority vote. The Clarity Act was generally well received outside of Quebec, and opinion there favored what appeared to be a more muscular federal policy. But federal involvement was not well received in Quebec where many argued that the Quebec community should be the one to determine Quebec's future. According to pollster Allan Gregg, 50 percent of Quebecers supported a simple majority outcome to decide independence, while 74 percent of the rest of Canada concluded that a simple majority was insufficient.[19]

It is not clear, however (see figure 13.3), that the promulgation of the Act has had much impact on Quebec opinion. Moreover, Canadians generally are relaxed about negotiating a partnership with Quebec. When asked whether the rest of Canada should negotiate the separation of Quebec—given a favorable referendum on that issue—62 percent of Canadians outside Quebec said Yes. In addition, English Canadians also seem relaxed over negotiating a partnership with Quebec (figure 13.7). They support negotiating a new partnership (after independence) with 72 percent approval. But the Clarity Act may well create a crisis between Quebec and the rest of the country. If Quebec ignores the resolution or resolutions of the House of Commons, insisting that only Quebecers can make the choices with respect to the clear wording or the clear majority, then Quebec and Canada may well find themselves unable to negotiate a solution, embittering both communities following a Yes vote. The Clarity Act works only if it prevents another vote on an ambiguous question, but it could make the situation worse, if Quebecers determine to launch a Third Referendum regardless of the terms.

CONCLUSION

Since the mid-1960s, opinion over Quebec's status has been divided both within and outside the province. Early efforts of the Front de Libération de Quebec (FLQ) to achieve independence through means of political terrorism were unsuccessful and even counterproductive. They remain so today. But democratic political agitation on both sides has created an environment in which negotiation of Quebec's future between Quebec authorities and the federal government is not ruled out. Given the Clarity Act, it is highly unlikely that narrow provincial approval of a hastily drafted Quebec provision for

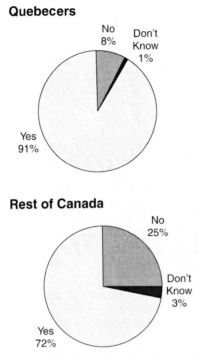

Figure 13.7. *Should the rest of Canada negotiate a partnership with an independent Quebec?*
Source: The Strategic Counsel

independence-association would lead to the demise of federal Canada. It might lead to negotiation, but most Canadians would not expect this to produce an independent Quebec. As Rhéal Séguin correctly says, "support for sovereignty appears to be more a reflection of Quebecers' anger toward the federal government than a deep-seated desire to achieve political independence." Independence for Quebec would also pose the real question of an independent status for the Inuit peoples in the North, to say nothing of the claims of the English-speakers in the South. Canada could break up in future, but this case brings out forcefully what is true in the other instances this volume studies: it is the policy of the federal government that is ultimately decisive in the question of further self-determination. An enlightened policy in Ottawa could continue to avoid political separation. The problem has been that Ottawa has not been very enlightened in its tactics up to now. And if by some chance an independence referendum was approved by voters in Quebec, the result would still depend on the outcome of negotiations with the federal government. Though they may prefer "independence," even Quebecois do not necessarily expect these to yield "independence."

NOTES

I want to thank POLLARA and its principals for their support for this project.

1. See particularly Kenneth McRae, "The Structure of Canadian History," in Louis Hartz, *The Founding of New Societies* (New York: Harcourt Brace, 1964).

2. In the opening chapter Rosecrance and Stein actually suggest three reasons for the increasing unlikely prospect of new states. Two are mentioned here but the third—the safety valve for the metropole to have discontented groups emigrate seems wholly inapplicable in the Canada and Quebec case.

3. One must be careful here for the Second Referendum in 1995 in Quebec barely failed to achieve a majority in favor of at least sovereignty-association, the rather complex and not completely transparent goal of Quebec nationalists.

4. The polling was undertaken by Strategic Counsel for the *Globe and Mail* and CTV News and reported by the *Globe and Mail* (October 22, 2005, p. 1). Allen Gregg, the president of Strategic Counsel, was the pollster for the Progressive Conservative Mulroney government from 1984 through 1993. The poll was taken from October 6 through October 13, 2005. The poll surveyed 1,000 Canadians and is assessed to be accurate to within 3.1 percentage points 95 percent of the time.

5. The Auditor General's Report was released to Parliament in November 2003. Chapters 3 and 4 focused a highly critical eye on the sponsorship programs of the federal government. The loud chorus of criticism in and outside of Parliament led the new Martin government to appoint the *Commission of Inquiry into the Sponsorship Program and Advertising Activities* by Order in Council on February 19, 2004. The Commission had a double mandate. The first required the Commission to investigate and report on questions raised, directly or indirectly, by chapters 3 and 4 of the November 2003 Report of the Auditor General of Canada. The second mandate called upon the Commission to make recommendations to the Government of Canada, based upon its factual findings, to prevent mismanagement of sponsorship programs and advertising activities in the future.

6. Following the "near-death" experience of the Second Referendum in 1995, the Sponsorship Program was designed by the Liberal Chrétien government to promote the federal presence in Quebec in the late 1990s through sponsorships of sporting and entertainment events.

7. The Auditor General in her report chronicled the mismanagement of the sponsorship management, suggesting, among other things, that much of the funding had failed to be accounted for properly and that funds had been provided to advertising agencies in Quebec for little or no work by these agencies. Portions of the funds paid to these executives were apparently passed to federal Liberal officials—in other words a "kick-back" scheme. In the Gomery inquiry, ad agency executives provided details of these payments including how funds found their way to Liberal Party officials and how in some cases those funds paid for workers at the agencies who worked for the federal Liberal Party.

8. Rhéal Séguin, "54% in Quebec Back Sovereignty," *Globe and Mail* (April 27, 2005). The high expression of support for sovereignty in 1998 was tied to the popular provincial campaign of PQ Premier Lucien Bouchard. The poll conducted by Léger was taken between April 21 and 24, 2005, and 1,008 interviews were con-

ducted with eligible voters throughout Quebec. The poll was considered accurate within 3.1 percentage points, 19 times out of 20.

9. In the Léger survey 37 percent of the respondents "said the scandal and the allegations of the Gomery Commission motivated their decision to support sovereignty."

10. The June 12th agreement was an undertaking by the PQ, BQ, and the Parti Action Démocratique du Quebec (ADQ) to work together to achieve a partnership with the rest of Canada after a Yes vote.

11. Quoted in Graeme Hamilton, "Sovereignty Question Not an If, But a When," *National Post* (October 29, 2005), p. A1.

12. Quoted in Brian Laghi, "Quebec Still Torn on Future in Canada," *Globe and Mail* (October 22, 2005), p. A1.

13. Referendums in Quebec are required by law to be conducted on a two-camp basis—those supporting the proposition and those opposing the proposition. Provincial law also regulates important issues such as funding.

14. We of course did the same for those in the rest of Canada who expressed support for independence.

15. Rhéal Séguin, "54% in Quebec Back Sovereignty," *Globe and Mail* (April 27, 2005).

16. Ibid.

17. In fact Commissioner John Gomery issued his first Report on November 1, 2005. His main findings included:

- clear evidence of political involvement in the administration of the Sponsorship Program;
- insufficient oversight by senior public civil servants;
- a veil of secrecy in administering the program;
- overcharging by communication agencies and subcontractors;
- the use of the Sponsorship Program for purposes other than national unity or federal visibility;
- avoidance in complying with federal legislation;
- a complex web of financial transactions involving a federal ministry, crown corporations, and communication agencies that led to kickback and illegal contributions to the federal Liberal Party in Quebec;
- evidence of certain agencies carrying on their payrolls individuals who in effect were working for the Liberal Party; and
- refusal of ministers, senior officials in the Prime Minister's Office, and public servants to acknowledge their responsibility for the problems of mismanagement that occurred.

18. *Clarity Act*, S.C., 2000, c. 26, as amended.

19. "Quebec Referendum Ten Years After," *Globe and Mail* (October 22, 2005), p. A12.

14

The Dilemma of Devolution and Federalism: Secessionary Nationalism and the Case of Scotland

Arthur A. Stein and Richard N. Rosecrance

In 1707, England and Scotland completed their union. Yet more than a quarter of a millennium later Scottish nationalism made a reappearance. The English-Scottish union is thus an exemplar of the success of a long-standing union and simultaneously epitomizes the continuing problem of secessionary nationalism in the modern world.[1] In terms of overarching globalization both England and Scotland are supporters of the modern world economy. After the "enclosures" were completed in the 18th century, Scotland and Glasgow were as much at the heart of the Industrial Revolution as Leeds and Manchester. Today they are equal partisans of globalization, making it easier for London to assuage Scottish concerns.

This chapter assesses the case of Scottish nationalism and argues that it exemplifies the dilemma of devolution and federalism. We argue that federations are constructed, and secessions are avoided, by providing autonomy, and yet the provision of autonomy makes possible a continuation of the very separateness that can again become the basis for later nationalist agitation. We also show that political integration is multifaceted and that this also leaves room for continued separateness and thus for national self-determination. Finally, we discuss the effect of supranational economic integration on demands for political separation.

THE UNION OF SCOTLAND AND ENGLAND

The peoples and kingdoms of England and Scotland share a long history of both conflict and peace, of both emergent sameness and continuing distinctiveness. They came to share a language but retain linguistic differences. They share and disagree in matters of religion.

Early in the last millennium, Scotland was being anglicized as its elite adopted English speech and manners and even institutions. English laws, religious institutions, economic arrangements such as land-tenure, and political institutions such as the sheriff and burgh charters were all adopted from England.

The process of assimilation was not always accompanied by peaceful interaction between the kingdoms, however. There were border disputes and territorial conflicts.

There were extensive periods of peace but the only attempt to unify the crowns failed. The intensively negotiated attempt to unify the crowns through marriage, the Treaty of Birgham-on-Tweed of 1290, ended prematurely with the death of the bride-to-be. The terms of this agreement stipulated that the two kingdoms would remain organizationally separate even after the succession to both crowns of the son who would be born of this royal marriage. The death of the maid, however, prevented the union of crowns.

England and Scotland were at war with each other in 1079–1080, 1214–1216, 1295–1296 (a war that led to England's annexation of Scotland), 1314–1328 (reestablishing Scottish independence), 1482, 1513, 1542–1549, and 1559–1560.[2] Their respective kings were periodically enticed to intervene in the other country, and their wars often involved France. By the 16th century, Scotland had a long-established tradition of allying itself with France as a counterweight to the English threat.

Unification of the kingdoms of England and Scotland proceeded in stages. It began with the unification of the Crown in 1603, when Scotland's King James VI, who had assiduously pursued good relations with England, inherited the English crown upon the death of Elizabeth I and became James I, King of England. From that point on, England and Scotland had the same monarch but separate parliaments.

The unified monarchy was beset by strains at every step. During their rule, monarchs found Scotland opposed to royal imposition from the south. During successions, Scots were often angered by the process and the outcome. During the English Civil War, the two fought a war as they parted ways about the nature of governance.

The kings who ruled England and Scotland resided in England. Their efforts to impose common structures met opposition in Scotland. Both James I (1603–1625) and his son Charles I (1625–1649) encountered substantial opposition to their efforts to make the Church of Scotland similar to the Church of England. Charles I went so far as to wage war on Scotland (the Bishops' War, 1639–1640), but eventually retreated when the English parliament refused to pay for the military campaign.[3] Despite Scottish support for monarchy and the restored rule of Charles II (1660–1685, see below), the Scots rebelled in both 1666 and 1679 to English religious pronouncements during his reign.

The Scots had problems not only with the unified monarchy but also with the alternative during the 17th century. Portions of the English Civil War were really a war between England and Scotland. Indeed, in Scotland it is known as the "War of the Three Kingdoms."[4] In response to England's execution of Charles I and its ending monarchical rule in favor of Cromwell's republic, Scotland crowned Charles II king. The war that ensued resulted in Scotland's military defeat and its incorporation into a commonwealth with what was perceived to be inadequate representation. The English restoration of monarchy and the crowning of Charles II in 1660 (nine years after the Scots had done so) returned the status quo ante.

The unified monarchy was tested with virtually every succession during the century in which Scotland retained a separate parliament. Repeatedly, the English parliament made key decisions about the crown without consulting the Scottish parliament, and the latter parted company from the former. In addition to steps such as the execution of Charles I, the English parliament made peremptory decisions about royal succession. When the English deposed James II (1685–1689) in the Glorious Revolution and replaced him with William and Mary, some Scots supported the decision but others rallied to James II militarily and were again defeated. The Scots negotiated over the religious and financial terms of their acceptance of William and Mary which came two years after their English coronation. Finally, in 1701, during the reign of Queen Anne (1702–1714) the English parliament selected the house of Hanover to succeed Anne at the end of her reign. They made this decision also without consulting the Scottish parliament, which refused to pass the English Act of Settlement, thus signaling that they were free to choose another successor. In short, the policy differences between the two parliaments extended to issues of succession. Nonetheless, English-Scottish union occurred during this period (1707).

The disagreements between the two parliaments led many in England to press for fuller integration. On a number of occasions, a complete union of England and Scotland was proposed by England. In 1700, and again in 1702, King William proposed a complete union to the Scottish parliament.

Union was not attractive to Scotland until economic disasters brought Scottish opinion around. First there were a series of poor harvests in the 1690s. Second there was a disastrous attempt to establish a colony in Panama. A Scotland that had thus lost a quarter of its liquid capital was then subjected to economic pressure by the English.

In 1705, the English demonstrated the benefits of economic union by closing off their market to Scotland. Although denied full access to England's colonies, half of Scotland's exports went to England. But the English market was closed in 1705 to linen, coal, and cattle from Scotland. In addition, Scots would be treated by England as aliens.

The two parliaments then negotiated a union. The benefits to Scotland were entirely economic. They regained access to the English market and obtained full access to England's colonies.[5] There would be common coinage and common weights and measures. In addition, the act of union included compensation of almost half a million pounds to those who had lost money in the failed colonization of Panama.

The Scots held out for as much autonomy as they could extract from the English. Giving up their parliament and accepting representation in the existing English parliament was a foregone cost for it was England's chief objective.[6] The Scots pressed for a federation and the English refused. But the Scots were able to retain their legal system, their educational system, and their church.[7]

The agreement worked out by a commission was received differently in England and Scotland. The treaty divided Scots and faced bitter opposition. It was debated at length in the Scottish parliament and in the streets. Stones were thrown at parliament, copies of the treaty were burned, and for a month, the city of Glasgow's streets were filled with demonstrators opposed to union. Finally the treaty passed the Scottish parliament 100–67 on January 16, 1707. By contrast, the treaty faced no opposition in the English parliament.

Union had been negotiated. Great Britain came into being. Scotland accepted the English royal house as its own, dissolved its parliament, and obtained the right to send its representatives to Westminster. There would be common tariffs and economic policies. But Scotland retained a degree of autonomy. It was allowed to keep its own Church, the Church of Scotland (known as the Kirk); it retained its own laws and its own education system.

Unification was mutually beneficial and accepted voluntarily and calculatingly. The English were eager to incorporate a land that had repeatedly allied itself with France and posed a security problem as a result. A Scotland that was part of England could no longer serve as a base for European (mostly French) attacks on England. In return, Scotland obtained access to the English market, including Britain's overseas colonies.

But the union faced strong (and continuing) opposition in Scotland. Giving up Scottish autonomy was perceived quite differently in the two societies. Ironically, this combination of a unification that allowed for a great deal of cultural autonomy and was a calculated exchange led one scholar to write more than two and a half centuries later that "The 'Britain' of 1707 created no new nationality; it was the fruit of an English desire for stability and a Scottish pursuit of economic modernization."[8]

The union with England divided Scots. The divisions between Protestant Lowlanders and Catholic Highlanders continued as did their sympathies for different kings and lines of succession. In both 1715 and 1745 there were rebellions in the Highlands by supporters of Stuart descendants (the rebels were called Jacobites after their support of King James II and his descendants). The first rebellion occurred when George I succeeded Queen Anne; the Jacobites then proclaimed James III (son of James II) as their king. This rebellion was defeated. In 1745, the arrival in Scotland of Prince Charles Edward Stewart, son of James III, resulted in a new uprising. When the English crushed the rebellion of 1745, they banned the symbols of the rebel, the tartan and bagpipes, and for thirty-six years Highland dress was prohibited.

SCOTTISH DEVELOPMENT WITHIN THE UNION

Although there were no more military rebellions after the two failed attempts of the first half of the 18th century, there remained substantial resentment against the English. In the last quarter millennium, Scottish demands for autonomy and independence have been pursued peacefully, exercising the perquisites of voice and representation provided to Scots by the United Kingdom.

Scotland benefited enormously from the union with England. First, it underwent the economic modernization that Scottish elites hoped for. Scotland experienced the full force of English industrialization, becoming a leading center for textile manufacturing. Indeed, Glasgow is synonymous with English textiles in the 19th century. It was also a major center of coal mining and a center for heavy industry in the late 19th and early 20th centuries.

Simultaneously, there was a rebirth of Scottish culture, literature, and language. Scotland during the second half of the 18th century (and the beginning of the 19th) produced David Hume, Robert Burns, Adam Smith, James Boswell, Walter Scott, and James McPherson, among others. David Hume noted the irony of the emergence of a Scottish literary tradition absent an independent Scotland:

> Is it not strange that, at a time when we have lost our Princes, our Parliaments, our independent Government, even the Presence of our chief Nobility, are unhappy, in our Accent & Pronunciation, speak a very corrupt Dialect of the Tongue which we make use of; is it not strange, I say, that, in these Circumstances, we shou'd really be the People most distinguished for Literature in Europe?[9]

Many of the symbols of Scottish distinctiveness are creations of the age of union and not remnants of an earlier independent history. In the words of one scholar, "Early nineteenth-century Scotland was remarkably fruitful in the manufacturing of myths, and a great deal of what today is considered the Scottish identity was created at this time."[10]

Scotland experienced the benefits and social disruptions of industrialization and developed a sense of its distinctiveness, but a substantial majority of

its people remained firmly unionist. Indeed, Scottish autonomy and independence were often brought up by others as an adjunct to British policy
about home rule for Ireland. At the beginning of the 20th century, the Liberal
Party was in power with substantial support from Scotland. The Labour party
was pushing home rule, including Scotland, but Scots overwhelmingly voted
unionist.

But Scotland was especially hard-hit economically in the period following
the First World War. Scottish industries were especially affected after the war,
during the depression, and their decline simply continued. The sense that
Scotland was not benefiting economically from the union led to renewed
demands for independence. But those demands had little traction until the
last third of the 20th century.

The key to the growth of Scottish nationalist demands came when the discovery of oil off the coast of Scotland combined with Scottish disaffection.[11]

The Scottish Nationalist Party (SNP) campaigned for independence, arguing "It's Scotland's oil." In the election of October 1974, the SNP received 30
percent of the Scottish vote. The growing pressures for independence led to
a 1979 referendum on devolution. Although devolution received 52 percent
of the vote, only 32.9 percent of the electorate took part. Both the small margin of victory and the failure of the required 40 percent turnout to materialize
signaled the failure of Scottish nationalism.

Scottish nationalism underwent resurgence in the 1990s. The key was a
campaign focused on the new possibilities for Scottish independence.

SCOTLAND AND DEVOLUTION

The UK was not one of the founding six members of the EEC customs union
in the late 1950s. Instead, with six others, Britain created the European Free
Trade Area (EFTA).[12] As its name suggests, EFTA was intended merely to create a free trade area, reducing the tariff barriers of members towards one
another to zero. The EEC was intended to be a customs union and required
that its members not only reduce their internal barriers to one another but
agree on a common tariff against nonmembers. The customs union is a
deeper form of economic association and portends higher levels of integration and harmonization. But within a decade and a half, the UK joined the
EEC and began the process of economic integration with the major European
economies.[13]

The clarion call of Scottish nationalists then became "Independence within
Europe," or as one might say, "Scotland in the EU." The phrase captured the
essence of a political objective of achieving Scottish independence while
maintaining the economic status of membership in the EU. In effect, its proponents claimed that the commercial benefits of integration with England

could be retained alongside the benefits of EU membership even while the political costs of subjugation to England would be terminated. The Scots could retain the benefits of union and still obtain the benefits of sovereignty and independence.

The EU option declined, however, as the British Labour Party pressed for devolution of powers to Scotland, without independence. The most important transformation in English-Scottish relations came with the return of Labour to power and the accession of Tony Blair and an associated Scottish ruling clique. Almost two decades of Conservative party rule and attempted centralization caused a resurgence of Scottish nationalism. British Labour, concerned with regaining solid Scottish support for the Labour Party and undercutting the flight of voters to the Scottish Nationalist Party, devised a system of "devolution" as a way of meeting Scottish demands while retaining support for the union. The election of 1997 that brought British Labour to power also saw the SNP obtain a mere 22 percent of the Scottish vote.[14]

A referendum for devolution received 71 percent of the vote and was followed by its implementation. Thus, after three hundred years, Scotland had once again achieved its own parliament. The Scottish parliament, however, has scarcely been a foil of Scottish nationalism, for Labour coalitions continue to govern there. In 2003, the SNP received only 23 percent of Scottish votes.

Demands for statehood were thus dealt with through increased autonomy within the union rather than independence from it. The autonomy provided for in the original union was no longer sufficient to head off nationalist aspirations. The devolution of central power to local authority has for the present dealt with the problem. While the Scottish National Party received considerable support when the Tories were in power in London (in the 1980s and early 90s), it declined precipitately when Labour returned to power in Westminster. Tony Blair's Labour also is populated by Scots at the helm in Britain. Expenditure on Scotland by the British central government exceeds per capita expenditure in England or Wales. The subvention to Scotland under the terms of the "Barnett formula" is so favorable that there is some question whether it can be indefinitely continued, or whether the formula must be changed.

CONCLUSIONS

The record of Scottish nationalism provides many insights into the dynamics of integration. It demonstrates the varied aspects of integration and the continuing challenge of nationalist aspirations.

For Scotland, English culture was both a source of attraction and repulsion. The desire to be English competed with the desire to remain different. Much as American culture today is both imitated and reviled, English culture generated a similar set of polar responses among Scots.

The Scots' ability to absorb large aspects of English culture while retaining their distinctiveness is an indication of the resilience of identity.[15] Nairn finds Scotland's historical path unique in Europe and labels it "cultural subnationalism."[16]

The rise and fall of Scottish nationalism even in the context of union with England provides important insights into the seeming vagaries of integration and secession.

First, historical efforts at integration failed. Efforts to unify the English and Scottish crowns flagged as did efforts to unify the parliaments. Integration was not smooth and linear. Failures did not immediately lead to renewed attempts. Monarchical (executive) integration did not directly lead to integrated policy.

Second, integration need not happen in one step. The union of England and Scotland proceeded in stages. Integration of executive authority (monarchy) was accomplished before legislative integration.

The history of other unions parallels this record. In the United States, an original confederation (1783) was seen as a failure and replaced by the federal arrangement (1787). In the European Union, integration has also proceeded in stages. It began as a customs union and only later developed into a more integrated arrangement. Indeed, the name changes of the institution reflect this, from the European Economic Community (EEC), to the European Community (EC) to the European Union (EU).

Third, the process of integration itself creates friction. During the 17th-century era of monarchical integration, the English legislature dominated the process and did not consult their Scottish counterparts, and this was a source of conflict. The very workings of a partially integrated system thus became a source of friction.

Fourth, dissatisfaction with monarchical (executive) integration stimulated both separatists and integrationists. The latter lay the source of problems at the doorstep of incomplete integration and pressed for more integration. Some pushed for the replacement of Scotland's parliament with Scottish representation in an enlarged parliament in London. On the other hand, others blamed the problems of existing arrangements on premature integration and pressed for dissolution. This was the case during the most recent outburst of nationalist demands in the 1990s.

Fifth, even voluntary unions contained some element of coercion. The union of England and Scotland in 1707 was a voluntary act. The parliaments of the two countries ratified the act of union. Yet there was a backdrop of coercion and pressure. The English pressured the Scottish into union as well as bribed them to accept it. Voluntary choice often had a component of coercion underlying it.[17]

Sixth, even voluntarily negotiated unions must be sustained by force against military uprisings. Twice during the first half century of complete union, there were rebellions in support of monarchical alternatives for the Scottish crown. The union was retained by military suppression.

The use of force to maintain a union adopted voluntarily was a theme evident in U.S. history as well. The United States was a negotiated federation in which individual states agreed to membership. Yet subsequently, when one group wanted to secede, the union was maintained by force. The North went to war to retain the union with the South.

Seventh, a voluntary union required ceding important elements of autonomy. Even against the backdrop of coercion, a voluntarily negotiated union depended on bargaining and compromise. The basis of the compromise was the retention of some aspects of autonomy. This was the case for Scotland in 1707 and it was also true for the Americans in 1776.

Eighth, the continuing dilemma of autonomy is that even though the concession of autonomy is the prerequisite for union, it underscores distinctiveness and thus provides the basis for subsequent efforts at secession. The original union in 1707 allowed Scotland to retain sufficient autonomy that it was able to retain its identity and press for later secession. Indeed, the Scots retained so much autonomy that they were able to create a greater sense of distinctiveness under the union. Here, too, the U.S. case was similar. The original federal arrangement allowed Southern slave states to retain sufficient autonomy that they developed along separate lines and sought secession less than a century later.

Ninth, nationalist sentiment can arise in dependent regions not animated by nationalism at the moment of union. Historically, nationalism was a post-1789 phenomenon.[18] Developmentally, nationalism is for many scholars a product of industrialization.[19] Ironically, therefore, Scotland's union with England predates the emergence of modern nationalism. Scottish nationalism was re-created during the era of union. Despite Scotland's adoption of much of English culture, despite England's being one of the great long-standing historic nations in Europe, and despite Scotland's benefiting from industrialization, Scottish nationalism later emerged.

This suggests that other countries could experience pressures for nationalist splintering in the future. The construction of a united country, even prior to the emergence of nationalism, provides no guarantee against its subsequent development.

Tenth, entry of the union into a larger more encompassing regional union provides secessionists with the argument that the commercial benefits of union could be retained even with a political separation. The "Scotland in the EU" argument has its counterparts in the arguments of Quebec nationalists about joining NAFTA once independence has been conceded by Ottawa (see Alexandroff in chapter 13).

Finally, negotiated increased autonomy can relieve the pressure for outright independence. Although force can suppress secessionary demands (true for both Scotland in the first half of the 18th century and for the United States in the mid-19th century), providing more autonomy can head off pressure for independence without the use of force. This is the story of devolution in Scotland, and also that of Quebec in Canada.

The case of Scotland is thus both sobering and affirming. It is sobering because it suggests that even very long periods of life in an integrated union are no guarantee that secessionist pressures will not arise later. Yet, it also suggests that the autonomy that nurtured a secessionary nationalism can also be the basis for resolving nationalist demands short of independence.

NOTES

1. See Michael Keating, *Nations against the State* (London: Palgrave-Macmillan, 2001). He refers to this as "minority" and "separatist nationalism."

2. George Kohn, *Dictionary of Wars* (FACTS ON FILE), 1986.

3. Ironically, when the English civil war then erupted, Charles negotiated with the Scots and by granting their demands obtained their military support for his restoration to the crown. Cromwell's victory resulted in Charles's execution.

4. Norman Davies, *The Isles: A History* (New York: Oxford University Press, 1999).

5. The English had not been willing to grant the latter in earlier negotiations over union.

6. Scotland would be represented by 45 members of parliament and 16 elected peers.

7. The Scots also retained some other minor privileges.

8. J. G. A. Pocock, "The Limits and Divisions of British History: In Search of the Unknown Subject," *American Historical Review*, no. 2 (1982), 328.

9. Quoted in Tom Nairn, *The Breakup of Britain* (London: New Left Books, 1981), 139.

10. See Keith Brown, "Imagining Scotland," *Journal of British Studies*, Fall 1992, p. 415. Despite their existence as a distinct people with different institutions and customs, the Scots are also a constructed and an imagined community. See Benedict Anderson, *Imagined Communities* (London: Verso, 1983), and Hugh Trevor-Roper, "The Invention of Tradition: The Highland Tradition of Scotland," in Eric Hobsbawm and Terence Ranger, eds., *The Invention of Tradition* (Cambridge: Cambridge University Press, 1986).

11. Scotland's nationalist reassertion combines both grievance and greed. See Paul Collier and Anke Hoeffler, "Greed and Grievance in Civil War," unpublished paper, Oxford University, 2002. They argue that empirically greed has been more of a factor in secession and civil war than grievance, and that grievance has often been manufactured to justify greed. The Scottish case certainly has a long history of grievance, and the discovery of a valuable commodity created a set of possibilities. But as pointed out below, so did the solidification of the EU.

12. Creating a Europe of sixes and sevens; see Emile Benoit, *Europe at Sixes and Sevens* (New York: Columbia University Press, 1961), and Miriam Camps, *Britain and the European Community* (Princeton, NJ: Princeton University Press, 1964).

13. Within the EEC and, subsequently, the EU, multiple paths and speeds toward economic integration were allowed as states were allowed to opt out of some integrative measures even as subsets of states committed themselves to tighter integration. An example of the latter are the subset of countries who adopted the Euro and gave up national monetary autonomy.

14. In that election, all Conservative party MPs from Scotland and Wales lost.

15. Much the same can be said about the resurgence of ethnic and racial identity in the U.S. belying the characterization of the U.S. as a melting pot.

16. See Carsten Hammer Andersen et al., "The Development of Scottish Nationalism" (Aalborg University, 1997). The authors refer to this as pseudo-nationalism.

17. This is a general point to address to economic analyses of politics. Indeed, it can be made about economic exchange itself. See the work of Jack Hirshleifer, *The Dark Side of the Force* (Cambridge: Cambridge University Press, 2001).

18. See Miroslav Hroch, *Social Preconditions of National Revival in Europe* (Cambridge: Cambridge University Press, 1985). The author identifies three phases of nationalism, the first of which began in 1789.

19. This position is associated with Ernst Gellner, *Nations and Nationalism* (Ithaca, NY: Cornell University Press, 1983).

15

The Taiwan-China Tangle: Divided Sovereignty in the Age of Globalization

Richard Baum

Globalization—the spread of transnational networks of production, commerce and communications, technology and popular culture—is commonly believed to exert a pacifying influence on those subject to its gravitational pull. By fostering economic interdependence and organizational convergence, as well as shared situational understandings and life experiences, globalization putatively helps to reduce the vast normative, institutional, and behavioral gaps that divide the inhabitants of widely separated societies and cultures.[1]

In an earlier essay I examined China's post-Mao involvement in transnational trade, investment, finance, and information networks, and in a wide array of multinational regimes and organizations, to test the hypothesis that increasing global interaction and functional interdependence would result in increasing normative convergence—and decreasing international tensions—between China and the West. The results of that investigation were inconclusive: in some respects China appeared to have absorbed and assimilated prevailing international norms, standards, and practices; in other respects China continued to dance to its own distinctive—and sometimes contrary—national tune. As opposed to the expectations of neoliberal internationalism, "the China difference," though visibly diminishing in the socioeconomic, scientific, and technical realms, continued to loom large in the political and military spheres.[2]

The present chapter focuses on another, related aspect of China's increasing global interconnectedness: its changing relations with the "breakaway province" of Taiwan. Examining the initial conditions and tortuous history of Taiwan's long separation from the Chinese mainland, I assess the impact on that separation of two parallel developments commonly associated with the process of globalization: China's stunningly successful market reforms and "opening up" to the outside world, and Taiwan's equally impressive transition from a one-party dictatorship to a multi-party democracy. My objective in examining the effects of these two parallel, loosely interconnected processes—Chinese marketization and Taiwanese democratization—is to understand how the forces of globalization are affecting the long-term prospects for peaceful integration and eventual reunification (or, alternatively, permanently divided sovereignty and possible war) across the Taiwan Strait.

HISTORICAL BACKGROUND

Following the flight of the defeated Kuomintang (KMT) regime from mainland China to Taiwan in 1949, rival governments on either side of the Taiwan Strait advanced conflicting claims of sovereignty. For more than three decades the government-in-exile of the Republic of China (ROC) in Taipei, under President Chiang Kai-shek, purported to represent all of China on the grounds that the "Communist bandits" (*gongfei*) in control of the mainland were temporary interlopers who would soon be overthrown. For its part, the People's Republic of China (PRC) in Beijing, under Mao Zedong, claimed Taiwan as an integral part of China—a "breakaway province" that would soon be "liberated" and reunited with the Motherland.

Beijing was prevented from realizing its objective of early liberation by the intervention of the U.S. 7th Fleet in the Taiwan Strait at the outset of the Korean War, and by the subsequent enactment of the U.S.-Taiwan Mutual Security Treaty of 1954. Thereafter, Beijing frequently and bitterly condemned the United States for its continued "illegal intervention" in the domestic affairs of the Chinese people.[3]

With the passage of time, Beijing's inability to liberate Taiwan in the face of continuing U.S. military support for the ROC, coupled with the manifest unreality of Chiang Kai-shek's pledge to effect an early return to the mainland, led to a virtual stalemate in the Taiwan Strait. Periodically the Chinese Communists would mount a military threat to Taiwan, bombarding the KMT-held offshore islands of Quemoy and Matsu; but the U.S. threat of "massive retaliation," reinforced by the U.S.S.R.'s growing reluctance to come to Beijing's aid in the event of a nuclear showdown with the United States, forced Mao Zedong to back down on at least two occasions, in 1954 and again in 1958.[4]

This uneasy military stalemate lasted until 1972, when Henry Kissinger and Zhou En-lai worked out the historic compromise that enabled the U.S. and China to sidestep the troublesome sovereignty issue in the interest of establishing a common front against Soviet expansionism. In the Shanghai Communiqué of February 1972 U.S. negotiators, taking advantage of the fact that both Beijing and Taipei claimed sovereignty over a single Chinese territorial entity that included both the mainland and Taiwan, deliberately obfuscated the sovereignty question by stating that "the United States *acknowledges* that all Chinese on either side of the Taiwan Strait maintain there is but one China and Taiwan is part of China. The United States *does not challenge* that view" (emphasis added).[5]

By means of such diplomatic legerdemain the United States was able to begin the process of normalizing relations with the PRC without having to accept Beijing's claim to legal jurisdiction over Taiwan. By the same token, Beijing could claim that America had conceded that Taiwan was part of China. Each side thus emerged with a partial victory—secured at the expense of the ROC on Taiwan, whose leaders felt betrayed by American concessions to the "bandit" regime on the Chinese mainland.

As the United States stepped up its economic, technical, and cultural contacts with the PRC in the early 1970s, the ROC faced the prospect of increasing diplomatic isolation. Capitalizing on the improving atmosphere of Sino-American relations, Beijing used its newfound diplomatic leverage to pressure the United Nations to expel the ROC from both the General Assembly and Security Council.[6] At the same time, Beijing insisted that any country wishing to establish diplomatic relations with China must first sever all governmental ties to Taiwan.[7]

As more and more countries jumped on the diplomatic bandwagon, recognizing the PRC and de-recognizing the ROC, the Taipei regime was powerfully constrained to redefine its traditional sovereignty claim. No longer insisting that a return to the mainland was either imminent or feasible, Chiang Kai-shek's son and presidential successor, Chiang Ching-kuo, ceased proclaiming the ROC's effective jurisdiction over the Chinese mainland. Thereafter, the Taipei regime changed its name officially, if rather ambiguously, to "The Republic of China *on Taiwan*." For its part, Beijing never wavered from its traditional insistence that "there is only one China; the government of the PRC is the sole legal government of China; and Taiwan is an inalienable part of China." The result was an asymmetrical situation in which both sides continued to lay claim to the name "China," but only one side insisted on the exclusivity—and territorial inclusiveness—of its own definition.

TAIWAN'S DEMOCRATIC TRANSITION AND THE "OPENING" OF CHINA

In the quarter century since the United States and China completed their normalization of relations in 1979, two long-term developments have significantly altered the cross-strait sovereignty equation. These are, first, the dramatic growth of the Chinese economy under the aegis of Deng Xiaoping's policy of reform and "opening up"; and second, Taiwan's equally dramatic drive toward full political democracy. While these two historic processes occurred within roughly the same time frame and in roughly parallel fashion, their effects on cross-strait dynamics have tended to work in diametrically opposite directions.

China's entry into the jetstream of globalized commerce, communications, and cultural diffusion in the 1980s was marked, among other things, by the rapid development of indirect cross-strait trade and investment ties. Although legally enjoined from engaging in direct commercial relations, Beijing and Taipei made creative use of cross-strait family connections, third-party go-betweens, and old-fashioned coastal smugglers to realize the benefits of the substantial economic complementarities that existed across the Taiwan Strait.

In Taiwan, massive amounts of American Cold War largesse in the aftermath of the Korean War made possible an impressive economic growth spurt beginning in the late 1950s. Further stimulated by the ROC government's creation of export-processing zones, by a mobile, disciplined Taiwanese labor force, and by its significant comparative advantage in small-scale, flexible manufacturing techniques, Taiwan's increasingly export-driven economy "took off" in the early 1960s, averaging over 12 percent annual GDP growth from 1965 to 1978.[8] Indeed, by the late 1970s—just as China was beginning to emerge from its self-imposed Maoist cocoon—Taiwan had already joined the ranks of East Asia's dynamic "Little Dragons."[9] Enjoying substantial capital reserves, sophisticated mid-range manufacturing capabilities, an educated, skilled labor force (but one marked by a growing shortage of low-wage workers), and a business culture that typically used family and overseas networks to facilitate technology transfer and market access, Taiwan was well positioned to take advantage of China's "opening" to the outside world. By the same token China, with its vast, untapped domestic market, its abundance of low-wage labor, industrial raw materials and energy supplies, its shortage of investment capital, and its need for mid-range manufacturing technologies to jump-start its export-led industrialization drive, was a natural magnet for Taiwanese trade and investment. Equally important, the two sides shared a common language and cultural heritage.

Under these circumstances, and notwithstanding the continued political and military impasse across the Taiwan Strait, indirect, unofficial commercial, financial, and technological flows between the two sides increased substantially in the 1980s, with two-way trade reaching $4 billion (U.S.) in 1990—a fourfold increase over 1985. This increase in commercial activity was accompanied by new PRC initiatives designed to encourage Taiwanese business enterprises and individuals to invest in China. Although the Kuomintang government, fearful of compromising its security, remained extremely wary of Beijing's attempts to lure Taiwanese "compatriots" to the mainland, a nascent wave of "mainland China fever" was nonetheless evident among Taiwanese industrialists and investors.[10]

In 1987, Chiang Ching-kuo unilaterally terminated the state of martial law imposed by his father some twenty-nine years earlier, following this up with a relaxation of restrictions on cross-strait travel. Between 1987 and 1992 more than 4 million Taiwanese visited Mainland China, with about 40,000 Chinese crossing in the opposite direction. In the same period, indirect cross-strait trade reached $10 billion (U.S.) a year, while cumulative Taiwanese investment in China totaled almost $10 billion.[11]

This dramatic—if largely extralegal—rise in cross-strait travel, trade, and investment increased the interest of leaders on both sides in creating a regular, quasi-official mechanism for handling practical issues of mutual concern. While Beijing and Taipei each continued to eschew direct political contacts in lieu of an agreement on the all-important sovereignty question,[12] the two sides agreed to set up unofficial, quasi-governmental organizations to engage in periodic contacts on a variety of nonpolitical issues. In late 1991, Beijing established an "Association for Relations across the Taiwan Strait" (ARATS) to conduct negotiations with its Taiwanese counterpart, the newly created "Straits Exchange Foundation" (SEF). Under the stewardship of senior officials seconded from their respective governments—Wang Daohan of China and Koo Chen-fu of Taiwan—from 1992 to 1995 ARATS and SEF held a series of meetings in neutral venues from Singapore to Hong Kong. Among the key topics under discussion at these early meetings was creation of the so-called "three links" (*san tong*) to provide direct air, postal, and shipping links across the Taiwan Strait. (In the absence of government-to-government relations, all cross-strait commerce and travel had to be routed through third party venues such as Hong Kong and South Korea.) The discussions quickly stalled, however, over Beijing's insistence that the "three links" could not be established without a prior Taiwanese acceptance of Beijing's traditional "one-China" principle—viz., that "there is only one China in the world; the government of the People's Republic of China is the sole legal government representing the whole of China; and Taiwan is an inalienable part of China." In turn, the Taiwan side insisted that "the two sides of the Strait have different opinions as to the meaning of one China. Taipei . . . considers one China to mean the Republic of China."[13]

In an effort to break this deadlock, ARATS leaders in 1992 proposed that the two parties temporarily shelve the question of the specific meaning of "one China." SEF leaders agreed (though not without putting their own spin on the agreement),[14] and within a year a series of four preliminary protocols were signed by ARATS and SEF governing the notarization of documents, the registering of mail, the convening of periodic meetings, and the designation of times and places for future meetings. For a brief period from 1992 to 1995, cross-strait relations thus appeared to be in a warming trend.[15]

In the event, the "honeymoon" was short-lived. By the mid-1990s PRC leaders had become increasingly alarmed over the mounting pro-independence diplomatic initiatives taken by Taiwan's new president, Lee Teng-hui. Lee was the first native-born Taiwanese to hold top-level executive office in the ROC. Under his presidency, the initial democratic reforms introduced by Chiang Ching-kuo in 1987 were dramatically expanded and broadened in scope. As Taiwan accelerated its transition to democracy in the early 1990s, many native Taiwanese, long alienated by the authoritarian, "carpetbagging" regime of the Kuomintang under Chiang Kai-shek, began to demand a stronger participatory role in the political life of the island. Within a relatively short time, a strong wave of local Taiwanese nationalism arose, challenging the very notion of "Chineseness" that had served as the foundation-stone of ROC self-identity—and cross-strait relations—for half a century.

DEMOCRATIZATION AND THE RISE OF THE TAIWAN INDEPENDENCE MOVEMENT

For two decades after the Kuomintang consolidated its political control of Taiwan by brutally suppressing all native opposition, the KMT had been perceived as a party of, and for, Chinese mainlanders.[16] All important government positions were monopolized by mainland-born officials, and all manifestations of local nationalism or pro-independence sentiment were harshly suppressed under the virtually unlimited police powers granted to the government under the 1949 martial law declaration.

Recognizing that strained relations between the mainland-born minority (3 million) and the increasingly affluent and articulate Taiwan-born majority (20 million) were exerting a negative impact on the political and economic vitality of the island, the KMT regime in the 1970s began to pursue a policy of gradual "inclusion," recruiting local Taiwanese into KMT youth organizations and permitting non-KMT candidates to run as individuals (i.e., without political organization) in local mayoral and council elections. When Chiang Ching-kuo selected the Taiwan-born Lee Teng-hui as his vice-presidential candidate in 1984, it neatly symbolized the KMT's gradual shift to a policy of political inclusion.

Under Lee Teng-hui, Taiwan's democratic transition accelerated dramatically. In May 1991 Chiang Kai-shek's "temporary articles" governing "Suppression of the Communist Rebellion" were cancelled, officially ending the 42-year-old civil war; this was followed by a series of constitutional amendments that, by the mid-1990s, effectively removed most of the remaining legal obstacles to the normal functioning of democratic institutions. By the end of 1991, political parties had begun to contest local elections. A year later Taiwan held its first direct parliamentary elections. And in 1996, the presidency itself was contested in the island's first direct popular presidential election.

The liberalization of Taiwan's political institutions and rules was accompanied, perhaps not surprisingly, by an upsurge of local nationalism. Long-simmering popular resentment against the mainlander-dominated KMT regime was manifested in increasing electoral support for the newly legalized, pro-independence Democratic Progressive Party (DPP). Successor to the long-suppressed underground Taiwan Independence Movement, the DPP remained a minority party throughout the 1990s; all the while, however, its avowedly pro-independence candidates won an increasingly larger share of the popular vote in legislative and mayoralty elections, capturing 31 percent of the votes in the 1992 parliamentary election, rising to almost 40 percent three years later.[17]

As Taiwanese nationalism thus gained a stronger purchase in domestic politics, President Lee Teng-hui began to shift his own—and the ROC's—long-established position on the "one China" question, distancing himself from the KMT's traditional pro-reunification rhetoric and identifying himself more closely with Taiwanese aspirations for separate statehood. Indeed, Lee's stunning transformation, after the death of Chiang Ching-kuo, from a loyal Kuomintang lieutenant to a militant Taiwanese nationalist is one of the more fascinating aspects of Taiwan's democratic transition.

Under Lee Teng-hui's guidance, in the early 1990s the ROC accepted a de-facto "divided China" formula, no longer insisting that only one China could be represented in international organizations. Under a policy of "pragmatic diplomacy," Taiwan now grudgingly accepted the PRC's existence, while seeking to carve out a separate space for itself in the international diplomatic and organizational arena. Shedding its traditional, anachronistic claim to speak for all of China, the ROC government now spent large amounts of money trying—with mixed results—to induce a number of smaller states in Central America, Africa, the Caribbean, and Asia-Pacific islands to recognize the Taipei regime as a separate, distinct entity. At the same time, the ROC applied for separate membership in a number of international organizations to which the PRC belonged (or was in the process of joining), such as GATT and WHO. And in its most audacious initiative, the Taipei government offered to pay the accumulated debts of the United Nations (up to $1 billion [U.S.]) in an unsuccessful attempt to secure ROC (re-)admission to that body and its affiliated organizations.

Observing these developments with disdain, Beijing accused Lee Teng-hui of pursuing a path leading to Taiwanese independence, thereby violating the framework of the SEF-ARATS "1992 consensus," which had tacitly affirmed that there was only "one China, albeit with different interpretations" (*yige zhongguo, gezi biaoshu*). To Beijing, it appeared that Lee

Teng-hui had virtually abandoned, in all but name, the KMT's traditional commitment to reunification across the Taiwan Strait.

Under these circumstances, when President Lee applied for a visa to visit the United States as a "private citizen" in the early summer of 1995—ostensibly to attend a reunion of his Cornell University graduating class—the Chinese government registered a vehement protest. Arguing that granting Lee Teng-hui a visa was tantamount to U.S. recognition of the "Taiwan authorities," Beijing threatened diplomatic reprisal if the visa were issued. At first the U.S. State Department advised against allowing Lee to attend his Cornell class reunion. Ever since the U.S. "derecognition" of Taiwan in 1979, top-level ROC officials had been permitted to touch down on U.S. territory only briefly and in transit, en route to non-U.S. destinations. This would mark a clear easing of such restrictions.

Under intense pressure from pro-Taiwan legislators in the Republican-dominated U.S. Congress, however, President Bill Clinton, acting against the advice of Secretary of State Warren Christopher, personally approved the visa in June 1995. Granted access to U.S. audiences and mass media, Lee Teng-hui gave a public address at his Cornell reunion in which he spoke enthusiastically, albeit elliptically, of Taiwan's long history of de facto national independence and sovereignty. Beijing's reaction was immediate. Branding Lee Teng-hui a "splittist" and accusing the U.S. of interfering in China's domestic affairs, the PRC launched a series of high-profile military maneuvers and missile tests off the Taiwan coast.[18]

As military tensions rose in the Taiwan Strait, the post-1987 "honeymoon" in cross-strait economic and cultural relations came to an abrupt end. Beijing unilaterally cancelled the next scheduled round of the ARATS-SEF talks; the "three links" were put on indefinite hold; and a fresh wave of anti-China sentiment swept across Taiwan. In a government-commissioned poll taken in the aftermath of the 1995 Chinese missile tests, three of every four Taiwan residents perceived Beijing as "hostile" or "unfriendly."[19] And in Taiwan's first direct presidential election, held against a background of stepped-up Chinese military pressure in March 1996, 78 percent of Taiwan's voters defied Beijing's threats and supported candidates advocating the island's de facto independence—including 54 percent who voted for the incumbent president, Lee Teng-hui.[20]

Further contributing to Beijing's mounting irritation, during his second term in office President Lee deftly played the "democracy card," suggesting that reunification would only be possible if and when the PRC underwent wholesale democratization, and interpreting Taiwan's democratic transition as a mandate for self-determination. Gone were the days, Lee averred, when a small handful of ROC oligarchs could sit down with their counterparts in Beijing to decide the fate of the 23 million people of Taiwan. Henceforth, the vox populi would have to be consulted before any change in Taiwan's status could be contemplated. With public opinion running between 3:1 and 4:1 against early reunification, Lee Teng-hui appeared to be on rather safe ground.[21]

CENTRIFUGAL POLITICS VS. CENTRIPETAL ECONOMICS

Paradoxically, the emerging nationalism of the Taiwanese people, unchained in the course of Taiwan's democratic transition, served sharply to counteract the integrative, conflict-softening effects of growing cross-strait commercial, cultural, and technological ties. With economic and political forces pulling in diametrically opposed directions, prospects for an early, peaceful solution of the divided sovereignty problem seemed dim.

In the decade of the 1990s, a pronounced shift in the ethnic and cultural self-identity of Taiwan's 23 million residents reflected a dramatic rise in the perception of Taiwanese distinctiveness. Between 1993 and 2000, the percentage of Taiwan respondents identifying themselves as "Chinese" dropped steadily, from 48.5 percent to 13.6 percent, while those labeling themselves as "Taiwanese" increased from 16.7 to 45 percent, with most of the remaining respondents identifying themselves as "both Taiwanese and Chinese."[22]

With a substantial majority of Taiwanese people displaying strong Taiwanese identity and an equally strong distrust of PRC motives and intentions, Lee Teng-hui edged closer to a declaration of full Taiwanese independence. In a July 1999 interview with the German magazine *Deutsche Welle*, Lee characterized PRC-ROC relations as a "special state-to-state relationship":

> [Our various] constitutional amendments have placed cross-strait relations as a state-to-state relationship, or at least *a special state-to-state relationship (guo yu guo tebie guanxi)*, rather than an internal relationship between a legitimate government and a renegade group, or between a central government and a local government. Thus, the Beijing authorities' characterization of Taiwan as a "renegade province" is historically and legally untrue (emphasis added).[23]

Lee further irritated PRC policy makers by deftly sidestepping Beijing's recurrent warning that a formal declaration of independence would trigger a war in the Taiwan Strait. Choosing his words carefully, Lee asserted that insofar as "Taiwan has been a sovereign state since it was founded in 1912 . . . there is no need to declare independence."[24]

In the wake of Lee Teng-hui's provocative "state-to-state relations" remarks, Beijing stepped up its verbal attack on Taiwan's "creeping independence." In a *White Paper* on "The One-China Principle and the Taiwan Issue," published on the eve of Taiwan's March 2000 presidential election, Beijing reiterated its traditional demand for reunification and renewed its earlier threat that any declaration of independence by the Taiwan authorities would be construed by the PRC as a *casus belli*, adding to this a new warning that "indefinite postponement"of reunification talks by the Taiwan authorities would be intolerable.[25]

In response to what was widely perceived as a crude Chinese attempt to intimidate the island's voters into rejecting the pro-independence DPP presidential candidate Chen Shui-bian, Taiwan's electorate produced a stunning upset. Prior to China's issuance of the February 2000 *White Paper*, Chen Shui-bian, the mayor of Taipei, had been regarded as something of a dark horse in a three-way presidential contest with the highly popular former provincial Governor James Soong, who had recently bolted the KMT to form his own party, the People First Party (PFP), and the colorless KMT candidate Lien Chan, who had been Lee Teng-hui's vice president. (Lee himself was constitutionally barred from seeking a third term in 2000.) When the ballots were counted, Chen Shui-bian secured a surprising victory with 39.9 percent of the popular vote to 36.8 percent for James Soong and 23.1 percent for Lien Chan. For the first time in ROC's 50-year existence on Taiwan an avowedly pro-independence, non-KMT candidate had been elected president. And in a stunning rebuke to the pro-unification New Party, less than 1 percent of the electorate voted for its presidential candidate. This result, of course, only took place because of the split in the KMT.

ECONOMICS "TAKES COMMAND"

In the face of deteriorating political-military relations across the Taiwan Strait in the late 1990s, Beijing and Taipei, each for its own reasons, continued to keep open the window of cross-strait economic ties. For their part, PRC leaders employed classic "united front" tactics, using the lure of enhanced access to Chinese resources, low-wage labor, and markets to induce Taiwanese businesspeople to step up their trade and investment activities on the mainland.[26] For his part, Lee Teng-hui envisioned the gradual expansion of cross-strait economic exchange as a means of "Taiwanizing" the Chinese mainland.[27]

Notwithstanding the growing commercial appeal of the vast China market, in the aftermath of the Taiwan Strait missile test crisis of 1995–96 Lee Teng-hui expressed the fear that, given the disparity in size between the two economies, burgeoning cross-strait trade and investment would increase Taiwan's economic dependency and technological vulnerability, thereby giving Beijing added political leverage over Taipei. Consequently, in 1996 President Lee laid down new guidelines for the expansion of cross-strait economic ties. Under a declarative policy of "no haste, be patient," he imposed restrictions on certain strategic mainland-bound investments and technology transfers in areas such as petrochemicals and information technology (IT).

Lee's concerns were not without merit. As Taiwan felt the ripple effects of the 1997–98 Asian financial crisis, followed by an even more dramatic economic downturn in 2000–2001, the "fatal attraction" of the China market increased, as more and more Taiwanese businesspeople looked to industrial and commercial operations on the mainland to bail them out of economic difficulty. By the end of October 2000, almost 23,000 ROC-invested firms had been approved for operation in Mainland China, with approved investments totaling $46.5 billion (U.S.)—approximately half of which had actually been utilized. By the year 2000 Taiwan had become Mainland China's third largest investor, after Hong Kong and the United States.[28]

Indirect trade also boomed in this period. In the decade of the 1990s two-way commerce increased annually, on average, by more than 20 percent, with the annual trade volume rising from $10 billion in 1992 to $32 billion (U.S.) in 2000. Taiwan enjoyed a huge surplus in this expanding two-way trade, with exports exceeding imports by a whopping 4:1 margin.[29] Along with the dramatic expansion of export trade came a massive outflow of Taiwanese visitors to the Chinese mainland. By October 2000, a total of more than 17 million Taiwan residents had visited Mainland China, while 550,000 PRC residents had traveled to Taiwan.[30] According to ROC government estimates in 2001, on any given day there were more than 500,000 ROC citizens in Mainland China, including 300,000 in Shanghai alone.[31] Clearly, Lee Teng-hui's "no haste, go slow" policy was having only a limited impact.

PROSPECTS FOR CROSS-STRAIT ECONOMIC INTEGRATION

After winning the presidential election in March 2000, Chen Shui-bian began to soften his pro-independence rhetoric. Throughout his political career Chen had been a vocal supporter of Taiwan independence. As president, however, he was constrained to reassure both his anxious domestic audience and American patrons that he would not drag the island, willy-nilly, into a shooting war with China. Toward this end Chen, in his inaugural address, introduced the so-called "one if and four no's." So long as the PRC refrained from using military force against Taiwan, he stated, he would not declare independence, change the national title (e.g., from ROC to ROT), push for a constitutional amendment incorporating the "state-to-state relations" formula, or hold a referendum on the question of independence. Nor would he seek to abolish Taiwan's National Unification Council and its 1991 "Guidelines for National Unification."[32] Notwithstanding Chen's verbal reassurances, however, Beijing remained suspicious. Criticizing the new president for his conspicuous failure to embrace the one-China principle, Chinese media commentators voiced deep distrust of Chen's motives. At the same time, the PRC government adopted an official stance of "watch and see" toward Taiwan's new president—i.e., "watch what he says, see what he does."[33] Shortly after taking office, Chen Shui-bian staked out a relatively conciliatory, if deliberately ambiguous position on the PRC's perennial demand for Taiwanese acceptance of the one-China principle. Acknowledging the common Chinese ancestry and cultural heritage of the people on both sides of the Taiwan Strait, he went so far as to suggest that "the question of a future one China" (*weilai yige zhongguo de wenti*) could be discussed in cross-strait negotiations.[34]

While Chen thus moderated his previous hard-line stance on cross-strait relations, the KMT, having endured a humiliating third-place finish in the February 2000 presidential election, appeared rudderless and disoriented. Stunned by their sudden reversal of fortune, many senior KMT leaders blamed Lee Teng-hui for their party's deepening woes. Some even suggested that Lee had *deliberately* conspired to lose the election by choosing the colorless, uncharismatic Lien Chan as the party's presidential standard-bearer. Whatever the case, unhappy KMT politicians began to distance themselves from the former president and his policies—including his theory of "special state-to-state relations." Reversing Lee's provocative embrace of local Taiwanese nationalism, the KMT now sought to "reinvent" itself, among other things, as the party of cross-strait compromise and reconciliation. Angered by the KMT's efforts to distance itself from his leadership, and alarmed by the party's sudden embrace of cross-strait reconciliation, Lee Teng-hui bolted the KMT in 2001, forming his own political party and creating a tactical alliance with Chen Shui-bian's pro-independence DPP.

Conspicuously, this repositioning coincided with the worsening of Taiwan's domestic economic woes. With the economy mired in recession, Taiwanese investors and businesspeople—many of them traditional KMT supporters—were eager to exploit economic opportunities on the Chinese mainland. Symptomatic of this new enthusiasm was the formation, early in 2001, of a $1.6 billion (U.S.) partnership between the son of one of Taiwan's wealthiest businessmen, Wang Yung-ching, and the son of Chinese President Jiang Zemin, for the purpose of manufacturing integrated circuits in Shanghai. For many in Taiwan, "integrated circuits" was fast becoming a metaphor for a profound shift in the nature of cross-strait relations.

With Taiwanese business interests clamoring for a more liberal trade and investment environment, some ROC political leaders now became "born again" champions of cross-strait economic integration. Led by former Premier Vincent Siew, deputy head of the KMT and a once-trusted associate of Lee Teng-hui, they now began to advocate a radically new approach to economic relations with the mainland.

Speaking at the American Enterprise Institute in January 2001, Vincent Siew argued that the globalization of business in the 21st century required "new thinking and new approaches"; and he went on to propose the creation of an EU-style "common market" to achieve economic—and ultimately political—integration across the Taiwan Strait:

The globalization of business . . . brings with it powerful incentives to create a new order. . . . The establishment of a "cross-strait common market" can help to overcome existing political and economic impasses by creating a framework for integration while implementing concrete projects along a timeline of 20 or 30 years.

Systematic pursuit of these aims would lead, over time, to the creation of a closely tied entity spanning both sides, beyond the tangible boundaries. Such economic unity would . . . pave the way for political integration. . . .

The future establishment of a "cross-strait common market" will reduce the areas where the one-China dispute is relevant, thus lessening mutual political arguments. . . . We can devise coalition mechanisms, via negotiation and cooperation, to manage specific aspects of mutual economic affairs. . . . These interim arrangements will lead to a "sharing of sovereignty" in the agreed areas. Under this concept . . . the one-China issue will be solved gradually as the jurisdiction of "A Greater China" is phased in.[35]

Vincent Siew's stunning proposal for cross-strait economic and political integration was echoed by a number of Taiwanese business leaders and economic analysts, many of whom noted that the imminent accession of both Taiwan and China to the WTO would inevitably draw the two parties into closer bilateral contacts, coordination, and cooperation. It was better, they argued, to get out in front of the WTO wave than to sit back and risk being overwhelmed by it.[36]

Responding to surging Taiwanese business demand for a liberalized trade and investment environment, in March 2001 a nongovernmental "Cross-strait Common Market Foundation" was established in Taipei. Cognizant that the island's recession-weary voters were generally supportive of expanded economic links, President Chen Shui-bian cautiously endorsed the new venture. Speaking at the inauguration of the Common Market Foundation, he urged his countrymen to "put cross-strait trade issues under the global framework and work to form a whole new economic model between the two sides."[37]

With domestic opinion divided over the costs and benefits of economic integration, Chen Shui-bian's DPP-led administration welcomed closer cross-strait cooperation within the multilateral framework of WTO, while warning against the dangers of relaxing Taiwan's vigilance. As one high-level government spokesman put it:

WTO membership offers an important venue for both Taipei and Beijing to interact constructively in a multilateral context. It also presents both sides with a valuable opportunity to transcend our differences in a pragmatic and mutually beneficial fashion. . . . Of course, Beijing still tries to undermine Taiwan's political status internationally. . . . Our thriving democracy stands in sharp contrast to its repressive, authoritarian form of government. But at the same time, the two of us are already commercially involved with each other to a sizable degree. So it is a complex relationship, to say the least. . . . For our part, the people and government of Taiwan are making every effort to be positive and pragmatic towards the PRC. We intend to pursue a constructive cooperative relationship of peaceful coexistence and mutual prosperity; and we won't jeopardize peace and stability. . . . Normalization of cross-strait relations . . . must begin with the normalization of economic and trade relations. . . . This is our long-term goal and our consistent policy.[38]

Further bowing to recession-induced economic pressures, Chen Shui-bian in 2001 relaxed restrictions previously imposed by Lee Teng-hui on Taiwanese investment in certain strategic mainland industries and sectors. Rescinding Lee's declarative policy of "no haste, be patient," Chen put forward a new slogan: "active opening up, effective management."[39] And he declared that "integration of our economies, trade, and culture can be a starting point for . . . a new framework of permanent peace and political integration."[40]

For its part, Beijing responded to the upsurge of "mainland fever" among Taiwanese investors and businesspeople by putting a somewhat softer, gentler spin on its traditional one-China principle. In the summer of 2000, PRC Vice-Premier Qian Qichen proposed a minimalist rendering of the "1992 consensus"—viz., "one China, subject to different interpretations"—as a basis for restarting the long-stalled SEF-ARATS talks.[41] When this initiative failed to elicit a positive response from Taipei, Qian went a half step further, indicating that China would be willing to finesse the question of sovereignty in order to resolve the long-stalled "three links" negotiations. "The issue of direct links is easy," he said, "so long as both sides agree that ships do not fly [national] flags in harbors." Qian subsequently amplified this proposal, suggesting that the PRC might drop its precondition that the ROC accept the one-China principle "if Taiwan were willing to start full direct air and shipping links and would agree that these would be considered 'special domestic links.'"[42] In a further attempt to sidestep perennial ROC objections to the one-China principle, Qian Qichen even hinted obliquely at the idea of shared sovereignty, announcing that the entity "China" included both Taiwan and the mainland ("*Taiwan he dalu doushi zhongguo de yibufen*")—a definition not necessarily coterminous with the PRC.[43] The Taipei government refused to be drawn into a discussion of the finer points of such ambiguous initiatives, however; and ROC spokesmen continued to insist that cross-strait negotiations should be resumed without any political preconditions. On the whole the Taiwanese public was supportive of initiatives designed to facilitate the process of cross-strait integration.

For its part Beijing, too, seemed increasingly optimistic about the prospects for long-term peaceful reunification. By mid-year 2001 Chinese leaders had evidently concluded that the resort to "coercive diplomacy" in the 1995–96 Taiwan Strait missile tests and again in the run-up to the 2000 Taiwan presidential election had been largely counterproductive, serving to stiffen Taiwanese resistance to PRC "bullying" and causing the new Bush Administration in Washington to declare its readiness to "do whatever it takes" to defend the ROC against a threat from China. In response, Beijing began to lower its military profile in the Taiwan Strait and to reduce its rhetorical provocations. By the same token, although Beijing had previously shunned all contact with the pro-independence DPP, in 2002 it began openly to court rank-and-file members of that party, reserving its cold shoulder for a "small handful of splitters" within the party leadership who continued to pursue the goal of Taiwan independence—a group that included both President Chen Shui-bian and Vice President Annette Lu.[44] In reducing the shrillness of their rhetoric, in welcoming direct cross-strait links, and in broadening their united front appeal to include members of Taiwan's political as well as business elite, PRC leaders appeared to be gaining confidence that time was now on their side.

Reflecting the new mood of cross-strait optimism, scholars inside and outside Taiwan began to examine seriously—for the first time—alternative models of political integration and shared sovereignty. Some found the concept of "federation" appealing; others preferred the idea of "confederation"; still others opted for a loosely structured notion of "commonwealth."[45] In general, by the autumn of 2002 there was a growing confidence that—eventually—the war of words over the one-China principle would be resolved by finesse rather than by fighting.

SARS AND THE REFERENDUM CRISIS OF 2003

As the Pan Blues moved closer to China, Chen Shui-bian moved in the opposite direction. Countering the Pan Blues' endorsement of the "1992 consensus," he now put forward his own, contrary formulation—"one country on each side of the strait" (*yibian, yiguo*). Domestic politics, it seemed, was once again driving the polarization of debate.

By the spring of 2003, opinion polls showed the Pan Blue ticket enjoying a narrow margin over Chen Shui-bian. At this critical juncture Mother Nature—in the form of an outbreak of the deadly SARS virus in southern China—intervened to provide Chen with a golden opportunity to blunt the opposition's soft-line offensive. As the SARS epidemic spread from China to Hong Kong and then to Taiwan in the late winter and spring of 2003, Beijing repeatedly blocked efforts to dispatch a World Health Organization epidemiological team to investigate the outbreak of SARS on Taiwan—a nonmember of WHO. As the death toll on the island mounted, approaching 100 fatalities by mid-June, Taiwanese resentment of Beijing's obstructionist tactics intensified. Capitalizing upon this resentment, Chen Shui-bian played the democracy card, proposing to hold an island-wide popular referendum on the question of Taiwan's entry into the World Health Organization.[46]

Chen's initiative proved instantly popular with Taiwanese voters, but it raised a firestorm of controversy internationally. China immediately criticized the idea of a referendum, calling it a clear violation of the one-China principle. And Beijing lobbied hard with the Bush Administration to persuade Chen Shui-bian to withdraw his proposal.[47] Despite Washington's misgivings, Chen refused to back down. Digging in his heels, he declared in June 2003 that it was his duty as president to "safeguard Taiwan's sovereignty, dignity and security." Defending the use of the referendum as a legitimate means of expressing the democratic vox populi, Chen went on to claim that "Only Taiwan's 23 million people have the right to decide Taiwan's future."[48] A few months later he averred: "I hereby want to clearly and solemnly tell you that the 23 million people and the DPP want to push for the birth of a new constitution."[49] Observers noted that this appeared to reverse Chen's May 2000 inaugural pledge not to alter the ROC's constitution.

In throwing down the gauntlet on the question of Taiwan's right of self-determination, Chen Shui-bian evidently calculated that the pro-Taiwan tilt of the U.S. Congress and the Bush Administration, together with Beijing's demonstrated desire to avoid another escalatory crisis in the Taiwan Strait, would suffice to shield him against both excessive U.S. pressure and forceful Chinese reprisals. Certainly, Chen expected a relatively benign U.S. response: Just two weeks earlier he had been permitted to spend two full days in New York City while ostensibly "in transit" to Panama. While in the Big Apple he addressed a rally of supporters and attended a $500-a-plate dinner in his honor, where he also gave a public address—the first time since 1979 a Taiwan president had been allowed to speak in a major American city. During the testimonial dinner the titular head of the quasi-official American Institute in Taiwan, Therese Shaheen, assured Chen Shui-bian that he had a "secret guardian angel here that's really responsible for tonight, and that is President George W. Bush."[50] In a further show of American goodwill, Chen was granted a telephone conversation with Deputy Secretary of State Richard Armitage; later, in Panama, he conspicuously shook hands with Secretary of State Colin Powell.

But Chen overplayed his hand. In response to the new referendum law, Beijing warned in late November that Chen's machinations had brought Taiwan close to the brink of disaster: "If Chen Shui-bian refuses to come to his senses, obstinately clings to his course, continues along the 'Taiwan independence' road, and creates a 'Taiwan independence' incident," warned a high-level Chinese official, "this is bound to . . . bring disaster on the Taiwan people, and we will certainly not sit idly by in such a case."[51] Another PRC official warned that China "must make necessary preparations to resolutely crush Taiwan independence-splittist plots."[52] The unusually somber tone of these warnings was clearly intended to convey to Taipei—and to Washington—the gravity of the situation.

Unsettled by Beijing's reaction, and irritated by Chen Shui-bian's stance, President George W. Bush issued a sharp warning to the Taiwan leader. With Chinese Premier Wen Jiabao standing at his side, President Bush on December 9 stated: "We oppose any unilateral decision by either China or Taiwan to change the status quo. . . . The comments and actions made by the leader of Taiwan indicate that he may be willing to make decisions unilaterally, to change the status quo, which we oppose."[53]

Although Wen Jiabao was clearly gratified by Bush's remarks, Chen Shuibian did not retreat. By mid-December Chen had drawn even with the Pan Blues in opinion polls.[54] With his popularity rebounding, Chen confirmed his intention to proceed with a "defensive referendum," to be held on election day, March 20, 2004, on the question of whether China should remove hundreds of short-range ballistic missiles aimed at Taiwan.[55] He further cautioned that if Beijing stepped up its military threats against Taiwan, this might push the island even farther down the road toward independence.[56]

Emblematic of deteriorating cross-strait relations, opinion polls show a hardening of Taiwanese attitudes toward the mainland. One survey released in late October 2003 showed that fully two-thirds of Taiwan's probable voters (up from 57 percent a year earlier) were now unwilling to accept the PRC's "one country, two systems" formula as the basis for future reunification. In another poll, 62 percent of the adults sampled identified themselves exclusively as "Taiwanese"—up six percentage points from the previous year, and the highest figure in the 15-year history of the poll.[57]

With popular attitudes hardening, the Pan Blues suddenly found themselves on the defensive, their pro-integration policy trumped by Chen Shuibian's display of patriotic bravado. Cognizant of this shift in opinion, Lien Chan began to backpedal on the reunification issue. Refusing to reaffirm either the KMT's traditional support for the "1992 consensus" or his party's longstanding goal of eventual reunification, Lien now opted for a watereddown pledge to hold talks with Beijing "within the framework of the status quo."[58] A week later he even endorsed Chen Shui-bian's controversial formulation "*yibian, yiguo*" (one country on each side of the strait). "If you put it simply," Lien averred, "since each side has one country, there should be no problem."[59]

THE DISPUTED PRESIDENTIAL ELECTION OF MARCH 2004

Lien Chan's sudden change of tack evidently helped neutralize the rising popularity of Chen Shui-bian's hard-line stance. As the presidential campaign entered its final stages, Lien and Chen ran neck and neck. On the eve of the election several unofficial polls showed Lien with a narrow edge.[60]

But then, fate intervened to secure Chen Shui-bian's victory. Less than twenty-four hours before the polls opened, a would-be assassin's bullet (or bullets) grazed the president and ricocheted off Vice President Annette Lu as they rode, unprotected, in a motorcade. The botched assassination attempt generated a wave of voter sympathy, erasing the opposition's erstwhile lead and enabling Chen to squeak through to victory. When the final vote tally was announced, the president had won reelection by a mere 29,000 votes out of almost 13 million cast.

Unwilling to concede defeat, angry Pan Blue supporters led massive demonstrations in front of Taipei's presidential palace. Implying that Chen's supporters had staged the shooting, Lien demanded a recount and even called for a new election.

Meanwhile, across the Strait, Chinese government officials employed shrill language, reminiscent of the Cold War, to warn that China would "not sit idly by" if conditions on Taiwan deteriorated into chaos. A crisis was averted when cooler heads on both sides—encouraged by U.S. officials from the quasi-governmental American Institute in Taiwan—prevailed. Chen agreed in principle to a ballot recount and brought in a team of independent American forensics experts to investigate the shooting. In exchange, the Pan Blues gave up their call for a new election.[61]

China's leaders now found themselves in an uncomfortable bind. While they repeated for public consumption their perennial one-China mantra— "There is only one China in the world and Taiwan is a part of China"—privately they faced the growing likelihood that they would either have to make good on their longstanding threat of military intervention, or else swallow their pride and accept some measure of Taiwanese autonomy.

Amid the deepening gloom of Beijing's election postmortem, there was one small bright spot. To Beijing's relief, Chen Shui-bian's controversial referendum, calling on China to remove hundreds of missiles from the Taiwan Strait area, failed to clear the high bar required for passage, thus averting an immediate cross-strait crisis.[62]

When Chen Shui-bian took his second oath of office on May 20, 2004 he downplayed the independence controversy, emphasizing instead the need to improve Taiwan's democratic governance, strengthen its rule of law, and reform its ossified administrative structures. Toward these ends, he pledged to undertake a wholesale constitutional makeover by the end of his second (and final) term in 2008. Citing the absence of a clear popular consensus on the question of Taiwan's national identity, however, he promised not to change Taiwan's name, flag, or legal status during his tenure in office.[63]

On the question of cross-strait relations, Chen's speech was generally moderate and restrained. Conceding that the Taiwanese people could "understand why the government on the other side of the Strait, in light of historical complexities and ethnic sentiments, cannot relinquish its insistence on the 'one China principle,'" he spelled out his hope for a peaceful future. If the two sides can make "a concerted effort to find some positive aspect of our differences and commonalities," he said, "perhaps we shall discover a wonderful opportunity, a catalyst for building a cooperative and mutually beneficial relationship." But he accompanied this with a sharp reminder to Beijing that "Taiwan's existence as a member of international society is also a fact. Such realities cannot be negated by anyone for any reason."[64]

THE WAR OF WORDS

China's initial reaction to such bravado was predictably frosty. Dismissing Chen's ostensible display of goodwill as "another sham," the official PRC media characterized the Taiwan president as "a complete troublemaker and crisis instigator."[65] And the government-owned *China Daily* observed that "the mainland has seen through Chen's nature as a politician who clings to a separatist stance and is notorious for his bad faith and lack of political credibility."[66]

In Washington, the response was upbeat, but the White House stepped up pressure on Chen to moderate his drive for independence—first evidenced in December 2003, when Bush famously stated that "We oppose any unilateral decision by either China or Taiwan to change the status quo"—reflected, in large measure, Washington's preoccupation with Iraq, terrorism, and the Middle East. With U.S. military resources stretched perilously thin, President Bush was unwilling to see Taiwan provoke a military confrontation in the Taiwan Strait.

China also added to its criticisms. In a statement dated May 17, 2004 the PRC's Taiwan Affairs Office blasted Chen Shui-bian for his "track record . . . of broken promises and bad faith" and laid down a clear marker on the question of independence:

> The Taiwan leaders have before them two roads: one is to pull back immediately from their dangerous lurch towards independence, recognizing that both sides of the Taiwan Strait belong to the one and same China and dedicating their efforts to closer cross-strait relations. The other is to keep following their separatist agenda to cut Taiwan from the rest of China and, in the end, meet their own destruction by playing with fire. The Taiwan leaders must choose between [these] two roads.[67]

At the same time, however, the May 17 statement also provided a tentative roadmap identifying a pathway toward mutual reconciliation. Omitting mention of China's perennial demand that Taiwan accept as a precondition for negotiations Deng Xiaoping's "one country, two systems" formula for reunification, the new statement held out—for the first time—the prospect of "equal-footed consultations" between the two sides to "address the issue

of international living space of the Taiwan region commensurate with its status." In return, the Taiwan authorities would be expected to acknowledge
that "both the mainland and Taiwan belong to one and the same China."
This new, more relaxed formulation was later elaborated upon in the Chinese media, which spelled out the possibility that direct cross-strait commercial and communications links could be resumed once the Taiwan side
accepted the so-called "1992 consensus," under which each side would be
permitted to retain its own distinct interpretation of the meaning of "one
China."[68]

Amid the sharply conflicting signals, Western scholars and diplomats noted
two small but apparently significant changes in China's treatment of Chen
Shui-bian. First, in the weeks following Chen's second inauguration, the deci-
bel level of Beijing's harsh anti-Chen polemics began to subside. A mood
of grim determination seemed to supplant the strident rhetoric of the past.
Second, Chinese officials began to hint that their military preparations for a
cross-strait conflict were nearing completion. As one Chinese scholar noted,
"before a tiger attacks, it remains calm and quiet."[69] Such signaling suggested
that China's intention was to boost the credibility—and hence the deterrent
value—of its warnings against further movement in the direction of Taiwan
independence.

Beijing's somber signals were aimed primarily at Washington. Since Chen
Shui-bien was a loose cannon, only Washington could stop Taiwan's destructive march toward independence.

GLOBALIZATION, DEMOCRATIZATION, AND DIVIDED SOVEREIGNTY

Notwithstanding the demonstrable rise in cross-strait tensions, the Taiwanese
economy continued to rebound from the recession of 2000–01. In 2003, the
island's GDP grew at a 4.2 percent annual rate, with industrial production rising 9 percent.[70] By mid-year 2004, the economy had picked up additional
momentum, expanding at an annualized rate of 6.3 percent.[71] Despite the
deadly SARS epidemic, cross-strait trade rose by 25 percent in 2003, surpass-
ing the $50 billion mark, while Taiwanese investment on the mainland regis-
tered a 43 percent increase, year-on-year.[72] With an average of $1.8 billion
dollars in new Taiwanese capital committed to the mainland each month,
the cumulative amount of contracted Taiwanese cross-strait investment
approached $70 billion by year's end.[73] Also by the end of 2003, fully 60 per-
cent of Taiwan's IT hardware was being produced in mainland China (up
from 49 percent in 2002), while Taiwanese-invested companies now produced more than 70 percent of China's total electronics output.[74] As more
and more Taiwanese firms located their production facilities on the main-

land, Taiwan's technological lead over China, estimated at 5–10 years in 2000, was now said to have declined to 3–5 years.[75]

In early 2004 an official from Taiwan's Mainland Affairs Council privately confirmed that there were as many as one million Taiwanese citizens residing on the mainland—a doubling of the 2001 figure—with 200,000 PRC citizens (the majority of whom were mainland wives of Taiwanese businessmen) living on Taiwan. For all the tough talk on both sides of the Taiwan Strait, the expanding stream of cross-strait trade, investment, and human migration continued to draw the two economies into an ever-tighter web of interdependent relationships.

THE OLYMPIC FACTOR

Some observers—including not a few Taiwanese analysts—have claimed that Beijing would be most unlikely to launch a military attack on Taiwan during the run-up to the 2008 Beijing Olympic Games. China, they argue, has too much riding on a successful Olympics to risk the international opprobrium, trade and investment losses, and military-industrial damage that would attend a cross-strait attack. According to this reasoning, Taiwan had roughly a four-year window of opportunity to employ its incremental "salami-slicing" tactics in pursuit of sovereign self-determination, with a reduced risk of Chinese military intervention.

To thwart such thinking, Beijing in 2004 ratcheted sharply upward its rhetoric of deterrence, issuing a series of sobering warnings reminiscent of the escalatory warnings that preceded China's entry into the Korean War a half century earlier. Privately, Chinese scholars and officials conveyed the clear, grim message that Chen Shui-bian's envelope-pushing behavior will, if not restrained by the United States, lead inevitably to military conflict, possibly sooner rather than later.[76]

While Chen Shui-bian responded to Chinese threats with an olive branch in one hand, he pushed the envelope of Taiwan independence further with the other. Toward the end of his October 10, 2004 speech, Chen claimed it was an "indisputable fact" that "Taiwan" and the "Republic of China" were wholly interchangeable geographical entities, calling the ROC "a country [*guojia*] of 36,000 square kilometers"—i.e., exactly coterminous with Taiwan's territorial area. This equation implicitly reinforced Taiwan's claim to independence from the mainland while at the same time setting the stage for a possible future constitutional change in the island's official name, from "Republic of China" to "Republic of Taiwan."

Beijing's reaction was predictably hostile. An official spokesman for the Taiwan Affairs Office of the State Council characterized as disingenuous Chen Shui-bian's claim of seeking to reduce cross-strait tension:

In his speech, he stubbornly insisted on the separatist stance of "each side is a [separate] country" [*yi bian, yi guo*]; further denied that Taiwan is a part of China; viciously slandered and attacked the mother mainland; and deliberately harmed cross-strait relations. As a result, he himself has exposed his lies.[77]

To increase the pressure on Taipei, Beijing announced in December 2004 that the National People's Congress would, at its forthcoming spring legislative session, pass an "Anti-Secession Law" designed to provide a legal basis for the use of military force in the event of a de jure declaration of independence.[78]

With the war of words heating up yet again, two new developments, on opposite sides of the Pacific, combined to put a damper on Chen Shui-bian's plans to promote his independence agenda. First, the reelection of George Bush to a second presidential term in November 2004 was followed by strong signals that the U.S. wanted Chen Shui-bian to avoid upsetting the status quo in the Taiwan Strait. Many analysts attributed Washington's new, tougher stance to U.S. recognition that it had too much at stake in its relationship with China to be manipulated and held hostage by Chen's unpredictable behavior; also U.S.-China collaboration was essential to break the deadlock in the stalled six-party talks on North Korean nuclear disarmament.[79]

The second new development was the unexpectedly poor showing by Chen Shui-bian's Pan Green alliance in the Taiwanese legislative elections of December 2004. The opposition Pan Blue coalition of the KMT and PFP won 113 seats in the 225-seat Legislative Yuan, to only 101 seats for Chen's DPP and its principal ally, Lee Teng-hui's TSU. In the view of a leading Taiwanese political analyst, the Pan Blues' narrow victory reflected a popular perception that "Chen's recent statements and policies are too radical."[80]

In the aftermath of the U.S. and Taiwan elections, a somewhat chastened Chen Shui-bian began to back down from his more provocative preelection rhetoric. In February 2005, he disavowed any intention to declare independence. At the same time, in a joint ten-point declaration with PFP leader James Soong, he called for renewed dialogue with Beijing, holding open the possibility of cross-strait reconciliation.[81] As Chen began to backpedal, China sought to exploit his electoral weakness, proposing to expand direct charter flights between the two sides and offering to open the Chinese mainland to Taiwanese farm products. This afforded a small opening, Hu Jintao in early March praised Chen's stance and pointed to "new and positive factors" in cross-strait relations.[82]

But a sharply discordant note was sounded with the NPC's final passage, in March 2005, of China's controversial Anti-Secession Law. In response, massive street demonstrations were held in Taiwan's major cities to denounce the new law. Upwards of 500,000 people participated, including Chen Shui-bian himself.[83] Negative response to the new ASL was also forthcoming from Washington, where Bush Administration officials (including Secretary of State

Condoleezza Rice) as well as influential members of Congress expressed disappointment at the new Chinese legislation.[84]

Stung by widespread criticism at a time when cross-strait relations seemed to be heading in a more favorable direction, Chinese officials and policy analysts sought to downplay the military threat implicit in the new law, suggesting instead that such legislation was a necessary step in the direction of achieving the "rule of law" in China.[85]

THE PAN BLUE PEACE OFFENSIVE

Buoyed by their electoral gains, the Pan Blues mounted their own peace offensive in the late spring of 2005. Responding to a new mainland offer to "negotiate with any Taiwanese political parties as long as they uphold . . . the '1992 consensus,'"[86] leaders of the Pan Blue coalition partners—the KMT and the PFP—announced their intention to visit the mainland. First to make the trip was KMT Vice Chairman Chiang Pin-kung, who received a friendly welcome in Guangdong province at the end of March. Chinese officials used the occasion of Chiang's visit to announce the ending of longstanding PRC tariffs on the import of agricultural products from Taiwan.

In the aftermath of Chiang's ice-breaking journey, KMT President Lien Chan traveled to China at the end of May. Visiting Sun Yat-sen's memorial in Nanjing and later speaking to a packed crowd at Peking University, Lien emphasized the common roots, traditions, and nationality of the people of China and Taiwan, declaring his firm opposition to Taiwan independence and his support for the "1992 consensus." His goodwill visit was capped by a cordial meeting with Hu Jintao.[87] With public opinion in Taiwan strongly favorable to Lien Chan's's cross-strait peace initiative,[88] Chen Shui-bian came under increased pressure to demonstrate his desire for peace. When PFP leader James Soong announced his intention to make a cross-strait sojourn of his own, Chen phoned Soong to wish him a successful trip, asking him to "convey some messages to the Chinese leadership" during his visit.[89]

When Soong touched down in China on May 5, the official *China Daily* referred to his visit as "a historic move of exchange and dialogue between the PFP and CCP" and predicted that Soong's visit "will push cross-strait relations in a healthy direction."[90] In a speech to students at Beijing's Tsinghua University, Soong, like Lien before him, affirmed his support for the "1992 consensus," receiving a standing ovation when he stated, "Taiwan independence is a road with a dead end."[91] Even the long-moribund New Party now got into the act as its chairman, Yu Muming, paid a visit to China in early July.

In July 2005, the KMT held an election for a new party chairman to replace the outgoing Lien Chan. In a mild upset, the charismatic mayor of Taipei, Ma Ying-jeou, defeated the favored legislative insider, Wang Jyn-pyng. Shortly thereafter, Chinese President Hu Jintao publicly congratulated Ma, saying, "I sincerely hope that the KMT and the CCP, together with compatriots on both sides of the Taiwan Straits, will continue to promote the peaceful and steady development of cross-straits relations, and join hands to create a bright future for the Chinese nation."[92] In the aftermath of Ma's victory, polls in Taiwan showed him handily defeating each of the leading DPP contenders in the 2008 presidential election.[93]

By the end of summer 2005, the momentum in cross-strait relations had shifted noticeably in the direction of quiescence. On both sides of the Strait, leaders were talking softly, downplaying threats and emphasizing the need for a new, more constructive political dialogue.[94] So striking was the mood of relaxation that when President Bush met with Hu Jintao in Beijing in mid-November, the subject of Taiwan received only perfunctory mention.

CONCLUSION: LULL OR DÉTENTE?

Under these circumstances, and with cross-strait economic integration continuing to increase rapidly,[95] it would be tempting to take comfort in the neoliberal internationalist faith in the pacifying influence of globalization's powerful economic attractors. But politics is often, in the first instance, local rather than global. And policymakers in pursuit of narrow political advantage can—and often do—defy the seemingly compelling logic of systemic rationality. While many mainland Chinese scholars and policy analysts note with satisfaction the placidity of the cross-strait situation since the summer of 2005, they continue to worry that Chen Shui-bian, if faced with imminent domestic political defeat, might use the "China threat" to provoke a crisis and rally patriotic support. An almost identical—though opposite—fear of excessive Chinese nationalist bravado is often expressed by Taiwanese analysts.[96]

Although oscillating periods of tension and relaxation have occurred often in the past, taking on the appearance of a well-choreographed ballet, the situation remains inherently dangerous. Cross-strait economic interdependence or no, the possibility of war cannot be dismissed as unthinkable. As the authors of a recent RAND Corporation study pointed out,

> Increasing economic integration is far from a guarantee of peace in the Taiwan Strait. Chinese leaders might very well be willing to bear the economic costs of a conflict if they calculated that military action was necessary to prevent the permanent separation of Taiwan from the mainland.[97]

With the dual imperatives of globalization—economic interdependence and national self-determination—continuing to pull in sharply divergent directions, Taiwan's future remains uncertain. The epic Newtonian struggle between politics and economics has produced no clear winner, only alternating cycles of tension and relaxation, with no end in sight. *Plus ça change, plus c'est la même chose.*

NOTES

1. See, for example, Ngaire Woods, ed., *The Political Economy of Globalization* (Basingstoke: Macmillan, 2000); Thomas L. Friedman, *The Lexus and the Olive Tree* (New York: Farrar, Straus and Giroux, 1999); and Richard Rosecrance, ed., *The New Great Power Coalition: Toward a World Concert of Nations* (Boulder: Rowman and Littlefield, 2001).

2. Richard Baum and Alexei Shevchenko, "China and the Forces of Globalization," in Rosecrance, ed., *The New Great Power Coalition*, ch. 5.

3. For a history of the "two Chinas" problem, see Ralph Clough, *Cooperation or Conflict in the Taiwan Strait?* (Boulder: Rowman & Littlefield, 1999).

4. On the genesis and resolution of the offshore islands crises of 1954 and 1958, see Chen Jian, *Mao's China and the Cold War* (Chapel Hill: The University of North Carolina Press, 2001).

5. The text of the Shanghai Communiqué appears in Richard Solomon, ed., *The China Factor* (Englewood Cliffs, NJ: Prentice-Hall, 1981), 296–300.

6. In the event, expulsion was unnecessary, as the ROC delegation, facing certain rejection, walked out of the UN in October 1971—before a vote could be taken on the question of Chinese representation.

7. In 1972 Japan fashioned a compromise with China under the terms of which Japan agreed to terminate all official governmental contacts with Taiwan, while being allowed to retain unofficial trade and cultural ties. Known as the "Japan formula," this compromise formed the basis for the subsequent U.S.-China normalization agreement of December 15, 1978.

8. See Christopher Howe, "Taiwan in the 20th Century: Model or Victim?" *The China Quarterly* 165 (March 2001), table 5, p. 52.

9. On Taiwan's "economic miracle," see Michael Y. M. Kau and Denis Fred Simon, *Taiwan: Beyond the Economic Miracle* (Armonk, NY: M. E. Sharpe, 1992).

10. See Linda Chao and Ramon H. Myers, *The Divided China Problem: Conflict Avoidance and Resolution* (Stanford: Hoover Institution, 2000), 19–21.

11. Ibid., 22.

12. For its part, throughout this period the ROC pursued a policy of "three no's" vis-à-vis the mainland—no official contacts, no negotiations, and no compromise; by the same token, the PRC refused to enter into political discussions with Taipei until the latter affirmed PRC sovereignty under the "one China" principle.

13. Quoted in Chao and Myers, *Divided China Problem*, 23.

14. The two sides' differing interpretations of this "1992 consensus" would later become a contentious issue. See below.

15. One reason for Beijing's more conciliatory line toward Taiwan in the early and mid-1990s was its desire to ensure a smooth, peaceful transfer of power in Hong Kong, which was due to be returned to Chinese sovereignty in 1997 under the "one country, two systems" formula.

16. The February 28, 1947 massacre of over 1,000 unarmed Taiwanese anti-KMT protesters by troops of KMT General Chen Yi—known as "the 2-28 incident"— served to cement the hostility of large numbers of Taiwanese citizens to rule by the Chinese Nationalists.

17. On electoral trends in Taiwan in the 1990s, see Shelley Rigger, *Politics in Taiwan* (New York: Routledge, 1999), chap. 7.

18. On these events, see Andrew Scobell, "Show of Force: The PLA and the 1995–1996 Taiwan Strait Crisis" (Honolulu: Asia/Pacific Research Center, Working Papers, January 1999).

19. Poll results reported in Rigger, *Politics in Taiwan*, 169–70. For similar results presented longitudinally over time, see "Public Opinion on Cross-strait Relations in the Republic of China," http://www.mac.gov.tw (Taipei: Mainland Affairs Council, May 2000).

20. In addition to Lee Teng-hui's 54 percent, pro-independence DPP candidate Peng Ming-min garnered 24 percent of the popular vote. By contrast, only 16 percent supported the candidate of the pro-unification New Party, which had split off from the KMT in protest, inter alia, over Lee Teng-hui's pro-independence policies.

21. In public opinion polls conducted on Taiwan between 1995 and 1999, combined support for "continuation of the status quo" (i.e., de facto separation) and "de jure independence" hovered between 68 and 78 percent, while support for "reunification" held relatively steady between 15 and 20 percent. See Alexander Ya-Li Lu, "The Significance and Consequences of Taiwan's 2000 Presidential Election," in Kenneth Klinkner, ed., *The United States and Cross-straits Relations: China, Taiwan and the US Entering a New Century* (Urbana: University of Illinois, Center for East Asian and Pacific Studies, 2001), 69, table 2. See also "Public Opinion on Cross-strait Relations."

22. "How People in Taiwan Identify Themselves, as Taiwanese, Chinese, or Both?" (Mainland Affairs Council, ROC, 2000), http://www.mac.gov.tw, 1. See also, "Public Opinion on Cross-strait Relations."

23. *Taipei Speaks Up: Special State-to-State Relationship* (Taipei: Mainland Affairs Council, August 1999), 1–2.

24. Ibid., 2.

25. See "Full Text of White Paper on Taiwan Issue," Xinhua (Beijing), February 21, 2000. The warning against indefinite postponement of reunification talks was strengthened and made more explicit in a subsequent PRC *White Paper,* issued in October 2000.

26. As early as 1985, when cross-strait trade and investment were first beginning to blossom, a CCP United Front Work Department report stated that "We can definitely, step by step, lead Taiwan's industries to further rely on our market. . . . Continuing to develop these efforts would effectively lead us to control the operation of Taiwan's economy that would speed up the reunification of the motherland." Quoted in Hsin-hsing Wu, *Bridging the Strait: Taiwan, China, and the Prospects for Reunification* (Hong Kong: Oxford University Press, 1994), 171.

27. Note, e.g., Lee's remarks to a visiting American delegation in June 1999: "Inspired by the Taiwan experience, the whole of mainland China is likely to be Taiwanized." Quoted in Paul J. Bolt, "Taiwan–Mainland China Economic Cooperation: Ties that Bind?" in Klinkner, *The United States and Cross-strait Relations,* 200.

28. See Vincent C. Siew, "Toward the Creation of a 'Cross-strait Common Market'" (Washington, DC: American Enterprise Institute, January 22, 2002), http://www.aei .org/sp/spsiew010122.htm.

29. Willem van Kaminade, "Taiwan: Domestic Gridlock, Cross-strait Deadlock," *The Washington Quarterly* 24:4 (Autumn 2001), 67.

30. Siew, "Toward the Creation of a 'Cross-strait Common Market.'"

31. Tsai Ing-wen, personal communication with the author, September 11, 2001.

32. "President Chen Shui-bian's Inauguration Speech" (Taipei Government Information Office, May 20, 2000).

33. See, e.g., "Taiwan's New Leader 'Lacks Sincerity,'" Xinhua (Beijing), May 20, 2000; and Douglas H. Paal, "Cautious Beijing Is Biding Its Time," *International Herald Tribune*, May 24, 2000.

34. "Taiwan President Chen Shui-bian's First News Conference" (Taipei: Chinese Television System, June 20, 2000; translated in FBIS CPP20000620000031).

35. Siew, "Toward the Creation of a 'Cross-strait Common Market.'"

36. See, e.g., Edward Gresser, "China in the WTO: Three Predictions and One Reminder," *Straits Times* (Singapore), November 10, 2001; and Sherman Katz, "WTO Accession of China and Taiwan" (Washington, DC: Center for Strategic and International Studies, November 2001), http://www.globalization101.org/projects.asp?PROJECT_ID=7.

37. Lin Mei-chun, "President Chen Backs Common Market Concept, *Taipei Times*, March 27, 2001.

38. Deputy ROC Foreign Minister Michael Y. M. Kau, "The Impact of WTO Accession on Political and Economic Relations between the Two Sides of the Taiwan Strait" (speech delivered at the Rayburn House Office Building, Washington D.C., July 23, 2002).

39. "Newsweek Asia Edition Interviews Taiwan President Chen," *Newsweek*, May 13, 2002; see also Katz, "WTO Accession of China and Taiwan."

40. Chen Shui-bian, "Cross-Century Remarks" (December 31, 2000), quoted in Byron S. J. Weng, "Modes of National Integration" (Taipei: Peace Forum, April 2001), http://www.dsis.org.tw/peaceforum/papers/2001-04/O0104001e.htm.

41. Van Kamenade, "Taiwan: Domestic Gridlock," 64.

42. "Chinese Vice-Premier Qian Urges Cross-strait Reunification," Xinhua (Beijing), January 22, 2001.

43. Quoted in Yang Jiemian, "A Partnership Worth Preserving," *New York Times*, March 21, 2001.

44. Also subject to Beijing's continuing boycott was former president Lee Teng-hui. These developments are examined in Alan Wachman, "The China-Taiwan Relationship: A Cold War of Words," *Orbis*, September 2002.

45. Alternative models of political integration are examined in Jacques de Lisle, "The China-Taiwan Relationship: Law's Spectral Answers to the Cross-strait Sovereignty Question," *Orbis*, September 2002; Weng, "Modes of National Integration"; and Siew, "Toward the Creation of a 'Cross-strait Common Market.'" See also Wachman, "The China-Taiwan Relationship"; Chao and Myers, *The Divided China Problem*; and Bolt, "Taiwan–Mainland China Economic Cooperation."

46. Chen also proposed a referendum on construction of a fourth nuclear power plant on Taiwan, with the two issues to be submitted to voters concurrently with the presidential election of March 20, 2004.

47. For an excellent review of these events and their historical antecedents, see Shelley Rigger, "New Crisis in the Taiwan Strait?" (Philadelphia: Foreign Policy Research Institute, September 5, 2003), www.fpri.org.

48. *Taipei Times*, June 23, 2003, http://www.taipeitimes.com/News/front/archives/2003/06/23/2003056387.

49. "Taiwan President Pushes New Constitution for 2006," Reuters (Taipei), September 29, 2003.

50. See Susan V. Lawrence, "United States and Taiwan: Diplomatic but Triumphal Progress," *Far Eastern Economic Review*, November 13, 2003. As a result of this and other diplomatic indiscretions, Ms. Shaheen was subsequently removed from her AIT post.

51. "PRC Taiwan Affairs Spokesman Warns against Taiwan Independence," Xinhua (Beijing), November 26, 2003.

52. Li Weiyi, quoted in Tyler Marshall, "Opposition in Taiwan Sheds China Policy," *Los Angeles Times*, December 17, 2003.

53. "Bush Opposes Taiwan Bid for Independence," Associated Press (Washington), December 9, 2003.

54. "Survey Shows Taiwan Poll Support," Associated Press (Taipei), December 15, 2003.

55. Central News Agency (Taipei), December 11, 2003, http://www.cna.com.tw.

56. "Opposition in Taiwan Sheds China Policy."

57. Survey results reported in *Lien-he Pao* (Taipei), October 20, 2003.

58. Ibid.; also *China Times* (Taipei), December 16, 2003.

59. Associated Press (Taipei), December 21, 2003.

60. Although Taiwanese law prohibits publication of poll results during the last ten days of a presidential election, pollsters in Taipei privately confirmed that Lien was leading as of March 19 by a margin of from two to five percentage points.

61. These events are examined in Richard Baum, "Chinese Puzzle," *San Jose Mercury News*, April 4, 2004.

62. In November 2003, Pan Blue lawmakers, who outnumbered Pan Greens in the Legislative Yuan, enacted a law stipulating that a referendum, in order to pass, must receive a total number of votes equal to (or greater than) the absolute majority of all eligible voters. Since several million eligible voters failed to cast ballots in the March election, Chen's missile referendum failed despite receiving an absolute majority of votes actually cast.

63. Material in this section is drawn from Richard Baum, "Washington Hopes for the Best; Beijing Prepares for the Worst," *YaleGlobalOnline*, May 24, 2004, http://yaleglobal.yale.edu/display.article?id=3963.

64. The full text of Chen's inaugural address is available at http://www.president.gov.tw/index_e.html.

65. "Taiwan Independence Never to Be Tolerated," *People's Daily* (online edition), May 20, 2004. http://english.peopledaily.com.cn/200405/20/eng20040520_143879.html.

66. Quoted in Joseph Kahn and Chris Buckley, "Taiwan's President Tones Down His Pro-Independence Oratory," *New York Times*, May 21, 2004.

67. "Taiwan Affairs Office Issues Statement on Current Cross-straits Relations" (May 17, 2004). The full text is available at http://www.china.org.cn/english/2004/May/95545.htm.

68. See note 2. The "1992 consensus"—which was informally discussed but never officially implemented—reportedly provided for the resumption of direct cross-strait links even while the two sides continued to disagree on the meaning of the one-China

principle (*yige zhongguo, gezi biaoshu*). Since the late 1990s, however, the Taiwan side has refused to recognize the validity (or even the existence) of the "1992 consensus."

69. "Beijing Expert Says People's Liberation Army Will Succeed in Eliminating 'Taiwan Independence' Forces," *Xianggang Shangbao* (*Hong Kong Commercial Daily*), March 31, 2004.

70. *The Economist,* December 13, 2003, p. 102.

71. *The Economist,* August 14, 2004, p. 90.

72. Agence France Presse (Beijing), December 21, 2003; Xinhua (Taipei), June 21, 2003. Taiwan enjoyed a $32 billion surplus in its cross-strait trade in the first ten months of 2003.

73. Craig Meer and Macabe Keliher, "Taiwan's Economic Leverage over China," *Asian Wall Street Journal,* August 12, 2003; Liu Yusheng, "PRC Official Urges Efforts to Stop 'Taiwan Independence,'" *Zhongguo Xinwen She* (China News Service, Beijing), January 3, 2004.

74. Michael Chase, Kevin Pollpeter, and James Mulvenon, *'Shanghaied'? The Economic and Political Implications of the Flow of Information Technology and Investment across the Taiwan Strait* (Santa Monica: Rand National Security Research Division, 2004).

75. Private communication from Prof. Chien-min Chao, National Cheng Chi University, Taipei, December 18, 2003.

76. Although no timetable has ever been definitively set by the Chinese side, there were authoritative reports in the summer of 2004 that the CCP Politburo had met to discuss setting a 2020 deadline for Taiwan's final reunification. See "China May Resolve Taiwan Issue by 2020," *Wen Wei Po* (Hong Kong), July 15, 2004.

77. "Text of PRC's Taiwan Affairs Office News Conference on Chen Shui-bian's Speech," Beijing CCTV-4 (in Mandarin), October 13, 2004, transl. in FBIS CPP20041013000040.

78. See Wang Yiwei, "China's Defensive Realism," *AsiaTimes* (online edition), December 22, 2004; also, "China's Dangerous Leap Backward," *Taipei Times,* December 20, 2004.

79. "U.S. Approach to Taiwan Is Set to Be Tougher," *Washington Post,* November 18, 2004.

80. Andrew Yang, quoted in "Taiwan Opposition Wins Parliamentary Majority," Reuters, December 11, 2004.

81. "Chen Hints at Softer Approach to Beijing," *International Herald Tribune,* February 25, 2005.

82. "MAC Hails Hu Jintao's Comments on Chen's 'Four Noes,'" *Taipei Times,* March 5, 2005.

83. Keith Bradsher, "Hundreds of Thousands Stage Mass Rally in Taiwan," *New York Times,* March 26, 2005.

84. Edward Cody, "China's Law on Taiwan Backfires," *Washington Post,* March 24, 2005.

85. Chinese leaders were aware that final passage of the ASL—which had been in the works for well over a year—would provoke a widespread backlash; however, once the legislation had worked itself through the legislative process and been placed on the NPC's calendar, they could not withdraw it without losing considerable international face. So they did the next best thing by watering down its more

threatening language (e.g., substituting "non-peaceful means" for "military force") and adding new sections emphasizing cross-strait economic, commercial, and cultural cooperation.

86. "Mainland Open to Talks with Taiwan Parties," *China Daily* (online edition), April 13, 2005.

87. See Associated Press, April 29, 2005; Agence France Press, May 1, 2005.

88. One opinion poll conducted in early June showed 56 percent of the public having a favorable view, with only 18 percent unfavorable.

89. "President Asks Opposition Leader to Convey Messages to China," *China News Agency* (Taipei), May 1, 2005.

90. "Soong's Visit Helps Promote CCP-PFP Ties," *China Daily*, May 9, 2005.

91. Reuters, May 12, 2005.

92. *People's Daily* (online edition, in English), July 17, 2005.

93. *Zhongguo Shibao*, July, 2005.

94. See, for example, *China News Analysis*, September 22, 2005.

95. In 2004, China accounted for 37 percent of Taiwan's exports and 66 percent of Taiwan's FDI. See *Taiwan Yearbook 2004*, http://ecommerce.taipeitimes.com/yearbook2004/P135.htm#4.

96. Such views were repeatedly expressed in the course of the author's visits to Taipei and Beijing in the latter half of 2005.

97. Chase, et al., *Shanghaied*, xx.

III

CONCLUSIONS

16

Who Will Be Independent?

Richard N. Rosecrance

International history has witnessed trends toward and away from the amalgamation of disparate political units—in Europe and elsewhere. After the Roman Empire broke into halves and then the halves themselves declined and splintered, new political entities emerged from the ruins. As trade dwindled and Mediterranean commerce faltered, more or less self-sufficient agrarian units initially took their place. Not until the end of the first millennium and the rise of the Ottoman Turks in the East and trading cities in the West, however, did commerce begin to revive. Even then, the territorial state did not initially appear. City states and the Hansa towns operated on coasts and rivers, but hinterlands remained relatively unorganized. After 1450, however, the gunpowder-toting territorial state became the residuary legatee of historical processes, forcing an ultimate consolidation among political units.

This evolution did not take place overnight. In 1500 Europe was still largely populated by "state-lets"—duchies, bishoprics, and semi-independent provinces—each owing allegiance to different masters. With the Reformation, the Church was divided, and princes were equally so. Five hundred political units were then scattered over the European landscape. But from then until 1900, states consolidated themselves, with the European numbers falling to about 25 territorial states at the end of the 19th century.

Since 1945, however, the trend has turned in the opposite direction. Now two hundred or more states inhabit world politics, and many observers have believed that the process of political subdivision would continue unabated, with the two hundred existing states perhaps becoming four hundred. This book reaches the conclusion, however, that this outcome is unlikely. For various reasons, the process of state formation has largely run its course and come to an end.

Why is that? First, the net effect of globalization has been to dwarf all political units. No country is now self-sufficient in raw materials, technology, trained manpower, and markets. All states need markets overseas, and most depend upon sources of foreign capital and technology. This would not be a problem if markets and capital were open to all on equal terms, but they are not. Larger states have greater access in most cases, and capital does not move fluidly to areas of labor abundance. Russia and America need the outside world as much as Singapore and Mauritius, but they also have large markets inside their countries on which they can rely in case of trouble. New (smaller) nations, therefore, cannot expect independence will solve their problems for them.

As the trend in political scale has begun to reverse, present-day countries have aimed to regain the advantages of bigness, though in altered form. As Arthur Stein shows, through trade pacts, customs unions, and currency linkages, nations have used organizations to make up for deficient size. Instead of relying wholly on market forces, they have sought specific contractual guarantees to protect themselves. By joining the European Union, NAFTA, WTO, or regional trade arrangements, countries have obtained protections that a single state could not obtain on its own. Southeast Asian countries suffered grievously in 1997–98 when capital flight undercut their growth. Since then, they have negotiated regional and international arrangements to prevent the crisis occurring again. In Latin America new trade preferences have been established. The United States, Canada, and Mexico have deepened their trade links. CAFTA—the Central American Free Trade Area—is in process of receiving privileged access to the American market, insulating its members (the Dominican Republic, Honduras, Nicaragua, El Salvador, Costa Rica, and Guatemala) from the perils of international, particularly Chinese, competition.

Provinces considering independence from their political masters thus have had to think what protections, if any, they might find in the globalized world. Some dissident factions undoubtedly believed they might enter the EU or NAFTA as independent states, but this prospect became less likely when charter members did not welcome them. They then began to reevaluate their status within the metropolitan regime. Potentially dissident Scotland, the Basques, Quebec, and other provincial populations have gradually come to see the federal-metropole as a less hostile environment, and their independence movements have declined in proportion. In the erstwhile Third World some, like the Palestinians, Southern Sudan, and Kosovo, still hoped for independence, and might in time gain it. But aside from these exceptions, few new states are likely to be created.

There are three primary reasons for this change. First, metropolitan governments have themselves embraced globalization, extending its benefits to potentially dissident provinces. The ability to buy, sell, and receive capital internationally has been accorded to regional authorities. Provinces have thus begun to recognize that independence might not represent a superior outcome—it might not even be useful. Second and perhaps more important, dissident elements can no longer legitimately use the threat of terrorism to gain independence from a reluctant metropolitan government. If they do so, they lose the support of other nations and the international community as a whole, undermining their position. Third, existing governments have rewarded dissident provinces which have remained within the central administrative fold. Scotland, for example, is not likely to be better treated (as soi-disant member of the European Union) than it is at the moment by the British government. The rewards of remaining within tend to exceed the benefits of going outside. Nor is membership in the EU, NAFTA, or other regional trade pacts likely to be automatically accorded to dissident provinces which seek independence.

When the metropole collapsed (as it did in the case of the old Soviet Union or federal Yugoslavia), the outcome changed. The remaining provinces then sought to make themselves eligible for membership in NATO or the European Union. But where the dissident province takes the initiative to sever communal bonds, the international response tends to be cautious or negative. And particularly if insurgents wage a long terrorist struggle to gain independence, the dissenters may sacrifice outside support in the process. Under these circumstances, the state-units populating the world may come to stabilize for the immediate future at around two hundred. Looking ahead, we may see surprisingly few new states. It is possible, even, that the number of fully independent states may decline as political units begin to merge with each other.

OUTCOMES IN DIFFERENT REGIONS

Europe and North America have presented the most compelling examples of restraint on potential new states. After accepting the independence of Russian and Yugoslav successor-provinces, the international community called a halt on the process of further subdivision. Spain, France, Belgium, and the United Kingdom took a negative view of further proliferation of states and acted to prevent a breakup of their own territories. Particularly after the September 11, 2001 attacks on the United States, the Madrid bombings of March 11, 2004, and the London bombings of July 7, 2005 European countries have renounced the terrorism associated with independence movements. Scotland, Chechnya, the Basques, Bretons, and Welsh will be expected to continue within their homeland states. (See Richard Rosecrance and Arthur Stein in chapter 1, and Deepak Lal in chapter 3.) Public opinion has turned against terrorism or even radical agitation designed to procure independence. Even the IRA and Sinn Fein have had to return to peaceful methods to gain acceptance in Dublin and Belfast. In North America, Quebec has benefited from

Ottawa's generosity, but also been constrained by the federal government's strictures on the terms of a plebiscite to achieve independence. If it were to be granted sovereignty, Quebec also would face the prospect of further splits in its territory—of the Inuit peoples in the North and English-speaking Canadians in the South. A general unraveling of the province was not in Montreal's interest, nor in Ottawa's. The status quo—with Quebec remaining within Canada—is the likely result. (See Alan Alexandroff in chapter 13.)

For a while it seemed that independence movements would more likely succeed in South and Southeast Asia. Kashmir had long-standing nationalist credentials, and they were generally recognized around the world. But when Kashmiri activists crossed the line of control to wreak havoc in Delhi, the crisis raised the danger of war between the two new nuclear states of Pakistan and India. India was also able to make the case that if Kashmir secedes today, it will be the Punjab, Mizo- or Naga-land tomorrow. A country cannot stand by and allow its provinces to use force to gain autonomy. (See Deepak Lal in chapter 9.) Such outcomes have to be negotiated if they are to be accepted internationally. As applied to Indonesia, these conclusions ratified the case for central control by Jakarta. If Aceh and Ambon were allowed separation, what would happen to Sulawesi and Sumatra? Island archipelagoes are particularly vulnerable to such unraveling. (See Etel Solingen in chapter 10.) East Timor was the last case in which Indonesian control would be generally disputed and independence conceded. In the East Timor case, the international community agreed that recent acquisitions were intrinsically more questionable than rule over long-established provinces.

Africa, of course, was a special case. The presence of oil, uranium, and precious stones and metals augured in favor of political subdivision—to develop the particularly sensitive regions which possessed those materials. But equally, no government would stand by as its richest province sought independence. Thus what might have been regional secession turned into civil wars, with central governments contending every step of the way to reestablish authority. In similar fashion in the Middle East, the Kurds could not capture the oil resources of Northern Iraq and then move to autonomy. They would have to share their riches with a central government which insisted on a strong federalism. (See Steven Miller in chapter 11.)

The occupations of Iraq and Afghanistan changed patterns in the Near East and beyond. Political independence of new regions, however, did not seem likely. The Kurds would indeed benefit from federalism, but they would not be conceded independence. Northern Afghanistan and other provinces might be ruled by erstwhile "war lords," but they would not become completely autonomous. Over time road building and new infrastructure would provide stronger links with Kabul. Growing political reform and gradual democratization also had a centralizing effect on the whole Middle East. With electoral reform and an extension of suffrage in the air, the popular stake in central political outcomes would rise accordingly, diluting regional orientations. More democratic regimes could use "voice" to stimulate "loyalty," making provincial autonomy even less necessary. New democratic regimes could thereby enfranchise dissidents and bring them closer to the center.

The Middle East, however, remained poised on a threshold of political indecision. As Etel Solingen demonstrates, regional outcomes depend upon the character of political coalitions within and outside the state. Backlash coalitions seeking to negate globalization operated within the Arab League, and they supported similar backlash coalitions within Arab League members. The modernizing force of globalization, then, could be contained within rigid receptacles embodying traditional order. Outside intervention within an individual Arab country—to produce globalist or democratic change—would be anathema to such authorities. This leaves the Arab world paralyzed between alternatives. (See Gitty Amini in chapter 7.)

On the one hand, the U.S. coalition's invasion of Iraq has forced Arab states to renew themselves politically. Challenged Arab regimes can no longer maunder around without political direction. They all need new political/military or economic justification to remain in power. They can get this by militant opposition to U.S. policy as has been the case in Iran and to some degree in Syria. They can also get it through some measure of accommodation to modernist influences as has increasingly been the case in Lebanon and Jordan. Egypt has just picked up the option of free trade with Washington and broadened the presidential vote. Saudi Arabia remains politically divided, and neither reform of the elementary schools nor new political leadership appears likely to emerge in the short run. Longer-term outcomes may depend upon how Iraq and Afghanistan fare economically and politically. Globalist modernization and democracy were highly desirable, but they were also brought by force to the Middle East. Traditionalists may well reject them both as Western implants. (See Gitty Amini in chapter 7.)

On the other hand, a simple anti-Western and anti-American posture will not suffice to reinsure the power of autocratic regimes. They will have to change, and economics is the safest short-term expedient to gain support. If change is confined to rearmament, plotting military campaigns against hostile neighbors, or voicing anti-imperialist rhetoric, it will achieve nothing. Capital will stay away, and what is there will leave. Investment will be even scarcer. Under these conditions, it is at least possible that some heretofore autocratic regimes will begin to learn Southeast Asian lessons and begin to pursue "trading" vocations in international politics. The temporary rise in oil prices, however, gave a new breathing room to regimes out of harmony with their populations.

Much depends as well on what happens in the Palestinian-Israeli context. An Abu Mazen (Mahmoud Abbas) who gains concessions from Israel may be better able to control his terrorist allies than Yasir Arafat was. If Arabs are allowed to filter back as workers into Israel, economic conditions in the West Bank could improve. And if, in response, terrorism and suicide bombing are put on hold, Ehud Olmert could then make further gestures to the new Palestinian leadership. This could improve economics on both sides of the green line and eventually lead to negotiations for a final settlement. Greater economic success for both Palestine and Israel—as they renounced violence—would be a beacon for the entire Middle East, favoring similar changes elsewhere. Given the nature of backlash coalitions among current Arab leaders, however, this outcome is possible, but not likely. Political power has always been more important than risking the uncertainties of economic change. Islamic Jihad does not necessarily follow the dictates of El Fatah now that Hamas has won Palestinian elections.

The Iraq War raised the prospect of civil war between Sunnis and Shiites, but it did not destabilize the larger Middle East as some had predicted. Arabs did not take to the street to denounce their feckless political leaders who were unable to stop America. Instead most saw it as a stimulus for change and perhaps one long overdue. In Iran, as Gitty Amini shows, the war led the Islamic leadership to cling even more tightly to their nuclear weapons program. They hoped to ride out negotiations with the Europeans and get a package of reforms which would not preclude a long-term nuclear option. This, however, would not be accepted by the European Three and the United States, who would then seek to force change in Iranian policy. Then just possibly, the mullahs would concede and put their weapons capabilities on hold or dismantle them. IAEA would resume intrusive inspections of Iranian capabilities. This result was not probable, but neither could it be entirely ruled out. Putin's Russia could play a facilitative role here.

Iran is a test case, not only of Middle Eastern outcomes, but also of the long-term relationship with China. If Iran reneged on the negotiations with Europe, America would bring the issue to the UN Security Council where China would be faced with the need to veto actions stemming from the complaint. Would it do so? That depends on a host of other factors, among them the situation in North Korea and the nature of relations with Taiwan. China will not save Iran from American wrath as a matter of the first priority. Its policies there are theoretical not practical ones. It does not want to set a precedent for international intervention in Tibet or elsewhere. But even more, it wants Taiwan to submit peacefully to reintegration with the mainland. (See Richard Baum in chapter 15.) This is not likely unless the United States also presses Taipei to make concessions. Further spread of nuclear weapons in the Middle East or Northeast Asia would embolden Taiwan as well. It could alter the South Korean abstention on such weapons. And afterward, Japan might also go nuclear. If Taipei followed suit, Beijing would not get Taiwan back, and the arms race would proceed unchecked, undercutting China's erstwhile peaceful rise.

This is not an outcome China desires, but avoiding it requires further Chinese initiative—first in regard to Pyongyang and second to induce Taiwan's cooperation. Hitherto Beijing has reacted to American and Taiwanese policies, largely in passive terms. But a waiting game will not suffice for the longer term. Unless China and the United States work together, North Korea will achieve a nuclear fait accompli. And that in turn will greatly complicate the cross-straits problem if Taipei moves in a similar direction. Pyongyang's energy and food dependence on China gives Beijing a decisive say in North Korean strategy. One possibility is a Chinese-American rapprochement in which China exerts leverage on Kim Jong-Il and the U.S. on Chen Shui-Bian. Neither problem will be solved without outside pressure. And a solution in Asia would make Iran more tractable in the Middle East. This outcome is theoretically possible, but not likely.

Whether nuclear weapons spread or not, few new states will be recognized in less developed regions of the world. The Middle East will not split apart under reformist pressures. It will more likely centralize. African civil wars will not foster the independence of contending provinces. In South Asia, the Tamils are unlikely to gain a state of their own, nor will India be subdivided into new countries. (See Deepak Lal in chapter 9.) Taiwan will not be given de jure independence, though it may get guaranteed internal autonomy from Beijing. (See Richard Baum in chapter 15.) In Europe and North America, subnational provinces do very well and have no pressing need to change their status.

GLOBALIZATION WILL CONTINUE

Some have hypothesized that globalization (like the Titanic) is sinking. A major war could scuttle economic cooperation and trade flows. A great depression would raise tariffs to new heights and end the international flow of capital. While neither is impossible, neither worst-case scenario is at all likely. The organizational structure of international economics favors "reward thy neighbor" outcomes, not bloodymindedness. There is even more international cooperation than one might expect, given public goods problems. Nor does globalization depend uniquely upon a particular power relationship in world politics. As many have shown, United States' hegemony is not the sine qua non of cooperation, and cooperation could increase if America were even less hegemonic. Despite the suggestions of Deepak Lal and Niall Ferguson, however, a British imperial model is not necessary to hold the world economy together. The economic cooperation of Great Powers is sufficient to do so, and it is not only possible but likely. And the prospect of further terrorism welds continents more solidly together to keep the world economy functioning.

This does not mean that weapons of mass destruction will never be used by terrorists against civilian targets with the objective of interrupting world trade and terminating globalization. (See Graham Allison in chapter 6.) The two attacks on the World Trade Center clearly had these as their goal. Suitcase bombs may find their way into terrorist hands, and they may someday be detonated in Western or industrial cities. The result could be catastrophic, but it would hardly be decisive. Commerce and trade would reestablish themselves; new ports and communications facilities would be opened. In Franklin Roosevelt's words, the greatest danger then would be "fear itself"—unreasoning fear that paralyzed action. John Mueller rightly claims that "overreaction" to terrorism could be more devastating than "terrorism" itself in that it could stop activity to mitigate damage and reconstruct infrastructure. As Mueller shows, the economic impact of 9/11 was less than many other events that afflict the world each year, such as auto accidents, epidemics, or chronic health problems. The world takes account of these unfortunate facts, but it does not grind to a halt because the latter occur. Indeed, Mueller's analysis might even be taken further. Humanity does not normally give up under crisis or attack, no matter how perilous the challenge. British production did not wither under the impact of the German Blitz in 1940 and 1941; aided by American Lend Lease, it actually increased at a substantial rate right through the rest of the Second World War. Forty thousand people were killed in the bombings, but the British people rallied and supported the war effort. More recently, suicide bombings did not paralyze the Israeli public nor did al-Qaeda bombings lead Londoners to give up traveling in the Underground. Normal life continued, and it is imperative for the United States—whose urban population was virtually never under threat—to behave similarly under the new conditions in which it finds itself. Some people will be killed in terrorist incidents, but this should not terminate a way of life or an economic medium—globalization—which sustains it.

Globalization will not only continue (see Luisita Cordero and Richard Rosecrance in chapter 2), it also takes a different form today. In the past, it was based fundamentally on local production stimulated by export markets. Industrialization had the initial effect of making large-scale economies more self-sufficient. They could produce more domestically—particularly consumer goods—and thus had less need to import from other advanced societies. This was altered to some degree by product differentiation. All industrial economies could produce autos, but some cars were better or at least different from others. German and Japanese cars became preferred items even when production capacity existed at home. Then it began to be recognized that some industries benefited from economies of scale. According to Brian Arthur, software, finance, and insurance were such industries. Others believed that autos and civilian aircraft were also industries in which costs decreased with greater output. If this was true, it was possible that some countries would have to buy from others as, say, software or advanced microprocessors were increasingly produced in only a few places around the globe. Interdependence thus became structural. If there were only five efficient producers of autos on a worldwide basis, most countries would have to buy from a foreign source. Even defense industries began to have economies of scale. Perhaps most countries will now have to buy weapons from other states.

This eventuality lessens economic viability for provinces seeking independence. They will inexorably have to buy from abroad. Do they then possess something essential that they can sell in return to finance their purchases? As economies of scale set in, this question reverberates without a clear answer. Aside from oil, does Mexico possess any economy-of-scale industries which are not presently migrating to China? Under the circumstances, which fledgling new state would like to inherit or adopt Mexico's problems? The barrier to achieving economies of scale is a formidable one.

TERRORISM, REPRESENTATION, AND INTERNATIONAL COOPERATION

Terrorism, of course, is a contemporary means of calling attention to one's plight even if independence does not constitute a full remedy for the difficulties encountered. But just as it is true that economic problems cannot necessarily be remedied by gaining independence, it is also true that potential terrorists can find another way of expressing themselves. In closed societies, those seeking political outlets cannot campaign for electoral reform. They will be promptly incarcerated if they do. But there is a link between national self-determination, terrorism, and the possibility of political change. Movements in favor of national self-determination flag if the metropolitan government responds by offering both sticks and carrots to potential dissenters. If terrorism is ruled out, those advocating provincial independence can either seek electoral representation or they can content themselves with benefits offered by the home government. One of the useful effects of the Iraq War was to raise the possibility of electoral representation for those who would otherwise support the insurgency. If—over time—Sunnis accept this course of action, insurgent terrorism will decline even if the United States does not immediately withdraw its troops. Incorporation within the political system thus at least partly substitutes for opposition mounted from outside it. As Albert Hirschman saw, the achievement of "voice" within a polity ultimately increases loyalty to it.

As Steven Miller shows, however, the benefits to the United States of its Iraq venture will be distinctly limited. Even if a quasi-democratic regime comes to power in Baghdad, it will have strong Shiite and Islamist colorations. It may be led by individuals that owe their allegiance to clerics in

Iran. Thus in Miller's formulation, if the U.S. loses, it loses and has to with-draw. But if it wins and establishes a proto-democratic government, it also may lose in political and religious terms.

Political representation is one means of defusing the terrorist impulse; another is international agreement to contain it. The two together constitute powerful remedies for discontent. The first reduces the demand to express terrorism; the second reduces the supply that can effectively be mounted. The threat of terrorism in China, the Middle East, and East Asia is also a stim-ulus to political and electoral reform. Leaders that might defect from a politi-cal state may sometimes be co-opted by democratic inclusion within it. Thus even countries like China, Egypt, and Saudi Arabia see the handwriting on the wall. They are cooperating in an international effort to root out terrorism, but—by preserving authoritarian political systems domestically—they are also generating the very movements they seek to combat. Ultimately, this could affect their ability to cooperate with other similarly minded states. Democratic reform cannot be attained overnight, but neither can it be entirely neglected if political decisions are to retain legitimacy.

The same is true for international cooperation. The global economy is now causing diverse political units to seek greater political scale to cope with eco-nomic crisis. No state—not even the United States—is large and economically self-sufficient enough to subsist on its own. As a variety of states attain much higher growth rates, competitors combine to achieve the scale to match their growth. But cooperation to effect "mergers" among states—as the European Union has brilliantly demonstrated—cannot take place where authoritarian regimes remain in place. Authoritarian pledges cannot ultimately be trusted because they are not sustained by democratic legislatures elected by popular vote, and so international cooperation itself depends upon political reform of existing autocratic regimes.

One of the major characteristics of the Great Power system today is that it is sustained not only by common economic interests but by a common com-mitment to exorcize terrorism. Great Power relationships including Russia and China (as well as India, Japan, Europe, and the United States) have recovered from the bruising disagreements over the Iraq War. They are now positioned to cooperate against terrorism as well as to keep the world econ-omy on an even keel. No Great Power wishes to see the further spread of weapons of mass destruction, certainly not to potentially terrorist states or groups and this adds to the strength of cooperation. In the aftermath of 9/11, 3/11, and 7/7, intelligence cooperation between the United States and Europe has increased despite the differences over Iraq. It will likely continue to do so. The basis of this cooperation—protecting and extending democratic governments and economic systems—is far more forward-looking than the intrinsically atavistic cooperation of the Concert of Europe in the 19th cen-tury. Then the aristocrats looked back, steadfastly striving to prevent liberal-democratic change. Their cooperation could not long continue and indeed collapsed after 1848. But authoritarian regimes today, as Bill Clinton said in China, are "on the wrong side of history." The tide of events is likely to increase Great Power cooperation as all the Great Powers liberalize in both economic and political terms. Russia has partly made this transition and only China awaits to do so. The continuing influence of globalization upon Beijing—bringing Shanghai's and Guangjou's influence to bear—will make that transition easier. China may actually have been right to postpone democratic reform until the economy had already made a liberal transition. Now, having solved the problem that eluded Gorbachev, it can begin to make change in politics as well. The Kuomintang did so in Taiwan and won democratic elections after it renounced authoritarian power. Under new conditions, a modernized Chinese Communist Party just possibly might begin to enjoy political tolerance if not popularity. As recent visits across the straits indicate, the Kuomintang is there to advise Beijing every step of the way. The notion, however, that the United States can discipline China by threatening to withhold capital or markets, however, is dubious, as Richard Cooper points out. China will develop at its own tempo, regardless of what America does.

FROM SPLITTING TO AGGLOMERATION?

It is premature to speculate on the ultimate future of world politics. But one possibility that cannot be ruled out is a gradual agglomeration of states—a reversal of the traditional national self-determination process. Despite what is occasionally said, globalization favors larger not smaller states. Smaller states do not have adequate sources of capital or sufficiently large markets. If tariffs rise, the free trade areas remaining will be those negotiated among larger states. And it has always been true that globalization applied more to capital flows than to trade. Trade has always been hemmed in by restrictions—on both industrial and agricultural goods. Indebted countries have always had difficulty quickly repaying their loans through enhanced exports. Frequently creditors held back on buying indebted country exports. Today even large countries threaten tariff hikes on crucial industries.

Foreign direct investment has been one way of circumventing this blockage. Even if one's exports are restricted, FDI can jump over the tariff barrier and produce the export within the tariff zone of the desired market. But at least until recently, indebted countries have not usually had the financial means to export their products via foreign direct investment. Thus developed country tariffs have been hardest to surmount. Instead, foreign direct investment has been used by the First World to export to the Third World, rather than the other way around. Thus Chinese tariffs have not prevented U.S. or German production of the goods the Western nations would have exported to Guangdong, Shanghai, or elsewhere. But U.S. and European tariffs have raised important barriers to Third World exports.

It is suggestive that customs unions or trading blocs are now the order of the day and not just in the Western and developed world. In East Asia new trade blocs or monetary funds have been proposed. In Latin America they are becoming a continual rejoinder to tariffs in the developed world. Bilateral agreements are offered as the Doha Round fails to make headway. In each case, multilaterally or bilaterally, countries are seeking to become bigger economic units.

Even the Great Powers are seeking to get larger, through merger with others. The European Union now has 25 members with more waiting in the wings, including Bulgaria and Ukraine. This is not likely to change despite defeats for the European Constitution in Paris and The Hague. The United States is now seeking to accompany NAFTA with FTAA, the Free Trade Agreement of the Americas, and is starting with CAFTA—the Central American Free Trade Area. China and Japan are moving outward to broaden their markets and access to raw materials through bilateral or multilateral trade pacts. Negotiated Largeness is increasingly replacing Smallness in the international system.

CONCLUSION

The international system is at a choice point in a variety of different areas. On nuclear weapons, countries can accede to further spread and hope that multilateral nuclear deterrence will prevent war, or they can strive to stop the spread and induce possible proliferators to stay their hand. If states abstain, the arms race would then be confined, and economic growth could flourish in its absence.

Terrorism will continue to be a problem, but if nuclear weapons are confined to present holders, terrorists will find it more difficult to get access to them. (See Graham Allison in chapter 6.) Great Power solidarity will increase to confront the danger of the uncontrolled spread of nuclear weapons and terrorism. Both possibilities threaten their leadership of the international system.

The future of globalization is a third pressing problem. If globalization collapses either as a result of unlimited terrorism or a new Great Depression, major powers will be left with the nationalist-mercantile state. As occurred in the 1930s, such "nationalist capitalism" will cut the ties with other nations and economies and strive to achieve some degree of national self-sufficiency. Since the Great Powers will have been accustomed to satisfying their needs through world trade and a massive movement of factors of production— engendered by economies of scale—they may well then seek to expand militarily to capture the areas on which they previously depended for economic sustenance. Wars over the sources of oil, raw materials, and grain could then take place, with the Middle East, Australia, the granaries of North America, and Argentina residing at the center of the disturbance. East Asia and Europe would have to expand rapidly to ensure their supplies of needed materials. Areas of particular economic efficiency like Northwestern Europe, the coastal United States, Guangdong, and Shanghai will become lighthouses of attraction to aggressors even though their capture is probably impossible.

Fortunately, globalization is unlikely to collapse. Foreign trade would then continue to offer access to all countries to the high technology, raw materials, and agriculture of the world, and military expansion would not be necessary. In theory, globalization could allow more provinces to seek independence, benefiting from an international free trade regime. Yet the globalization which presently operates favors capital movements over the free movement of trade. Capital can leave markets in an instant, and trade may not fully compensate for its departure. East Asia showed in 1997–98 that it could not pay back its loans quickly enough through exports. Some countries—like Malaysia and Chile—have instituted capital controls to compensate for the disadvantage. In the circumstances, provinces have hesitated to brave the financial winds of the globalized international economy by seeking independence. Pressed by metropolitan governments to remain within the national fold, they have found few international allies supporting a move to external sovereignty. Few new states may therefore be created in the years ahead.

Tom Friedman, *New York Times* columnist, has responded to this situation by declaring that "the earth is flat." But it is not flat. All countries do not have corporate champions contending on a level playing field. Economies of scale apply, and some firms and industries do better than others. This concentrates industrial power in fewer hands. All countries will not possess economies of scale industries though they will still have comparative advantages in some goods. Even a China that makes auto components for the world may still not have the strongest auto company. An India that concentrates on software and services may still not possess the strongest technology/internet provider. New countries will have to buy important goods and services from large corporations located somewhere else. Labor will need employment and will seek to migrate to areas which possess such industries. Even the largest countries will be dependent on markets, funds, and raw materials located outside their borders. Independence movements just gaining autonomy will have the greatest difficulty. That is why there will not be many of them, and the world will stabilize at or near its present number of states. Under certain circumstances, as nations merge together, the number of states could actually decline.

Index

About the Contributors

Alan S. Alexandroff is Research Director of the Program on Conflict Management and Negotiation at the Munk Centre of the University of Toronto. He examines the Chinese economy and the question of global institutional reform.

Graham Allison is Douglas Dillon Professor of International Politics at the Kennedy School, Harvard University. He works on terrorism, weapons of mass destruction, and US-Russian relations.

Gitty M. Amini is Associate Professor of Political Science at the University of La Verne and author of a forthcoming volume on rewards and punishments in international strategy. Her other interests include the Middle East, Northeast Asia, and the proliferation of weapons of mass destruction.

Richard Baum is Distinguished Professor of Political Science at UCLA and currently Visiting Professor of International Studies at Peking University. He is working on the impact of globalization on Chinese domestic and international politics.

Richard N. Cooper is Professor of Economics at Harvard University and is engaged in a long-term study of the impact of globalization on interdependence among major powers.

Luisita Cordero is Research Associate of the Carnegie Project on Globalization and National Self-Determination at UCLA. Her work centers on the comparative and international politics of Southeast Asian nations.

Barbara Koremenos is Associate Professor of Political Science at the University of Michigan. She is examining how to design robust structures of international law, given the pressures of international and domestic politics.

Deepak Lal is James S. Coleman Professor of International Development at UCLA. His most recent work on *The Invisible Hand* will be published next year by Princeton University Press.

Steven E. Miller is Director of the International Security Program, The Belfer Center, Kennedy School of Government, Harvard University. He focuses on Middle Eastern and East Asian aspects of proliferation.

John E. Mueller is Woody Hayes Professor of Military History at Ohio State University. He is currently working on a book entitled *Devils and Duct Tape: Terrorism and the Dynamics of Threat Exaggeration.*

John Reppert is Dean of the College of International and Security Studies, Marshall European Center for Security Studies. He focuses on the security structures of Eurasian nations and their adaptation to new opportunities and threats.

Richard N. Rosecrance is Distinguished Research Professor of Political Science at UCLA and Senior Fellow, Belfer Center for Science and International Affairs, Kennedy School of Government, Harvard University. He is examining "agglomeration processes" in international politics.

Alexei Shevchenko is Lecturer at the University of Southern California. His research compares the logic and dynamics of Chinese and Russian elites' adaptation to market conditions.

Etel Solingen is Professor of Political Science, University of California (Irvine). Her current projects include studies on the relationship between globalization and regionalism, competing theories of East Asian security, and contrasting nuclear trajectories in East Asia and the Middle East.

Arthur A. Stein is Professor of Political Science at UCLA. He centers his attention on nationalism, regimes, and the impact of globalization.